MODELS OF QUALITATIVE RESEARCH

MODELS OF QUALITATIVE RESEARCH

AN OXFORD HANDBOOK OF QUALITATIVE RESEARCH IN AMERICAN MUSIC EDUCATION

Volume 3

Edited by
COLLEEN M. CONWAY

UNIVERSITY PRESS

Oxford University Press is a department of the University of Oxford. It furthers
the University's objective of excellence in research, scholarship, and education
by publishing worldwide. Oxford is a registered trade mark of Oxford University
Press in the UK and certain other countries.

Published in the United States of America by Oxford University Press
198 Madison Avenue, New York, NY 10016, United States of America.

© Oxford University Press 2020

All rights reserved. No part of this publication may be reproduced, stored in
a retrieval system, or transmitted, in any form or by any means, without the
prior permission in writing of Oxford University Press, or as expressly permitted
by law, by license, or under terms agreed with the appropriate reproduction
rights organization. Inquiries concerning reproduction outside the scope of the
above should be sent to the Rights Department, Oxford University Press, at the
address above.

You must not circulate this work in any other form
and you must impose this same condition on any acquirer.

CIP data is on file at the Library of Congress
ISBN 978-0-19-092097-5

1 3 5 7 9 8 6 4 2

Printed by Marquis, Canada

Contents

Preface	vii
Colleen M. Conway	
List of Contributors	xi
1. Qualitative Research in Early Childhood Music Education Alison M. Reynolds	1
2. Qualitative Research in General Music Education Ann Marie Stanley	24
3. Instrumental Music (Winds, Brass, Percussion) Chad West	49
4. Instrumental Music (Strings) Margaret H. Berg	68
5. Qualitative Choral Music Research Bridget Sweet	88
6. A Critical Analysis of Qualitative Research on Learning to Teach Music in Preservice Music Teacher Education Mark Robin Campbell and Linda K. Thompson	107
7. Inservice Music Teacher Professional Development Colleen M. Conway and Scott N. Edgar	139
8. Community Music Education Nathan B. Kruse and Erin M. Hansen	161
9. Qualitative Research Examining Students with Exceptionalities in Music Education Ryan M. Hourigan	185

10. Intersectionalities: Exploring Qualitative Research, Music
    Education, and Diversity   200
    BRUCE CARTER

11. World Musics and Cultural Diversity in the Music Classroom and
    the Community   214
    YIANNIS MIRALIS

12. Teaching Qualitative Research Experientially and Aesthetically   232
    LIORA BRESLER

Index   263

Preface

Models of Qualitative Research in Music Education

THE chapters in *Models of Qualitative Research in Music Education* are a resource for music education researchers, music education graduate students, and P–12 music teachers. Authors in the book examine the use of qualitative research in answering important research questions regarding music teaching and learning in a variety of diverse music education contexts. Each author examines key studies and provides suggestions for future questions that qualitative researchers may consider. Contexts examined in the chapter include: early childhood music, general music, instrumental music (winds, brass percussion), instrumental music (strings), choral music, preservice teacher education, teacher professional development, community music education, music for students with special needs, music education and issues of diversity, and world music. Authors had the dual challenge of presenting what was important about qualitative research in their area as well as what the profession has learned about the topic (e.g., instrumental music) through qualitative research. In most cases authors also needed to define their field (e.g., early childhood or community music) as part of the work. I am proud of the ways in which these authors grappled with this challenge and believe what has resulted will be valuable for the field.

The future of qualitative research lies in preparing the next generation of scholars; thus, the final chapter in the book addresses the teaching of qualitative research. Experienced qualitative researcher Liora Bresler lets the reader "in" on her specific approach to the task of teaching about qualitative research, and her chapter includes a syllabus from her course as well as analysis of student work.

Consideration of Issues Not Represented in the *Handbook*

The challenge for any book Editor is often to define the scope of the volume. Authors for this text were instructed to focus their chapters on qualitative research in American music education. The decision to be exclusive to studies conducted in North America (Canada and the US) was made to help focus and contain the volume. Many authors struggled with this restriction as there is a rich traditional of qualitative research within international contexts. Another delimitation aimed at focusing the scope of this book was that authors include only qualitative studies that appear in published journals or as dissertations; not conference presentations or unpublished manuscripts.

Decisions regarding inclusion of contexts for music education centered around organizing the chapters so that there would not be too much overlap between topics but that all contexts that have been examined through a qualitative literature base would be addressed. I was initially concerned about overlap between early childhood music and general music, but these two authors were able to negotiate clear divisions in their chapters. I had considered a separate chapter on composition and improvisation, but eventually decided to encourage authors to include studies in this area within their context (i.e., general music, band, choral, and strings). There was some potential overlap between community music education and the chapters on choral, band, and strings, but again authors worked well together to address this. Studies that address adult musical learning appear within the community music education chapter. The chapter on pre-service teacher education includes studies up through undergraduate education, and the inservice teacher professional development chapter then includes beginning teacher induction, graduate education, and teacher professional development.

In terms of what might be "missing," the constructs of culturally relevant pedagogy and multiculturalism are not fully explored. Yiannis Miralis, author of the world music chapter, has written about the challenge of defining the terms associated with world music including: multicultural, multiethnic, and world music (Miralis 2002, 2006), and Bruce Carter, who authored the music education and diversity chapter, addresses definitions as well. However, both chapters had space only to gesture to the concepts of culturally relevant pedagogy and multiculturalism. I was unable to secure an author to address these concepts more completely.

Finally, there are important issues in music education not addressed in the text because qualitative researchers have not examined these areas. The most glaring example, to me, is in the area of music and arts education policy. In the Epilogue of their most recent *Sage Handbook of Qualitative Research* (4th ed.), Denzin and Lincoln (2011) suggest:

> One of the many myths surrounding qualitative research is that policy formulation utilizing such research is either difficult or impossible (Lincoln, 2011). Frequently dismissed as "anecdotal" by its detractors, qualitative research has often turned inward, addressing its own community of believers, who choose their own, less global, more locally focused means to effects social change. (717)

They go on to suggest that there are emerging trends in meta-analysis of qualitative data that may assist researchers, and they conclude by suggesting: "An exploration of these options, with a direct focus on their applicability for policy purposes, is the centerpiece of new and future efforts at addressing the cumulation issue" (717). Several researchers have published work in *Arts Education Policy Review* (*AEPR*) based on qualitative inquiries (Conway, Krueger, Robinson, Hacck, and Smith 2002; Edgar 2012; Robinson 2005; West 2011). These researchers have had to adjust their style of writing to reflect policy analysis as well as reporting of research. With music programs around the country under intense scrutiny, it may be time for all researchers to turn their energies toward policy work.

References

Conway, Colleen M., Patricia Krueger, Mitchell Robinson, Paul Haack, and Michael V. Smith. 2002. "Beginning Music Teacher Mentor and Induction Policy: A Cross-State Perspective." *Arts Education Policy Review* 104 (2): 9–17.

Denzin, Norman K., and Yvonne S. Lincoln. 2011. "Epilogue: Toward a "Refunctioned Ethnography." In *The Sage Handbook of Qualitative Research*, 4th ed., edited by Norman K. Denzin and Yvonne S. Lincoln, 715–18. Thousand Oaks, CA: Sage Publications.

Edgar, Scott. 2012. "Communication of Expectations between Principals and Entry-Year Instrumental Music Teachers." *Arts Education Policy Review* 113 (4): 136–46.

Lincoln, Yvonne S. 2011. "Policy from Prose: The Perfect Adequacy of Policy Formulation from Qualitative Research." Paper presented at the American Educational Research Association, New Orleans.

Miralis, Yiannis C. 2002. "Multicultural-World Music Education and Music Teacher Education at the Big-Ten Schools: Identified Problems and Suggestions." Doctoral dissertation, Michigan State University. *Dissertation Abstracts International* 54 (8): 2939A.

Miralis, Yiannis. 2006. "Clarifying the Terms 'Multicultural,' 'Multiethnic,' and 'World Music' Education through a Review of Literature." *Update: Applications of Research in Music Education* 24: 54–66. doi:10.1177/87551233060240020106

Robinson, Mitchell. 2005. "The Theory of Tensegrity and School/College Collaboration in Music Education." *Arts Education Policy Review* 106 (3): 9–18.

West, Chad. 2011. "Teaching Music in an Era of High Stakes Testing and Budget Reductions." *Arts Education Policy Review* 113 (2): 75–79.

Contributors

Margaret H. Berg, Professor of Instrumental/String Music Education, University of Colorado, Boulder

Liora Bresler, Professor of Curriculum and Instruction, University of Illinois

Mark Robin Campbell, Professor of Music Education, State University of New York, Potsdam

Bruce Carter, Member of the National Council on the Arts, National Endowment for the Arts

Colleen M. Conway, Professor of Music Education, University of Michigan

Scott N. Edgar, Associate Professor of Music, Lake Forest College

Erin M. Hansen, Assistant Professor of Music Education, University of Illinois

Ryan M. Hourigan, Professor of Music Education and Director, School of Music, Ball State University

Nathan B. Kruse, Associate Professor of Music Education, Case Western Reserve University

Yiannis Miralis, Associate Professor of Music Education, European University–Cyprus

Alison M. Reynolds, Professor of Music Education, Temple University

Ann Marie Stanley, Associate Professor of Music Education, Louisiana State University

Sandra L. Stauffer, Professor of Music in Music Education, Arizona State University

Bridget Sweet, Associate Professor of Music Education, University of Illinois

Linda K. Thompson, Professor in Music Education, Lee University

Chad West, Associate Professor of Music Education, Ithaca College

MODELS OF QUALITATIVE RESEARCH

CHAPTER 1

QUALITATIVE RESEARCH IN EARLY CHILDHOOD MUSIC EDUCATION

ALISON M. REYNOLDS

> Would it not be salutary for them and for music if our children, having lived a free musical life..., could grow into adults who are able and accustomed to create such intimate music for themselves and for the delight of others, within social groups that music may help to integrate into unassuming but principled creative societies? Might we not hope then to hear new kinds of music, new ways of using the limitless language of sound—a language that can be used with creative freedom only by those... who do not allow the voice of tradition to prevent them from hearing the voice that speaks within them?[1]

In February 1937, a pair of individuals who thought of children as spontaneous music-makers embarked on a multi-year journey with 14 young children[2] and a few other adults. With today's equivalent of a million dollars of funding from the Pillsbury Foundation for the Advancement of Music Education, along with advice from conductor Leopold Stokowski, they started the Pillsbury Foundation School. Their initial focus? Creating a fluid, music-object-rich environment to facilitate young children's musical play and study their spontaneous music-making (Wilson 1981).

As facilitator-observers, the pair extensively chronicled children's musical, expressive play through data sources now familiar to qualitative music education researchers: text, music notation, audio recordings, and photographs. Their results? First, evidence from their long-term, systematic documentation that, while in a preschool setting three hours daily[3]—young children express emergent musicality through individual and socially interactive moments of spontaneous music-making. Second, a historically important moment for early childhood music education qualitative researchers, most of whom now know the individuals relative to the Pillsbury Foundation Studies (1937–1945), even if only by name: Moorhead and Pond.

Though Moorhead and Pond were not trained as early childhood music teachers or qualitative researchers, their work represents the first early childhood music education qualitative research in the United States. In 2013, just over 75 years after they began, their work continues to represent overlapping contextual considerations for early childhood music education qualitative researchers: philosophical, historical, political, ethical, methodological, musical, and technological.

Within this chapter, I trace events supporting the intersections of early childhood music education and qualitative research, celebrating the continued relevance of Moorhead and Pond's contributions. I offer points of view about expanding notions of adults' and young children's roles in the research processes and honoring young children's capacities to collaborate as both music-makers and researchers. Finally, after surveying qualitative approaches and topics in publications in early childhood music education research in the twenty-first century,[4] I offer how the collective professional experience within the profession might continue to propel qualitative research in early childhood music education forward.

1.1. Early Childhood, Music Education, and Qualitative Research: Interdependent Histories

Though researchers have offered evidence that music for young children has been of interest long before the settling and colonization of the United States (e.g., Humphreys 1985), their systematic study of its history has been infrequent. Alvarez (1981) completed a comprehensive dissertation chronicling in separate chapters the history of early childhood music education in the United States from 1900 to 1980, and *early childhood music education* as practice and a research focus. A contemporary review of those histories (with the goals of considering the interdependence of those histories alongside understanding whom music educators had included in those histories) provides a backdrop to begin to understand the emergence and applications of qualitative research within early childhood music education.

In 1874, when the National Education Association formally established nursery school for children three and four years old, and kindergarten for children five years old, children typically began formal schooling when six years old (Alvarez 1981). In the late 1880s, G. Stanley Hall began studying young children quantitatively by age groups, influencing researchers in psychology to study young children *systematically* and *scientifically* (Humphreys 1985), and report general characteristics of children based on age ranges for various stages of development. Practitioners in early childhood education accepted researchers' recommendations about children's needs, believing "that research... on the development of young children was directly relevant to early childhood education" (Spodek and Saracho 1998, viii). As structured models for day care and curriculum within schooling began to emerge in the 1900s, education scholars also began to categorize and study children by age (Beatty 1998) rather than studying them in contexts of mixed ages. Meanwhile, music teachers used the "personal experience method" (Barr, Davis, and Johnson 1953; as cited in Mark 1992, 48) rather than research (Draper and Gayle 1987) to guide their work with children.

Moorhead and Pond's research in the late 1930s and early 1940s marks the first evidence of music-specific research in early childhood settings in the United States, championed as the beginning of a "new phase in the history of early childhood music education" (McDonald and Simons 1989, 15). At that time, Moorhead and Pond's specific interests in documenting children's spontaneous music-making fit well with tenets in the prominent Progressive Education movements, which valued play and music-making as integral to nurturing young children's creative self-expression and social and emotional development (Alvarez 1981). As the 1930s and 1940s were unfolding, however, music educators began to weigh in about striking a balance between unstructured tenets of those movements and increasing structured experiences to ensure children's achievement of specific music concepts such as singing, listening, and playing instruments. Additionally, music educators focused on developing curriculum based on those concepts, evaluating programs and course content, and measuring individuals' music achievement (Alvarez 1981).

In 1949—four years after the Pillsbury Foundation Studies (the Studies) ended, recordings of the children's music-making while attending the Pillsbury School were released. By then, music educators might have known about "the four Pillsbury Foundation Studies, the recordings, and a pamphlet made by the Pillsbury Foundation" (Kierstead 1994, 214). That same year, the Music Education Research Council (MERC) publicly declared the importance of music in the lives of preschool children (Morgan 1949 as referenced in Alvarez 1981). MERC supported music education for children between two and six years old, described mothers' music-making with their children as well as children's music-making on their own, recommended 20 minutes of daily music activities, and called attention to the need for teachers to teach music to preschool age children (Alvarez 1981).

By 1951, music educators acknowledged that young children under six years old were being cared for in various settings: "nursery schools, kindergartens, church and community groups, and in the home" (Alvarez 1981, 30). Although educators needed to begin considering appropriate music education practices for that age group as different from practices appropriate for elementary general music, and their music-learning contexts as more diverse before elementary school than when in elementary school, the profession concentrated on teachers' needs to direct activities to ensure children's achievement of music skills demonstrating understanding of music concepts. Throughout the 1950s and into the 1960s, combined challenges of replicating aspects of the Pillsbury School and the incompatibility of the Pillsbury School tenets with the concept movement seemed to have silenced interests in any practice or qualitative research resembling Moorhead and Pond's work.

In 1965, the US government funded the national preschool program Head Start for children three and four years old, partly a response to the increasing numbers of young children whose mothers had entered the workforce after both world wars, and partly a reflection of the increasing awareness of educational needs among impoverished children (Spodek and Saracho 1998). Even though children younger than three years old were not included in the initial Head Start movement (Perkins-Gough 2007), the program created opportunities for music education researchers and teachers, as the young children attending Head Start preschools came from different socioeconomic backgrounds from the children to whom music educators previously had access.

Two years later, participants from the Tanglewood Symposium convened, forming the subcommittee Music for Early Childhood. They agreed that music programs and teacher preparation should include preschool and very young children (Mark 1999). Specifically, the Committee on Critical Issues stated

> We recommend that MENC,[5] recognizing the unrealized potentials of education in general and particularly of music in the lives of children from the ages of three to eight, (a) establish a commission that would cooperate with recognized leaders in the field of early childhood education and of Head Start and of other programs to develop a systematic plan of action and content for the effective use of music; (b) apprise college and university music departments of the necessity to ... prepare music education students to teach music to three- to eight-year-old children from all economic, social, and cultural backgrounds; and (c) charge its Music Education Research Council with the responsibility of defining areas of research related to the use of music for this age group. (Choate 1968, iii)

The Music Educators National Conference (MENC) adopted goals and objectives after Tanglewood, including "[to involve] people of all ages in learning music" (Mark 1999, 19). Music educators delegated only ages 3–11 years as "the optimum ages for developing musical interest, skills, and attitudes of young children" (Choate 1968, 136). Perhaps because children younger than three typically were not in settings with music educators, they were excluded from their decree of *music for all ages*.

In 1971, Moorhead and Pond surfaced in a published research-focused article. Zimmerman (1971/2011) published an article bridging research and practice, focusing mostly on elementary school-aged children. In it, she referenced Moorhead and Pond's original publication once, under the musical characteristic *manipulative development*: "Some researchers view the imaginative playing of instruments as an extension of sounds made by their own body" (25–26).

Roughly throughout the 1970s, scholars published practical texts for teachers working with children in kindergarten or younger (e.g., Andress 1980; Aronoff 1969;

Boardman and Andress 1981; Choate 1970; Leonard 1968; Marsh 1974; McDonald 1979). Greenberg (1979) appears to have been the first to describe in early childhood music texts the ways a developing baby in utero responds to sounds. Greenberg also described music behaviors for children between birth and three years old. Although many authors stitched narratively descriptive vignettes into their texts, providing realistic glimpses of young children's music-making within music activities and perhaps foreshadowing the profession's adoption of ethnographic and narrative approaches to describe learning and teaching interactions in early childhood music education, through the mid-1970s, Moorhead and Pond's continued to be the only qualitative study in early childhood music. Music scholars seemed to be unaware of, were unsure how to apply, or perhaps discounted Moorhead and Pond's work.[6]

Shirley Shelley and Bruce Wilson, colleagues at University of Maryland, began to change that. When one of Shelley's graduate students wrote about the Studies for an assignment, Shelly became curious (Kierstead 2006). Together, Shelley and Wilson began a quest to understand more about Moorhead and Pond's study of children's spontaneous music-making. Their pursuit led them in 1975 to stakeholders in the School: "an original trustee, some parents of former students" (Wilson 1981, 20)—one of whom "[transcribed] the Daily Observation Notes" (Kierstead 1994, 214), which were the index cards on which Moorhead or Pond wrote text, notation, and (in Moorhead's case), invented notation. The contemporary pair, Shelley and Wilson, conducted interviews with pioneers Moorhead and Pond. By 1978, Wilson had completed the process of archiving artifacts from the School, and its trustees approved housing them at the MENC Archives at the University of Maryland (Wilson 1981).

1.1.1. Sparking Interest in Early Childhood Music Education Qualitative Research

In 1978, a few events occurred that, together, represent another pivotal moment in defining early childhood within qualitative music education research. First, Pond spoke at the annual MENC convention, "breaking a self-imposed silence of thirty-three years" (Kierstead 2006, 285). Second, the Pillsbury Foundation, in response to music educators' heightened interest, re-published the four original studies as *Music of Young Children* (Wilson 1981). Third, Pond began a period in which he would publish additional responses to and reflections about his work at the School. Fourth, Shelley (1981) began a qualitative project studying spontaneous music-making among children ages three to five years. She reported that Moorhead and Pond's findings from the Studies continued to be relevant in a "contemporary music setting" (29). Aside from Moorhead and Pond's studies, she cited philosophical contributions from two additional sources as related research: "the Contemporary Music Project on Creativity (1966), and the Manhattanville Music Curriculum Program (Thomas, 1970)" (27). She seems to have been the first to cite Pond's then-recent MENC speech as related research. After this point, scholars increasingly included Moorhead and Pond's work among their references within early childhood texts and research.

Shelley (1981) essentially highlighted a need for researchers to study children's music culture using qualitative techniques. Influenced, perhaps, by Pond's comments in the introduction of the re-publication of the Studies (1978), she acknowledged that children's "self-initiated music activity can be misleading to adult musicians" (26) who might characterize the activity as "undisciplined" and "lack[ing] purpose" (26). She encouraged the profession to understand that young children have their "own music." Additionally, Shelley referred to Pond's MENC address, reminding the profession:

> Children must be free to make their own music in their own ways. They need freedom to move, freedom to play instruments, freedom to make choices, and freedom to construct sounds.... We should encourage children to acquire improvisational skills and techniques, for it is through such participation that the child develops aural discrimination, knowledge of sound, and the ability to think sound. (27)

Finally, Shelley offered evidence from her studies that Moorhead and Pond's observations of young children—from a different setting and decade—were transferrable to her situation: "children pursue[d] musical activities on their own during a free activity period" (29). Amidst Pond's re-emergence, Shelley's and Wilson's re-presenting the Studies, and Shelley's qualitatively based studies, researchers had a newly laid path to study young children's music-making in context, as fluid, flexible, and spontaneous.

Wilson reflected on the dry spell of research preceding this "rediscovery" (Kierstead 2006, 285) of Moorhead and Pond, observing that the original research "came and went when the music education profession was not ready for [it].... Very few musicians specialized in early childhood music and the profession was ill-equipped to study the musical development of the very young. Graduate research in music education was in its infancy.... [and] few people [were] looking for the answers suggested in the Pillsbury Foundation School..." (Wilson 1981, 15). In contrast to the dry spell during the previous 35 years, the 1980s would represent a watershed moment in the United States for early childhood music education qualitative research.

In 1980, members of MENC officially founded the Early Childhood Special Research Interest Group (EC SRIG). Members of the EC SRIG notably declared that early childhood encompasses children from infancy through at least six years old. They sought to promote early childhood research by encouraging research and collaborations, identifying appropriate measurement tools, and disseminating findings—including through meetings and publications. Five Task Groups formed to direct activity into understanding needs assessment, the nature of teaching, the identification of children's social and musical behaviors, the nature of musical development in infants, and music development relative to early childhood development (L. M. Walker 1991).[7] Despite a lack of models for qualitative approaches to research, members chose language that, in hindsight, could accommodate them.

Apparently, Pond's conference appearance and the re-publication of the Studies in 1978 stirred controversy. In 1981, Pond addressed the profession, opening his article with the following statements.

> I want to make it perfectly clear... what I was *not* doing—what I did not set out to do. There were in the beginning misunderstandings (some of them no doubt genuine) thirty-three years ago, and they have persisted even to the present time. (1)

First among the things he hoped to clarify? His intentions to document what he learned from and with the children musically, rather than to test, measure, or evaluate children based on music variables determined a priori. The remainder of the address represents his restorying—taking a reflexive look at—his journey that led him to discover, to his surprise, that young children are spontaneous, creative music-makers and his challenges documenting evidence of that.

Pond's re-emergence coincided with the emergence of doctoral students who chose qualitative methodologies to study music in early childhood. Researchers from over a dozen universities across the United States produced dissertations using a variety of approaches, such as case study (Fox 1982), ethnography (J. R. Zimmerman 1983), or naturalistic observation (Metz 1986; Miller 1983). Two dissertation researchers featured both qualitative data and quantitative data (Bedsole 1987; Bennett 1981); and one specifically inquired into and described the benefits of using multiple methods within one research project (Fiedler 1982).[8]

Not long after, the National Association for the Education of Young Children (NAEYC) established age parameters for the term *early childhood* as the years from at least birth through eight years old (Bredekamp 1987). Andress asserted that the starkly different general developmental characteristics within such a broad age group made it difficult for music practitioners to apply "early childhood" research results. She proposed distinguishing among *preschool* and *primary age* children, suggesting that preschool encompass "neonate/infant (0–18 mo.); toddler (18–36 mo.); three year old; four year old; [and] kindergartner (5–6 yrs)" (11), and primary encompass "children six through eight years of age" (1986, 11). She recommended that researchers study children within those age groups to learn more about characteristics of typical *music* development.

Tuition-based early childhood music-specific programs, many with university affiliations, provided venues for parents to introduce music education to their children. Most offered weekly classes for children 18 months or older in age groups similar to those Andress suggested. Defining early childhood music programs by their curriculum, methodologies, or age groups (introducing programs with infants in the early 1990s) inspired a few studies during the early to mid-1990s, in which researchers studied aspects of those programs qualitatively (e.g., Collier-Slone 1991; Hicks 1993; Reynolds 1995; Yang 1990).

1.1.2. Reporting on Qualitative Research in Early Childhood Music Education

In the mid-1980s, early childhood music education researchers promoted studying young children's music "in dynamic natural contexts" (M. P. Zimmerman 1984, 75) using naturalistic, observational, ethnographic, narrative, and interpretive approaches. Peery, Peery, and Draper (1987) published early childhood music education qualitative and quantitative research chapters side by side. J. C. Peery described the collection as "systematic studies" (vii) about music's role in young children's lives. He shared the editors' collective hopes that "beyond [contributing to] academic research, [the studies will encourage] an occasional teacher, or even possibly a parent, . . . to consider broader implications, and perhaps broader involvements of music in children's lives" (viii). Peery recognized, perhaps, that the research in the United States described a very narrow slice of children as well as contexts for music education. As the 1980s were drawing to a close, McDonald and Simons (1989) published a practical text for adults working with young children birth through six, within which they summarized as the Studies. Their publisher's formatting style offered readers citations of Moorhead and Pond alongside recommendations for teaching creativity and improvisation, sound exploration and timbre, children's music preferences, and use of instruments in the classroom. Additionally, they cite Shelley (1981) and her observations about learning environments that nurture children's music creativity.

In 1992, in a chapter summarizing early childhood music-learning research, Scott-Kassner (1992) planted *early childhood* squarely between the years birth to age eight, citing NAEYC. She described qualitative studies by Moorhead and Pond, Shelley, Metz, and Miller amidst a "generally clinical" (634) landscape in which qualitative research is "often viewed with suspicion by traditional, trained researchers" (634). J. C. Peery (1993) noted the profession lacked a "specific conceptual or editorial method or approach that separates early childhood material from the broader context [of music development]" (207). Not long after, MENC (1994) published music standards for students in kindergarten to 12th grade; and, another year later, standards for children two to four years old (MENC 1995).

During the 1990s, the number of qualitative early childhood music education dissertations more than doubled as compared to the 1980s, without the authors subsequently publishing research articles based on their dissertations. By the end of the 1990s, though, the landscape in general early childhood education research had shifted again. Scholars referred to a wider and more rapid acceptance of "studying children in context" (Graue and Walsh 1998) using qualitative research techniques, and these studies gained visibility in the field through qualitative conferences (Hatch and Wisniewski 1990) and publications (e.g., Hatch 1995b; Spodek, Saracho, and Pellegrini 1998). The beginning of the twenty-first century would be the next watershed moment.

In 2002, *The New Handbook of Research on Music Teaching and Learning* (Colwell and Richardson 2002) featured early childhood music teaching and research—including qualitative references—more prominently than in the first. By 2010, the number of qualitative early childhood music education dissertations again increased over the last decade, and the combined number in 2010 through 2011 already had approached half the total number from the first decade of the twenty-first century. Overall, variety in approaches persisted. Specifically, researchers (e.g., Schonauer 2002; Dansereau 2005; and Hardy 2011) increasingly collected both qualitative data and quantitative data. Time will tell the extent to which twenty-first-century early childhood music education qualitative researchers subsequently publish their dissertation studies.

Just over 75 years after the Pillsbury Foundation Studies, and 30-plus years since Moorhead and Pond's rediscovery, there is clear historical evidence that the profession has increased its attention to early childhood music education and research (Alvarez 1981; Overland and Reynolds 2010). Music educators have made strides in offering definitions of both *early childhood music education* and *qualitative early childhood music education research*. Many music educators now embrace ages for early childhood endorsed by NAEYC (birth to eight years); and support National Association for Music Education's (NAfME) call for musically rich environments for all children from birth, and *Music Standards* for children two years of age and older. At the time of this writing, NAfME is spearheading a revision of its music standards, which will contribute to the continued evolution of early childhood music education within the United States.

1.2. Stakeholders in Early Childhood Music Education: Considerations for Qualitative Researchers

In 1966, Kodály shared, "I used to think the ideal age for beginning a child's musical education was nine months before birth. Now I think it is nine months before his mother's birth" (Salty Saint 1966, 41). His observation suggests consideration of several beliefs asserted within music education: each person—including those youngest and mostly invisible in the historical definitions of early childhood music education—is born musical (Blacking 1973) or musically literate (Reynolds, Long, and Valerio 2007); makes music spontaneously (Moorhead and Pond 1978); occupies a "cultural and historical" space relative to others (Graue and Walsh 1998, 9); lives as an active agent in her music education; and possesses powerful epistemological orientations to policy, research, and practice. Also, Kodály's observation challenges music educators to consider that each member of society plays a role in the music education of the youngest children.

Including each person as integral to another's music education suggests value in featuring the voices of all stakeholders in early childhood music education research, including children, parents, general and music-specific preservice and in-service teachers, paraprofessionals, administrators, and policymakers. Specifically, it makes sense to include them, as they are "the very people ... who say they want to see children develop fully as thinkers, 'feelers,' and doers, [so] they may fulfill their potential—now, in their childhoods, and later, in their maturity" (Campbell 1999, 8).

Early childhood qualitative research scholars have reminded researchers that *early childhood* is an adult construction (e.g., Graue and Walsh 1998; Hatch 1995a). As illustrated in the previous section of this chapter, teachers and researchers have most influenced construct notions of *early childhood* within music education. In addition to defining children by their chronological age, adults define children "physically, developmentally, socially, culturally, discursively, historically, linguistically, [and] politically" (Graue and Hawkins 2005, 45) from a "generational perspective" (Mayall 2002). That means adult qualitative researchers enter a site with a different role to fill, organized in part by their research purpose and questions relative to the children and context. In those sites, they interact with other adults. Each carries a unique perspective about children as individuals. Each also carries a unique perspective of the construct *music education in early childhood*. With multifaceted combinations for defining children come multifaceted ways to learn from and about children in research. Recognizing the confluence of perspectives emphasizes qualitative researchers' needs to adopt consistent reflexivity (Davis 1998). One's research purpose and questions position adults and children within the research and its dissemination, even when projects lack children's voices. The purpose and questions also suggest roles for the researcher in early childhood settings.

Lahman (2008) collected researchers' descriptions of various roles they adopted or felt were applied to them when entering the research site, such as Corsaro's (2005) "reactive role" to describe waiting to be invited before interacting with children; Thorne's (1993) "adult visitor" role in relation to the research site, including attempts to avoid being defined as "mother or teacher"; Fine and Sandstrom's (1988) "adult friend" role; Mandell's (1988) "least adult role"; Christensen's (2004) "an unusual type of adult or a different type of adult who is interested in children's perspectives"; or Wolcott's (1972) "teacher as an enemy." To summarize, "the positioning of researcher as [constituting] a variety of adults in relation to the children they research allows for multi-faceted, changeable relationships in the research site with a variety of children who will [in turn] invariably perceive adults in different ways" (Lahman 2008, 290).

Lahman's reference to "children they research" (2008, 290) reflects a frequent scenario among researchers: adults respectfully conduct research *on* children. Adults typically make all decisions throughout a study; attain consent from other adults (children ages 7–17 years old could refuse to assent); and collect, analyze, and disseminate the research. Although children generate the data, they have not owned them. In such research, children would be easy to *locate* (Janzen 2008). That is, adults position children as the focus in research reports, yet have chosen which words children will "speak." They have "othered" children (Lahman 2008, 282). Researchers reflexively work to be mindful in such adult-centric settings "whether [their] capturing a moment in time is capturing the child's reality or whether it is the researcher's representation of the child's reality, given his or her own filter and assumption" (Jipson and Jipson 2005, 42). After all, "we who work with children are no longer children ourselves" (Campbell 1999, 7). How, then, do researchers ensure "[children's direct engagement] in the process of meaning making and knowledge production?" (Jipson and Jipson 2005, 42). How do researchers avoid making children objects they are studying (e.g., Christensen and James 2000)? Scholars have considered potential answers to those questions, some of which are discussed in the section that follows.

1.3. Researching within a Qualitative Early Childhood Music Education Landscape

MacNaughton, Smith, and Davis (2007) suggest reconsidering children's roles in research. They recommend that researchers shift from the traditional adult-centric research process toward at least a more equal process. Liberally, they favor tipping the process in favor of a child-centric research process in which "children initiate and direct research. Children have the initial idea . . . and decide how the project is to be carried out. Adults are available to the children but do not take charge" (172). Adults—as providers of primary care—do choose or prepare the setting that offers possibilities to children as researchers and guide or scaffold children's research processes.

Teachers adopting the Reggio Emilia philosophy embrace the view that adults create an environment in which children's natural inquisitiveness, collaborative spirits, and active agency as co-constructors of knowledge thrive. In Reggio-inspired settings, young children's inquiry, coupled with adults' provision of materials and availability for scaffolding children's learning, enriches the experience of co-construction of knowledge for all (e.g., Kim 2012). Children, early childhood teachers, parents— even the environment, the "third teacher"—collaborate on *projects*. Children use their "hundred languages" (Infant-Toddler Centres 2010) to express themselves and to make learning visible. Projects require virtually every aspect of qualitative research, with two chief distinctions. First, adults offer provocations based on children's initiations of inquiry. The adults become *co-researchers with children*. Second, teachers typically document and display results of the co-constructed research only within the school community.

How did Moorhead or Pond view their adult roles as teachers or researchers? Did they view children as children, students, collaborative researchers, or subjects? We know more from Pond than from Moorhead about potential answers to those questions.[9] Reflecting on his time at the School, Pond (1980) described being with children for "almost eight years of creative companionship" (39), ready to listen and watch, "to discover how creative music activity was provoked and generated in young children" (39). "I was always ready, when invited, to join in the children's music making . . . not so much as a teacher, but as a musician and composer . . . available but never [imposing]" (39); "by collaborating with them in their improvising whenever they asked me to—which was frequently" (Pond 1981, 10); or "help[ing] them to learn to read and write musical notation, in a manner . . . agreeable to their perceptions and not inhibitory of their spontaneity, [and only] after they had told me they wanted to learn" (11).

Moorhead and Pond created text and notation to share children's musicing. Children have a prominent position throughout the Studies. Hence, readers can easily *locate* children as most important in the reports. Though evidence suggests the music environment moved from child-initiated to more teacher-centered as early as fall 1938 (Kierstead 2006), it seems that Moorhead and Pond strove to honor viewpoints important in contemporary qualitative research: children's "authentic voice and participation," "young people [as] valuable experts in their cultures . . . and therefore integral partners in the research process" (Janzen 2008, 289). It seems possible, at least, that children at the Pillsbury Foundation School felt integral to the project. Pond quoted one child as having said, "Everybody stand up and raise your hands to the sky. That means you're all members of this music; we're all members of that tune we were playing" (Wilson 1981, 20).

A researcher's report of children's music-making, movement, or conversation—especially the youngest—has most often represented children's voices within early childhood qualitative music education research (see volume 2, chapter 7). Reports and audio documentation of research in the United States that stems from purposeful intentions similar to those behind Moorhead and Pond's research are nonexistent in peer-reviewed journals or books. Reasons for that seem simple: early childhood music education researchers—typically full-time music teacher educators—have lacked opportunities (and funding) to spend unstructured music time with children longitudinally in a context established primarily with a belief that children are spontaneous music-makers.

Contemporary early childhood music education qualitative research examples approaching Moorhead and Pond's experiences resonate with researchers using tenets of Project Zero and Reggio Emilia, settings in which adults work with children to "make learning visible" (Harvard 2006). In Reggio Emilia projects, early childhood researchers adopted the roles of *Music Pedagogues* or *Music Atelieristas*, listening for and scaffolding child-initiated and child-directed music and music projects—or offering music-based provocations for children to consider (Burton 2011; Reynolds, Cancemi, et al. 2012; Reynolds, Filsinger, et al. 2012; Smith 2011). In each study, researchers provided evidence to support children as capable of initiating and developing projects when adults spend extended lengths of time with children, accept that the youngest of children indeed initiate music-making and music-based inquiry, facilitate and scaffold children's music-learning interests as their music-making and music-focused projects unfolded over time—including children's documentation of their music-making or music-focused projects—and ensure that children's thoughts and feelings are represented alongside the music-making or other music-based data that unfolds.

Pushing beyond Moorhead and Pond's accomplishments, examples are emerging of children successfully providing initiation, design, and presentation[10] of research. To date, although children are featured as co-constructors of inquiry in early childhood settings (e.g., Clark 2007), they remain invisible as co-authors. Until we create venues for them to be co-authors and co-disseminators, we only can imagine the powerful influence their voices could have.

As the 21st century continues to unfold, researchers likely will be alternately relieved and overwhelmed by resources specific to early childhood qualitative research.[11] Prominently, authors emphasize the necessity for adults to listen to children's voices. Listening to children's voices through spoken or musical expression requires adults to spend extended time in context with children as they play naturally. Doing so honors the children and their natural interests, and fosters relationships with them, a critical component for both the child and the adult. "Data must be generated before it can be collected" (Graue and Walsh 1998, 91). Otherwise, researchers must realize that children "who sense marginalization have often become experts at illusion, telling investigators what they want to hear but possibly little of what they might be thinking at any moment in time" (Malewski 2005, 220).

As children generate data, using video recordings to collect that data is both easier as technology improves, and continuously fraught with technical challenges (e.g., Walsh, Bakir, et al. 2007)—including ones Shelley (1981) identified. Even so, video provides ways to re-view many (but not all) details about actors in complex contexts. Pond likely would have valued using video-recording devices in his work, as he took copious observation notes "to have an intelligible picture of the music of these young children, to consider the social and individual activities as a related background, and to observe the fringing activities of speech, physical movement and any production of sound" (Moorhead and Pond 1978, 8), and had only audio recordings of children's music-making. Likely, too, he would have agreed that when studying children's music-making in dynamic contexts, inevitably, amounts and types of data are time-consuming to organize, analyze, and write up.

Qualitative early childhood music education researchers typically rely on various technologies to provide evidence for their findings as they analyze, triangulate, and audit data. Increasingly, they use technology to share, store, and report data, particularly for presentations and, more recently, for disseminating via online publishing. As technologies evolve, researchers must work to ensure that file formats remain accessible yet secure. Researchers and their readers may find data collected as pictures are worth a thousand words, in audio files data worth double that of pictures, and in video, triple. Many children already are experts at using diverse applications on computers and portable devices like iPhones, iPods, and iPads, a skill that will help them as they assume more sophisticated roles as researchers. Their data generation, collection, sharing, and more formal dissemination—whether through text, notation, photographs, audio files, or video files—will be priceless. Regardless, everyone's use of such files continues to require utmost sensitivity to the children (see volume 2, chapter 1).

1.3.1. Surveying Twenty-First-Century Qualitative Approaches to Early Childhood Music Education Research

A survey of journals and edited books featuring twenty-first-century early childhood music education qualitative research reveals that researchers most frequently select theoretical approaches to orient their research (see volume 1, chapter 4). Researchers have addressed multifaceted considerations from various stakeholders in early childhood music education using diverse models in their reports, such as an ethnomusicological/phenomenological study illuminating complex dimensions of children's musical cultures (Campbell 2010); a phenomenological study about interactive improvisation between adults and children (Custodero 2007); a phenomenological, particularistic case study regarding preservice music teachers' perceptions of teaching children with special needs (Hourigan 2009); a mixed methods study about students with special needs and conditions that best support their music learning (Gerrity, Hourigan, and Horton 2013); a heuristic study from a three-year music-play-based relationship among a music teacher educator/researcher, mother, two music education graduate students, and a child with autism (Valerio, Sy, Gruber, and Stockman 2011); narrative accounts from early childhood or general music teachers (Neely 2007; Reynolds 2012; L. N. Walker 2009); case studies in which teachers notice music's influence on children with special needs (McCord 2009; Taggart, Alvarez, and Schubert 2011); and case studies describing parents'—and sometimes children's—engagement with the early childhood music teacher via social media networks (Koops 2011, 2012).

Researchers have applied Denzin's steps of interpretation to learn about singing practices in families (Custodero 2006); content analysis to describe ways parenting magazines feature music information (Sims and Udtaisuk 2008); conversation analysis to describe vocal and movement-based music interactions (Reynolds 2006); Csikszentmihalyi's flow to their own teacher/researchers' reflections (Custodero and St. John 2007); and symbolic interactionism as elementary general music teachers consider the meaning of music aptitude (Reynolds and Hyun 2004) or reflect on their teaching (Valerio 2009; Valerio and Freeman 2009) or service-learning fieldwork (e.g., Reynolds, Jerome, Preston, and Haynes 2005).

Researchers have also applied community of practice (e.g., Gruenhagen 2009; Hornbach 2011); philosophical inquiry (e.g., Ilari 2011); play theory (e.g., Berger and Cooper 2003; Koops 2011); caregiving theory (Custodero and Johnson-Green 2008); Super and Harkness's (2002) developmental niche framework (Custodero 2009); theories of language acquisition (Burton 2002, 2011); Gordon's (2003) *Music Learning Theory for Newborn and Young Children* (Reynolds 2006; Valerio, Seaman, Yap, Santucci, and Tu 2006); or developmentally appropriate practice (e.g., Miranda 2004) as they apply to music acquisition, early childhood music teaching, or early childhood music-teacher education. Occasionally, researchers share techniques for analyzing their data, rather than articulating a codified theoretical approach (e.g., Cooper and Cardany

2011; Kastner 2011; McCord 2009; Scott, Jellison, et al. 2007).[12] And, when relevant, researchers consistently reference Moorhead and Pond.

1.4. THE FUTURE: CONSIDERATIONS FOR EARLY CHILDHOOD MUSIC EDUCATION QUALITATIVE RESEARCHERS

Early childhood has long been a collection of diverse constructions, constituting multiple realities in diverse settings during a time when children typically develop and change most rapidly. Since the Pillsbury Foundation Studies, the profession increasingly agrees that "music happens to children, ... much of it is 'visible'—and surely audible—in many settings and circumstances" (Campbell 1999, 7), and is of importance to children. The profession also increasingly agrees that qualitative research is viable for learning more about children's music-making in dynamic contexts (McCarthy 2010). What Pond said about the Studies in 1981 continues to resonate: "*I believe this research ... may continue to be useful to researchers who are working today*" (Pond 1981, 11). In addition to the Studies, early childhood music education qualitative researchers have books, journal articles, and dissertations within and outside the United State to guide them. What might be their next steps?

As music educators grapple generally with the relevance of out-of-school music to *music education*, researchers might help communicate that, until children are required to attend school, and then, until required schooling requires music, all of children's music-making and music education happens out-of-school. As Pond (1981) and, subsequently, researchers who have documented children's emergent and co-constructed music have reported, children are musical long before they reach school music settings. Continuing to use qualitative approaches to document ways diverse stakeholders successfully validate and extend children's predispositions will help practitioners guide children to "create ... intimate music for themselves and for the delight of others, within social groups that music may help to integrate into unassuming but principled creative societies" (Pond 1978, 4). Collaborative research among stakeholders in children's lives (including children themselves) across disciplines and across the globe likely will help the profession better articulate research into how all children—from at least birth—fit in the relevance, context, and best practices within music education, music-teacher preparation, music-researcher preparation, and teaching in higher education curricula. As technologies for collecting data generation, their analyses, and dissemination advance, researchers should think about advancing their research sensibly, yet creatively—"not allow[ing] the voice of tradition to prevent them from hearing the voice that speaks within them" (Pond 1978, 4).

Qualitatively, researchers can gather the profession's collective early childhood initiatives, seek consistency within the profession by using the term *early childhood* as encompassing children from at least birth to eight years old, establish research collaboratives, construct broad-scale studies in which researchers unify the purpose and essential research questions, and increase efforts to study diverse settings to learn about diverse children. Generally, they should prioritize the continued dissemination of their research—particularly dissertations—with authentic, compelling, articulate, persistent, and far, up-reaching voices. United efforts to feature audio, video, and photographs in research dissemination likely will advance understandings about early childhood music education among children, parents, teachers, and policymakers.

In closing, the combined economic, environmental, and political climates in the United States make the future of music education for our nation's youngest children difficult to predict. Very recent successful efforts among advocates petitioning the elimination of school music education programs suggest that, when children and stakeholders directly deliver messages about the meaning of music and music education in their lives, decision-makers listen. Maintaining rigor and adding cohesion to qualitative dissemination efforts that prominently feature diverse children's and stakeholders' musical and spoken voices about music in relation to their health, education, and welfare may deliver powerful insights that, in turn, may strengthen policymakers' cohesive commitments to the music education of each person in the United States—from the age of "nine months before [the child's] birth" (Salty Saint 1966, 41). "There is still very much to be done" (Pond 1981, 11); qualitatively, there is much we could accomplish together.

Notes

1. Pond, 1978, 3–4.
2. Children in the first study were 1.5–8.5 years old (Moorhead and Pond 1978, 7).
3. Moorhead and Pond, 1978, 79.
4. Excluding dissertations.
5. The Music Educators National Conference (MENC) changed its name in 2011 to the National Association for Music Education (NAfME).
6. Aronoff (1969) and M. P. Zimmerman (1971/2011), for example, are exceptions.
7. In 1991, the Sengstack Educational Foundation provided funding to the EC SRIG for their creation of an academic journal. After one issue—with citations of qualitative research—publications ceased.
8. See volume 1, chapter 10.
9. Wilson (1981) describes Pillsbury Study materials, which are archived at the MENC Historical Center at the University of Maryland.
10. Although this example is with co-researchers slightly older than eight years, note Filsinger 2011.
11. See, for example, Aubrey, David, et al. 2000; Christensen and James 2000; Graue and Walsh 1998; Greene and Hill 2005; Hatch 1995b, 2007; Heath, Hindmarsh, and P. Luff 2010; MacNaughton, Rolfe, and Siraj-Blatchford 2001; Nutbrown 2002; Soto and Swadener 2005; Spodek and Saracho 2005; Spodek, Saracho, and Pellegrini 1998; and Tisdall, Davis, and Gallagher 2009.

12. See Hatch (2007b, 230) for remarks on this topic, specifically in relation to early childhood qualitative research.

REFERENCES

Alvarez, B. J. 1981. "Preschool Music Education and Research on the Musical Development of Preschool Children: 1900 to 1980." PhD diss., University of Michigan.

Andress, B. 1980. *Music Experiences in Early Childhood*. New York: Holt, Rinehart and Winston.

Andress, B. 1986. "Toward an Integrated Developmental Theory for Early Childhood Music Education." *Bulletin of the Council for Research in Music Education* 86: 10–17.

Aronoff, F. W. 1969. *Music and Young Children*. New York: Holt, Rinehart and Winston.

Aubrey, C., T. David, R. Godfrey, and L. Thompson, eds. 2000. *Early Childhood Educational Research: Issues in Methodology and Ethics*. London: Routledge/Falmer.

Barr, A. S., R. A. Davis, and O. Johnson, eds. 1953. *Educational Research and Appraisal*. Chicago: J. B. Lippincott.

Beatty, B. 1998. "From Infant Schools to Project Head Start: Doing Historical Research in Early Childhood Education." In *Yearbook in Early Childhood Education*, vol. 8: *Issues in Early Childhood Educational Research*, edited by B. Spodek, O. N. Saracho, and A. D. Pellegrini, 1–29. New York: Teachers College Press.

Bedsole, E. A. 1987. "A Descriptive Study of the Musical Abilities of Three- and Four-Year-Old Children." PhD diss., University of Illinois at Urbana-Champaign.

Bennett, P. D. 1981. "An Exploratory Study of Children's Multi-Sensory Responses to Symbolizing Musical Sound through Speech Rhythm Patterns." PhD diss., University of North Texas.

Berger, A. A., and S. Cooper. 2003. "Musical Play: A Case Study of Preschool Children and Parents." *Journal of Research in Music Education* 51 (2): 151–65.

Blacking, J. 1973. *How Musical Is Man?* Seattle: University of Washington Press.

Boardman, E., and B. Andress. 1981. *The Music Book: Teacher's Reference Book, Grade K*. New York: Holt, Rinehart and Winston.

Bredekamp, S., ed. 1987. *Developmentally Appropriate Practice in Early Childhood Programs Serving Children from Birth through Age 8*. Washington, DC: National Association for the Education of Young Children.

Burton, S. L. 2002. "An Exploration of Preschool Children's Spontaneous Songs and Chants." *Visions of Research in Music Education* 2. http://www-usr.rider.edu/~vrme/v2n1/visions/burton-an%20exploration%20of%20preschool%20children.pdf.

Burton, S. L. 2011. "Language Acquisition: A Lens on Music Learning." In *Learning from Young Children: Research in Early Childhood Music*, edited by S. L. Burton and C. C. Taggart, 23–38. Lanham, MD: Rowman and Littlefield.

Campbell, P. S. 1999. "The Many-Splendored Worlds of Our Musical Children." *Update: Applications of Research in Music Education* 18 (1): 7–14.

Campbell, P. S. 2010. *Songs in Their Heads: Music and Its Meaning in Children's Lives*. 2nd ed. Oxford: Oxford University Press.

Choate, R. A., ed. 1968. *Documentary Report of the Tanglewood Symposium*. Washington, DC: Music Educators National Conference.

Choate, R. A. 1970. *New Dimensions in Music: Music for Early Childhood.* New York: American Book.
Christensen, H. 2004. "Children's Participation in Ethnographic Research: Issues of Power and Representation." *Children and Society* 18: 165–76.
Christensen, H., and A. James, eds. 2000. *Research with Children: Perspectives and Practices.* London: Routledge/Falmer.
Clark, A. 2007. "A Hundred Ways of Listening: Gathering Children's Perspectives of Their Early Childhood Environment." *Young Children* 62 (3): 76–81.
Colwell, R., and C. Richardson, eds. 2002. *The New Handbook of Research on Music Teaching and Learning: A Project of the Music Educators National Conference.* Oxford: Oxford University Press.
Collier-Slone, K. 1991. "The Psychology of Humanistic Life Education: A Longitudinal Study." PhD diss., The Union Institute.
Contemporary Music Project. 1966. *Experiments in Musical Creativity.* Washington, DC: Music Educators National Conference.
Cooper, S., and A. B. Cardany. 2011. "The Importance of Parents in Early Childhood Music Program Evaluation." In *Learning from Young Children: Research in Early Childhood Music*, edited by S. L. Burton and C. C. Taggart, 95–112. Lanham, MD: Rowman and Littlefield.
Corsaro, W. 2005. *The Sociology of Childhood.* 2nd ed. Thousand Oaks, CA: Sage Publications.
Custodero, L. A. 2006. "Singing Practices in 10 Families with Young Children." *Journal of Research in Music Education* 54 (1): 37–56.
Custodero, L. A. 2007. "Origins and Expertise in the Musical Improvisations of Adults and Children: A Phenomenological Study of Content and Process." *British Journal of Music Education* 24 (1): 77–98.
Custodero, L. A. 2009. "Musical Portraits, Musical Pathways: Stories of Meaning Making in the Lives of Six Families." In *Musical Experiences in Our Lives: Things We Learn and Meanings We Make*, edited by J. L. Kerchner and C. R. Abril, 77–92. Lanham, MD: Rowman and Littlefield.
Custodero, L. A., and E. Johnson-Green. 2008. "Caregiving in Counterpoint: Reciprocal Influences in the Musical Parenting of Younger and Older Infants." *Early Childhood Development and Care* 178 (1): 15–39.
Custodero, L. A., and A. St. John. 2007. "Actions Speak: Lessons Learned from the Systematic Observation of Flow Experience in Young Children's Music Making." In *Listen to Their Voices: Research to Practice: A Biennial Series*, 3rd ed., edited by L. R. Bartel (series ed.) and K. Smithrim and R. Upitis (vol. eds.), 211–27. Waterloo, ON: Canadian Music Educators Association.
Dansereau, D. R. 2005. "The Musicality of 3-Year-Old Children within the Context of Research-Based Musical Engagement." PhD diss., Georgia State University.
Davis, J. M. 1998. "Understanding the Meanings of Children: A Reflexive Process." *Children and Society* 12: 325–35.
Draper, T. W., and C. Gayle. 1987. "An Analysis of Historical Reasons for Teaching Music to Your Children." In *Music and Child Development*, edited by J. C. Peery, I. W. Peery, and T. W. Draper, 194–205. New York: Springer-Verlag.
Fiedler, S. K. 1982. "A Methodological Study of Three Observation Techniques—An Observation Schedule, Participant Observation and a Structured Interview—In Two Elementary Music Classrooms." PhD diss., Northwestern University.

Filsinger, K. B. 2011. *Side-by-Side: Guiding Young Composers.* Workshop co-presented with research participants at the NYSSMA Winter Conference, Rochester, NY, December 2–4.

Fine, G. A., and K. L. Sandstrom. 1988. *Knowing Children: Participant Observation with Minors.* Newbury Park, CA: Sage Publications.

Fox, D. B. 1982. "The Pitch Range and Contour of Infant Vocalizations: Volumes I and II." PhD diss., The Ohio State University.

Gerrity, K. W., R. M. Hourigan, and P. W. Horton. 2013. "Conditions That Facilitate Music Learning among Students with Special Needs: A Mixed-Methods Inquiry." *Journal of Research in Music Education* 61 (2): 144–59. doi:10.1177/0022429413485428.

Gordon, E. E. 2003. *A Music Learning Theory for Newborn and Young Children.* Chicago: GIA.

Graue, E., and M. Hawkins. 2005. "Relations, Refractions, and Reflections in Research with Children." In *Power and Voice in Research with Children*, edited by L. D. Soto and B. B. Swadener, 45–54. New York: Peter Lang.

Graue, M. E., and D. J. Walsh. 1998. *Studying Children in Context: Theories, Methods, and Ethics.* Thousand Oaks, CA: Sage Publications.

Greenberg, M. 1979. *Your Children Need Music: A Guide for Parents and Teachers of Young Children.* Englewood Cliffs, NJ: Prentice-Hall.

Greene, S., and M. Hill, eds. 2005. *Researching Children's Experience: Approaches and Methods.* Thousand Oaks, CA: Sage Publications.

Gruenhagen, L. M. 2009. "Developing Professional Knowledge about Music Teaching and Learning through Collaborative Conversations." In *Research Perspectives: Thought and Practice in Music Education*, edited by L. Thompson and M. Campbell, 125–51. Charlotte, NC: Information Age.

Hatch, J. A. 1995a. "Studying Childhood as a Cultural Invention: A Rationale and Framework." In *Qualitative Research in Early Childhood Settings*, edited by J. A. Hatch, 117–33. Westport, CT: Praeger.

Hatch, J. A., ed. 1995b. *Qualitative Research in Early Childhood Settings.* Westport, CT: Praeger.

Hatch, J. A., ed. 2007. *Early Childhood Qualitative Research.* New York: Routledge, Taylor and Francis Group.

Hatch, J. A., and R. Wisniewski, eds. 1990. "Qualitative Studies in Early Childhood Contexts." *Special Issue, International Journal of Qualitative Studies in Education* 3: 209–302.

Hardy, W. L. 2011. "Arts in Early Childhood Education and the Enhancement of Learning." PhD diss., Walden University.

Harvard Graduate School of Education. 2006. *Making Learning Visible: Understanding, Documenting, and Supporting Individual and Group Learning.* Boston: Project Zero. http://www.pz.harvard.edu/mlv/.

Heath, C., J. Hindmarsh, and P. Luff. 2010. *Video in Qualitative Research: Analysing Social Interaction in Everyday Life.* Los Angeles: SAGE.

Hicks, W. K. 1993. "An Investigation of the Initial Stages of Preparatory Audiation." PhD diss., Temple University.

Hornbach, C. M. 2011. "Building Community to Elicit Responses in Early Childhood Music Classes." In *Learning from Young Children: Research in Early Childhood Music*, edited by S. L. Burton and C. C. Taggart, 63–78. Lanham, MD: Rowman and Littlefield.

Hourigan, R. M. 2009. "Preservice Music Teachers' Perceptions of Fieldwork Experiences in a Special Needs Classroom." *Journal of Research in Music Education* 57 (2): 152–68.

Humphreys, J. 1985. "The Child-Study Movement and Public School Music Education." *Journal of Research in Music Education* 33 (2): 79–86.

Ilari, B. 2011. "Twenty-First-Century Parenting, Electronic Media." In *Learning from Young Children: Research in Early Childhood Music*, edited by S. L. Burton and C. C. Taggart, 195–214. Lanham, MD: Rowman and Littlefield.

Infant-Toddler Centres and Preschools Istituzione of the Municipality of Reggio Emilia. 2010. *Indications: Preschools and Infant-Toddler Centres of the Municipality of Reggio Emilia*. Reggio Emilia, Italy: Reggio Children.

Janzen, M. D. 2008. "Where Is the (Postmodern) Child in Early Childhood Education Research?" *Early Years* 28 (3): 287–98.

Jipson, J., and J. Jipson. 2005. "Confidence Intervals: Doing Research with Young Children." In *Power and Voice in Research with Children*, edited by L. D. Soto and B. B. Swadener, 35–43. New York: Peter Lang.

Kastner, J. D. 2011. "Elementary Music Teachers' Role-Identities in and Perceptions of Teaching Prekindergarten Students with Special Needs." In *Learning from Young Children: Research in Early Childhood Music*, edited by S. L. Burton and C. C. Taggart, 113–31. Lanham, MD: Rowman and Littlefield.

Kierstead, J. K. 1994. "The Pillsbury Foundation School (1937–1948) and Beyond." *The Bulletin of Historical Research in Music Education* 15 (3): 183–219.

Kierstead, J. K. 2006. "Listening to the Spontaneous Music-Making of Preschool Children in Play: Living a Pedagogy of Wonder." PhD diss., University of Maryland, College Park.

Kim, B. S. 2012. "Shades of Pink: Preschoolers Make Meaning in a Reggio-Inspired Classroom." *Young Children* 67 (2): 44–50.

Koops, L. H. 2011. "Music Play Zone: An On-Line Social Network Site Connecting Parents and Teacher in an Early Childhood Music Class." In *Learning from Young Children: Research in Early Childhood Music*, edited by S. L. Burton and C. C. Taggart, 181–94. Lanham, MD: Rowman and Littlefield.

Koops, L. H. 2012. "'Now Can I Watch My Video?' Exploring Musical Play through Video Sharing and Social Networking in an Early Childhood Music Class." *Research Studies in Music Education* 34 (1): 15–28. doi:10.1177/1321103X12442994.

Lahman, M. K. E. 2008. "Always Othered: Ethical Research with Children." *Journal of Early Childhood Research* 6 (3): 281–300.

Leonard, C. 1968. *Discovering Music Together: Early Childhood*. Chicago: Follett.

MacNaughton, G., S. A. Rolfe, and I. Siraj-Blatchford. 2001. *Doing Early Childhood Research: International Perspectives on Theory and Practice*. Buckingham, UK: Open University Press.

MacNaughton, G., K. Smith, and K. Davis. 2007. "Researching with Children: The Challenges and Possibilities for Building 'Child Friendly' Research." In *Early Childhood Qualitative Research*, edited by J. A. Hatch, 167–84. New York: Routledge.

Malewski, E. 2005. "Epilogue: When Children and Youth Talk Back: Precocious Research Practices and the Cleverest Voices." In *Power and Voice in Research with Children*, edited by L. D. Soto and B. B. Swadener, 215–22. New York: Peter Lang.

Mark, M. 1992. "A History of Music Education Research." In *Handbook of Research on Music Teaching and Learning*, edited by R. Colwell, 48–59. New York: Schemer.

Mark, M. 1999. "MENC: From Tanglewood to the Present." In *Vision 2020: The Housewright Symposium on the Future of Music Education*, edited by C. K. Madsen. Reston, VA: MENC.

Marsh, M. V. 1974. *The Spectrum of Music with Related Arts: Kindergarten*. New York: Macmillan.

Mayall, B. 2002. *Towards a Sociology of Childhood: Thinking from Children's Lives*. Buckingham, UK: Open University Press.

McCarthy, M. 2010. "Researching Children's Musical Culture: Historical and Contemporary Perspectives." *Music Education Research* 12 (1): 1–12.

McCord, K. A. 2009. "Improvisatory Musical Experiences in the Lives of Children with Severe Disabilities." In *Musical Experiences in Our Lives: Things We Learn and Meanings We Make*, edited by J. L. Kerchner and C. R. Abril, 127–43. Lanham, MD: Rowman and Littlefield.

McDonald, D. T. 1979. *Music in Our Lives: The Early Years*. Washington, DC: National Association for the Education of Young Children.

McDonald, D. T., and G. M. Simons. 1989. *Musical Growth and Development: Birth through Six*. New York: Schirmer Books.

Mendel, N. 1988. "The Least Adult Role in Studying Children." *Journal of Contemporary Ethnography* 16: 433–37. doi:10.1177/0891241688164002.

Metz, E. R. 1986. "Movement as a Musical Response among Preschool Children." PhD diss., Arizona State University.

Miller, L. B. 1983. "Music in Early Childhood: Naturalistic Observation of Young Children's Musical Behaviors." PhD diss., University of Kansas.

Miranda, L. M. 2004. "The Implications of Developmentally Appropriate Practice for the Kindergarten General Music Classroom." *Journal of Research in Music Education* 52 (1): 43–63.

Moorhead, G. E., and D. Pond. 1978. *Music of Young Children*. Santa Barbara, CA: Pillsbury Foundation for Advancement of Music Education.

Morgan, H. B. N., ed. 1949. *Music Education Source Book*. Chicago: The Music Educators National Conference.

Music Educators National Conference. 1994. *The National Standards for Arts Education*. Reston, VA: MENC.

Music Educators National Conference. 1995. *Performance Standards for Music: Prekindergarten*. Reston, VA: MENC.

Neely, L. 2007. *Musical ConverSings with Children*. New York: Noval Science.

Nutbrown, C., ed. 2002. *Research Studies in Early Childhood Education*. Stoke-on-Trent, UK: Trentham Books.

Overland, C., and A. M. Reynolds. 2010. "The Role of MENC: The National Association for Music Education in Early Childhood Music Education, 1980–2007." *Journal of Historical Research in Music Education* 32 (2): 99–117.

Peery, J. C. 1993. "Music in Early Childhood Education." In *Handbook of Research on the Education of Young Children*, edited by B. Spodek, 207–24. New York: Macmillan.

Peery, J. C., I. W. Peery, and T. W. Draper, eds. 1987. *Music and Child Development*. New York: Springer-Verlag.

Perkins-Gough, D. 2007. "Giving Intervention a Head Start: A Conversation with Edward Zigler." *Early Intervention at Every Age* 65 (2): 8–14.

Pond, D. 1978. "Introduction." In *Music of Young Children*, eds. G. E. Moorhead and D. Pond, 3–4. Santa Barbara, CA: Pillsbury Foundation for Advancement of Music Education.

Pond, D. 1980. "The Young Child's Playful World of Sound." *Music Educators Journal* 66 (7): 38–41.

Pond, D. 1981. "A Composer's Study of Young Children's Innate Musicality." *Bulletin of the Council for Research in Music Education* 68: 1–12.

Reynolds, A. M. 1995. "An Investigation of the Movement Responses Performed by Children 18 Months to Three Years of Age and Their Caregivers to Rhythm Chants in Duple and Triple Meters." PhD diss., Temple University.

Reynolds, A. M. 2006. "Vocal Interactions during Informal Early Childhood Music Classes." *Bulletin of the Council for Research in Music Education* 168: 35–49.

Reynolds, A. M. 2012. "General Music Teachers Talk Professional Development: Kindling the Spark, Fanning the Flame, and Keeping an Eye on the Fire." In *Narrative Soundings: An Anthology of Narrative Inquiry in Music Education*, edited by M. Barrett and S. Stauffer, 275–86. Dordrecht: Springer.

Reynolds, A. M., J. Cancemi, C. Weston, B. Folliett, Children ... at the Early Learning Center, Yokohama International School. 2012. "Musical Moments in a Reggio-Inspired Preschool." Paper Presentation, Yokohama International School, Yokohama, Japan, April 27.

Reynolds, A. M., K. R. Filsinger, K. Chayot, and K. Goldenberg. 2012. "Co-Constructing Music-Rich Environments." Research-Based Workshop Presentation at the Early Childhood Education Commission Conference, International Society for Music Education, Corfu, Greece, July 9–13.

Reynolds, A. M., and K. Hyun. 2004. "Understanding Music Aptitude: Teachers' Interpretations." *Research Studies in Music Education* 23: 18–31.

Reynolds, A. M., A. Jerome, A. L. Preston, and H. O. Haynes. 2005. "Service-Learning in Music Education: Participants' Reflections." *Bulletin of the Council for Research in Music Education* 165: 79–91.

Reynolds, A. M., S. Long, and W. H. Valerio. 2007. "Language Acquisition and Music Acquisition: Possible Parallels." In *Listen to Their Voices, Research to Practice: A Biennial Series*, vol. 3, edited by L. R. Bartel (series ed.) and K. Smithrim and R. Upitis (vol. eds.), 211–27. Waterloo, ON: Canadian Music Educators Association.

"Salty Saint of Budapest." 1966. *Time* 88 (9): 41.

Schonauer, A. L. M. 2002. "Teaching at the Foundation: Role Development and Identification among Elementary General Music Teachers." PhD diss., University of Oklahoma.

Scott, L. P., J. A. Jellison, E. W. Chappell, and A. A. Standridge. 2007. "Talking with Music Teachers about Inclusion: Perceptions, Opinions and Experiences." *Journal of Music Therapy* 44 (1): 38–56.

Scott-Kassner, C. (1992). "Research on Music in Early Childhood." In *Handbook of Research on Music Teaching and Learning*, edited by R. Colwell, 633–50. New York: Schirmer Books.

Shelley, S. 1981. "Investigating the Musical Capabilities of Young Children." *Bulletin of the Council for Research in Music Education* 68: 26–34.

Sims, W., and D. B. Udtaisuk. 2008. "Music's Representation in Parenting Magazines: A Content Analysis." *UPDATE: Applications of Research in Music Education* 26 (2): 17–26.

Smith, A. 2011. "The Incorporation of Principles of the Reggio Emilia Approach in a North American Preschool Music Curriculum." In *Learning from Young Children: Research in Early Childhood Music*, edited by S. L. Burton and C. C. Taggart, 79–93. Lanham, MD: Rowman and Littlefield.

Soto, L. D., and B. B. Swadener, eds. 2005. *Power and Voice in Research with Children*. New York: Peter Lang.

Spodek, B., and O. N. Saracho, eds. 1998. "Introduction: Reflections on the Past." In *Yearbook in Early Childhood Education*, vol. 8: *Issues in Early Childhood Educational Research*, edited by B. Spodek, O. N. Saracho, and A. D. Pellegrini, vii–xiii. New York: Teachers College Press.

Spodek, B., and O. N. Saracho, eds. 2005. *International Perspectives on Research in Early Childhood Education*. Greenwich, CT: Information Age.

Spodek, B., O. N. Saracho, and A. D. Pellegrini, eds. 1998. *Issues in Early Childhood Educational Research*. New York: Teachers College Press.

Super, C. M., and S. Harkness. 2002. "Culture Structures the Environment for Development." *Human Development* 45 (4): 270–74.

Taggart, C. C., J. Alvarez, and K. Schubert. 2011. "The Role of Early Childhood Music Class Participation in the Development of Four Children with Speech and Language Delay." In *Learning from Young Children: Research in Early Childhood Music*, edited by S. L. Burton and C. C. Taggart, 245–58. Lanham, MD: Rowman and Littlefield.

Thomas, R. B., ed. 1970. *Manhattanville Music Curriculum Program*. (OE-HEW Final ReNo. 6-1999), ED 045865. Washington DC: US Government Printing Office.

Thorne, B. 1993. *Gender Play: Girls and Boys in School*. New Brunswick, NJ: Rutgers University Press.

Tisdall, E. K. M., J. M. Davis, and M. Gallagher. 2009. *Researching with Children and Young People: Research Design, Methods and Analysis*. Los Angeles: Sage Publications.

Valerio, W. H. 2009. "From the Teacher's View: Observations of Toddlers' Musical Development." In *Musical Experiences in Our Lives: Things We Learn and Meanings We Make*, edited by J. L. Kerchner and C. R. Abril, 39–58. Lanham, MD: Rowman and Littlefield.

Valerio, W. H., and N. K. Freeman. 2009. "Pre-Service Teachers' Perceptions of Early Childhood Music Teaching Experiences." *Bulletin of the Council for Research in Music Education* 181: 51–69.

Valerio, W. H., M. A. Seaman, C. C. Yap, P. Santucci, and M. Tu. 2006. "Vocal Evidence of Toddler Music Syntax Acquisition: A Case Study." *Bulletin of the Council for Research in Music Education* 170: 33–45.

Valerio, W. H., A. Sy, H. Gruber, and C. G. Stockman. 2011. "Examining Music Experiences with Anthony, a Child Who Has Autism." In *Learning from Young Children: Research in Early Childhood Music*, edited by S. L. Burton and C. C. Taggart, 259–81. Lanham, MD: Rowman and Littlefield.

Walker, L. M. 1991. "Historical Overview of the Early Childhood Special Research Interest Group (SRIG)." *Music in Early Childhood: A Research Journal for the Early Childhood Special Research Interest Group* 1 (1): 1–2.

Walker, L. N. 2009. "Stories from the Front." In *Narrative Inquiry in Music Education: Troubling Certainty*, edited by M. S. Barrett and S. L. Stauffer, 179–94. Springer.

Walsh, D. J., N. Bakir, T. B. Lee, Y-H. Chung, K. Chung, and Colleagues: H. Campuzano, Y-T. Chen, Y. Kedem, W. Liu, Y. Ozturk, S. Sung, A. Tufekci, and N. Waight. 2007. "Using Digital Video in Field-Based Research with Children: A Primer." In *Early Childhood Qualitative Research*, edited by J. A. Hatch, 43–62. New York: Routledge/Taylor and Francis Group.

Wilson, B. 1981. "Implications of the Pillsbury Foundation School of Santa Barbara in Perspective." *Bulletin of the Council for Research in Music Education* 68: 13–25.

Wolcott, H. F. 1972. "The Teacher as Enemy." *Practical Anthropology* 19 (5): 226–30.

Yang, I. Y. 1990. "The Influence of Music Instruction on Two-Year-Old Children's Responses to Unfamiliar Music Stimuli." PhD diss., the University of Rochester, Eastman School of Music.

Zimmerman, J. R. 1983. "The Musical Experiences of Two Groups of Children in One Elementary School: An Ethnographic Study." PhD diss., The Ohio State University.

Zimmerman, M. P. 1971/2011. "Musical Characteristics of Children." *Visions of Research in Music Education* 17. Retrieved from http://www-usr.rider.edu/~vrme/v17n1/visions/article8.pdf.

Zimmerman, M. P. 1984. "State of the Art in Early Childhood Music and Research." In *The Young Child and Music: Contemporary Principles in Child Development and Music Education*, edited by J. Boswell, 65–78. Reston, VA: Music Educators National Conference.

CHAPTER 2

QUALITATIVE RESEARCH IN GENERAL MUSIC EDUCATION

ANN MARIE STANLEY

In 1979, then president of the Music Educators National Conference James Mason issued a statement calling for the formation of a National Council for Elementary General Music within MENC.[1] He wrote:

> Persons working in the elementary general music area provide the basic foundations upon which a musically and culturally sensitive citizenry is developed. Many within our profession feel that such a base in music education must be systematically planned for, supported in its development, and carefully evaluated. (Kenney 2010, 12)

General music is arguably the most diverse, inclusive component of music education in the United States. The "heart of the school music program" (Hoffman 1981), general music is indeed *general,* or not confined to any particular specialization, and *foundational,* meaning that a thorough, comprehensive general music education is a crucial building block for other types of musical endeavors.

General music, especially in elementary school, is perhaps the only segment of a typical music education curriculum offered to all children and may reach the largest number of students. No auditions, private lessons, or instrument purchases are required; as Hoffman (1981) wrote: "We don't screen children out of a program because they are not the best. We are the single most democratic part of music education because we say it's for everybody" (42). Because general music is the way music education provides foundational musical knowledge for an entire population, its importance warrants a careful, research-based approach to curriculum planning and evaluation. To that end, researchers have consistently sought new and more effective ways to investigate general music teaching and learning.

In 1991, Atterbury criticized the lack of research basis evident in the general music textbooks and curriculum documents. She suggested researchers could make maximum impact on teaching practice by studying how and when to teach musical concepts, singing techniques, rhythm syllables, and listening. She advocated attention to student assessment, and criticized the lack of research on various methodologies. Atterbury also criticized researchers' overreliance on student reading, writing and motor skills in participant response methods, especially in the early grades. She faulted researchers' tendencies to ignore variables and include inadequate numbers of subjects, as well as their failure to allow enough time for their interventions to make a difference. While Atterbury's article was an effective reminder that general music practice should be research-based, she took a decidedly positivist stance, asking for attention to control of all variables, the need for replication, and external validity in general music research.

In contrast, Boardman (1990) asked for a global change in the way researchers approached general music education. She advocated for research that would go beyond specifics of method and techniques. She cited a shortfall in research on why there was such a pervasive gap between the stated goals of general music education and related student musical achievement:

> Studies dealing with specific aspects of general music would seem to offer great potential, yet it will be essentially impossible to implement their results in a way that will significantly change the profile of general music from what it is today until we understand why there is such a chasm between ideal and real. (8)

Boardman asked for "sophisticated research techniques... holistic in intent and design," versus the prevailing "reductionist research strategies" (14).

Qualitative researchers have played an important part in answering Boardman's call for more sophisticated, holistic depictions of general music. Researchers' diverse methodological approaches—paired with increased attention to the complex diversity of general music classroom activities—have in the last quarter century resulted in a more complete understanding of music teaching and learning in general music. The studies reviewed in this chapter represent an attempt at an inclusive view of how general music curricula intersect with teaching practice, the learning environment, and the developmental level, desires, and propensities of students.

2.1. Organization of Chapter and Definition of General Music

In this chapter I first select representative research to illustrate ways qualitative researchers have examined music teaching and learning within the panorama of typical elementary general music classroom activities. One choice researchers have made is between the insider and outsider viewpoints: the authors of studies reviewed here often straddled the emic and etic perspectives. I divide section 2.2 according to the positioning and identity of the researcher vis-à-vis the researched phenomenon. The groups are arranged depending on whether the research involved (a) outsider observers studying students; (b) outsider observers studying teaching practice; (c) insider/outsiders, defined as teachers studying students; and (d) insiders: teachers studying their *own* students.

I contrast the studies in the first part of section 2.2 with those in which researchers have examined musical behaviors *out* of the classroom, in order to focus on the nature of student learning without the need to account for classroom unpredictability. These studies fall into two groups: those that present (a) an outsider perspective, outside the classroom or (b) an insider-outsider hybrid viewpoint. In section 2.3, I include research on the general music teacher, in terms of her unique working conditions and needs. I summarize selected research on teachers' general music content knowledge and teaching practice, including a brief discussion on the interesting phenomenon of teachers studying teaching practice and how some of these music education researchers (experienced teachers themselves) dealt with their preconceived notions or value judgments about teaching practice.

In sections 2.4 and 2.5, I further deconstruct methodological and epistemological considerations. To bridge Boardman's chasm between "ideal and real," researchers have chosen particular stances along the etic-emic perspective continuum, depending on the research questions and the specific general music phenomenon being studied. The issue of researcher stance plays a complicated and important role in the interpretation of general qualitative research. It would be easy, but inaccurate, to assert that out-of-the-classroom studies performed by outsiders—or those adopting a removed, disinterested viewpoint—represent an "ideal" or pure look at children's learning in general music tasks. Likewise, studies at the other end of the continuum are not automatically more "real," even though teachers doing research in their own classrooms may make pedagogical decisions based on naturally emerging data from the authentic complexity of the classroom. Analysis techniques in these qualitative studies generally tend toward the personal, situated, and recursive, as opposed to objective, impartial, and strictly sequenced. Each researcher in this chapter has chosen a balance between embracing classroom complexity and isolating individual student or teacher actions; these decisions are discussed at length in sections 2.4 and 2.5. In section 2.6, I make recommendations for future research given the issues unique to qualitative inquiry.

First, some definitions and boundaries for this chapter: Boardman (1990) wrote, "General music will refer to those aspects of the total school music curriculum that focus on outcomes to be attained by all students . . . the primary objective of the general music class is not demonstration of accomplishment through public performance" (5). While public performances are not unusual in general music, typically general music is focused on music teaching and learning processes inside the classroom. At the elementary level, general music may be called, variously, "elementary general music," "classroom music," "vocal music," "vocal-general." In grades 6–12, these curricula are called "secondary general" and often encompass all other musical offerings not included under the broad umbrella of "ensembles" (e.g., music appreciation, composition classes, music technology). Due to space limitations, I will exclude many studies on children's musical life outside of the general classroom (e.g., Harwood 1998; Lum and Campbell 2007), studies about music integration within general education (e.g., Bresler 1993, 1995, 1996; Miller 1996, 2003; Whitaker 1996), and studies on specific courses like technology or guitar (e.g., Ruthmann 2006; Tobias 2010).

2.2. THE PANORAMA OF ELEMENTARY GENERAL MUSIC ACTIVITIES: SEEKING A "SLICE OF LIFE"

Qualitative researchers have sought ways to delve deeply into the real world of the music classroom. By investigating the panoramic array of typical elementary general music activities and gathering data on music teaching and learning within these experiences, researchers have captured moments that illuminate the intrinsic nature of general music learning.

Reese (1981) performed one of the first qualitative studies in general music. He wrote a cogent explanation for the need for his research methodology to encompass the entire classroom milieu: "Since [Reese's] study was more concerned with developing a comprehensive understanding of a complex setting—with obtaining a 'slice of life'—than with causal explanations of human behavior, it was important to preserve the naturalistic context to the maximum degree possible" (9). In this section, I look at ways various researchers have approached capturing Reese's "slice of life" in general music. Studies are categorized according to the placement and orientation of the researcher. I also categorize the studies based on whether the research questions focused more on *student* or *teacher* actions and characteristics. Sections 2.2.1: "Outside Observers Studying Students" and 2.2.2: "Outside Observers Studying Teaching Practice" concern those researchers who are not connected with the classroom or phenomenon under investigation. Section 2.2.3: "Insider/Outsider: Teachers Studying Students" concerns researchers who are intimately connected with—and are usually the teachers themselves of—the classroom or phenomenon under investigation but who wrote from a more neutral, detached perspective. Section 2.2.4: "Insiders: Teachers Studying Students" relates to teachers researching their own students and teaching settings; in several cases these researchers write about how the process of doing research affected their teaching decisions during the study itself. Section 2.2.5: "Outsider Perspective, Outside the Classroom" details studies performed by outsider researchers in laboratories or in other settings outside the classroom milieu. Section 2.2.6: "Insider-Outsider Hybrid" studies are those in which researchers chose methodologies that enabled views of general music teachers and activities both inside *and* removed from the classroom.

2.2.1. Outside Observers Studying Students

DeLorenzo's (1989) research was one of the first forays into naturalistic, non-laboratory settings of children's musical creativity, including students' classroom environment and social interaction. She sought to understand creative problem-solving and decision-making in sixth-grade general music classes in four different schools, by observing and analyzing classroom videotapes. DeLorenzo's work was unique in that she examined not only individual students' creative processes, but the context: the classroom and the teacher-directed activities. DeLorenzo maintained an outsider stance throughout; while she conducted some informal interviews with the students, she characterized student responses as "guarded" (193), indicating that she probably did not have, nor seek, a personal relationship with student participants.

Holdridge used the word *naturalistic* in the title of her 1991 dissertation "Music in Our Lives: A Naturalistic Study of Three High School General Music Classes." Like DeLorenzo, Holdridge relied on outsider observations and teacher interviews as she examined implementation of a general music curriculum in New York. Holdridge observed classrooms for a year and collected data on classroom aspects such as student ability and interest, the learning climate in the school, and student-teacher respect. Like Holdridge (1991), Wayman (2004) took an outsider's look at secondary general music, but put the spotlight on student voice in her study. She interviewed three middle school general music students for 60 minutes each about their attitudes toward music education, general music class, and the importance of music in their lives. She did not know the participants before her study and selected them based on their teacher-perceived ability to speak compellingly about their experiences.

Claire (1993/1994) investigated how social interactions influence student creativity. She observed three fifth-grade classes in different elementary schools, and wrote about the need for researchers to attend to all elements of classroom functionality when studying student work: "It would be a great folly to disregard the interactive complexity inherent in classroom life when attempting to gain an understanding of learning environments conducive to creative activity in any discipline" (26). Kaschub (1997) also investigated group processes in her study of a high school choir and sixth-grade general music class. Both groups, led by professional composers, collaboratively composed pieces. Kaschub wrote that she had few models to guide her in documenting group interaction in the classroom: "Further research is needed to address group learning in music settings. Only a handful of studies examine how students work together in group composition projects or examine the role of the individual in collaborative processes" (26).

2.2.2. Outsider Observers Studying Teaching Practice

Brummett's 1993 dissertation investigated two teachers' use of a process-oriented assessment framework in sixth-grade general music. Brummett's research perspective was etic; her data were derived from interviews, field notes, classroom observations, and school district documents. She also studied the classroom context to understand teachers' assessment practice within actual music classroom activity.

Three researchers in this chapter used case study methodology to examine the intersection of teaching practice and student learning. Miranda (2004) took an outside observer view in a multiple case study of aspects of developmentally appropriate teaching practice (DAP) by three kindergarten music teachers. Data included 90 videotaped observations, field notes, interviews, and classroom artifacts. Individual lapel microphones worn by two children in each class recorded certain students' talk during free time. Miranda sought feedback on her analysis from knowledgeable outside reviewers: their questions helped confirm or disconfirm her initial findings.

Kelly-McHale (2011) examined how an elementary general music teacher's practices and beliefs influenced the musical identity of four immigrant students. Kelly-McHale looked at students' interaction with their teacher's curriculum: students became fluent in notation, singing, and playing instruments, but the teacher's practice lacked cultural responsiveness that could have helped the children integrate their musical- and self-identities. Kelly-McHale used observation and interview data but set a boundary based on maintaining an etic perspective: "I felt that if I became a part of the music classroom as a participant-observer, my role as researcher would become biased because my identity as a music teacher would begin to influence how I viewed the actions and reactions in the music classroom. Based on these insights, I did not feel that it was professionally or ethically advisable for me to position myself as another teacher in the music classroom" (136). Salvador (2011) likewise collected "naturalistic observation" data about three elementary music teachers' assessment practices by observing those teachers instructing selected music classes for one- to two-month periods. In her collective case-study dissertation, Salvador wrote, "I attempted to be as unobtrusive as possible in order to have the least impact, but I recognized that my presence in the classroom had the potential to change the classroom climate" (72.) So while Salvador does not further interrogate her etic perspective by pursuing the idea of whether her presence did in fact change the atmosphere of the research site, she does elsewhere in her dissertation write thoughtfully about her own personal background as vocalist, music teacher, music therapist, and assessment scholar, in an effort to help the reader understand that her own history helped her interpret the data and findings meaningfully and sympathetically.

2.2.3. Insider/Outsider: Teachers Studying Students

The three studies in this section are characterized by researchers' attempts to examine phenomena within their own classrooms (as insiders) yet simultaneously maintain a distance from the study (as outsiders). Emmons (1998) shifted between teacher/researcher roles in a multiple case study examining the compositional process of five of his own seventh-grade general music students. Emmons-as-researcher collected data in the forms of open-ended interviews with students, parents, and classroom teachers, transcribed lesson videotapes, and artifacts. Expert observers provided a viewpoint yet another step removed: two other general music teachers had access to all the data and commented on Emmon's analysis. Emmons also collected insider data in the form of his own teacher and student journals—the latter documenting student voice through their reflections on the composition lessons—and his notes on his in-the-moment decisions. He also asked students to watch videotape of their own composition and comment on their ideas and process. Emmons noted his instruction throughout the study had an observable effect on student composition, especially in "students making creative decisions in order to please the teacher ... they were conscientious students" (170). This is similar to effects mentioned by Perconti (1996) and Gromko (1996), written about in this chapter's sections 2.2.4 and 2.2.5.

In a study of her own fourth- and fifth-grade students' expressive movement to music, Ferguson (2004) took a hands-off approach to data collection, a tactic which she wrote made her role as teacher-as-researcher difficult. The students did not work at their highest developmental level—nor did they emulate their most highly skilled peers—when she moved into an observational, less instructional role. She also repeatedly negotiated the research space between studying individual students and their interactions with peers; in data analysis she alternated between the larger perspective of analyzing videotape of entire classes over long periods and a more microanalytic view of individual and small groups.

This recursive process of analysis is a hallmark of qualitative general music research. In this case, the back-and-forth between narrow and wide foci broadened Ferguson's understanding of movement in general music. Looking at certain students' movements increased her awareness of elements she needed to look for in the entire group: "This study began with questions about individual listeners in relation to a classroom context but as the study progressed, the questions about individual learners seemed impossible to answer without first studying classroom groups" (84).

Hamilton (1999) shadowed six children in their normal routine of student composition, interaction, and musical play in three sixth-grade music classrooms. She wrote: "I was curious about what and how my students were learning in the context of the classroom as I taught it. I was not satisfied that looking at the products of their work gave me the kind of insight I was seeking" (261). Hamilton let the data collection unfold as naturally as she could and avoided letting the study affect her pedagogical decisions: "*After* I completed data collection and analysis I examined my teaching practice and let the results of the research inform my future teaching" (63, emphasis added). However, Hamilton wrote that researchers working in their own classrooms could use the results of data collection right away to affect their teaching practice, a process she referred to as "closing the teacher-researcher loop." Next, I describe studies that do close that loop. In studies reviewed in the following section, researchers used data to immediately inform pedagogy.

2.2.4. Insiders: Teachers Studying Students

In contrast to the previously mentioned researchers' removed stances as the observant other, Wiggins (1993, 1994, 1994/1995, 1995, 1999/2000) completely embraced the insider viewpoint in papers she published about research in her own general music classroom. She asserted: "As a profession we must begin to look at more than discrete activities in a laboratory setting in order to develop effective music education practice" (Wiggins 1995, 72). For studies published in 1993, 1994, and 1994/1995, Wiggins collected five months' worth of videotape, audiotape, field notes, interviews, and artifacts from everyday happenings in her music classroom. She wrote that observing the situation from her vantage point as teacher *and* involved participant gave her a different view of the data, a slant which she could not definitively characterize as positive or negative. She wrote, "my intense involvement in the situation may have made it difficult to see what needed to be seen . . . that same close involvement may have made it possible to see more than an outsider might have seen" (1994/1995, 32).

Wiggins continued to explore insider immersion through qualitative research in her own classroom. Her studies are pioneering efforts to account for the role of classroom interactions between learner, peers, *and* teacher, as students work to gain musical understanding. Wiggins drew a sharp contrast between the situated perspective of her research and that which preceded:

> The studies on which these [prior] theories [of musical understanding] are based have been conducted under laboratory conditions. . . . In looking at learners' interaction with music, it is important to also consider the potential impact of interaction with other people on an individual's musical learning. In music education, the influences of such interaction on musical learning has only begun to be investigated. (Wiggins 1994, 233)

Wiggins also explored the idea of shadowing, or tape-recording with lapel microphones, the verbal and musical statements of one or two children throughout their experience in music class. To study collaboratively how teacher expertise and student learning interact, Wiggins and Bodoin (1998) examined multiple audio- and videotapes of typical activities in Bodoin's second-grade music classroom. To provide an observer's view, a stationary camera was used to videotape nine class periods over four months. To generate data about how the typical student in her class might learn, Bodoin had two students wear lapel microphones and carry mini-tape recorders. The researchers sought a multidimensional understanding through documenting researcher, student, and teacher perspectives; Bodoin as teacher-researcher wrote that the 18-month collaborative data analysis provided her an in-depth opportunity to examine her own practice.

In some of her studies, Wiggins acknowledged that the line between teacher-researcher roles grew faint: in fact, her actions as researcher were similar to what she habitually did as a teacher. She wrote that during the five-month study (1993, 1994), she re-evaluated children's needs and developed lessons in the moment. However, in Wiggins's (1999/2000) in-depth look at six representative instances of elementary general music students' interactions within group improvisation or composition, she was able to darken the teacher-researcher boundary. In this study, she took a macro-look back at audio- and videotaped evidence of student musical creative processes from five of her previous studies, three of her graduate students' research projects, and over 600 sample creative projects collected in her own classrooms.

Like Wiggins, Perconti (1996) also made a multi-year study of the processes of composition and active learning in her general music classes. She wrote, "qualitative inquiry allowed the study to take place in the natural setting where the interrelationship between classroom opportunities and student progress as well as the process and meaning of composing in the early elementary general classroom could be investigated" (44). Perconti also attended to the representation of the students' voice in her study. She periodically asked students to reflect in writing to questions like "What did you learn in music class today?" She collected 190 reflections to analyze participants' views. Perconti freely admitted how her questions, assistance, and prompting altered and affected student composition and student work, which in turn affected her teaching.

Student voice and the sense of the real classroom atmosphere resonate strongly throughout Greher's (2002) study. She examined the creation and use of music listening software intended to capture the interest of inner-city middle school general music students in three classes. While she was not the formal teacher for these classes, she took on teaching responsibilities for several months to instruct and guide the students' use of the software. She was participant-observer in this study and actively sought formal and informal input from the student participants in the creation, revision, and use of the software.

Student viewpoint vis-à-vis teacher-researcher questioning is also a salient feature of Beegle's (2010) classroom-based study. Beegle examined student interactions within small-group improvisation in her weekly general music classes. Over three months, teacher-researcher Beegle focused on students' musical and social roles in four-student "focus groups" (222) engaged in constructivist learning tasks. Like other researchers discussed in this chapter, Beegle collected data in the form of audio- and videotaped observations, her own reflections and field notes, and questionnaires. However, Beegle also garnered the children's viewpoint through individual and small-group interviews. As students watched video excerpts of their group improvisations, she asked broad, probing questions such as, "'Do you have anything you want to tell me about that performance?' and 'What were you thinking about as you were performing?'" (222).

Miller (2004) wrote about practical considerations of designing developmentally appropriate compositional tasks for her own elementary general music students' "wide intellectual and emotional diversity" (61). Calling her work "naturalistic action research," Miller engaged in a cycle of planning lessons, evaluating the resultant student work (alone and with colleagues), and then re-teaching similar lessons to numerous classes. Miller called the project "ongoing" and representative of her "continued professional growth" (62): maintaining an orientation toward research as useful for the reflective practitioner seeking feedback on the success of her own classroom initiatives. While Miller writes about her research from a "contextualized ... personal" stance (67), she also reminds readers that her teaching situation is so similar to many general music teachers' settings that these developmentally appropriate compositional activities—shaped through many cycles of teaching, observation, and reflection in one classroom—likely would have wide applicability.

Like Miller, Strand (2005) studied a cycle of developing, field-testing, and evaluating her own curriculum, intended to promote transfer of conceptual learning in listening and performing lessons to composing. She sought to "examine a theory-based curriculum in a real classroom" (33). While Strand studied this curriculum in a somewhat atypical setting—eight students between ages 9–12 attended music class together for 32 hours one summer—she nonetheless completed four, four-step cycles of planning, teaching, observing results, and reflecting on results: a reasonable replication of what a general music teacher would do in the school year. Her data collection methods were similar to Emmons (1998) in that she created a balance between obtaining data available only to the teacher insider (her own daily field notes and reflections), as well as that observable by expert outsiders (compositional artifacts and videos). Interestingly, Strand wrote about "tempering" (20) her analysis during reflection and planning by using the input of two expert observers and a third person who independently analyzed the coding of the transcript data. Strand wrote that she sometimes disagreed and debated instructional strategies with each of the three; these outsiders had a distinct impact on Strand's implementation of her own curriculum. She wrote: "I adopted a revision to instruction only after I and the expert observers agreed that the revision would change instruction for the better" (20). Strand eventually found evidence for the theory of learning transfer, and wrote about ways teachers might enhance learning based on transferal of deep concepts.

2.2.5. Outsider Perspective, Outside the Classroom

In her dissertation, Barrett (1990) used a structured interview/task setting outside the classroom for her study of fourth-grade students' mental processes and strategies for melody recall and reproduction. She stated that studying students' musical explorations had the possibility to yield rich data, but that at the time of her study, "few models for this qualitative view of cognitive phenomena in music were available" (199). To help future researchers, Barrett wrote about several methodological strategies to manage the quantity and depth of data associated with qualitative inquiry. She suggested using a small sample size in order to pursue longer, more detailed interviews or observations. She also recommended techniques to aid in data analysis, such as recording time markers within interviews, and using software to easily record students' musical maneuvering.

Gromko (1996) published a study of young children's compositions and musical manipulations. Five children, ages six to nine, worked with Gromko in individual interviews in her office. Gromko's study did not utilize the "natural setting" of Perconti's (1996); however, like Perconti, Gromko took care to collect data on the individual experience of each student as they worked one-on-one with her to compose. Gromko pointed out one disadvantage of the side-by-side-with-researcher compositional work: the language used to shape student ideas was too often affected by researcher inquiries: "my questions often led them where they would otherwise not have gone" (49).

Younker (2000) examined the musical thought processes and patterns of 8-, 11-, and 14-year-olds in compositional decision-making. In decisions congruent with Barrett's (1990) suggestions, she used a small sample size (nine) in composing/interview sessions, and used music software to capture the students' musical experimentation. She studied the students' verbal responses in a "think-aloud" setting while composing, to distinguish age-specific thought processes and to identify any developmental patterns that might emerge. Because Younker was able to closely interact with her few participants outside the classroom, she was able to observe them in a detailed, almost microscopic way as they made manifest their musical thinking.

In an example of how an outside-of-school environment provided richer answers to certain research questions than a classroom-based methodology could have, Stauffer (2002) researched sixth-graders' musical compositions. Building on her earlier study of the creativity of one student in a computer laboratory (Stauffer 2001), Stauffer used the same setting for this work. Six students came weekly to after-school computer music sessions at the university music education computer lab. These students were "faithful participants" (304) for nearly three years in this after-school computer music experience.

Stauffer (2002) wanted to study the connection between students' musical and life experiences and their compositions. In order to garner the purest look at student composition and to trace influences between their "real life" and their compositions in the most uncomplicated way possible, Stauffer used a "non-intervention protocol" (303). She provided no compositional instruction and assigned no tasks. Stauffer found that socio-cultural context was influential on student composition: students composed music they liked, in response to inspiration from wide swaths of their life. It is likely that Stauffer's ability to trace these influences would have been sharply limited had students been composing in the classroom and undoubtedly would have been affected by the immediate influence of peers and teachers. However, Stauffer said her unfettered-by-teaching methodology hindered the ability of two students to express themselves compositionally: their lack of experience in "musical ways of thinking" (318) may have inhibited their work.

2.2.6. Insider-Outsider Hybrid

Another way to examine general music has been to blend both the insider and outsider approaches. Kerchner (2000) used an innovative hybrid methodology for a study of her own second- and fifth-grade music students' listening processes. This methodology enabled her to effectively use classroom elements *and* a more individual, focused look at students performing musical tasks outside the classroom. She conducted individual listening tasks/interviews outside the classroom milieu, yet in a way that was familiar to students. The tasks were similar to regular class activities, and the person prompting them was Kerchner, their regular music teacher: "I considered it important that the students felt comfortable in performing the music listening tasks in the presence of a familiar person" (34). In "a familiar educational setting for both the researcher and participants" (34), students provided multisensory responses to express their perceptions of musical examples in two individual sessions with Kerchner. In an additional, seamless bridging between research and the classroom, Kerchner wrote that these opportunities, for students to reflect on listening and learning in multiple ways, were not rarefied laboratory-style actions: they could easily be reproduced within the classroom. She also wrote about the value of general music teachers using "research skills"—interviewing and questioning—in practice: "Asking children to tell their story about their music experiences . . . can be quite revealing. Yet, I found that children only provided rich answers to well-constructed questions. The amount of information that I received was often the reflection of the quality of the question that I posed" (48).

Bartolome (2009) studied the practice strategies of successful beginning recorder students. The teacher-researcher conducted semi-structured interviews with her third-grade recorder students about their self-regulation of practice. Like Kerchner's, Bartolome's study is unique in its attention to participant voice and the resultant clarity of the nine-year-olds' explanations of their practicing, due to Bartolome's practice of re-stating responses for confirmation and asking probing, clarifying questions of her participants.

Like Bartolome, I sought a hybridized insider-outsider perspective in my own research. Stanley (2009, 2012) is a hybrid in two ways: (1) The social constructivist methodology enabled all participants and the researcher to adopt insider and outsider viewpoints at various times; and (2) the study was a look at student *and* teacher learning. I formed and facilitated a collaborative teacher study group (CTSG) which met seven times to discuss elementary music student collaboration by analyzing video from each participant's classroom. The three elementary music teacher members of the CTSG toggled between insider and outsider, depending if they were analyzing the teaching practice and student learning in video from their own classroom or from that of the other participants. Using a discussion protocol helped orient the participants' discussion toward either viewpoint. The group was able to summarize the role of collaboration in student general music learning in three principles of collaboration. I investigated teacher learning, as well as changes in my own perceptions of student musical collaboration, by tracing the evolution of the teachers' viewpoints within statements they made in the group meetings and individually.

One of my most important findings was that the process of learning together in a group combated the isolation often felt by general music teachers. The following section begins with the work of selected researchers who also sought to understand the isolation and need for support often inherent in the general music teacher's job. I then write about research on teacher learning and teacher knowledge.

2.3. Research on the General Music Teacher

In this section I write about how researchers have investigated general music teachers' unique working conditions, particular pedagogical content knowledge, and ways of teaching, and ways in which researchers have written about bias toward certain types or styles of teaching during studies.

2.3.1. General Music Teachers' Need for Support

Robbins (1994/1995) studied the formation of a general music teacher network for support in implementing new concepts from an Orff-Schulwerk teacher training course. She wrote: "For music teachers, talking together is a rare and unfamiliar event that they simultaneously fear and crave" (48), and in her group of teachers (dubbed OrffSPIEL) she combated isolation and established conversation through common goals of inquiry and reflection. Using journals and meeting transcripts to examine the OrffSPIEL experience, Robbins found that participants considered the experience empowering and validating. I (2011, 2012) drew upon Robbins's work in examining how collaborative teacher study groups (CTSGs) can support elementary general music teachers in increasing their confidence, expertise, and disposition toward reflection.

Several researchers have characterized the work of general music teachers as isolated. By virtue of often being the only music teacher at their site, many general music teachers lack access to collegial support or the wisdom of other general music teachers. Tagg (1997) and Morrissey (2004) commented on isolation and marginalization as well as issues of elementary music teacher burnout, scheduling, and vocal health in their single case studies of elementary vocal music teachers.

2.3.2. Teacher Knowledge

A group of researchers have examined qualitatively how a general music teacher organizes and uses her knowledge of music and teaching. Duling (1992) studied two exemplary secondary general music teachers to determine factors contributing to their acquisition of "pedagogical content knowledge (PCK)" (Shulman 1987, cited in Duling 1992, 5). Through interviews, observations, examining lesson plans, and by asking questions while viewing video of participants' teaching with them (stimulated recall), Duling created a detailed image of not only how these teachers acquired and used PCK, but also the teachers' classrooms and teaching styles: knowledgeable, organized, and enthusiastic, yet serious. Alig (1992) investigated how six general music teachers used knowledge and skill to develop into national leaders in general music education. In his multiple case study, Alig was able to use interview data to connect events in participants' lives with their growth in leadership. Both Duling and Alig treated participants as portrait subjects, and the "voice and vitality" of each participant (Alig 1992, 173) were strongly present.

Eshelman (1995) examined the beliefs, practices, and types of knowledge of four exemplary general music teachers through interviews, videotaped observations, and field notes. Eshelman documented and illustrated the relationship between content and pedagogical instructional knowledge and how these components related to Elliott's (1995) model categories of music teacher knowledge. Eshelman created the Model of Exemplary Elementary Teachers' Instructional Knowledge, which included interwoven examples from these teachers' everyday lives in the classroom.

Like Eshelman, Anderson-Nickel (1997) sought to identify different types of teacher expertise but emphasized how musical and pedagogical knowledge places teachers on a novice-expert continuum. Like Duling, Anderson-Nickel used data collection methods of videotaping classes and stimulated recall, and interviews focused on reflective responses. Anderson-Nickel connected teaching practice with level of expertise and found the relationship paralleled prior researchers' findings about the continuum of expertise. Expert teachers employed reflective self-awareness, smoother routines, and more efficient use of information in the moment. Delaney (2011) analyzed the content of teachers' commentary on video of music classrooms. She used stimulated recall in individual interviews, during which teachers viewed three of their own videos, stopping freely to discuss aspects of teaching practice. Teachers also viewed one video of another teacher outside the study. Delaney found the process motivated reflective conversation about the art of teaching.

Several researchers have found the storytelling capabilities of narrative inquiry methodology helpful in drawing rich pictures of music teacher life. Niebur (1997) used narrative inquiry (based on ethnographic techniques of observations, teacher shadowing, group meetings with the participants, and interviews) to write colorful stories about four general music teachers and how they assess students. Lemons (1998) also used narrative inquiry based on researcher observation and participant interviews while watching videos of their own teaching, to study how teacher knowledge is affected by teachers' history, perceptions, assumptions, and previous experience.

2.3.3. Teachers Studying Teachers

When researchers knowledgeable about general music observe general music teaching, they choose to handle their preconceived notions and beliefs in different ways. Lemons (1994/1995) wrote about how her subjectivity underwent a "process of taming" (58) to move past her prior beliefs about teacher quality. On the other hand, Chen (2000) embraced her subjectivity in a stance as "researcher-as-instrument" (39) when she studied one exemplary teacher's reflective practice and constructivist elementary general music classroom. Chen's prolonged presence in the classroom for interviews led her eventually to interact with specific students, assist the teacher, and answer student questions. Her "personal perspectives and perception inevitably influenced the construction and re-construction of this teacher's lived experience" (Chen 2000, 35).

McDonald (2001) examined the value of guided critical reflection with peers on the topic of classroom management in general music. In a collective case study, McDonald analyzed results of her "Creating Positive Discipline and Management" (35) workshops with 100-plus teachers over several years. McDonald wrote about the influence of the workshop on the participants' practice, and how her presence affected the findings: teachers enrolled in these workshops to seek help with classroom management and then formed a relationship with the classroom management expert who was also the researcher. Like Stanley (2009, 2012) and Robbins (1994/1995), McDonald was concerned about teachers' lack of supportive networks in their own school sites: "participants may have left the workshop having received personal attention and constructive suggestions... yet will not be offered further opportunities for dialogue or critical reflection about their concerns at their school settings" (44)

2.4. Discussion of Researcher Perspectives

The issue of "insider" versus "outsider" perspectives is a perdurable one in qualitative research, and a useful framework for a discussion of literature reviewed in this chapter. Each researcher cited here has written about his or her rationale for choosing a certain etic or emic vantage point from which to scrutinize the phenomenon under study; in the following section I offer commentary on the epistemological implications of such choices.

2.4.1. A Slice from the Outside, A Slice from the Inside

Some of the authors discussed in this chapter presented the "slice of life" from a distance. For them, this removal may enhance objectivity and perhaps result in more truthful, accurate findings. Even researchers who took great care to place themselves at a significant distance from their participants often chose to confirm findings with outside auditors, seeking a once-removed and ostensibly less subjective "other" to evaluate the researchers' conclusions.

However, not being a member of a community, school, or classroom is not a guarantee of objectivity. Being outside a situation does not automatically mean one is not still intimately acquainted with it. Most of the authors in this chapter had a background in general music teaching before they became researchers on general music, and many understandably were curious about and sought to examine research questions in situations that bore close resemblance to former teaching assignments. This deep, empathetic understanding of the field of general music precludes true outsider-ness.

For example, Kelly-McHale (2011) wrote about her struggle to honestly situate herself as an outside "observer," given that she herself was a veteran general music teacher who (1) taught in the same district as the participant teacher she was studying, and (2) had years of experience using the same methodology—Kodály—with comparable student populations. Kelly-McHale chose to make her inner conflict as transparent as possible by writing extensive autobiographical notes along with her data analysis:

> [M]y experience in this closely related setting could potentially influence my descriptions and data analysis based on a tendency to evaluate the teacher's instructional delivery or the performance of the students. I became aware of the need to continuously reflect on my experience as a general music teacher in order to interrogate my analysis of the data as it emerged. I engaged in several conversations with my advisor that helped me recognize when I was allowing my personal feelings to drive assumptions and to ensure that I was allowing the data to speak for itself. I also kept autobiographical notes to better understand the role that my feelings and actions played in the research setting. (142)

Objectivity was not the goal of some researchers discussed in this chapter who took the outsider viewpoint. For example, I chose a hybrid stance of omniscient observer, facilitator, *and* group member in my research. My observer role was not adopted to seek objectivity, but rather, to provide knowledgeable commentary on our group's interactions from one more perspective. I wrote, "there is no superior vantage point from which to survey the intrinsic beliefs, perceptions, and learning of an individual or a community, I knew that my roles . . . would privilege me to understand what happened in our meetings, or as a result of our meetings" (Stanley 2009, 4).

Other authors mentioned in this chapter took on the ultimate insider role, by examining their own work in their own classrooms. However, being closely involved in a situation does not guarantee a full understanding of *all* elements within, nor is that understanding necessarily deeper than what an outside researcher could obtain. Consider Wiggins, who wrote: "Despite my active role both in interacting with the children and in determining the environment for the study, my view as teacher-researcher was still really that of an outsider. Although I was not an outsider to the situation, I had no choice but to be an outsider to the children's thought processes" (1994, 236–37). And Beegle (2010) explained that although she was using the teacher-as-researcher paradigm in order to "provide insight that is difficult or impossible for a researcher from outside the classroom to obtain" (221) she thought that same insight, her prior knowledge of the students as their teacher, might even "jeopardize" her ability to understand exactly what the children meant to do. Therefore, she asked the students to confirm or dispute her conclusions.

Hammersley (1993), writing about the insider-outsider continuum, recommended "a judicious combination of involvement and estrangement . . . no position, not even a marginal one, guarantees valid knowledge; and no position prevents it either" (145). It appears that most researchers discussed in this chapter tried to combine both angles thoughtfully, albeit in varying proportions, and write clearly and convincingly about their choices.

2.4.2. Writing about Researcher Positioning

"I now accept that I can use the insider/outsider situation to my advantage, if through a process of self-reflection, I understand who and what I am" (Richardson 2000, 929). The most important aspect of researcher positioning is how the author reflects on and comes to know her stance in the context of the study, and then how she explains it in her writing. Perhaps it is time to add more personal and less static, oppositional terms than "insider-outsider" to our considerations of stance.

In 2002, Labaree published a review of the literature analyzing the insider-outsider issue. He wrote, "Many contemporary researchers are focusing on their desire to look beyond this methodological dichotomy. . . . This conceptualization of research creates a polarizing effect that undermines the ability of the researcher to move beyond understanding insiderness and outsiderness as an either/or proposition" (99; 101). But even placing the stance on a continuum to avoid dichotomy is problematic. Hellawell (2006) wrote, "We are . . . not talking about one continuum but about a multiple series of parallel ones. There may be some elements of insiderness on some dimensions of your research and some elements of outsiderness on other dimensions" (490). What is important is the researcher's ability to make measured decisions regarding her inside/outside stance(s) and parse these judgments for the reader in precise ways to better illuminate the researcher's identity as situated within the particular project. See Tobias (2010) for a detailed discussion of researcher portrayed as the "least adult" presence (118), someone who "credibly maintained ignorance as to what [participants] were doing" (119), and was therefore able to access insider data about students' understanding of their own creative projects without inserting himself. Tobias also described shifts between stances using one of three lenses: "monological, subjective, and dialogical" (119).

The increased visibility of these processes and judgments within published research reports would be extremely valuable. However, inclusion of discussion related to these topics would require that qualitative projects be given more space and words to do justice to the issues: certainly more than the one or two sentences about "researcher orientation" that have become boilerplate. Perhaps the insider-outsider notion could be reconceptualized as "researcher visibility-invisibility" within the text. The reader needs to know explicitly how and when the role of the researcher was made visible, or hidden, at points throughout the study. Researchers would benefit from more precise analysis and reflection about insider/outsider identities throughout *all* phases of the project—from proposal to the final report—rather than one decision made in the very beginning as just one of many methodological choices.

These decisions should be given space in qualitative reports of research. For example, often reading a dissertation yields a more nuanced understanding of shifts in researcher stance than does the 20-page distillation of the study published in research journals (cf. Younker 1997, 2000; Miranda 2002, 2004). Younker (1997, 2000) called her study "descriptive" and transcribed carefully what her participants said and did while they composed. Because of this care, she did not choose to seek triangulation from an outside source, other than a short comparative analysis performed by her advisor. Younker (2000) wrote convincingly and in detail about what the students did and said while they composed; for her, it appears no more corroboration was necessary in her journalistic, storied view of participants' compositional strategies. However, in her 1997 dissertation, Younker wrote about her need to encourage students during their process of using unfamiliar software, during which she asked them to explain what they were thinking and doing. At this point, Younker described herself as "facilitator" (1997, 30) versus outside researcher. Similarly, in her dissertation, Miranda (2002) described her study as "constructivist," necessitating an immersion viewpoint (2002, 74) and situated herself as "observer/observer-participant" (2002, 75). These descriptions represent a much finer distinction of stance than emerges from the 2004 short journal article about her dissertation study.

Likewise, regarding trustworthiness: a single sentence is currently commonplace in journal articles, one about how "outside experts" reviewed the data for confirming/disconfirming ideas, and that triangulation was used to verify the credibility of the analysis. The reader deserves more: the issue of goodness and accuracy being monitored and substantiated by "outsiders" is problematic. "Outsiders" coming to the same or different conclusions as the "insider"—or, for that matter, the *other* "outsider," the researcher—is not automatically good, nor inevitably bad. Rather, the *process* that led to confirmation or disconfirmation deserves serious, robust treatment in the paper so the reader can understand the fine shades of identity and meaning that qualitatively affect these judgments. Those responsible for the dissemination of qualitative research in general music could explore ways to include detailed descriptions of this practice.

2.5. THE RESEARCHER'S FOOTPRINTS

Another perennial question in qualitative research, related to the insider-outsider discussion, is, "How does the act of being observed change the 'observed one'?" The studies in this chapter varied, but most were not intended to change or alter the phenomenon under study (except perhaps the work in section 2.2.4). Much research in general music is intended to offer readers that "slice of life" as it exists in a given moment, not changing it in the process of presentation.

However, it seems that most researchers acknowledge that their research had some sort of influence—even unintentional—on the participants. We can infer ways in which research in section 2.3.2 affected the teachers being studied. Anderson-Nickel (1997) stated that she did not interact at all with participants: "the study was not experimental and was not intended to intervene or influence the classroom environment" (44). She did, however, state that she "acknowledged concerns . . . relating to the dignity and self-respect of the teachers" who may have had "concerns" about being videotaped (45). It seems logical, too, that in addition to videotape effects, the teachers who experienced Anderson-Nickel's research protocol (responding to stimulated recall prompts while watching video of their own teaching, and answering open-ended interview questions designed to elicit reflective thinking) likely experienced a change in thinking about teaching practice, or in their perceptions of their own teaching. While these changes might have been profound, or not, tracing them was outside Anderson-Nickel's inquiry.

While Duling (1992) wanted to merely observe the teachers in his study, his presence affected them. One teacher-participant drew him into participatory dialogue as he was observing the class, stating later that Duling served as her surrogate for a close co-teacher colleague who had been transferred to another school. One teacher, with whom Duling had no interaction while observing, nonetheless stated that Duling's presence fueled in him "an energy I need to apply to my teaching" (80) and that he was always more "on" on days when Duling was there, even after he left: "My work with the whole set of morning classes is influenced even after you [leave for the day]. I think a little more clearly—keep my focus" (99).

Delaney (2011) wrote honestly about her efforts *not* to influence participants: "As this researcher observed the videotape . . . [she] attempted to refrain from commenting on the instruction, but at times, these thoughts were discussed with the teachers. This researcher's experience and education influenced the questions asked and the direction of the discussion" (47). On the other hand, researchers Chen (2000), McDonald (2001), and Stanley (2009, 2012) all embraced the effect they had on participants. McDonald and Stanley wrote of their concern that anything their participants learned by being in the study would not last if they were not supported in their classroom environments by colleagues and administrators.

Consider one of Lather's (2003) "goodness criteria": validity as catalyst, assessed through the value of the findings for instigating action. Lather defines catalytic validity as "the degree to which the research process re-orients, focuses, and energizes participants . . . respondents gain self-understanding, and, ideally, self-determination through research participation" (191). Lather's lens gives us a way to look at the reaction of participants to research: were they affected by being in a study? How? And what lingering role does the research play in their self-understanding or self-determination? If we ignore this aspect of doing qualitative research in general music, we may lose important insights.

2.6. Recommendations for Future Research

In this section, I provide recommendations for research which could ensure all voices within general music are better-represented in qualitative scholarship. I also offer suggestions for topics which so far have been under-researched: culturally relevant pedagogy and age-appropriate pedagogy.

2.6.1. Let All Voices Be Heard

Future researchers should find ways to strengthen all voices within qualitative research on general music. The voice of the researcher will be made stronger and increasingly trustworthy if researcher processes, decision-making, and shifts in attitude are more explicitly written about. The voice of the participants—general music teachers and students—could be fortified in terms of (a) researchers' efforts to determine the effect of research on participants and write about it; and (b) researchers' seeking student perspective on general music education.

In terms of the effect of research on participants, I reject the view that the background knowledge, or participation, of the researcher threatens validity. Rather, I argue in favor of mediating bias through an increased inclusion of two perspectives currently missing from the literature: the *participant view* of the insider/outsider positioning of the researcher, and the *participant view* of the researcher's role in the production of knowledge. Qualitative researchers could probe, through a variety of means, the participants' outlook on researcher stance, researcher involvement, and researcher effects on the phenomena of music teaching and learning under study. To omit these views seems to eliminate valuable glimpses of the interactions, relationships, relative distance or closeness, hierarchy, or power differential between researchers and their participants.

Regarding the second point, student perspective, Griffin (2010) wrote a review of the literature connecting children's school music experiences with their daily lives. She asked for a stronger "linkage between children's perspectives on their musical activities and what actually occurs in elementary music education" (47): a child-oriented connection between research and practice:

> Children's perspectives need to be heard and their voices acknowledged as a central catalyst in shaping the planning, enacting, and experiencing of music curricula … up until now their voices have not played as important a role as may be possible. (48)

This voice-as-catalyst comparison recalls Lather's "catalytic validity" construct. One way to gauge the success of qualitative research in general music is if and when researchers can confirm that their projects instigated needed curricular innovations, and that those innovations heeded the voiced needs of students. (See Reynolds, volume 3, chapter 1 in this volume, for more on children's voice in research.)

2.6.2. Investigate Culturally Responsive, Age-Appropriate Pedagogy

The topic of culturally responsive pedagogy is a rich one for qualitative investigation, especially as "culture" pertains to contemporary views of music, or even "youth" (Tobias 2010, 116). Recent calls for a reformed general curriculum that incorporates elements of popular or specific ethnic cultures relevant to students' lives might be strengthened by more research in this area (e.g., Abramo 2011). The relationship between secondary general music and music education reform warrants further study: Is secondary general music a "catch-all" course, a required fine arts credit, or "a recasting of curricular options beyond large ensembles to address needs of students marginalized from traditional music programs" (Tobias 2010, 4)? There is little qualitative research in secondary general music environments. Tobias wrote, "Although a growing number of music educators are calling for expanded curricular offerings beyond the secondary large ensemble context, few empirical studies of such curricula exist" (2010, 83).

2.6.3. Conclusion: Meaningful Investigations

Our profession needs to ask more questions about the relationship between commonly used general music classroom activities and student musical achievement. Especially in the current era of high-stakes teacher accountability for student learning, the connection between the activities children do in music class and what they learn from them is a crucial one. For example, how does classroom singing affect children's ability to match pitch, audiate, and understand the basic harmonic building blocks of music? Or does classroom singing teach children more about community, teamwork, and democracy? How do movement and circle games affect children's deep and enduring understanding of music? How do creative music-making activities like composition and improvisation factor into students' acquisition of lifelong musicianship skills? We actually know very little about the three-way connection or intersection between (a) many common general music activities, (b) how they are taught, and (c) how children learn from them.

Qualitative research, with its varied methodologies and potential for creative, insightful exploration of the intersection of music teaching and learning, can offer an in-depth, powerful picture of student musical skills and behaviors. Researchers should investigate what defines lasting musical learning in general music, and whether we are achieving that through some of the activities we are currently using and believe to be valuable.

Similarly, qualitative researchers should seek different lenses through which to view and understand the musical growth that occurs throughout the multiple years students are usually involved in general music. For example, Younker (1997, 2000) offers a longer-term developmental perspective. Longitudinal, collaborative efforts to examine student learning are especially needed, recognizing of course that these types of lengthy multi-researcher qualitative studies require a combination of resources, time, and money. Perhaps it is a matter of being more realistic about how long meaningful qualitative inquiry may take. Kleinknecht, Puddephatt, and Sanders (2012) wrote, "No matter how tempting new and trendy methods and conceptual styles may be, there is never any good substitute for the long periods of time required to sufficiently immerse oneself into, and collect rich and rigorous data about, the social worlds of others" (8). Snapshots of musical learning in one moment, or over the course of one unit, are illuminating. However, to realize general music classes' potential as—recalling Mason's significant claim in 1979—the "basic foundations upon which a musically and culturally sensitive citizenry is developed," researchers now need to focus their work on deeper issues of student musical learning and achievement that will confirm the extraordinarily important, foundational nature of general music, and secure its place as the basic building block for all future musical endeavors.

Note

1. Now the National Association for Music Education (NAfME).

References

Abramo, J. M. 2011. "Gender Differences of Popular Music Production in Secondary Schools." *Journal of Research in Music Education* 59 (1): 21–43.
Alig, K. J. 1992. "Factors in the Development of Leading General Music Educators." PhD diss., Arizona State University.
Anderson-Nickel, J. D. 1997. "Teacher Expertise among Elementary General Music Teachers." PhD diss., Arizona State University.
Atterbury, B. W. 1991. "Some Directions for Research in Elementary General Music." *Bulletin of the Council for Research in Music Education* 109: 37–45.
Barrett, J. R. 1990. "Melodic Schemata, Forms of Representation, and Cognitive Strategies Used by Fourth-Graders in the Recall and Reproduction of Familiar Songs." PhD diss., University of Wisconsin-Madison.
Bartolome, S. J. 2009. "Naturally Emerging Self-Regulated Practice Behaviors among Highly Successful Beginning Recorder Students." *Research Studies in Music Education* 31 (1): 37–51.
Beegle, A. C. 2010. "A Classroom-Based Study of Small-Group Planned Improvisation with Fifth-Grade Children." *Journal of Research in Music Education* 58 (3): 219–39.
Boardman, E. 1990. "Needed Research in General Music." *Bulletin of the Council for Research in Music Education* 104: 5–15.

Bresler, L. B. 1993. Music in a Double-Bind: Instruction by Non-Specialists in Elementary Schools. *Bulletin of the Council for Research in Music Education* 115: 1–14.

Bresler, L. 1995/1996. "Curricular Orientations in Elementary School Music: Roles, Pedagogies and Values." *Bulletin of the Council for Research in Music Education* 127: 22–27.

Brummett, V. M. 1993. "The Development, Application, and Critique of an Interactive Student Evaluation Framework for Elementary General Music." PhD diss., University of Illinois at Urbana-Champaign.

Chen, C. D. 2000. "Constructivism in General Music Education: A Music Teacher's Lived Experience." PhD diss., University of Illinois at Urbana-Champaign.

Claire, L. 1993/1994. "The Social Psychology of Creativity: The Importance of Peer Social Processes for Students' Academic and Artistic Creativity in Classroom Contexts." *Bulletin of the Council for Research in Music Education* 119: 21–28.

Delaney, D. W. 2011. "Elementary General Music Teachers' Reflections on Instruction." *Update: Applications of Research in Music Education* 29 (2): 41–49.

DeLorenzo, L. C. 1989. "A Field Study of Sixth-Grade Students' Creative Music Problem-Solving Processes." *Journal of Research in Music Education* 37 (3): 188–200.

Duling, E. B. 1992. "The Development of Pedagogical-Content Knowledge: Two Case Studies of Exemplary General Music Teachers." PhD diss., The Ohio State University.

Emmons, S. E. 1998. "Analysis of Musical Creativity in Middle School Students through Composition Using Computer-Assisted Instruction: A Multiple Case Study." PhD diss., University of Rochester: Eastman School of Music.

Eshelman, D. A. 1995. "The Instructional Knowledge of Exemplary Elementary General Music Teachers: Commonalities Based on David J. Elliott's Model of the Professional Music Educator." PhD diss., University of Oklahoma.

Ferguson, L. S. 2004. "I See Them Listening: A Teacher's Understanding of Children's Expressive Movements to Music in the Classroom." PhD diss., University of Illinois at Urbana-Champaign.

Greher, G. R. 2002. "'Picture This!' 1997: An Interactive Listening Environment for Middle School General Music." PhD diss., Teachers College, Columbia University.

Griffin, S. M. 2010. "Inquiring into Children's Music Experiences: Groundings in Literature." *Update: Applications of Research in Music Education* 28 (2): 42–49.

Gromko, J. E. 1996. "In a Child's Voice: An Interpretive Interaction with Young Composers." *Bulletin of the Council for Research in Music Education* 128: 37–58.

Hamilton, H. J. 1999. "Music Learning through Composition, Improvisation and Peer Interaction in the Context of Three Sixth Grade Music Classes." PhD diss., University of Minnesota.

Hammersley, M. 1993. "On Practitioner Ethnography." In *What's Wrong with Ethnography*, edited by M. Hammersley, 135–58. London: Paul Chapman.

Harwood, E. 1998. "Go on Girl! Improvisation in African-American Girls' Singing Games." In *In the Course of Performance: Studies in the World of Musical Improvisation*, edited B. Nettl, 113–25. Chicago: University of Chicago Press.

Hellawell, D. 2006. "Inside out: Analysis of the Insider-Outsider Concept as a Heuristic Device to Develop Reflexivity in Students Doing Qualitative Research." *Teaching in Higher Education* 11 (4): 483–94.

Hoffman, M. E. 1981. "The Heart of the School Music Program." *Music Educators Journal* 68 (1): 42–43.

Holdridge, J. R. 1991. "Music in Our Lives: A Naturalistic Study of Three High School General Music Classes." PhD diss., New York University.

Kaschub, M. 1997. "A Comparison of Two Composer-Guided Large Group Composition Projects." *Research Studies in Music Education* 8 (1): 15–28.

Kelly-McHale, J. L. 2011. "The Relationship between Children's Musical Identities and Music Teacher Beliefs and Practices in an Elementary General Music Classroom." PhD diss., Northwestern University.

Kenney, S. 2010. "A History of the Society for General Music." *General Music Today* 24 (1): 4–14.

Kerchner, J. L. 2000. "Children's Verbal, Visual, and Kinesthetic Responses: Insight into Their Music Listening Experiences." *Bulletin of the Council for Research in Music Education* 146: 31–50.

Kleinknecht, S., A. Puddephatt, and C. B. Sanders. 2012. "Introduction to the Special Issue. Qualitative Analysis Conference 2011: Contemporary Issues in Qualitative Research." *Qualitative Sociology Review* 8 (1): 6–9.

Labaree, R. V. 2002. "The Risk of 'Going Observationalist': Negotiating the Hidden Dilemmas of Being an Insider Participant Observer." *Qualitative Research* 2 (1): 97–101.

Lather, P. 2003. "Issues of Validity in Openly Ideological Research." In *Turning Points in Qualitative Research: Tying Knots in a Handkerchief*, edited by Y. S. Lincoln and N. K. Denzin, 185–215. Walnut Creek, CA: AltaMira Press.

Lemons, M. L. 1998. "Image, Context, and Knowledge in the Practice of Two Elementary Music Teachers." PhD diss., University of Illinois, Urbana-Champaign.

Lemons, M. L. 1994/1995. "Curriculum in Elementary Music: A Critical Reflection on Subjectivity." *Bulletin of the Council for Research in Music Education* 123: 53–58.

Lum, C. H., and P. S. Campbell. 2007. "The Sonic Surrounds of an Elementary School." *Journal of Research in Music Education* 55 (1): 31–47.

McDonald, N. L. 2001. "Reflective Practices: Collective Case Studies of Selected K–8 General Music Teachers in Peer Problem-Solving Discipline and Management Workshop Settings." PhD diss., University of San Diego.

Miller, B. A. 1996. "Integrating Elementary General Music: A Collaborative Action Research Study." *Bulletin of the Council for Research in Music Education* 130: 100–15.

Miller, B. A. 2003. "Integrating Elementary General Music Instruction with a First Grade Whole Language Classroom." *Bulletin of the Council for Research in Music Education* 156: 43–62.

Miller, B. A. 2004. "Designing Compositional Tasks for Elementary Music Classrooms." *Research Studies in Music Education* 22 (1): 59–71.

Miranda, M. L. 2002. "The Seasons of Kindergarten: Developmentally Appropriate Practice in the Kindergarten Music Classroom." PhD diss., Arizona State University.

Miranda, M. L. 2004. "The Implications of Developmentally Appropriate Practice for the Kindergarten General Music Classroom." *Journal of Research in Music Education* 52 (1): 43–63.

Morrissey, M. L. 2004. "Intensification and the Vocal Health of an Elementary General Music Teacher." PhD diss., University of Wisconsin-Madison.

Niebur, L. L. 1997. "Standards, Assessment, and Stories of Practice in General Music." PhD diss., Arizona State University.

Perconti, E. S. 1996. "Learning to Compose and Learning through Composing: A Study of the Composing Process in Elementary General Music." PhD diss., University of Idaho.

Reese, S. 1981. "An Implementation of the CEMREL Aesthetic Education Program by Elementary Classroom Teachers: A Qualitative Observation." PhD diss., University of Illinois at Urbana-Champaign.

Richardson, L. 2000. "Writing: A Method of Inquiry." In *Handbook of Qualitative Research*, edited by N. K. Denzin and Y. S. Lincoln, 923–48. Thousand Oaks, CA: Sage Publications.

Robbins, J. 1994/1995. "Levels of Learning in Orff SPIEL." *Bulletin of the Council for Research in Music Education* 123: 47–53.

Ruthmann, S. A. 2006. "Negotiating Learning and Teaching in a Music Technology Lab: Curricular, Pedagogical, and Ecological Issues." PhD diss., Oakland University, Rochester, MI.

Salvador, K. 2011. "Individualizing Elementary General Music Instruction: Case Studies of Assessment and Differentiation." PhD diss., Michigan State University, Lansing, MI.

Stanley, A. M. 2009. "The Experiences of Elementary Music Teachers in a Collaborative Teacher Study Group." PhD diss., University of Michigan.

Stanley, A. M. 2012. "What is Collaboration in Elementary Music Education? A Social Constructivist Inquiry within a Collaborative Teacher Study Group (CTSG)." *Bulletin of the Council for Research in Music Education* 192: 53–74.

Stauffer, S. L. 2001. "Composing with Computers: Meg Makes Music." *Bulletin of the Council for Research in Music Education* 150: 1–20.

Stauffer, S. L. 2002. "Connections between the Musical and Life Experiences of Young Composers and Their Compositions." *Journal of Research in Music Education* 50 (4): 301–22.

Strand, K. 2005. "Nurturing Young Composers: Exploring the Relationship between Instruction and Transfer in 9–12 Year-Old Students." *Bulletin of the Council for Research in Music Education* 165: 17–36.

Tagg, B. M. 1997. "The Jane Rand Story: A Case Study of an Elementary Vocal Music Teacher." PhD diss., Syracuse University.

Tobias, E. 2010. "Crossfading and Plugging in: Secondary Students' Engagement and Learning in a Songwriting and Technology Class." PhD diss., Northwestern University.

Wayman, V. E. 2004. "An Exploratory Investigation of Three Middle School General Music Students' Beliefs about Music Education." *Bulletin of the Council for Research in Music Education* 160: 26–37.

Whitaker, N. L. 1996. "Elusive Connections: Music Integration and the Elementary Classroom." *Bulletin of the Council for Research in Music Education* 130: 89–99.

Wiggins, J. H. 1993. "The Nature of Children's Musical Learning in the Context of a Music Classroom." PhD diss., University of Illinois at Urbana-Champaign.

Wiggins, J. H. 1994. "Children's Strategies for Solving Compositional Problems with Peers." *Journal of Research in Music Education* 42 (3): 232–52.

Wiggins, J. H. 1995. "Building Structural Understanding: Sam's Story." *The Quarterly Journal of Music Teaching and Learning* 6 (3): 57–75.

Wiggins, J. H. (1994/1995). "Teacher-Research in a General Music Classroom: Effects on the Teacher." *Bulletin of the Council for Research in Music Education* 123: 31–35.

Wiggins, J. H. 1999/2000. "The Nature of Shared Musical Understanding and Its Role in Empowering Independent Musical Thinking." *Bulletin of the Council for Research in Music Education* 143: 65–90.

Wiggins, J., and K. Bodoin. 1998. "Painting a Big Soup: Teaching and Learning in a Second Grade General Music Classroom." *Journal of Research in Music Education* 46 (2): 281–302.

Younker, B. A. 1997. "Thought Processes and Strategies of Eight, Eleven, and Fourteen Year Old Students While Engaged in Music Composition." PhD diss., Northwestern University.

Younker, B. A. 2000. "Thought Processes and Strategies of Students While Engaged in Music Composition." *Research in Music Education* 14: 24–38.

CHAPTER 3

INSTRUMENTAL MUSIC (WINDS, BRASS, PERCUSSION)

CHAD WEST

WHILE American school band programs have been around for a century, it was only as recent as the 1980s that such programs have been explored through qualitative research methods. The first qualitative study examining American school band programs appeared in 1980 as an article in the *Journal of Band Research* that described the characteristics of five college band directors (Yarberry 1980). Since that first study, approximately 50 published qualitative studies have addressed American school band programs. Of those, 36 have been dissertations and 14 have been journal articles. Within the peer-reviewed music education journals, six have appeared in the *Bulletin of the Council for Research in Music Education* (*CRME*), three have appeared in the *Journal of Research in Music Education* (*JRME*), two were published in the *Journal of Band Research* (*JBR*), two were published in *Music Educators Journal* (*MEJ*), and one appeared in *Contributions to Music Education* (*CME*). This chapter explores the qualitative band studies published as dissertations and journal articles from 1980 through 2011.[1] The first section (3.1) of this chapter, "Teaching Band," presents findings related specifically to documenting band teaching practices, jazz band, teaching students with special needs, composition, band students' learning, and band student perspectives. The second section (3.2) of this chapter, "Beyond Teaching Band," presents findings from studies that have explored broad facets of band programs such as the social aspects of band, gender, adult learners, histories, and the lives of band directors.

3.1. TEACHING BAND

Much of the quantitative band research through the years has examined aspects directly related to teaching and learning—mainly student cognition and teaching techniques.

Since the 1980s qualitative band researchers have begun studying similar topics, albeit with a different worldview, using different methods and suggesting different implications. Since the first qualitative band study in 1980, researchers have documented effective teaching practices, looked at ways of teaching jazz and composition, brought attention and understanding to band students with special needs, conducted action research in their own classrooms, and sought to understand student perceptions of band.

3.1.1. Documenting Band Teaching Practices

Through personal interviews and document examination, Yarberry (1980) explored the previous music experiences, commitment to the profession, philosophies, and professional education of five outstanding college band directors. While the author did not identify his study as qualitative and used language that today we associate with quantitative research, his method of interviewing participants regarding their perceptions was indeed consistent with what we identify today as qualitative research. The researcher even went so far as to examine (presumably with permission) the diaries and personal letters of these directors. With research techniques still dominated by a quantitative worldview in 1980, the author was careful to defend the interview as a valid form of data collection: "The research interview appeared to be a powerful instrument for the study . . . particularly the involvement of the conductor with the development of his own band!" (24).

Jachens (1987) interviewed six well-known band directors who taught during the 1920s and 1930s regarding their teaching techniques, materials they used, and their philosophies and goals in teaching band. Additionally, the researcher studied artifacts such as newspaper clippings and concert programs. The author presented findings according to how the participants taught tone, intonation, technique, and interpretation. In addition, Jachens suggested that these band directors felt that in the 1920s and 1930s, the focus was on technique rather than tone, intonation, and expression.

In 1988, Casey sought to identify successful teaching practices for preparing students to sight-read at band festivals and competitions. The researcher observed and video-recorded the comments and behaviors of successful band directors in simulated sight-reading sessions. After each session, the researcher then interviewed each director regarding his/her means of organizing time and use of teaching strategies to prepare students for the contest sight-reading session. Based on the recorded observations and interviews, Casey constructed a composite conductor profile that band directors could use to prepare students for contest sight-reading.

Looking at band pedagogy more broadly, Buell (1990) examined effective teaching and conducting practices within high performing symphonic band and wind ensemble settings. Through observing band rehearsals and interviewing the band directors and their students, the researcher found that effective teaching and conducting was not linked to any single factor, but rather to a combination of positive learning environments, the appropriate linking of teaching strategies to instructional goals, and using varied instructional techniques according to individual differences in students. Continuous development of personal musicianship and thorough score-study were also found to aid effectiveness in teaching band.

Similar to Buell, in an effort to identify common factors of success, Dugle (1991) observed rehearsals and interviewed the parents, administrators, students, and staff of three high-achieving band programs in Illinois. The researcher found common characteristics such as teacher traits, teacher teamwork, adequate financing, private lessons, the community arts environment, and parental and administrative support. Students perceived the reason for success of the programs were the social aspects afforded by participation in band.

In 1993, Prather interviewed and observed a college band director and his two graduate student protégés. The researcher described patterns of personal and professional mentoring practices between the director and his mentees, including how the mentor passed on information to the protégés regarding warm-ups, concept of tone quality, teaching of rhythm, use of literature, approach to discipline, baton technique, structure of the band program, team concept, personal mannerisms, and philosophies.

Six years later, Conway (1999) interviewed four experienced band directors (one elementary, two middle school, and one high school) and observed their teaching practices to develop teaching cases for use in instrumental music education courses. Specifically, the researcher documented the participants' daily interactions, decision-making skills, and use of pedagogical content knowledge. Within the cases, Conway described and discussed curricula and objectives, program administration, recruitment and balanced instrumentation, scheduling, literature choices, classroom management strategies, motivation, assessment techniques, musicianship, and rapport with students.

Similar to Buell, Dugle, and Conway, Gonzalez (2001) examined the philosophies and rehearsal procedures of three public school band directors and three college band directors known for their strong programs and excellent reputations. The researcher video-recorded each participant during a typical rehearsal and surveyed each regarding his/her rehearsal procedures and philosophy. Gonzalez coded the data according to areas where the philosophy and procedure aligned and found that these conductors all utilized effective pacing, systematic rehearsal formats, timely interjections of instructional comments, and a philosophically based plan for the use of rehearsal procedures.

Using both qualitative and quantitative techniques, Schopp (2006) studied the use of improvisation and composition among high school band directors in the state of New York. For the qualitative portion of the study, the researcher observed five high school band programs and interviewed their directors to identify possible teaching strategies for incorporating improvisation and composition into the high school band program. Findings from both data sets suggest that while band directors generally supported the teaching of improvisation and composition, most offered little regular instruction in these areas. The researcher found that this is most often the result of lack of time due to rehearsal and performance commitments, as well as teacher and student anxiety when engaging in these experiences. Schopp suggested that successful programs use approaches that begin simply, foster non-threatening environments, and incorporate student improvisations and compositions into performances. The researcher also found that while teacher education programs are preparing new music educators to teach improvisation and composition, band directors are often unable to incorporate such instruction into their direction of large ensembles such as concert band.

In another mixed methods study, Bazan (2007) sought to describe teaching strategies of band directors who reported a student-directed teaching style. Bazan used quantitative techniques to identify such teachers and invited three of the most student-directed teachers to participate in the qualitative portion of his study. The researcher then observed and video-recorded five rehearsals of each participant and interviewed each participant after each rehearsal. Bazan found that even the teachers who self-reported the highest usage of student-directed teaching strategies still most frequently utilized teacher-directed instruction. Other findings described potential student-directed band rehearsal strategies and the challenges these band directors faced when implementing them.

Perhaps the qualitative band literature on teaching practices could be grouped into two categories: (a) studying the general thoughts and actions of high-performing band directors, and (b) studying band directors through a specific lens. For instance, researchers such as Yarberry, Jachens, Buell, Dugle, Prather, Conway, and Gonzalez explored and documented general thoughts and actions of high performing band directors. More specifically, Casey examined a band director through the lens of preparing a band for sight-reading, Schopp looked at how band directors in New York were teaching composition and improvisation, and Bazan observed ways that band directors used student-directed teaching styles.

3.1.2. Jazz Band

The earliest qualitative study examining school jazz band was Leavell (1996), who explored middle school students' perceptions of jazz band, including their views about playing individualized parts, improvising, and interpreting and articulating swing rhythms. Leavell found that students struggled with the musical differences between concert band and jazz band, such as (a) the playing of individualized parts, (b) swing and straight patterns within the same song, (c) changes in articulation, and (d) improvisation. With regard to student perceptions, students felt that (a) group improvisation and rhythmic embellishment of familiar melodies were relatively non-threatening forms of improvisation, (b) they could more freely express themselves in jazz band, and (c) the most effective instructional strategies were student-centered activities. Leavell also found that a clique formed between the students who were the most willing improvisers.

Ten years later, Dyas (2006) examined the students, directors, curricula, repertoire, and instructional techniques in two exemplary high school jazz programs. The researcher found that the students (a) became interested in playing jazz by being inspired by a jazz musician (whether professional or student), (b) listened to jazz and practiced often, (c) took private lessons, (d) played local professional gigs, (e) felt that they learned most in the combo setting as opposed to the large ensemble, (f) learned most from their peers, and (g) planned to become professional musicians.

One year after Dyas's study, Goodrich (2007) used ethnographic techniques (prolonged engagement in the field, interviews, artifacts) over the course of one academic year to explore the culture within a successful high school jazz band. The researcher observed and interviewed student jazz band members, the director, the assistant director, adult mentors, a guidance counselor, a principal, parents, and non–jazz band students. Five themes emerged: (a) mentoring from the adult perspective, (b) peer mentoring for musicianship, (c) mentoring in rehearsals, (d) mentoring outside jazz band rehearsals, and (e) social mentoring. Much of the motivation to practice and get better came from younger students modeling themselves after older students. Mentoring also occurred when high school students played for junior high students. Using the same research site and ethnographic techniques, Goodrich (2008) examined whether elements of historic jazz culture could be fostered in a traditional school jazz band setting. The researcher suggested that under the supervision of the director, such a culture could be fostered in terms of listening for style, improvisation, and learning the lingo.

Rummel (2010) studied music educators within different subgroups regarding their experience in jazz-related activities. Using quantitative techniques, the researcher found one's primary instrument to be significantly correlated to one's previous experience and that self-directed study was the primary source of jazz improvisation experience. To better understand the quantitative findings, Rummel then interviewed eight participants from different subgroups. Qualitative findings both confirmed and clarified the quantitative correlation between instrument choice and experience with jazz; specifically, that when one plays a typical or traditional jazz instrument there are more opportunities to learn to improvise and thus more opportunities to participate in jazz activities.

In a mixed methods study, West (2011) observed and interviewed two veteran and expert middle school band directors (one of them being a noted middle school jazz educator) three times each to explore their experiences, thoughts, and actions regarding middle school jazz. Similar to Rummel, findings suggested that among the previous experiences that most prepared these band directors to teach middle school jazz was their professional playing experiences outside of their college preparation. Findings regarding these directors' thoughts and actions about middle school jazz were compared and contrasted in relation to the following themes: (a) the value of middle school jazz, (b) differences and similarities with concert band, (c) teaching the rhythm section, (d) teaching style, (e) modeling, (f) improvisation, (g) peer mentoring, (h) literature, (i) non-traditional jazz instruments, and (j) student difficulties.

The thread that can be seen throughout all of these qualitative studies on school jazz is that people have tended to learn the most about jazz outside of school, or at least apart from the school band director. Leavell indicated that students preferred self-guided learning, Dyas and Goodrich indicated that students learned most from their peers, and Rummel and West indicated that experiences playing outside of school were those that most prepared band directors in their studies to teach jazz ensemble. Certainly, school jazz ensembles are where many students are introduced to jazz and which provide an opportunity for students to come together and play jazz, but the research thus far seems to indicate that the most valued experiences in learning jazz come outside of the band room and apart from the band director.

3.1.3. Teaching Band Students with Special Needs

The earliest qualitative study to examine students with special needs was Tooker (1995), who in 1995 presented a case study of eight students within a high school special education beginning band class. The teacher-researcher video-recorded 15 weeks of classroom instruction, used each student's individualized education program to develop individual music objectives, solicited feedback from four music educators and four special education professionals who observed the band class, and interviewed school and district level administrators. Tooker found that when adjusting the pace of instruction, modifying notation and classroom management strategies, and maintaining high expectations, some of the special learners were able to perform at levels commensurate to their general education peers.

Ten years later, Lapka (2005) studied the inclusion practices of a high school band in which one-quarter of its members had severe disabilities. Through observing rehearsals and interviewing faculty, staff, students, and parents, Lapka documented the inner workings of this program and described relationships between the students with disabilities and their non-disabled peers. In particular, the researcher found that (a) both general education and special education teachers in the school embraced the band program's inclusion practices, (b) inclusion was implemented gradually, (c) there was much parental and peer support, (d) the band had to be creative and flexible in solving problems, and (e) some modification of band curriculum was needed to accommodate these students.

To document the challenges of a child with special needs in band, and to do so through the eyes of the participant, Hourigan (2009) presented a case study of a child (Jason) who suffered from traumatic brain injury syndrome. Specifically, the author described the interactions between Jason, his classmates, his band director, his parents, and his school district from Jason's perspective. The author suggested that many of the issues that emerged are critical to all students, rather than just those with special needs. Hourigan offered the following suggestions to band directors for fostering an inclusive social atmosphere: (a) model appropriate social behavior, (b) initiate icebreaker activities at the beginning of the year to help students break down social barriers, (c) utilize opportunities for peer teaching, (d) carefully monitor for signs of bullying or hazing, and (e) remember that you do not have to shoulder the responsibility alone. Evidence from Tooker, Lapka, and Hourigan all suggests that two of the keys to educating band students with special needs are modification of materials and collaboration between parents, administrators, faculty, and staff.

3.1.4. Composition in Band

Whereas most of the qualitative research previously discussed (i.e., teaching techniques, jazz band, and students with special needs) has focused on band director actions, most of the qualitative research on composition in band has dealt with student perceptions. For instance, Tutt (2002) examined the specific criteria used by four high school band members to evaluate compositions they had previously rehearsed or performed. The researcher observed these students and interviewed them, their parents, and the band director. Tutt found that students evaluated compositions based on the variety of musical components used, the technical challenge and complexity, and their own personal connection with the composition.

One year later, Allsup (2003) examined the composition processes of two groups of band students through the lens of democracy. Over the course of three months, the researcher met with the students 11 times for two-and-a-half-hour meetings. Utilizing the students in the design, delivery, and analysis of the study, Allsup recorded all interactions and interviewed students at different stages in the process. One group of students chose to create music for electric guitar, bass, synthesized piano, and drums, while the other chose to create music using traditional concert band instruments. Findings suggested that whereas participants found classical music unsuitable for group composing or community making, they perceived composing in jazz or popular styles to be fun, nonobligatory, self-directed, personally meaningful, and suitable for cultivating interpersonal relationships.

For the qualitative portion of a mixed methods study, Stringham (2011) explored personal perspectives about improvisation and composition among high school band students in a program in which the curriculum emphasizes singing, moving, and playing by ear to learn melodies, bass lines, tonal patterns, rhythm patterns, and voice leading. Focus-group findings suggested that these students believed that the nature of their curriculum was helpful in learning to improvise and compose. Through class observations, Stringham suggested that teaching improvisation and composition in high school band is a practical, meaningful, and musical objective, and suggested that individual musicianship, understanding of music teaching and learning, interaction, making connections, and a positive learning environment are important factors in achieving this objective.

3.1.5. Action Research

The vast majority of published qualitative band research has been conducted by researchers outside the context of K–12 education (e.g., college professors and doctoral students); relatively missing are studies conducted by band directors with their own students. In one such publication, a collaborative action research study, Conway and Jeffers (2004) examined the implementation of new assessment procedures in a beginning band class. Through a teacher's log, a student instrumental music questionnaire, a parent evaluation of the assessment report, telephone interviews with parents, focus group interviews with students, a teacher interview, and the collaborative researcher's log of study interactions, the researchers documented the perceptions and suggestions of the students, challenges of implementation, and the connections between curriculum and assessment. While the main objective was to document and describe the collaborative action researcher process, findings from the study suggested that while most parents appreciated seeing a detailed report of their child's development in band rather than just a letter grade, some parents still wanted to see a letter grade since "that is easier for [them] to understand" (4).

Interested in incorporating informal learning processes into the formal music classroom, Davis (2008) conducted an action research study to explore the learning strategies used by her students to create their own musical meaning. Over the course of six months, the researcher observed the music learning processes of her fifth-grade beginning band students. Davis found that enabling students to discuss their own musical connections, even when seemingly unrelated to the task, encouraged students to make meaning of their understanding and take ownership of their learning.

3.1.6. Band Student Perspectives

One of the earliest studies to explore student experiences of band was Owens (1992), who observed and interviewed 12 middle school and college band students (6 from each group) regarding their perceptions of what makes appealing and effective band rehearsals. The researcher found that a majority of the middle school students preferred to receive instruction visually, while the majority of the college students expressed a kinesthetic preference. All of the students believed that the most appealing and effective rehearsals consisted of a variety of instructional strategies, direct involvement for a majority of time, and expressive use of language and metaphors.

Eleven years later, Kraus (2003) explored if and how students in a university wind ensemble setting experience Csikszentmihalyi's notion of flow. In addition to observing rehearsals and interviewing students, the researcher solicited information from eight students about their immediate psychological states at various points during rehearsal. Kraus found that these students did indeed experience the dimensions of flow in the wind ensemble rehearsal; specifically, students experienced them late in rehearsals and, similar to Owens, during extended periods of performance activity uninterrupted by frequent stops in the rehearsal. Findings indicated that experiencing flow in this setting is also dependent on the traits, actions, experience levels, and abilities of others in the group.

Curious about the "average" student's perceptions of middle school band, Scheib (2006) studied one such student's ("Lindy's") perspective. Over the course of two months, the researcher observed Lindy in small group and ensemble settings and interviewed her and her band director regarding her perceptions of band. Scheib found

Lindy to be highly achievement-oriented and motivated primarily by a competition for chair placements. Void from her perceptions of the band experience were any musical, artistic, or aesthetic descriptions.

Regarding student practice, Oare (2007) studied goal setting and self-assessment within the personal practice sessions of six middle school band students. The researcher analyzed three videotaped practice sessions of each student and interviewed each student after the practice sessions. In addition, the researcher conducted focus group interviews both before and after the observation cycle and interviewed the participants' band director. Oare found a cyclical practice process in which students moved from motivation, to goal setting, to strategy use, to assessment, and back to motivation. The researcher also found that students who were motivated by learning the material employed more effective practice techniques than students who were motivated by performance objectives, although all students' practice goals tended to lack specificity and direction.

Also interested in student motivation, Legutki (2010), as part of a mixed methods study, interviewed nine high school students regarding their motivation for participating in band and organized the qualitative findings according to (a) performing, (b) outside-of-school experiences, (c) musical motivators vs. extra-musical motivators, (d) types of music that these students enjoy playing, (e) the role of competition, (f) early feelings of success and other seminal moments, and (g) the role of music in their future careers. The author suggested that music teachers should focus on student-centered approaches that provide support for psychological needs and intrinsic motivation in order to help them develop meaningful long-term engagement in music activities.

Buck (2011) explored band students' perceptions of the use of recorded aural models for practicing. The researcher first supplied eight students with sheet music along with a recording to serve as an aural model, then surveyed and interviewed the participants regarding their experiences using the aural model as a practice aid. Buck found that although students enjoyed using the aural models and felt that they increased their confidence, most of them expressed no increased motivation to practice; instead, most students viewed the aural models simply as a definitive source of how their sheet music should be interpreted.

When we ask our students about their perceptions of band, their responses can often surprise us. From the qualitative research conducted thus far, band directors are reminded that the band experience often extends well beyond the intrinsic or aesthetic. Though we teach an aural art, Owens, Oare, and Buck all remind us that our students may learn and be motivated by factors other than sound. While we want our students to experience and enjoy music for its expressive possibilities, Kraus, Scheib, and Legutki remind us that our students often value extra-musical elements of the band experience. Being a band director requires understandings and skills beyond teaching techniques and an understanding of student cognition. Extra-musical elements such as social interactions and gender influences also play into the mix of the band experience. Teaching band can extend beyond the K–12 setting into areas such as New Horizons bands, and even teaching music to the incarcerated and hospitalized. Other areas of interest to qualitative band researchers have included topics such as band directors' professional and personal lives, perceptions of their roles, stresses and challenges of their jobs, and elements that make up a band culture and band-directing culture. The next section of the chapter examines the research done in those areas that go "beyond teaching."

3.2. Beyond Teaching Band

3.2.1. Social Aspects of Band

In addition to collecting artifacts and completing field observations, Albrecht (1993) interviewed three band student leaders, three non-band student leaders, three lead teachers, the principal, and the band director within a single high school to extrapolate participants' shared beliefs, values, and traditions regarding high school band; specifically, the researcher examined perceptions of band service activity within the school culture. Albrecht found (a) that both the band director and the principal accepted the band's role as a service activity in school culture, (b) school culture is a present phenomenon frozen in memory upon graduation, and (c) whereas the band director, and to some extent, band students, viewed band as an instructional class, the principal, teachers, and non-band students viewed the band simply as service activity.

Using what he called "naturalistic form of inquiry," Robinson (1997) explored high school band students' perceptions of band. Specifically, the researcher wanted to see if there was a difference in perception among students in the upper band and students in the lower band. The researcher observed and administered a questionnaire to 45 high school band members from the same program and interviewed five students: three from the lower band and two from the upper band. Robinson found that students in both groups valued their high degree of social standing within the school community, similar to winning sports teams in the school. Students from both groups also valued the division of players into two separate groups, although for different reasons: members from the upper group valued the challenge and pursuit of higher performance standards, whereas students from the lower group valued the social nature of band.

Using discourse analysis and participant observation, Dobbs (2005) studied how the naturally occurring talk within a band class shaped the teaching and learning of music and the social community. The author observed, video-recorded, and analyzed both large group band ensemble classes and small group instruction for which the following themes emerged: (a) teacher talk and actions, (b) student talk and actions, (c) talk and actions related to music, (d) talk and actions related to social/community building, and (e) talk and actions related to carrying on school/administrative business. The author further coded each utterance according to whether they occurred as representatives, directives, commissives, expressives, or miscellaneous speech acts. Findings suggested a discursive feedback loop illustrating student knowledge and comprehension of musical concepts, and a repetition device reinforcing both curricular knowledge and the building of social relationships within the classroom. The author found differences in discourse patterns between the ensemble and small group contexts, as well as between teacher and students.

Three years later, Hoffman (2008) explored the intergroup processes and role identities of six middle school band students. Students were from the same band class but all played different instruments. The researcher collected data over a period of nearly six months in the form of classroom observations, open-ended interviews, and weekly student journals. Hoffman found that these middle school band students made choices of whether to continue in band based on influences (rejection or affirmation) of those around them. These students initially chose to enroll in band because friends, teachers, and family members encouraged them to do so. Then, based on others' affirmation or rejection of their competency in such roles, they re-evaluated whether they felt they belonged in the band; those who felt rejected or less competent chose to quit band. The students who felt like successful contributing members within the band identified with the group more strongly.

3.2.2. Gender

Jackson (1996) studied the experiences of 12 female college band directors from across the country representing various age groups and experience levels. Through telephone interviews with each participant, the researcher found that the older women band directors in her study encountered overt discrimination, while the younger directors encountered more subtle types of discrimination, if any. The respondents perceived the gender imbalance among college band directors to be partially due to the military heritage of the college band program.

Regarding gender and instrument choice among students, Conway (2000) interviewed 37 high school band students and found that all of them perceived certain associations between gender and instrument choice. Students who had broken gender stereotypes did so in an attempt to be different from their peers. Students who played instruments traditionally stereotyped with their gender cited family and peers as the most common influences. While students were generally supportive of females playing traditionally stereotyped male instruments, many were less supportive of males playing traditionally stereotyped female instruments, especially the flute. When asked about the influences for choosing a particular instrument, students often cited the characteristics of the instrument itself including size, sound, volume, and its role in band.

Ten years after Jackson's study, Sears (2010) examined how 11 female high school band directors perceive and engage with issues of isolation, discrimination, and stereotyping and how perceptions of gender roles have influenced their teaching identities. The researcher found that to succeed in the profession, participants often developed and projected a powerful, tough, assertive, competitive, and confident persona and felt they must work harder than their male counterparts to earn respect. While some participants felt that there are qualities unique to female directors, others rejected the idea that gender had any effect on their teaching. Participants felt that the masculine history of the profession, the struggle to balance work and family, and the belief that administrators may question a woman's ability to handle the job were reasons contributing to an underrepresentation of female band directors. Sears suggested that transparent hiring practices, in combination with increased visibility of female role models, guest conductors, and festival adjudicators, can help secondary instrumental music education to become a more gender-equitable profession.

3.2.3. Adult Learners

Interested in the practice habits of adults, Rohwer (2005) video-recorded three adult beginning saxophone players for three weeks while they practiced at home. Among these adult beginners, the researcher found a lack of systematic rhythm skill practice. Repetition was the main strategy for addressing errors, as players generally did not understand how to break the remediation of errors into smaller steps. Even after practice, players also could not always accurately judge whether an error had been corrected.

Alfano (2008) studied the experiences of adults who participate in an intergenerational band program. Specifically, the researcher sought to understand ways in which these adults interacted musically, socially, and educationally both with their own age cohort and with the adolescents in this co-learning environment. Through observations, interviews, and document analysis, the researcher described the personal, social, and intellectual benefits reported by the participants and concluded that these adults felt that the intergenerational co-learning experience resulted in a greater understanding, acceptance, care, respect, and appreciation of one age group for another.

3.2.4. Lives of Band Directors

Since at least 1993, when Wohl (1993) described the recurring events and daily routines in the life of a small town band director, qualitative band researchers have tried to capture essences of the profession through documenting the perceptions, actions, and stories of its professionals. One of the first was Thompson (1998), who interviewed experienced band directors regarding their perceptions of their roles as marching band directors. Thompson found that the participants viewed their roles as producers, directors, and managers of student behavior, and saw themselves as responsible for the band's public relations.

Five years later, Lamkin's (2003) phenomenological study explored the question, "what does it mean to be a high school band director?" The method included recalling and documenting the author's own lived experiences as a band director, exploring the profession through the etymology of the term "band director," unpacking the idiomatic phrases associated with the term "band director," and interviewing and documenting the lived experiences of a retired band director. The author described what it means to be a band director through these lived experiences as they relate to the ways the participants experienced time, being with others (including band students), and their world in general.

Peterson (2005) studied the challenges and experiences of three first-year band directors. Over the course of the participants' first year of teaching, the researcher regularly interviewed them by phone, observed them, and had them keep journal records of their experiences. The researcher also interviewed parents, administrators, mentors, and students. Peterson found that common among these beginning band directors was the desire to be liked by the students. Common challenges were working with band parents, selecting appropriate music for their ensembles, and setting limits for student behavior.

Conway, Eros, et al. (2007) observed and interviewed four beginning music teachers regarding their experiences in college secondary instrument methods classes to determine the most valuable experiences of those classes and suggest changes that would have made these classes more valuable in preparing these individuals to become band directors. The researchers found that (a) such classes prepared them to teach beginners more than they prepared them to teach high school students, (b) they regularly referred to and valued their course notebooks, (c) participants were split on whether performance faculty or education faculty should teach such classes, (d) the participants valued both playing the instruments and learning to teach them, and (e) the participants felt that on-the-job training was needed beyond the methods courses.

Concerned by a 2005 study indicating declining enrollment in Texas band programs, Jolly (2008) interviewed eight Texas music educators regarding their perceptions of the reasons contributing to the decline. Jolly found scheduling demands, overemphasis of band competition, decreasing family support, and the inability of many band programs to remain relevant to modern-day students to be the most perceived challenges and barriers to band enrollment.

The same year, Vandivere (2008) studied the nonverbal communication behaviors and role perceptions of preservice band directors, and whether participation in theater seminars enhanced those behaviors and perceptions. After participating in three theater seminars, participants were asked to journal and communicate with their peers online regarding their teaching. The researcher then video-recorded their classroom teaching and interviewed the participants. Findings suggested that these preservice band directors felt that participating in theater seminars enhanced their awareness of nonverbal communication behaviors in the classroom and had the potential to influence their perceptions of their roles as teachers.

Interested in how band directors acquire successful rehearsal techniques, Chaffin (2009) examined the perceptions of two third-year band directors. Over the course of three days, the researcher observed both band directors, interviewed them, and interviewed their colleagues. Chaffin found that participants in his study credited their colleagues, reflection-on-action, and recording their rehearsals as the most influential factors in helping them acquire effective planning, pacing, repertoire selection, and classroom management skills.

Henry (2009) examined the history of the Prairie View Interscholastic League (PVIL), which was created for black high school bands to participate in band contests from 1938–1970. Through interviews with 15 band directors who participated in the PVIL, the researcher documented and described the structure of the PVIL band contests, repertoire, preparation of the contests, and the importance of the PVIL to its participants and to the local black community. Henry also described the effects of segregation on these directors' band programs, in particular with regard to equipment and facility inequities.

That same year, Samuels (2009) interviewed, observed, and participated with Alfred Watkins, director of bands at Lassiter High School, to describe the components that have contributed to the success and national recognition of his high school band program. To provide a model for practicing high school band directors, Samuels described Watkins's philosophy of the program, curriculum, organization, and other unique qualities that have contributed to the success of the program. The researcher suggested that the findings from this study could inform practicing band directors and could be used to help shape the curriculum of undergraduate music education programs.

To both create a historical narrative and provide a model for college band directors navigating social, political, and economic changes, Bouldin (2010) documented the career of former Auburn University director of bands, Dr. Billy G. Walls. Through semi-structured interviews with Dr. Walls and his former colleagues and students, Bouldin described the social, economic, and political issues that affected the Auburn band program and Dr. Walls from 1961–1991. The author also described the change that Dr. Walls brought to music education in Alabama and throughout the Southeast, including the SEC's (Southeastern Conference's) first African-American drum major, the first female drum major, the first wind and percussion ensembles, and the first band graduate assistant.

3.2.5. Discussion

Although neither Yarberry nor Jachens, authors of the first two qualitative band studies, used terminology we now associate with qualitative research, and neither described the studies as *qualitative*, they each, nevertheless, explored band from a qualitative worldview and used qualitative research techniques, and thus might be considered the pioneers of early qualitative band research. Yarberry's study was published as an article derived from his dissertation completed six years earlier, indicating that qualitative band research was being conducted as early as 1974.

The first three qualitative studies in band research that were *self-described* as such occurred within three years of one another, were all doctoral dissertations, and all focused on documenting effective teaching practices (see Table 3.1). The first self-described qualitative band journal article, Conway (1999), did not appear until 11 years and 11 dissertations after the first self-described qualitative band dissertation (Casey

1988). This may have been because the research journals within the profession were slow to welcome qualitative methodology, because senior researchers were not conducting and submitting qualitative studies, or due to some combination of the two. The first self-described qualitative band study published in a journal that was not derived from a dissertation was Conway's phenomenological study on gender and instrument choice, published in the *Bulletin of the Council for Research in Music Education* (2000). After Conway's two studies, we see a more regular stream of qualitative band research published in music education journals. Still, it seems that senior researchers were either reluctant to conduct qualitative band research or unable to publish it in the professional journals, as we can see that only five journal articles have been published that were not derived from dissertations (i.e., Conway; Conway and Jeffers; Rohwer; Scheib; and Chaffin). Another possibility for the relative scarcity of such articles may be that researchers were more inclined to conduct studies that explored a topic from a broader perspective not limited specifically to band.

In addition to Yarberry, there are several other authors that could be considered "pioneers" in qualitative band research in that they were the first to explore a particular topic. The first qualitative band study to examine student perspectives was Owens, who in 1992 interviewed students regarding their perceptions of what makes appealing and effective band rehearsals. The first of its kind to study the lives of band directors was Wohl in 1983, who described the recurring events and daily routines in the life of a small-town band director. In 1995, Tooker was the first qualitative researcher to study band students with special needs. The very next year, Jackson and Leavell were the first to study gender and jazz, respectively. In 2002, Tutt and Allsup were the first to qualitatively study composition in band, Conway and Jeffers in 2004 were the first qualitative band researchers to publish an action research study, and Rowher in 2005 was the first to qualitatively study older adults' participation in band.

We have seen a wide variation of the use of terminology among qualitative band researchers when describing or classifying their methodologies. Many researchers referred to their studies simply as "qualitative" and some did not classify their study by any name, but rather described the (qualitative) methods used. It was not until 12 years after the first self-described qualitative band study that we find research (Conway's phenomenological study in 2000) described as something other than "qualitative" or "case study." After this study in 2000, we see the inverse from the previous 12 years; from 2000–2011 qualitative band researchers began using terms such as "phenomenology," "ethnography," "action research," "discourse analysis," and "mixed methods." Buell, in 1990, was the first qualitative band researcher to classify his study as a "case study." Other pioneers include Conway in 2000, who classified her study as phenomenological; Allsup in 2003, who published an ethnography; Conway and Jeffers in 2004, who conducted action research; Dobbs in 2005, who used discourse analysis; and Schopp in 2006, who used mixed methods.

The qualitative band studies since 1980 have examined topics as diverse as program profiles, social aspects, gender, lives of band directors, teaching practices, conducting and rehearsal techniques, assessment, student perspectives, jazz, student mentoring,

Table 3.1 Chronology of Qualitative Band Research Studies, 1980–2011

Author	Date	Topic	Design	Publication
Yarberry	1980	Teaching Practices	Qualitative	JBR
Jachens	1987	Teaching Practices	Qualitative	JBR
Casey	1988	Teaching Practices	Qualitative	Dissertation
Buell	1990	Teaching Practices	Case Study	Dissertation
Dugle	1991	Teaching Practices	Qualitative	Dissertation
Owens	1992	Student Perspectives	Qualitative	Dissertation
Prather	1993	Teaching Practices	Qualitative	Dissertation
Albrecht	1993	Social	Case Study	Dissertation
Wohl	1993	Lives of Band Directors	Case Study	Dissertation
Tooker	1995	Special Needs	Case Study	Dissertation
Jackson	1996	Gender	Qualitative	Dissertation
Leavell	1996	Jazz	Qualitative	Dissertation
Robinson	1997	Social	Qualitative	Abstract (BCRME)
Thompson	1998	Lives of Band Directors	Case Study	Dissertation
Conway	1999	Teaching Practices	Case Study	JRME
Conway	2000	Gender	Phenomenology	BCRME
Gonzales	2001	Teaching Practices	Case Study	Dissertation
Tutt	2002	Composition	Case Study	Dissertation
Allsup	2003	Composition	Ethnography	JRME
Kraus	2003	Student Perspectives	Case Study	Dissertation
Lamkin	2003	Lives of Band Directors	Phenomenology	Dissertation
Conway et al.	2004	Action Research	Action Research	BCRME
Lapka	2005	Special Needs	Case Study	Dissertation
Dobbs	2005	Social	Discourse Analysis	Dissertation
Rohwer	2005	Adult Learners	Case Study	CME
Peterson	2005	Lives of Band Directors	Case Study	Dissertation
Schopp	2006	Teaching Practices	MM (Case Study)	Dissertation
Dyas	2006	Jazz	Case Study	Dissertation
Scheib	2006	Student Perspectives	Case Study	MEJ
Conway et al.	2007	Lives of Band Directors	Self-Study	BCRME
Bazan	2007	Teaching Practices	MM (Qualitative)	Dissertation
Goodrich	2007	Jazz	Ethnography	JRME
Oare	2007	Student Perspectives	Case Study	Dissertation
Goodrich	2008	Jazz	Ethnography	BCRME
Davis	2008	Action Research	Action Research	Dissertation
Hoffman	2008	Social	Case Study	Dissertation
Jolly	2008	Lives of Band Directors	Qualitative	Dissertation
Vandivere	2008	Lives of Band Directors	Case Study	Dissertation
Alfano	2008	Adult Learners	Case Study	Dissertation
Hourigan	2009	Special Needs	Case Study	MEJ
Henry	2009	Lives of Band Directors	Case Study	Dissertation
Samuels	2009	Lives of Band Directors	Qualitative	Dissertation
Chaffin	2009	Lives of Band Directors	Qualitative	BCRME
Sears	2010	Gender	Qualitative	Dissertation
Bouldin	2010	Lives of Band Directors	Qualitative	Dissertation
Legutki	2010	Student Perceptions	MM (Qualitative)	Dissertation
Rummel	2010	Jazz	MM (Qualitative)	Dissertation
West	2011	Jazz	MM (Case Study)	Dissertation
Stringham	2011	Composition	MM (Qualitative)	Dissertation
Buck	2011	Student Perceptions	Qualitative	Dissertation

students with special needs, identity construction, composition, democratic learning, practice habits, and adult learners. Topics that have not been studied qualitatively as they apply specifically to band include teaching for democracy in band, the role of popular music in schools, and non-band students' perceptions of band, to name a few. Future qualitative band researchers could ask questions such as (a) What could teaching for democracy look like in school band? (b) What are perceived obstacles to teaching for democracy? (c) What perceptions do band directors, band students, and preservice music teachers hold about including vernacular music making activities and ways of learning into the school band program? (d) How can music teacher education change to better prepare future band directors to deliver a product more relevant to twenty-first-century students?

Note

1. Studies were searched using terms such as the following: qualitative, case, ethnography, narrative, phenomenological, grounded theory, and naturalistic. Studies that (a) were not qualitative, (b) were not conducted in the United States, or (c) were broader than just "band" (e.g., "instrumental" including strings) were not reviewed in this chapter. Last, for instances in which a journal article is derived from a dissertation, only the article is presented in this chapter.

References

Albrecht, Gary L. 1993. "Administration of Service Activity in the School Band Program within School Culture." PhD diss., The University of Wisconsin–Madison.
Alfano, Christopher J. 2008. "Seniors' Participation in an Intergenerational Music Learning Program." PhD diss., McGill University (Canada).
Allsup, Randall Everett. 2003. "Mutual Learning and Democratic Action in Instrumental Music Education." *Journal of Research in Music Education* 51 (1): 24–37.
Bazan, D. 2007. "Teaching and Learning Strategies Used by Student-Directed Teachers of Middle School Band." PhD diss., Case Western Reserve University.
Bouldin, Thomas Gordon. 2010. "Dr. Billy G. Walls and the Auburn University Bands, 1961–1991: A Story of Impact, Influence and Innovation." PhD diss., Auburn University.
Buck, Wayne A. 2011. "Rural Band Students' Perceptions of Practice Aids Created by Music Notation Software." EdD diss., Northcentral University.
Buell, Donald SeCheverell. 1990. "Effective Rehearsing with the Instrumental Music Ensemble: A Case Study." PhD diss., The University of Wisconsin–Madison.
Casey, J. Warren. 1988. "An Analysis of Band Conductor Sight Reading Behavior and Ensemble Preparation for Sight-Reading." PhD diss., The University of Oklahoma.
Chaffin, Charles R. 2009. "Perceptions of Instrumental Music Teachers Regarding the Development of Effective Rehearsal Techniques." *Bulletin of the Council for Research in Music Education* 181: 21–36.
Conway, Colleen M. 1999. "The Development of Teaching Cases for Instrumental Music Methods Courses." *Journal of Research in Music Education* 47 (4): 343–56.
Conway, Colleen M. 2000. "Gender and Musical Instrument Choice: A Phenomenological Investigation." *Bulletin of the Council for Research in Music Education* 146: 1.

Conway, Colleen M., J. Eros, Ryan Hourigan, and A. M. Stanley. 2007. "Perceptions of Beginning Teachers Regarding Brass and Woodwind Instrument Techniques Classes in Preservice Education." *Bulletin of the Council for Research in Music Education* 173: 39–54.

Conway, Colleen M., and Tom Jeffers. 2004. "Parent, Student, and Teacher Perceptions of Assessment Procedures in Beginning Instrumental Music." *Bulletin of the Council for Research in Music Education* 160: 16.

Davis, S. 2008. "Fostering a Musical Say: Enabling Meaning Making and Investment in a Band Class by Connecting to Students' Informal Music Learning Processes." PhD diss., Oakland University.

Dobbs, Teryl L. 2005. "Discourse in the Band Room: How Talk Shapes Teaching, Learning, and Community in a Middle School Instrumental Music Classroom." PhD diss., Northwestern University.

Dugle, Jon Richard. 1991. "An Assessment Profile of Quality Secondary Band Programs in Illinois." EdD diss., University of Illinois at Urbana-Champaign.

Dyas, J. B. 2006. "A Description, Comparison, and Interpretation of Two Exemplary Performing Arts High School Jazz Programs." PhD diss., Indiana University.

Gonzalez, Luis Samuel. 2001. "Rehearsal Effectiveness: An Analytical Study of Rehearsal Philosophies and Procedures of Selected Public School and Postsecondary Wind Band Conductors." DMA diss., University of Cincinnati.

Goodrich, Andrew. 2007. "Peer Mentoring in a High School Jazz Ensemble." *Journal of Research in Music Education* 55 (2): 94–114.

Goodrich, Andrew. 2008. "Utilizing Elements of the Historic Jazz Culture in a High School Setting." *Bulletin of the Council for Research in Music Education* 175: 11.

Henry, John P., Jr. 2009. "The Prairie View Interscholastic League Band Contests from 1938–1970, with an Emphasis on Black High School Bands and Band Directors in Texas." DMA diss., University of Houston.

Hoffman, A. 2008. "'Like Who You Are': Socially Constructed Identity in the Middle School Band." PhD diss., University of Maryland, College Park.

Hourigan, Ryan M. 2009. "The Invisible Student: Understanding Social Identity Construction within Performing Ensembles." *Music Educators Journal* 95 (4): 34–38.

Jachens, D. L. 1987. "The Pedagogical Approaches of Eight Important Midwestern Band Conductors During the Late 1920s and 1930s." *Journal of Band Research* 22 (2): 44–55.

Jackson, Cheryl Ann. 1996. "The Relationship between the Imbalance of Numbers of Women and Men College Band Conductors and the Various Issues That Influence the Career Aspirations of Women Instrumental Musicians." PhD diss., Michigan State University.

Jolly, D. 2008. "Music Educator Perceptions of Declining Enrollments in Texas Band Programs." EdD diss., Stephen F. Austin State University.

Lamkin, John R., II. 2003. "Beyond the Podium: A Phenomenological Investigation of the Lifeworlds of Experienced High School Band Directors." PhD diss., University of Maryland, College Park.

Lapka, Christine M. 2005. "A Case Study of the Integration of Students with Disabilities in a Secondary Music Ensemble." EdD diss., University of Illinois at Urbana-Champaign.

Leavell, Brian Keith. 1996. "'Making the Change': Middle School Band Students' Perspectives on the Learning of Musical-Technical Skills in Jazz Performance." PhD diss., University of North Texas.

Legutki, A. 2010. "Self-Determined Music Participation: The Role of Psychological Needs Satisfaction, Intrinsic Motivation, and Self-Regulation in the High School Band Experience." PhD diss., University of Illinois at Urbana-Champaign.

Oare, S. "Goals and Self-Assessment in the Middle School Learner: A Study of Music Practice Habits." PhD diss., Michigan State University, 2007.

Owens, Garry Wright. 1992. "Student Perceptions of Appealing and Effective Music Rehearsals: Toward Retention and Transfer of Learning." PhD diss., The University of Wisconsin–Madison.

Peterson, E. 2005. "Expectations and Experiences: Case Studies of Three First-Year Instrumental Music Teachers." DMA diss., Shenandoah University.

Prather, Belva Worthen. 1993. "Are There Identifiable Patterns of Personal and Professional Mentoring Relationships between Instrumental Music Educators and Their Students?" EdD diss., University of Arkansas.

Robinson, M. 1997. "Band: A Qualitative Study of Students' Perceptions of the High School Band Experience." *Bulletin of the Council for Research in Music Education* 131: 38–39.

Rohwer, Debbie A. 2005. "A Case Study of Adult Beginning Instrumental Practice." *Contributions to Music Education* 32 (1): 45–58.

Rummel, Jason Robert. 2010. "Perceptions of Jazz Improvisation among Pennsylvania Music Educators." DMA diss., Boston University.

Samuels, Sue. 2009. "Alfred Watkins and the Lassiter High School Band: A Qualitative Study." PhD diss., Auburn University.

Scheib, John W. 2006. "Lindy's Story: One Student's Experience in Middle School Band— Do Students Perceive School Music to Mean Simply Competition, Achievement, and Discipline? Or Can Teachers Communicate Music's Intrinsic Attributes?" *Music Educators Journal* 92 (5): 32.

Schopp, Steven Edward. 2006. "A Study of the Effects of National Standards for Music Education, Number 3, Improvisation and Number 4, Composition on High School Band Instruction in New York State." EdD diss., Teachers College, Columbia University.

Sears, C. 2010. "Paving Their Own Way: Experiences of Female High School Band Directors." EdD diss., Teachers College, Columbia University.

Stringham, D. 2011. "Improvisation and Composition in a High School Instrumental Music Curriculum." PhD diss., University of Rochester, Eastman School of Music.

Thompson, Gerald Wayne. 1998. "Responses of Marching Band Directors to Their Professional Roles and to an Instructional Framework for Teaching Marching Band Shows." EdD diss., University of Maryland College Park.

Tooker, Paul Arthur. 1995. "A Case Study of a High School Special Education Beginning Band Class." EdD diss., Columbia University Teachers College.

Tutt, Kevin Joseph. 2002. "High School Band Members Criteria for Evaluating Performed Music: A Collective Case Study." PhD diss., The Pennsylvania State University.

Vandivere, Allen Hale. 2008. "An Investigation of the Nonverbal Communication Behaviors and Role Perceptions of Pre-Service Band Teachers Who Participated in Theatre Seminars." PhD diss., University of North Texas.

West, C. 2011. "Teaching Middle School Jazz: An Exploratory Sequential Mixed Methods Study." PhD diss., University of Michigan.

Wohl, Mark Alan. 1993. "The Small Town Band Director: A Descriptive Case Study." PhD diss., University of Oregon.

Yarberry, G. A. 1980. "An Analysis of Five Exemplary College Band Programs." *Journal of Band Research* 15 (2): 23–45.

CHAPTER 4

INSTRUMENTAL MUSIC (STRINGS)

MARGARET H. BERG

4.1. INTRODUCTION

OVER the past decade, there has been an increased number of venues for the distribution of research on stringed instrument teaching, learning, and performance. Syntheses of research focused on stringed instrument instruction, study, and performance include Kantorski's (1995) content analysis of doctoral research in string education between 1936–1992 and Barnes's (2003) edited book *Applying Research to Teaching and Playing Stringed Instruments*. The *String Research Journal* (formerly the *Journal of String Research*) was created in 2000 for the publication of investigations of a philosophical, historical, or scientific nature that contribute to the understanding of the teaching and learning of strings. To date, published qualitative research on stringed instrument teaching, learning, and performance is limited, with the *String Research Journal/Journal of String Research* having published only two articles, or 9 percent of the total number of articles, that use qualitative methodology. However, given the increased number of research poster sessions at the National American String Teachers Association (ASTA) Conference, several of which use qualitative research design, we might expect an increase in the number of published qualitative studies on stringed instrument teaching and learning in this journal and other music education research journals.

This chapter is a review of extant research on American stringed instrument instruction, study, performance, program models, and curriculum. More specifically, studies are clustered into the following topic areas: teacher socialization, lived experience, models, and approaches; students' experience of learning to play a string instrument; professional and amateur performers; and school orchestra and alternative styles program components and curriculum. Studies that focused on preservice string teacher education are reviewed in volume 1, chapter 5 of the *Handbook*.

4.2. Teachers: Socialization, Lived Experience, Models, and Approaches

4.2.1. Teacher Socialization and Lived Experience

The majority of studies reviewed were focused on string teachers and/or string teaching. Studies on teacher socialization and lived experience explored role stressors, the impact of significant others (e.g., parents, teachers, peers, and professional colleagues) on teacher socialization, the impact of music-making activities on identity development and teaching, and novice orchestra teachers' focus of attention. Utilizing concepts from work organization stress research, Scheib (2003) explored the role stressors of four Midwestern high school music teachers, one of whom was an orchestra teacher. Data were collected via observation, interviews, and document analysis. While role ambiguity and nonparticipation issues were less of a concern for the participants, issues related to role conflicts, role overloads, and resource inadequacy were substantial. The burden of administrative responsibilities, the constant need for music education advocacy, conflicts between personal and professional roles, and tension created by scheduling conflicts due to the increasingly busy schedule of students were among the most significant stressors. Notably, the orchestra teacher participant focused his efforts on recruiting and seemed to report less tension and stress than the other participants. However, inter-role conflict was experienced with respect to student retention, as the teacher attempted to balance "making orchestra fun" and performance demands.

In 2008, Cox investigated the impact of significant others on the socialization of three experienced school orchestra teachers. Through in-depth interviews, Cox identified specific individuals who encouraged participants toward music involvement and teaching during pre-college, college, and post-college years. During primary socialization, mothers or fathers especially encouraged participants to become musicians and teachers, and high school ensemble directors and private music teachers were also sources of encouragement for seeking a college education, as well as for majoring in music education. During college years, the influence more often came from an ensemble director, from oneself, or from a private teacher. In post-college years, participants noted the impact of colleagues, other classroom teachers, administrators, parents, and family.

Music-making activities have also been found to impact teachers. Pellegrino (2010) described the identity development and teaching of a maximum variation (with respect to participant background) sample of four full-time, public school orchestra teachers. Utilizing a phenomenological case study design, data were generated through background surveys, three interviews with each individual, videotaped classroom observations, a focus group interview that included music-making and conversation, a researcher self-interview, and researcher journals. For the researcher self-interview, Pellegrino read interview questions aloud, then responded while simultaneously audiotaping. Individual participant music backgrounds and current music-making values and activities were presented, as well as a within-case and cross-case analysis of the intersection of music-making and teaching. Participants connected music-making to the formation of identity and with their well-being. Music-making intersected with teaching in multiple ways by reminding participants why they valued playing, providing insight into pedagogical issues, and helping them be more compassionate toward their students. Teachers used performance while teaching to remain focused, to inspire and gain credibility with students, to address classroom management, and to model technique, musicality, and their love of music-making. Pellegrino's dissertation is an exemplar based on the richness of the data presented and the application of various frameworks to the interpretation, including Wenger's (1999) Community of Practice model.

First-year orchestra teachers' focus of attention was the topic of Barnes's (2010) study. Data were collected over the course of one year through journals and in-depth interviews with five teachers. Overall, participants focused on students, administrators, and the self. Within these categories, participants attended to student behavior, music learning, administrative support, personal relationships with students, classroom discipline skills, and teaching efficacy. Barnes noted a need for increased preparation to teach in diverse contexts as well as the need for effective administrator support. While Barnes' findings illustrate general beginning teacher issues rather than string teaching specific issues, this study provides useful information on first-year orchestra teachers' lived experiences.

4.2.2. Teaching Models and Approaches

4.2.2.1. *Studio Setting*

Five studies of studio teaching models and approaches examined teacher-student interpersonal dynamics, the impact of Suzuki method instruction, and teaching strategies of artist-level teachers, including Dorothy DeLay and Donald McInnes. One study was an analysis and application of the tone production exercises of nine respected teachers (Brian Lewis, Stephen Shipps, Shi-Hwa Wang, Kathryn Plummer, Marilyn Seelman, Tanya Carey, Jeffrey Solow, Lawrence Hurst, and William Ritchie).

Using Freud's concept of "defense mechanisms," Gustafson (1986) analyzed the interpersonal dynamics during studio lessons of four violin teachers and eight of their aged 11–17 students. Data were collected via videos of 12 lessons and teacher interviews. Four vignettes displayed instances of lesson content and interactions being dominated by unconscious aims of either or both members of the dyad. Diagnostic and remedial content was impacted by projection, ineffective interaction patterns, and latent personal agendas.

The only study to use a phenomenological design, Collier-Slone (1991) examined the perceived impact of Suzuki method instruction on students' life experience. In-depth interviews were conducted with 28 adults (ranging in age from 25–62) who participated in Suzuki-based instruction from preschool through high school as students or parents. Three themes were aggregated from 14 meaning clusters including: the contribution of Suzuki method instruction to the development of significant interpersonal relationships with parents, peers, and teachers; the impact on the internal self (e.g., self-esteem, attitudes and values, spirituality, awareness of the existential nature of music) of Suzuki method participation; and the integration, internalization, and professional benefit of developing musical skills and discipline via the Suzuki method.

One of three studies focused on artist-level teaching, Gholson (1998) identified and characterized patterns of DeLay's teaching practice. Over a period of 13 months, field notes (with accompanying audiotapes) of 65 lessons, teacher interviews, and artifacts were collected. A theory of proximal positioning, based on Vygotsky's (1978) zone of proximal development, was posited. Preparatory (e.g., getting acquainted, creating goals, and probing for student frame of reference) and facilitative (e.g., goal development, cognitive magnification, use of metaphor, and creation of a comforting atmosphere to encourage risk-taking) strategies emerged as global patterns of teaching practice. Gholson's dissertation (1993), on which this article is based, includes a thorough description of coding and validation procedures, as well as the creative application of Schenkerian analysis to coding procedures.

Duke and Simmons (2006) examined 25 hours of private lesson video recordings by three artist-teachers, one of whom was renowned viola teacher Donald McInnes. Following the creation of narrative descriptions for each lesson, 19 elements were identified in each teacher, which were organized into three categories: goals and expectations, effecting change, and conveying information. While interviews with the teachers could have served as another data source, video excerpts of the elements for each teacher are viewable on the Center for Music Learning website (http://cml.music.utexas.edu), thus serving as a valuable resource.

In the third study of artist-level teaching, Moss (2006) identified favored sound production exercises of selected contemporary violin, viola, cello, and double bass studio teachers. Exercises were then adapted and field-tested with middle and high school orchestra students from nine programs. Sound production exercises were gathered during interviews and email exchanges with studio teachers, while data on the need for and effectiveness of the exercises was gathered via a questionnaire and interviews with orchestra directors. Selected exercises from studio teachers and literature formed the basis for three areas of focus in the adapted exercises: (1) developing right-hand finger flexibility; (2) focusing the tone; and (3) varying the bow's speed. Participating school orchestra directors used exercises as a warm-up activity, applied them to repertoire students were learning, and perceived improved tone production as a result of using the exercises.

4.2.2.2. *School Setting*

Six studies focused on aspects of beginning- and intermediate-level school orchestra teacher approaches including motivation techniques, sequence of instruction, rehearsal priorities, instructional approach, postural teaching techniques, and precollegiate guitar teaching methods. Parker (2001) examined the motivation strategies of an exemplary middle school orchestra teacher. Data were collected during five observations, an in-depth teacher interview, two student focus group interviews, interviews with 10 students, and a researcher journal. Findings suggest that the teacher's unique personality and genuine care for his students contributed to his success in motivating his seventh-grade orchestra students. Noteworthy motivation strategies were his lack of competition in the classroom in order to avoid student comparison, sense of humor, ability to make his students feel valued and respected in and out of the classroom, inviting accomplished performers into the class, relating concepts to repertoire, and choosing appropriate literature based on student level and variety. The researcher also noted the impact of teacher longevity in the position and accompanying success on local community support of the music program.

Lyne (1991) explored the sequence of instruction used by the researcher while teaching 19 beginning strings classes in six elementary schools. The teacher incorporated principles and activities from Rolland, Orff, and Kodaly in the teaching approach. A model of a teaching sequence was developed that included teacher assessment, diagnosis, and prescription. Areas of learning that were the focus of instruction were students' playing technique, understanding of musical concepts, and intrinsic motivation with regard to pacing. Questions were used by the teacher to determine student skill level, prescribe developmental or remedial teaching, and evaluate the prescription results. The sequence used by the researcher might be used by others who lack a mentor with music teaching expertise to foster professional growth.

In a related study, Kotchenruther (1998) investigated the rehearsal priorities of 12 middle school teachers. The design and analytical approach are indicative of the study publication date. Data were collected via two interviews and three rehearsal videos of each teacher as well as written evaluations of videotaped student performances completed by the participants. Videos were analyzed using the researcher-constructed Rehearsal Priorities Analysis Form based on the Flanders' Interaction Analysis System. Results based on stated and demonstrated priorities indicated that teacher rehearsal priorities divided into four areas: (1) notes/intonation, rhythm, posture; (2) ensemble, bowing, technique, note reading, dynamics; (3) tone, style, musicality, articulation, expression, phrasing, vibrato, balance; and (4) following conducting gestures, precision/clarity, interpretation, theory/history, independence, tempo, blend, energy, and unique problems. Findings suggest that middle school string teachers prioritize fundamental criteria highest, followed by physical criteria, then expressive and interpretive criteria.

Scruggs (2009) examined whether and in what ways a learner-centered classroom environment nurtured musical growth and independence in four suburban middle-school orchestra classrooms over four months. Using a mixed method triangulation design convergence model (Creswell and Plano Clark 2011), quantitative and qualitative data were collected and analyzed separately, followed by a comparison of results, leading to a final interpretation that incorporates both quantitative and qualitative findings. Qualitative data were collected via bi-weekly classroom observations, student focus group interviews, teacher interviews, and weekly journal entries by teachers. Several themes emerged, including "I vs. They"; Teacher Transformation; Development of Student Leaders, How Students Prefer to Learn, and Striking a Balance. While no differences in music performance outcomes between learner-centered and teacher-centered ensembles were found, students in learner-centered classrooms exhibited greater musical independence and indicated having more choice and leadership opportunities in their classrooms. Learner-centered teachers reported increased engagement and leadership skills from their students. Although the findings from this study suggest positive outcomes of learner-centered teaching, further study is needed on the implementation of this approach in diverse environments by teachers at various career stages.

Using a mixed methods design defined by the author as constructivist grounded theory, Hudnall (2012) administered an online survey to 230 middle or high school orchestra teachers on postural teaching methods and students' performance-related problems. Follow-up interviews and observations were conducted with three teachers during implementation of a researcher-designed postural teaching techniques program. Individual and cross-case analysis highlighted the importance of postural awareness, consistent definitions of postural elements, the impact of equipment, and common techniques used to teach relaxed posture. Researcher-designed techniques, with the exception of one exercise, were found to increase student and teacher awareness of posture that they might integrate into rehearsals.

Of these six studies, the only research on guitar teaching was by Merry (2010), who studied two precollegiate classical guitar methods—one at a public charter school utilizing a Suzuki method approach and the other in a private studio based on traditional pedagogy. Based on observations of and interviews with teachers, both teachers had defined goals and selected high-quality and age-appropriate repertoire. While both models were effective, differences in emphasis on sight-reading, tone production and listening, parent involvement, and age of beginners were found.

4.2.2.3. *Chamber Music Setting*

Although the chamber music ensemble was the unit of analysis in other studies, only one study focused on chamber music coaching, specifically the strategies used by the Cavani Quartet to foster collaborative student rehearsals. Cotter-Lockard (2012) collected data via interviews with the Cavani String Quartet and student quartet members. Also, post-coaching interviews that included review of video excerpts of the coaching session were conducted with select participants. The concept of chamber ensemble as a generative team was created to characterize the environment, communication, and ensemble members' ability to consider various perspectives fostered during coaching sessions.

4.3. STUDENTS

Studies that focused on students' experience of learning to play a string instrument clustered by grade level (elementary school, middle school, high school, and collegiate).

While the participants in some studies included band and orchestra students, the findings discussed in the following will focus on orchestra students.

4.3.1. Elementary and Middle School Level

Four studies investigated factors that contributed to beginner or elementary-school-level orchestra students' motivation to participate, fifth-grade instrumentalists' descriptions of music, sixth-grade instrumentalists' self-regulation, and seventh-grade student practice strategies. Over nine months, Stofko (2002) collected field notes and interviews (with teachers and students) during beginning band and orchestra rehearsals. Data were initially coded deductively using sports socialization agents concepts. Normative vignettes were created to illustrate the presentation of themes. While students joined the ensemble for a variety of reasons, the most influential factor in selecting an instrument was family influence, followed by timbre preferences. Band students reflected a greater degree of gender stereotyping of instruments than orchestra students. Although both band and orchestra instructors used similar pedagogical techniques, the personality of the instructors was a factor contributing to the effectiveness of each teaching technique. Differences between band and orchestra were also the result of the unique characteristics of the school setting.

One study explored eight fifth-grader instrumentalists' (four band, three string, one both) categorization and descriptions of 15 excerpts from unfamiliar music (Johnson 2003). Data were collected using a Q-sort technique, interviews, and written descriptions of pieces. Four categories of descriptors emerged: Elemental Music, Extramusical Associative, Affective, and Other (comparison to other pieces). The participants used elemental music terms most often, yet also included a substantial number of extramusical associations and affective descriptors.

Two studies explored beginning students' practicing. Using a mixed method triangulation design, Austin and Berg (2006) explored 224 band and orchestra students' practice motivation and regulation. A validating quantitative data model was used (Creswell and Plano Clark 2011), where quantitative and qualitative data were collected and analyzed separately, followed by an elaboration on quantitative results based on qualitative findings. Sixth-grade instrumentalists completed a 36-item practice inventory and produced two narratives depicting a typical practice session and a practice episode involving a difficult piece of music. Written narratives revealed that some students employ a range of practice and regulatory strategies, while others follow practice routines that are not considered strategic. Practice motivation was reflected in student comments about personal interest, effort, and emotional responses experienced while practicing.

In a follow-up study, Berg (2008) used a case study design to describe the practice strategies and function of music practice for two seventh-grade string students. Data were collected over 14 weeks during 56 videotaped practice sessions and audiotaped interviews with the participants, parents, and school orchestra teacher. Although both participants were motivated by a practice time requirement, the use of different practice routines, strategies, environments, and behaviors, as well as motivational catalysts, contributed to varied practice effectiveness. Findings suggest that music practice served multiple and varied functions for these two adolescent-aged instrumentalists.

4.3.2. High School and Collegiate Level

High school- or collegiate-level string students were the focus of five studies on the following subjects: musical experience during orchestra rehearsals, improvisation experiences in two alternative style ensembles, musical experiences of six arts magnet high school students, All-State orchestra member self-efficacy sources and other influences on changes in music competence perception, and college string majors' self-regulated practice behaviors.

Through observation, interviews, questionnaire administration, and analysis of three videotaped rehearsals, Johnson (1990) identified three aspects of musical experience (psychosocial, teacher role, and awareness) during orchestra rehearsals, each encompassing several dimensions. Given the diversity of student perspectives found in this setting, students' musical experience in the secondary orchestra classroom is likely to be multidimensional and varied.

Lasinger (2006) investigated the impact of improvisation on the learning experiences of string players in two high-school-level alternative (primarily fiddling or Celtic) style ensembles. Study participants included 32 (violin, viola, bass guitar, or acoustic guitar) students from the two ensembles, ensemble directors, and an undergraduate student who was a former member of one of the ensembles. Data were collected over a period of six weeks via individual interviews; two focus group interviews (which included researcher-student improvisation and discussion) with students; a student background survey; and rehearsal field notes. Students reported being more comfortable improvising during individual rather than group practice. When improvising during individual practice, students fused styles. Students were found to have three areas of focus when improvising: perception of improvisational ability by self and/or peers; memory of the repertoire; and a focus on right arm/left hand technique. Although each director advocated establishing safe environments for students during improvisation, many participants still struggled with comparing themselves to their peers. Students who were comfortable with improvisation were more likely to report coordinated focus on their left hand and right arm through consideration of the key signature and meter, while students who were uncomfortable with improvisation often shifted their focus toward the left hand because of their concern for playing the "right" notes. Varied student motivations for alternative ensemble participation included being able to play relevant music and the challenge of performing alternative style music.

A unique contribution to extant research on American students' string instrument learning, Thibeault (2007) studied the musical experiences of six arts magnet high school students. Over the course of a school year, 219 observations with accompanying informal interviews were conducted during rehearsals and performances in multiple settings, including school ensembles (orchestra, chamber ensemble, and jazz band); youth orchestras; garage bands; and bluegrass jam sessions. Eight hours of video, 329 digital photos, CD recordings of three students, Internet data, and artifacts (concert programs and handouts) also served as data sources. A distinction emerged between score-centered and setting-centered musical practices. Score-centered practices organize musical experiences around a fixed musical work, while setting-centered practices organize musical experiences around the musicians and context, allowing the musical work to be changed based on features of the setting. Thibeault's (2009) subsequent narrative presentation of one of the 2007 study participants highlighted tensions experienced between classical and bluegrass music performance and the associated instructional approach (guided vs. opportunity for exploration). Thibeault offers a vision of music education that embraces both score- and setting-centered practices, thus affording more creative opportunities for orchestra students. Thibeault's (2007) study is an excellent model of an ethnography given prolonged engagement, use of multiple data sources, and substantial methodological (research question development, data management, and data collection) information included in an appendix.

In another study of high school students, Hendricks (2009) examined All-State orchestra member self-efficacy sources and other contextual and intrapersonal influences on changes in music competence perception. A concurrent nested, semi-integrated mixed method design (Creswell, Plano Clark, Gutmann and Hanson 2003) was used for simultaneous collection of qualitative and quantitative data. Qualitative data were used to enhance the quantitative analyses, while inferences from qualitative analyses led to further statistical analysis. Qualitative data were collected by six researchers via observation of rehearsals and post-rehearsal discussions with students. Semi-structured interviews were conducted with all students following seating auditions, while follow-up interviews were completed with selected students based on initial interview and questionnaire responses and observed behaviors including emotional reactions. Data from observations and interviews were used to illustrate findings from the quantitative analyses as well as to provide more nuanced illustrations of sources of self-efficacy. Analyses suggest that students with higher self-efficacy beliefs were influenced by the sources of self-efficacy, with a primary influence from enactive mastery experience. Students with high self-efficacy beliefs were also positively influenced by (a) positive and negative conductor feedback; (b) encouragement from other students; (c) seeing other students succeed; and (d) issues of fatigue. Students with low self-efficacy beliefs felt more capable after seeing that other students were struggling. Variations in self-efficacy perceptions were also based on gender, orchestra placement, section in the orchestra, and relative number of same-school peers at the festival. While the findings seem to indicate that self-efficacy perceptions in a socially comparative environment are most closely associated with the ability to impress others and least associated with the ability to perform expressively, students can be taught to act as agents of their own cognition, motivation, and musical development. Hendricks's dissertation is a strong example of mixed method design given the detailed description of methodology and findings.

One of two studies that focused on collegiate-level students, Kim (2010) described four college string majors' self-regulated practice behaviors that promoted efficiency and independence. Data were collected over a period of two weeks via a researcher-constructed semi-structured practice diary and two interviews with each participant. Participants demonstrated a range of self-regulatory skills, although some similar characteristics in the ways college music students self-regulated their learning during practice were noted. Age-related development in skillful self-regulation was identified. Furthermore, the semi-structured practice diary seemed to be an effective tool to investigate self-regulated learning in instrumental practice as well as to encourage self-regulated learning, particularly for less regulatory students.

Although Black (2012) also explored collegiate-level student experience, data were collected post-hoc during interviews with 11 professional multi-stylists. Aspiring multi-stylists' unique needs, as well as the perceived impact of collegiate program configuration (university-based, monostyle conservatory, or multistyle conservatory) on participants' professional performing career preparation, were topics explored in this study. Eight needs were identified that clustered into three categories: supportive teachers, mentoring, and environment; relevant and flexible repertoire and performance opportunities; and opportunities to develop creative skills. Each program configuration was found to have strengths and limitations for pre-professional preparation.

4.4. Professional/Amateur Performers

Three studies focused on professional or amateur performer learning influences, improvisational thinking, socialization via significant others, or identity and self-efficacy development. Heaney (1994) explored educational background variables that contributed to the development of professional orchestra performers. In-depth interviews with seven Philadelphia Orchestra string section members and one former professional orchestra member (for the pilot study) were conducted. Findings were presented by variable categories and realist tales, with transcript excerpts included in each tale. An 11-variable model of string music education was created that included sub-variables. The 11 variables were: parent, teacher, listening, performance, age, independence, lessons, practice, social, peers, and repertoire. Variables not common to all participants included: values, expectations, talent, discipline, neighbor's support, and personal satisfaction. The changing roles of the teacher and parent over time and impact of this change for promoting active student learning were noted.

In the only study of professional jazz performers, Norgaard (2011) described the improvisational thinking of seven artist-level jazz musicians, two of whom were string instrument performers (Darol Anger and Rufus Reid). After recording an improvised blues solo, participants simultaneously listened to the recording and looked at the notation of their solo as they were interviewed about the thinking processes that led to their improvisations. In order to focus verbal comments on decision-making and structure, each interview began with the same prompt. As phrases of the solo were played, the artist described each phrase and other aspects of the performance. When necessary, the researcher asked clarification and elaboration questions. Artists described making sketch plans, which outlined one or more musical features of upcoming passages, monitoring and evaluating their output as they performed, and making judgments that often were incorporated into future planning. Four strategies for generating the melodic content of the improvisations emerged: recalling well-learned ideas from memory and inserting them into the ongoing improvisation, choosing notes based on a harmonic priority, choosing notes based on a melodic priority, and repeating material played in earlier sections of the improvisation. Norgaard's (2008) dissertation is an important contribution to the literature not only for its unique focus on improvisational thinking, but also as an excellent model of creative research design and detailed description of analysis procedures.

The first of two studies of amateur performers, Cox (2009) explored the impact of significant others on the socialization of amateur string quartet members. Individual interviews were initially conducted in a group setting as the group traveled to and from performances, with follow-up interviews carried out via email. The researcher, a participant in the quartet, described her contrasting experiences as a more-skilled quartet member while noting her role in their socialization. Participants were able to report both positive and negative influences during their pre-college years from influential family members. However, all reported negative influences from parents, the self, or degree requirements (e.g., having to play a recital) when choosing a college degree. Once a college degree was determined, influential persons and reference groups from non-music fields of study were identified. The socialization of these amateurs was characterized as evolving over time and growing into the role through successful performances.

Eaton (2013) explored the impact of string music performance on the development and maintenance of identity, self-efficacy, and well-being of six adult community music program participants. Data were collected via interviews and participant observation during orchestra rehearsals, a chamber music workshop, and self-structured chamber ensemble rehearsals. Participants conceived of themselves as amateur musicians who played regularly for emotional, cognitive, and social benefits. Family support, a variety of performance opportunities, and goal-setting contributed to participants' personal identity, perceived self-efficacy, and overall sense of well-being.

4.5. School Orchestra and Alternative Styles Programs and Curriculum

Studies focused on school orchestra and alternative styles program components and curriculum included case studies of an award-winning program, a parent education class, chamber ensembles, peer tutoring, an alternative concert format, implementation of composition, a school-based Celtic ensemble, a summer alternative styles program, and a summer fiddling and dance camp.

The development and features of the award-winning Upper Arlington, Ohio, orchestra program was the focus of Fu's (2009) research. Data were collected over the period of one month during four observations of elementary, middle school, or high school classes; teacher interviews; and curriculum document review. The history, structure (funding, teacher schedules, performance calendar, teacher qualifications, curriculum, enrichment activities), and current participation and attrition rates of the program were presented. Faculty qualifications with respect to being able to teach all levels of string classes contributed to the creation of an organized curriculum and the design of goal-directed instructional plans that were aligned with district curriculum documents. The ability to teach collaboratively helped to sustain this successful program.

Moss (1991, 1992) designed and implemented a class for parents of beginning elementary string students. The goals of the class were to give parents an opportunity to play an instrument, help parents become more involved in their child's music education, and foster positive public relations. Ten parents with a range of educational, occupational, and musical backgrounds volunteered to meet weekly for eight weeks. Parents learned necessary skills to perform "Twinkle, Twinkle Little Star" as well as home-based activities. Parents were recognized at the first concert, where they were given the opportunity to perform alongside their child. Data were gathered via videotaped class sessions, parent and student interviews, a teacher-researcher class observation diary, and questionnaires. The adult class was found to be an effective way to educate and motivate parents and their children. Parent perceptions of the class program were positive, expressing value in this shared experience with their child, with most parents being interested in additional instruction. Students were also positive about parent participation in the class, as they appreciated the parent's ability to assist at home, as well as the student's ability to offer critique to the parent. Orchestra teachers noted the positive impact of parent class-participation on students' attitudes toward learning to play a stringed instrument.

In the first of two studies on chamber music programs and related student experiences, Berg (1997) explored how students in two chamber music ensembles reached conclusions about musical interpretation through social interaction. Two chamber music ensembles from different programs—a quartet and a violin, piano, horn trio—were observed over a period of five months during 33 student rehearsals, coaching sessions, and performances. Additional data were collected during 11 semi-structured interviews with ensemble members (some of which included reviews of rehearsal videos) and coaches, and informal interviews. Four global patterns of musical thought and action were identified. These included: (1) musical topics covered in rehearsals; (2) amount and nature of the music rehearsed during each rehearsal; (3) types and frequency of verbal and nonverbal activity used by participants; and (4) use of a sequence of student activity during rehearsals, including orienting and assisted-learning activities. The analysis revealed several similarities between the two ensembles. Ensemble members challenged each other to work at a higher developmental level by requiring peers to clarify, elaborate on, or justify a problem solution. Also, the use of varied social participation structures as well as others' rehearsal strategies and musical ideas facilitated learning. Differences were noted in ensemble member role exchange and use of unique rehearsal strategies. Gendered use of language and status within the group contributed to a student's ability to assume a leadership role (Berg 2000). Intersubjectivity was found to develop in unique ways given the nature of musical problems. This study demonstrated that collaborative learning in a musical context can be multifaceted, complex, and filled with the potential to both encourage and hinder growth in musical understanding.

In another case study of a high school student chamber ensemble, Hendricks (2010) described the impact of accompanying music history and theory instruction on student chamber ensemble engagement and expressive performance. Two diverse teaching approaches were introduced sequentially by the teacher-researcher as students learned two movements of Schubert's "Death and the Maiden" Quartet. The first movement was taught using performance-based instruction only, while the second movement was taught with a combination of performance-based instruction and music history and theory lessons. Twenty-four coaching sessions were videotaped for subsequent analysis by the researcher and weekly questionnaires were completed by students. Student comments and teacher observations revealed that the incorporation of music history and theory lessons into performance instruction was motivational to students, a catalyst for expressive performance, and an effective use of rehearsal time given the rating for performances of each movement by an independent adjudicator. Hendricks recommended that teachers balance time spent on music history and theory as compared to technical performance instruction by spending more time playing than talking or listening during coaching sessions, using homework assignments to teach historical and theoretical aspects of a work, and gauging student readiness when introducing music history.

Although similarly focused on peer learning, Webb (2012) explored the instructional choices, thought processes, and knowledge construction of four high-school-aged peer tutors who taught middle school students from within the school districts' orchestra program. Concepts from constructivism, motivation research, and Vygotskian theory contributed to the theoretical framework. Data were collected through observation and video-recording of twelve 30-minute private lessons, initial and post-lesson interviews, and short post-lesson journal reflections. Findings for each participant were presented through four vignettes, while cross-case analysis resulted in five themes, including pedagogical choices based on prior experiences, reorganization and communication of musical concepts, enjoyment and value of tutoring, tutor perception of roles, and tutor's pedagogical comfort zone. Several suggestions for tutor preparation and guidance were provided, thus contributing to the application of this study to teaching.

The only study to focus on a concert experience, Berg's (2009) narrative display of an alternative middle school concert format depicted a model (titled "Strings Attached: The Reality Show") of a first concert of the year created by a middle school orchestra director. Based primarily on interviews and artifact collection, realist tales of associated events (writing a script, concert setup), and the concert precede a theme-based analysis of the narratives. This analysis includes a discussion of the unique features of the model, including the use of a lottery to determine concert order, the informal atmosphere, audience participation (including parent performance), and varied student participation based on musical skills and dispositions. This concert model promoted student ownership and community development. While this model has many positive outcomes, challenges of this concert model with respect to logistics and teacher role are also identified.

Chartier (2009) designed and implemented a 10-week composition project (distributed over approximately 400 minutes of instruction) into an eighth-grade orchestra curriculum. Student-determined groups (based on like instrument and friendships) of two to three students composed an original theme and one to three variations utilizing upper positions. Data included field notes (made during direct observation, video review of classes, and a final performance of compositions), student compositions, student reflections, and assessment rubrics. Overall, students had positive attitudes about composing and working in groups, which was manifested in a perceived increase in enthusiasm during orchestra class. Patterns were noted in group dynamics, more effective use of class time over the course of the project, the need for additional time to complete composition activities, and student challenges with playing their compositions. While the project helped some students improve shifting skills, the researcher suggested that the time used to compose during rehearsals may have had a negative impact on the orchestra's overall intonation, technical facility, and sound, due to the decrease in rehearsal time. However, caution must be used when applying these findings, given that quantitative measures were not used to substantiate findings related to individual student motivation and performance achievement. Still, Chartier's study does point out the challenge orchestra teachers face when attempting to offer varied experiences for students during rehearsals, given time constraints.

Also focused on creative activity, albeit through an alternative ensemble offering, Oare (2008) described the Chelsea House Orchestra (CHO), a Celtic folk ensemble offered within a respected traditional orchestra program. Research questions centered on the value of the CHO to the school's music program, development of the CHO, teacher musical background, and how the CHO incorporated principles of democratic education. Data were collected over four months through weekly observations of the CHO and traditional orchestra rehearsals, five interviews with the orchestra teacher, and a focus group interview with four CHO students. Four themes were identified in the data: social music-making, the balance between classical and folk music education, evolving authenticity, and the creolization of musical transmission. Social music-making consisted of the development of a community of learners, collaborative student empowerment, having creative freedom, and experiencing musical enjoyment. While the orchestra teacher thought his primary purpose was to teach music from the classical Western European tradition, given CHO students' preference for classical music, participants valued multiple styles of music, as evident in the variety of styles played by the traditional orchestra. The teacher and student did not learn Celtic music in the way the style is traditionally taught through immersion, but rather incorporated aspects of traditional school pedagogy and folk methods. This study is a model of a multicultural instrumental ensemble for teachers interested in developing an ensemble that aligns with the cultural backgrounds of their students. The impact on student retention and learning when incorporating an alternative ensemble into a traditional orchestra program was noted.

In another study of an alternative styles program, Fetter (2011) examined whether *String Jam*, a one-week alternative styles summer camp, can be framed as a model of postmodern curriculum design while also exploring identity development in two adolescent participants. Following an in-depth discussion of *String Jam* program design and implementation, Fetter noted how classical string technique from the past was used to connect students to the present *String Jam* experience to help students "try on" various ways of being musical. Criterion-sampling was used to identify two students who participated in *String Jam* consecutive years, and who were still in secondary school and involved in music. Data were collected via in-depth interviews with accompanying descriptions of home practice environment and resources. Four themes were identified: complexity of and influences on musical identities, engaging in exploration through improvisation and experimentation, challenges of an alternative styles experience, and future musical activities. Private teachers and *String Jam* were found to influence current music activities and identity construction. Postmodern curriculum theory concepts of self-organization and proleptic vision were evident in the impact of *String Jam* on one student's continued experimentation and openness to diverse musical styles. At the same time, lack of adult high-level musician role models who continue to play while having a career was noted for one participant. Implications included teacher openness to development of varied student musical identities, fostering exploration and learning by ear, addressing challenges surrounding implementation of alternative styles in a public school orchestra program, and nurturing possible musical selves for students through presentation of a variety of adult musician role models and post-secondary musical involvements. Fetter's dissertation is an excellent and unique model, given the analysis of a program via curriculum theory and case study design as well as the integrated presentation of literature review, researcher background, and findings.

Similar to Fetter, given its focus on an extracurricular alternative styles program, Dabczynski's (1994) study of the 1991 Northern Week at Ashokan, a fiddle and dance summer workshop, explored fiddle teaching and learning characteristics, motivational features of the camp, and aspects of the camp experience and repertoire that could be incorporated into a school music program. Data were collected via a questionnaire, field notes on various camp events, three formal interviews with each of the three focus participants, informal interviews with teachers and other participants, and documents. Videos of teaching sessions were analyzed using a modified version of the Master Teacher Profile observation form designed by Robert Culver. Stylistic competence was primarily acquired through oral-based learning, although growing acceptance of printed music was noted. Participants were motivated not only to learn new repertoire and improve as fiddlers, but also to participate in a community that included frequent social and musical interactions, shared growth and support, opportunity for lifelong learning, interaction with highly competent teaching models, and aesthetically gratifying experiences. Features recommended for adoption into school settings included building community through the development of a collective sense of purpose and musical connection and use of non-coercive leadership.

4.6. Conclusion

A review of extant qualitative research in the American string/orchestra setting included studies on teacher socialization, lived experience, and models, including approaches and instructional strategies used by studio teachers, school teachers, and chamber music coaches; beginning through advanced student practice, retention, description of music and musical experience, self-efficacy, and varied school and extracurricular performance experiences; adult professional or amateur performer skill, identity, and/or self-efficacy development, improvisational thinking, and socialization; school orchestra program development, ensemble offerings (including alternative styles ensembles and chamber music); and unique peer tutoring, concert, parent class, composition and alternative styles programs that resulted in multifaceted learning experiences for students. Of the 44 studies that were reviewed, the majority of studies focused on string teaching and teachers, followed by students, then school orchestra and alternative styles programs and curriculum, and finally professional or amateur performers. This distribution is contrasted with Kantorski and Stegman's (2006) content analysis of qualitative dissertations written between 1998–2002, where multicultural curriculum implementation was the most researched topic, followed by school music programs, teacher education, curricular integration, instructional strategies, ensemble members, and learning process. Some topics that were the focus of research reviewed for this chapter (for example, composing, adults, private lessons and practicing, teaching process) appeared in Kantorski and Stegman's content analysis, but were less frequently the focus of doctoral research. These differences in frequency distribution of research study topics may be the result of varying foci for dissertation vs. post-dissertation research. At the same time, researchers engaged in qualitative research in the school orchestra setting may tend to focus on multicultural offerings vis-à-vis nontraditional ensembles or extracurricular alternative styles programs. Furthermore, the more frequent study of string teaching and teachers may be a result of our tendency as string teachers to focus on teaching instrument technique, as well as to frequently consider expert models of instruction.

Given the relatively few number of studies on American stringed instrument instruction, study, performance, school orchestra and alternative styles programs, and curriculum, most topics were addressed by one study, with the noted exception of artist-level teaching strategies or exercises (Duke and Simmons 2006; Gholson 1998; Moss 2006), student practice (Austin and Berg 2006; Berg 2008; Kim 2010), and unique musical experiences provided by various nontraditional curricular and extracurricular or community-based offerings (Berg 2009; Black 2012; Chartier 2009; Dabczynski 1994; Eaton 2013; Fetter 2011; Oare 2008; Moss 1991; Thibeault 2007, 2009; Webb 2012). Researchers have a prime opportunity to add to this corpus of qualitative studies for topics that have been the focus of prior research in order to begin to establish a larger body of research on American string/orchestra teaching and learning. At the same time, given the increased frequency of performance-related injuries, school guitar classes, and students with multi-style backgrounds, these topics warrant further research.

In addition, topics related to those already examined outside of the string teaching, learning, and performance context might be explored, perhaps in conjunction with prior quantitative studies. For example, while there are some qualitative studies on expert teachers and successful programs, there are few qualitative studies of new string teachers and no qualitative studies on the development of new school orchestra programs. Follow-up case studies of teachers or programs could provide additional perspectives on quantitative results. (For an example of a quantitative study of new school orchestra programs, see Gillespie and Hamann 2010.) Other topics related to string teaching and learning that might be addressed using a qualitative research design as recommended by other authors (Heaney 1994; Kantorski 1995; Kantorski and Stegman 2006) include: string program evaluation; viola and double bass teaching; the role of parents; listening activities; social activities in string student learning; string teacher professional development; and use of technology. In particular, use of technology during instruction as a means for offering a broader educational experience seems a relevant and fertile topic for future research.

In addition to considering the topics addressed in the reviewed research, the reviewed research can also be categorized based on the qualitative methodology used. Similar to Kantorski and Stegman's (2006) review of qualitative dissertations and Merriam's (2009, 22) assessment of the corpus of qualitative research in education, case study design was used in the majority of studies. Action research or narrative research methods were used in three studies, while ethnography, phenomenology, and grounded theory were only used in one study each. In comparison with Kantorski and Stegman's (2006) review, a smaller percentage of the total number of qualitative studies in the American string/orchestra setting used ethnography and phenomenology. While methodology used may reflect the breadth of methodological training received during doctoral program study, the string music education researcher community has an opportunity to begin asking different types of questions about American string instrument teaching, learning, and performing that are aligned with various methodologies (Creswell 2006).

In addition, the breadth and depth of discussion on design in published qualitative studies in the American instrumental (string) setting overall can be expanded. In particular, researchers need to provide more detailed descriptions of sampling strategies, researcher background, researcher role and its impact on reflexivity, trustworthiness strategies (beyond member checks of transcripts and triangulation), and coding procedures. Some of these suggested improvements were also identified by Lane (2011) in a review of qualitative research published in two eminent music education research journals. As the string music education research community matures, we might expect not only an increase in the quantity and quality of published qualitative research, but also the emergence of more varied presentation formats beyond text, even within the confines of the traditional journal format. Certainly, there is a need and ample opportunity for additional qualitative research that will contribute to our understanding of the status and complexity of string teaching, learning, and performance.

References

Austin, J. R., and M. H. Berg. 2006. "Exploring Music Practice among 6th-Grade Band and Orchestra Students." *Psychology of Music* 34 (4): 535–58.

Barnes, G. V., ed. 2003. *Applying Research to Teaching and Playing Stringed Instruments*. Reston, VA: ASTA.

Barnes, G. V. 2010. "Teaching Music: The First Year." *Bulletin of the Council for Research in Music Education* 185: 63–76.

Berg, M. H. 1997. "Social Construction of Musical Experience in Two High School Chamber Music Ensembles." PhD diss., Northwestern University.

Berg, M. H. 2000. "Thinking for Yourself: The Social Construction of Chamber Music Experience." In *On the Sociology of Music Education II: Papers from the Music Education Symposium at the University of Oklahoma*, edited by R. Rideout, 91–112. Amherst: University of Massachusetts.

Berg, M. H. 2008. "Getting the Minutes in: A Case Study of Beginning Instrumentalists' Music Practice." In *Advances in Music Education Research*, edited by L. Thompson and M. Campbell, 45–65. Charlotte, NC: Information Age.

Berg, M. H. 2009. "Strings Attached: The Reality Show. In *Musical Experience in Our Lives: Things We Learn and Meanings We Make*, edited by J. Kerchner and C. Abril, 165–81. Lanham, MD: Rowman and Littlefield.

Black, M. E. 2012. "Forging Musical Paths: The Experiences of Multistyle String Players in Undergraduate Programs." PhD diss., Teachers College, Columbia University.

Chartier, K. 2009. "Integrating Composition into One Eighth-Grade Orchestra Classroom." MME thesis, University of Massachusetts–Lowell.

Collier-Slone, K. (1991). "The Psychology of Humanistic Life Education: A Longitudinal Study." PhD diss., The Union Institute.

Cotter-Lockard, D. 2012. "Chamber Music Coaching Strategies and Rehearsal Techniques That Enable Collaboration." PhD diss., Fielding Graduate University.

Cox, P. H. 2008. "Professional Socialization of Arkansas Music Teachers: A Follow-up Study." In *Sociological Explorations: Proceedings of the 5th International Symposium on the Sociology of Music Education*, edited by B. Roberts, 81–95. St. John's, Newfoundland: The Binder's Press.

Cox, P. H. 2009. "The Socialization of Members of a String Quartet towards Their Roles as Musicians." Research Presentation: 6th International Symposium on the Sociology of Music Education, Limerick, Ireland.

Creswell, J. W. 2006. *Qualitative Inquiry and Research Design: Choosing among Five Approaches*. 2nd ed. Thousand Oaks, CA: Sage Publications.

Creswell, J. W., and V. L. Plano Clark. 2011. *Designing and Conducting Mixed Methods Research*. Thousand Oaks, CA: Sage Publications.

Creswell, J. W., V. L. Plano Clark, M. L. Gutmann, and W. E. Hanson. 2003. "Advanced Mixed Methods Research Designs." In *Handbook of Mixed Methods in Social and Behavioral Research*, edited by A. Tashakkori and C. Teddlie, 209-40. Thousand Oaks, CA: Sage Publications.

Dabczynski, A. H. 1994. "Northern Week at Ashokan 1991: Fiddle Tunes, Motivation and Community at the Fiddle and Dance Camp." PhD diss., University of Michigan.

Duke, R. A., and A. L. Simmons. 2006. "The Nature of Expertise: Narrative Descriptions of 19 Common Elements Observed in the Lessons of Three Renowned Artist-Teachers." *Bulletin of the Council for Research in Music Education* 170: 7-19.

Eaton, K. G. 2013. "Finding the Fountain of 'You': A Case of Older Adult String Players' Identity, Self-Efficacy and Wellbeing as Community Musicians." PhD diss., New York University.

Fetter, J. P. 2011. "Alternative Styles in String Music Education: Identity Development and Curriculum Design in the Postmodern Era." PhD diss., University of Rochester.

Fu, W. M. 2009. "A Case Study of an Award Winning Public School String Program." MM thesis, Bowling Green State University.

Gholson, S. A. 1998. "Proximal Positioning: A Strategy of Practice in Violin Pedagogy." *Journal of Research in Music Education* 46 (4): 535-45.

Gholson, S. A. 1993. "Proximal Positioning: A Strategy of Practice in Violin Pedagogy." PhD diss., University of Cincinnati.

Gillespie, R., and D. Hamann. 2010. "An Investigation of New String Programs Established in American Schools between 1999 and 2009." *String Research Journal* 1: 25-38.

Gustafson, R. I. 1986. "Effects of Interpersonal Dynamics in the Student-Teacher Dyads on Diagnostic and Remedial Content of Four Private Violin Lessons." *Psychology of Music* 14 (2): 130-39.

Heaney, M. F. 1994. "Developing a String Research Agenda by Identifying the Components of a String Education: A Qualitative Study of Selected Members of the Philadelphia Orchestra String Section." PhD diss., The Florida State University.

Hendricks, K. S. 2009. "Relationships between the Sources of Self-Efficacy and Changes in Competence Perceptions of Music Students during an All-State Orchestra Event." PhD diss., University of Illinois at Urbana-Champaign.

Hendricks, K. S. 2010. "Investing Time: Teacher Research Observing the Influence of Music History and Theory Lessons upon Student Engagement and Expressive Performance of an Advanced High School String Quartet." *Bulletin of the Council for Research in Music Education* 184: 65-78.

Hudnall, C. R. 2012. "Teaching Relaxed, Healthy Posture: An Investigation of Pedagogical Approaches and String Musicians' Performance-Related Problems." PhD diss., Mercer University.

Johnson, D. C. 2003. "Fifth-Grade Instrumentalists' Descriptions of Music." *Bulletin of the Council for Research in Music Education* 158: 81-95.

Johnson, S. R. 1990. "A Description of Selected Aspects of Musical Experience from the Students' Perspective within the Context of a Secondary Orchestra Rehearsal: A Qualitative Case Study." PhD diss., Northwestern University.

Kantorski, V. J. 1995. "A Content Analysis of Doctoral Research in String Education, 1936-1992." *Journal of Research in Music Education* 43 (4): 288-97.

Kantorski, V. J., and S. F. Stegman. 2006. "A Content Analysis of Qualitative Research Dissertations in Music Education, 1998-2002." *Bulletin of the Council for Research in Music Education* 168: 63-73.

Kim, S. J. 2010. "A Study of Self-Regulated Learning in College String Majors." *String Research Journal* 1: 39–54.

Kotchenruther, M. J. 1998. "A Descriptive Study of the Rehearsal Priorities of Middle School String Teachers." PhD diss., University of Michigan.

Lane, J. 2011. "A Descriptive Analysis of Qualitative Research Published in Two Eminent Music Education Research Journals." *Bulletin of the Council for Research in Music Education* 188: 65–76.

Lansinger, K. 2006. "A Study of Improvisation in High School Alternative String Ensembles." MME thesis, University of Michigan.

Lyne, J. K. 1991. "Beginning Strings Class Instruction: Practice and Theory." EdD diss., University of Arizona.

Merry, R. 2010. "A Paradigm for Effective Pre-College Classical Guitar Methodology: A Case Study of Two Models of Effective Instruction." DA diss., University of Northern Colorado.

Moss, K. D. 1991. "The Design, Conduct, and Study of an Adult Beginning String Class for Parents of Beginning Elementary String Students." MME thesis, University of Cincinnati.

Moss, K. D. 1992. "Involving Today's Parents." *Music Educators Journal* 79 (2): 44–46.

Moss, K. D. 2006. "Favored Sound Production Exercises of Selected Violin, Viola, Cello, and Double Bass Pedagogues: An Analysis and Adaptation." PhD diss., University of Florida.

Norgaard, M. 2008. "Descriptions of Improvisational Thinking by Artist-Level Jazz Musicians." PhD diss., University of Texas-Austin.

Norgaard, M. 2011. "Descriptions of Improvisational Thinking by Artist-Level Jazz Musicians." *Journal of Research in Music Education* 59(2): 109–27.

Oare, S. 2008. "The Chelsea House Orchestra: A Case Study of a Non-Traditional School Instrumental Ensemble." *Bulletin of the Council for Research in Music Education*, 177: 63–78.

Parker, J. M. 2001. "The Motivation Techniques of an Exemplary Orchestra Teacher: A Case Study." MME thesis, Michigan State University.

Pellegrino, K. 2010. "The Meanings and Values of Music-Making in the Lives of String Teachers: Exploring the Intersections of Music-Making." PhD diss., University of Michigan.

Scheib, J. W. 2003. "Role Stress in The Professional Life of the School Music Teacher: A Collective Case Study." *Journal of Research in Music Education* 51 (2): 124–36.

Scruggs, B. B. 2009. "Learning Outcomes in Two Divergent Middle School String Orchestra Classroom Environments: A Comparison of a Learner-Centered and a Teacher-Centered Approach." PhD diss., Georgia State University.

Stofko, D. L. 2002. "A Comparative Study of the Beginning Band and Beginning Orchestra Experience." DMA diss., Arizona State University.

Thibeault, M. D. 2007. "Music Making Lives: Score and Setting in the Musical Experiences of High School Students." PhD diss., Stanford University.

Thibeault, M. D. 2009. "Violin and Fiddle: Narratives of Music and Musician in a High-School Setting." In *Musical Experience in Our Lives: Things We Learn and Meanings We Make*, edited by J. Kerchner and C. Abril, 255–74. Lanham, MD: Rowman and Littlefield.

Vygotsky, L. S. 1978. *Mind in Society: The Development of Higher Psychological Processes*. Cambridge, MA: Harvard University Press.

Webb, R. S. 2012. "Construction of Musical Understandings: An Exploration of Peer Tutoring in the School Orchestra Program." PhD diss., Northwestern University.

Wenger, E. 1999. *Communities of Practice: Learning, Meaning and Identity*. Cambridge, UK: Cambridge University Press.

CHAPTER 5

QUALITATIVE CHORAL MUSIC RESEARCH

BRIDGET SWEET

> If we wish for singing and choral music to become part of the "self" of adolescent boys and girls, we must listen to the experiences of young adolescents as expressed through their words and stories. Then, we can reflect what we learn from them in our teaching and rehearsing as the culmination of a constantly renewing cycle of inquiry, theory, research, and practice.
>
> (Freer 2006, 77)

5.1. Introduction

A comprehensive review of qualitative choral music education research conducted in the United States revealed diverse examinations that have created a valuable foundation for choral music educators and the music education profession. Research included in this chapter shares a core focus of choral music education, regardless of individual purpose statement or selected participant. Studies placed within a choral setting but focused on elements other than choral music have been excluded from this discussion. For example, Krueger's (1985) groundbreaking qualitative research explored the influences of hidden curriculum on perspectives of student teachers of music. Although a choral classroom was the setting for Krueger's study, the inquiry truly focused on student teacher perspectives and not choral music.

The following section examines research pertaining to choir as a safe place; section 5.3 explores various facets of participation in choral music, from student perspective to teacher participation. The final section of this chapter offers a brief summary and identifies areas of need in qualitative choral research.

5.2. Choir Is a Safe Place

Students experience conflict in many ways, "overt and covert, obvious and subtle, individually prompted and institutionally embedded" (Stengel 2010, 524). As a result, teacher awareness of student fears provides opportunity to better meet student needs through actions of appropriate interpretation and response within a safe environment. A safe place defuses student fear and establishes a sense of safety (Stengel 2010); a safe place empowers students to take control of their own lives (Toraiwa 2009).

Many researchers consider the choral classroom to be a safe place (Adderley, Kennedy, and Berz 2003; Freer 2009c; Kennedy 2004; Mills 2008; Parker 2009, 2010; Sweet 2008, 2010). Some students and teachers will go as far as to regard choir as a home away from home (Adderley et al. 2003; Borst 2002; Huff 1989), a place of escape (Borst 2002), or as a place of sanctuary (Kennedy 2004; Mills 2008). "Chorus is a place that never produces stress. It is a good place to come and say, 'Oh, good I have chorus . . . it is a good place to let things go'" (Parker 2010, 348). Within this section of the chapter, choral music research that clearly established a conversation about a safe classroom environment is presented; research that also pertained to issues of participation in choir will be discussed in section 5.3.

Our discussion begins with Borst (2002), who used observations, interviews, and thick and rich description to determine and discuss how two high school teachers' personal attributes influenced their processes of teaching choral music. Through cross-case analysis, five themes emerged regarding qualities of the two exemplary choral teachers: personal professionalism, class climate, relationship with students, discipline strategies, and teaching strategies. Themes did not exist independently, but rather "the themes form a web of choral music teacher qualities that coexist within a single complex. They coalesce to the extent that each thematic category blends with the others, forming an amalgamation of effective choral teaching" (117).

In addition to upholding high musical expectations and standards, the two teachers fostered hospitable classroom environments, which the teachers and their students considered a sort of home or family. Borst (2002) posited that a healthy classroom atmosphere encourages choral members to feel good about their tasks and abilities, potentially resulting in desires to participate more fully. "Because of the positive feeling-tone of the classroom environment in which they interact, the choral students behave in most any way to achieve the excellence for which the teacher-conductor is striving" (123). Although technically accurate choral behavior is possible without teacher-student relationships, it is incomplete. "Without the cultivation of positive human relationships and personal identities, technically proficient choirs may be missing a key ingredient in the recipe for artistic excellence" (124–25).

Through phenomenological inquiry, Haywood (2006) provided the perspective of Deborah, a 15-year-old choral student who alternately used a walker and a wheelchair for mobility due to a physical challenge. An effervescent teenager who loved to sing,

Deborah struggled with participation in school choirs as a result of her inability to access rehearsal spaces (i.e., no elevator at the School for the Arts) and choral director bias and ignorance. The bulk of data emanated from semi-structured interviews; grounded theory assisted in the interpretation of all data sources gathered throughout the case study, including interview transcriptions, field notes, and historical documentation.

Deborah's journey toward participation in an inclusive community choir was influenced by three emergent categories of data: barriers to inclusion, creating inclusive environments through advocacy, and building relationships (Haywood 2006). The third category, building relationships, pertained specifically to Deborah's musical and social bond with her present community choir director: "She was looking at me as a musician, as a singer. She was not looking at me physically which I find is just magnificent!" (414). As a result of her experiences in the inclusive choir environment, Deborah gained the musician identity that she openly desired. In Deborah's words:

> Music in general has made me a person. Has defined me. But I've become more. I'm learning more, which will in turn help me vocally. And that's how I've changed: I've become a person. I have my own identity. And that's the truth! (415)

The Northridge Children's Choir was the focus of Mills's dissertation research (2008) and accompanying article (2010) for which she examined how experiences within this choir, as well as interactions with peers and the conductor, influenced the formation of choristers' personal and musical identities. Data included two focus group interviews with six choir members (ages 12–14) and individual follow-up interviews with three focus group members and their parents, one adult former children's choir member, and the choir's conductor, as well as rehearsal observations, a choir background questionnaire, and observation field notes.

Mills (2008) concluded that the Northridge Children's Choir was a safe place for choral members, but the facilitation of this environment was a result of the students and not the director, Mrs. Talbot. Although Mrs. Talbot believed her choir to be a "place of sanctuary" (256), her goal was to be respected by students and to not develop close relationships with students.

> As a mentor and a model of beautiful singing . . . I hope I'm a model . . . When I think back on the teachers I love most, they were mentors. They were models. They were by *no means* friends and I knew that. You would never call them by their first name. They were people to be *respected*. And the frosting on the cake for a few of them . . . they were *loved*. But the *most important* thing is to be *respected*, and so that's all I care about (Interview, Mrs. Talbot, January 29, 2008). (Mills 2008, 264, emphasis in original document)

Mrs. Talbot, herself, recognized and acknowledged that the student choir leaders "are largely responsible for cultivating the atmosphere of love and acceptance that binds the choristers together in friendship" (267).

In contrast to Mrs. Talbot, who wished to remain at a distance from her choristers, Sweet's (2008) ethnographic case study of Deb Borton revealed a middle school choir teacher who worked diligently to build connections and relationships with choir students. Although Deb maintained autocratic teaching practices, she unintentionally achieved democratic goals, including the establishment of a supportive environment and community, student awareness of others, and musical independence. "Safe Place" was cornerstone to Deb's philosophy and classroom practice, and maintained as the official framework for her choral program. In her own words:

> And this whole concept of "Safe Place" that is *so* integral to my classroom—that not only when you are singing a solo, you get to be safe in here. You answer a question, we are respectful of you. Period. And nobody gets a second chance to hurt somebody's feelings because it's not *ever* accidental if you are unkind. (Sweet 2008, 91, emphasis in original document)

In addition to data collection through classroom observations, concert attendance, and formal interviews with Deb, a focus group was conducted with four eighth-grade female choir students and a separate group of five eighth-grade male choir students. Deb's students recognized the efforts she made and, as a result of her classroom environment, student musicianship flourished. "I think Mrs. Borton has strong opinions on pressure because she had bad experiences with too much pressure and singing and it gets personal when you're singing so she likes to keep as little pressure on us as possible" (100). This student comment supported Sweet's (2008) finding that, within a safe middle school choral environment, students are provided opportunities "to be themselves without inhibition, in a culture of acceptance" (202).

Through the framework of action research, Parker (2010) investigated high school choral students' definitions of social belonging and the factors of membership that contributed to experiences of belonging. Participants included 26 tenth- through twelfth-grade choral students from the same Northeastern high school, selected by intensity (students who demonstrated a noticeable, strong sense of belonging in choir) and purposeful random sampling. Within small groups of three to four students, choristers described their experiences of belonging within their choral ensemble. Interviews were audiotaped and transcribed; data also included Parker's notes of verbal and nonverbal interactions and body language between participants.

"Chorus as safe space suggests that the psychological benefits of choral singing in schools have potential for significant stress reduction" (Parker 2010, 350). Participation in singing, as well as "regular and consistent interaction" (350) between students (especially participation in trips), contributed to students' experiences of belonging in choir.

> In a school as sanctuary, students feel ready to learn because they are accepted as individuals, and are, as a result, more successful and relaxed in the classroom climate. Jackie and Tess seem to also indicate that chorus is a healthy and caring context where they can excel because they are accepted for who they are as individuals. (348)

Choral teachers in Parker's study influenced student belonging, as well as the classroom environment and the establishment of a safe choral space.

5.2.1. Less Safe Places

A discussion of choir and safe space would be incomplete without the acknowledgment of unfavorable spaces as well. Freer (2006) used memory pictures as autobiographical portraits of sequenced events (Fottland 2004) to share his self-story as a student, teacher, and researcher. His three autobiographical accounts, provided through the theoretical framework of narrative inquiry, offered insight into "understanding how the trivial, perhaps mundane, first encounter of an adolescent boy with his changing voice can potentially affect involvement in music later in life" (73).

Upon his return to fifth grade, Freer's (2006) voice began to change and "it was a particularly rapid, unwieldy, and not so subtle process" (73). His music teacher instructed him to "stand in the back of the choir and mouth the words. These were not instructions I wanted to hear. Believing that I could not sing, I immediately quit choir" (73). Although he eventually did pursue music in college, the negative influence of one elementary teacher—later followed by the positive influence of a college professor—impacted the course of his life as a musician and professor of music education.

Teacher influence was also an emergent factor in research by Abril (2007), who provided perspective on three female elementary education majors' anxieties about singing. Of the elementary majors enrolled in an elementary music methods course, three students "expressed serious concerns regarding taking this course because of their fear of singing and general lack of musical ability" (4). For this narrative inquiry, data involved structured interviews, participant journals, and field texts (observations of participants in the classroom setting, details of informal conversations, e-mail correspondence, and Abril's interpretations of events).

The three elementary majors individually revealed a poignant adolescent experience involving a choral director or teacher that caused each student to permanently fear or stop singing in front of peers and/or family. Although each of the women provided insightful vignettes, Melissa's story reflected the kinds of experiences that negatively impacted them all:

> When I was in sixth-grade we had the option of being in the choir. I wanted to be in [it] so badly—I thought I might be picked despite what my family said about me. For the audition, the teacher went around the room, knelt by each person, and took notes. . . . I was terrified as he came to me because I knew it was all or nothing (I remember my heart thumping so loudly). . . . Well, I didn't make the cut . . . and what made it worse was that all my friends did. I was devastated! I quit singing after that because I figured all these people must be right about me—my music teacher was the music expert! That really shattered my musical self-image. Since then I've felt pretty incapable. (Abril 2007, 6)

The implications of Abril's (2007) findings about singing and social anxiety are glaring for choral teachers, especially in respect to constructing and maintaining a safe choral space. "While teachers should not coddle students, they might use caution when assessing students' singing especially during the vulnerable period of adolescence. Assessment should focus on ways of helping students improve rather than assigning judgment" (13).

The idea of safe space in the choral classroom—or lack thereof—reoccurs within all research reviewed thus far in this chapter. Perspectives of choral teachers are specifically examined in two studies (Borst 2002; Sweet 2008) and perspectives of choral students (whether prospective or actual participants) are examined in four studies (Abril 2007; Freer 2006; Haywood 2006; Parker 2010). Mills (2008, 2010) considered insight from students, parents, and the choral director in her examination of chorister identity development. Although methodologies varied among research, each of the reviewed choral studies employed observations and interviews as methods of data collection, with the exception of Freer's (2006) self-study.

It should be noted that, within the majority of reviewed research, efforts by the choir teacher or director were credited for the creation of a safe choral environment; the exception was Mills (2008, 2010), who reported that the choristers, themselves, fostered the safe choral environment of the Northridge Children's Choir and not the choral director. In Abril (2007) and Freer (2006), actions by a choir teacher or director were identified as the reasons for adolescent choristers to discontinue their participation in choir or singing.

5.3. Perceptions of Participation in Choir

Concerns about student participation in choir reach beyond matters of attrition and retention, as evident by lines of questioning in qualitative choral music research. "Why do students join choir?" and "Why do students stay in choir?" have given way to deeper inquiries such as, "What do students perceive about their participation in choir and singing?" and "How do various aspects of choral experiences impact student involvement?" The influence of social factors on choral participation has also become prominent in examinations of involvement in choir.

The focus of this section will remain on different perspectives of participation in choir and involve a broad range of participants from high school students to intergenerational choir members to choral teachers. Current choir members provided perspective for the majority of qualitative choral studies. Although the perspective of former choir members has been encouraged in qualitative research (Conway and Borst 2001; Freer 2006; Parker 2009), only Freer (2009a, 2009b, 2009c) offered insight from non-choral students in his inquiries.

5.3.1. High School Participation in Choir

Through action research, Conway and Borst (2001) examined both personal and non-musical factors that influenced continued participation in Borst's choirs from middle school into high school. Of the high school students who studied with Borst for three years in middle school, six agreed to participate in this study and underwent individual interviews. In addition, the six students were interviewed as a six-person panel during Concert Choir rehearsal to measure potential peer-influence on interview responses. One parent of each of the six participants was interviewed about parental observations of their child, including observations of the meaningfulness of singing experiences between middle and high school.

Students and parents found it difficult to articulate reasons for student participation in choir, but enjoyment of singing was identified as a primary motivation (Conway and Borst 2001). In addition, non-musical outcomes—including social reasons, personal gain, and entertainment—influenced student participation in choir, as did positive experiences with teamwork, camaraderie, and opportunities to work within a group. Borst, himself, acknowledged personal and professional gains from this study, including a greater understanding of his teaching methods and goals. He recognized the need to develop aesthetic-awareness strategies, foster student involvement, and maintain a focus on teamwork within the choral student body as well as within the music faculty.

Adderley, Kennedy, and Berz (2003) broadened the scope of Conway and Borst's (2001) study beyond the choral classroom and focused on choir, band, and orchestra ensembles to qualitatively examine student motivations and insights on participation. Structured, individual interviews with 20 participants from band, choir, and orchestra (a total of 60 students) provided a balanced perspective from the three disciplines. "Accessibility rather than randomness was the major determinant in choosing the participants" (195) and balance was also achieved between girls and boys, as well as students from 10th, 11th, and 12th grades.

Although students placed great meaning and value on music participation and experiences, the importance of social aspects on participation in musical ensembles was significant.

> The social climate of these ensembles is important to each member and provides many with an outlet that they might not have had to meet others from within the larger school setting, or to form relationships away from the home environment that assist them in negotiating the often turbulent high school years. (Adderley, Kennedy, and Berz 2003, 204)

Findings aligned with earlier research regarding participation and meaningfulness of music ensemble experiences "providing a stronger case for the claim that students are intellectually, psychologically, emotionally, socially, and musically nurtured by membership in performing ensembles" (Adderley, Kennedy, and Berz, 2003, 204).

Social identity development was the focus of Parker's (2009) grounded theory research on adolescent choral singers. Data included 49 interviews with 36 different Mixed Choir participants within three Midwestern high school choral ensembles; 13 participants completed a second interview for member check procedures. In selecting choral participants, Parker used purposive random sampling, snowball sampling, and intensity sampling; directors from each of the choral programs underwent interviews as well.

Choral participation strengthened high school singers' sense of self and supported their social development (Parker 2009). "Feelings of confidence and increased self-concept gave participants the desire to give back in the form of leadership and performance, as well as willingness to engage in the larger choral legacy at their schools" (256). As with Adderley et al. (2003), Parker's participants "wore" their ensemble participation "as a badge to the larger school community" (257) and group excellence was important to the choral students. "Through the daily group goals of working together toward excellence, students leave class with feelings of competency and belonging to something bigger than themselves" (258).

Perspective gathered from six male high school students on music, musical vs. school lives, effective instructional practice, and peer interaction initially contributed to a book chapter by Freer (2009a) and subsequently led to two qualitative journal articles (2009b, 2009c). The boys selected for participation attended the same private school in the Southeastern United States and represented one of three categories: those who had sung in school choral ensembles continuously, those who sang but later withdrew from choral music, and those who did not sing at all.

For his first article, Freer (2009b) examined narratives of the boys' choral music experiences via flow theory and focused on "elements that enhanced their motivation to seek continued experiences in choral music" (143). Flow theory was defined as a "proximal theory of motivation" (146) through which students seek to replicate an experience because of the enjoyment they encounter as a result of the experience.

> By understanding how these boys' comments reflected qualities of flow, it is hoped that choral music educators may be able to design pedagogy and rehearsal techniques that enable the emergence of these optimal experiences. (Freer 2009b, 147)

Several significant connections emerged between flow theory and the boys' choral music experiences, including the importance of establishing clear and appropriate goals for students and the importance of an optimum balance between task challenge and student skill (Freer 2009b). In addition, Freer acknowledged the significance (and complexity) of feedback from the choral director in the development of student self-awareness within a choral ensemble.

Three of the aforementioned six male high school participants were again interviewed on three occasions for Freer's second article (2009c) about the construct of "possible selves" (Markus and Nurius 1986)—a notion about the kind of people we strive to become or fear becoming. One student was a current choral student, one a former choral student, and one had never participated in choral music. The boys discussed their previous musical experiences (past selves), current involvement (present self), and expectations for future involvement in music (possible selves).

Teenage singers—specifically male singers—may more successfully persevere through physical, social, academic, and musical transitions prevalent in adolescence through a focus on possible selves (Freer 2009c).

> Music educators can lay a foundation for this return to singing by purposefully encouraging their male choristers to develop conceptions of possible selves that involve choral music. These images, then, can be the focus of teacher-student conversations when boys decide to withdraw from choral music participation during secondary school. Such conversations need to reinforce—rather than diminish—the hoped-for possible self of each boy as an adult chorister. (351)

In response to his findings, Freer proposed a Possible Selves Program in Music for use specifically within the choral classroom.

High school immigrant students provided insight on their experiences in a non-auditioned American choir for Carlow's (2004) dissertation investigation of their acculturation process. The central research question for her collective case study, "What are the experiences of immigrant students who sing in high school choir?" (58), was supported by secondary questions: "What are the past and present musical experiences of immigrant students who sing in high school choir?" (58), "How do immigrant students perceive the repertoire, rehearsals, performance requirements, and traditions of high school choir?" (59), "To what extent and in what ways do immigrant students feel that they belong to, contribute to, and benefit from their high school chorus?" (60). During 10 months of data collection, Carlow interviewed four female choristers who had attended high school in the United States for no more than three years.

Although each participant had prior experience with music, encounters were of oral traditions rooted in folk or religious music; no previous experiences involved Western classical choral music. As a result, these students acknowledged linguistic frustrations and culture shock within the American choral setting. However, the immigrant students also identified benefits from participation in an American choir as:

> feelings of belonging to a school group, opportunities to practice English text, a lower-stress mainstreamed environment, the ability to earn credit toward high school graduation, and the ability to enhance the attractiveness of their college applications by including their membership in an extracurricular school group. (Carlow 2004, 310)

The story of Irina Choi—a 16-year-old Russian immigrant from Korea—was especially poignant in Carlow's (2004) dissertation and subsequently was published in a separate journal article (Carlow 2006). Irina had been very involved with singing and her school chorus while living in Russia and Kazakhstan. However, since moving to the United

States, she was incredibly unhappy and detached from others within her American high school choir.

> When I'm in the chorus, I know that I'm—like—I don't have to sing. I don't even have to open my mouth and sing. 'Cause there are a lot of people, and they can sing for me (personal communication, January 12, 2004). (Carlow 2006, 71)

Contradictory to Irina's participation in the American choir class was her involvement in the International Night show at the school, which featured student performers from the International Club. Through this venue, Irina focused heavily on her "identity as a solo pop singer" (71).

In response to Irina's story, Carlow (2006) encouraged music educators to acknowledge that students' "previous experiential backgrounds provide both a point of departure and an anchor for new learning" (75). Also stressed was the need for choral teachers to recognize the "varying stages of culture shock" (2006, 75) experienced by foreign students as they acculturated to the class and school setting. By acknowledging differences between students, music teachers will more amply meet the needs of foreign students within traditionally structured choral programs.

In examining adolescent choral singers' philosophical ways of thinking regarding music-making, Parker (2011) focused on "adolescent beliefs regarding music and its role within their lives, how adolescents describe the experience of music-making, and how adolescent philosophical beliefs serve to reflect, challenge and/or elucidate prominent ideas within music philosophy" (306). A constructivist paradigm was used to investigate both the "how" and "why" of the formation of adolescent belief systems; a pragmatic paradigm was also employed under the guise of effecting change within the music education community.

Participant interviews with 18 mixed choir members from three different mid-sized high schools in the Midwestern United States revealed four themes: (1) music-making as a simultaneously feelingful experience; (2) musical knowing as interpersonal knowing; (3) expressed music as expressed feeling; and (4) music-making as enlightening. In addition, commentary and insight from adolescent choristers connected with "aesthetic perception, expressiveness by convention, music-making as distinctly human, praxis as working understanding, art as self-unification, dialecticism, and individual's embodiment of musical experiences" (Parker 2011, 314), thereby confirming writings of philosophers such as Dewey, Elliott, Jorgensen, Langer, Reimer, Sparshott, and Stubley.

5.3.2. Middle Level Participation

Examination of choral research within middle grade levels begins with Kennedy (2002), who investigated the experiences and perceived benefits of participation in choir as reported by 11 junior high male choristers. Five questions guided this study:

(a) What are the motivating factors that encourage boys to join junior high choral ensembles? (b) What musical skills, knowledge, and attitudes do they acquire while belonging to these groups? (c) What are their perceptions of the "choral experience"—what do they like and what benefits do they reap? (d) What factors cause them to remain in choir year after year? (e) Is range-appropriate repertoire a factor in their enjoyment and participation in choir? (27).

Interviews provided the bulk of data, supported by observations, informal conversations, field notes, jottings, and material artifacts.

Junior high boys have "varied reasons for belonging to the choir, but strong similarities exist among the group" (Kennedy 2002, 35). Three primary factors influenced the boys' participation in choir: love of singing, teacher influence (in this case, a positive factor), and a cohort of friends. Students also expressed enthusiasm for their acquisition of musical skills and knowledge, but "by far the majority of comments concerned social aspects of the choir class" (33). Kennedy's inquiry about the range-appropriateness of choral repertoire and its influence on decisions of participation in choir revealed that the boys were quite clever at overcoming vocal range limitations and enjoyed participation in choir unanimously, regardless of stage of voice change. In fact, the boys found it more important to sing repertoire that they liked than to be concerned about vocal range.

In 2004, Kennedy conducted a second qualitative study that also focused on middle-level male singers. Through ethnography, she examined the culture of boys at the American Boychoir School (ABS), where the goal was (and continues to be) to nurture boys through the physical stages of voice change. "The American Boychoir School attracts educators with a particular interest in nurturing boys through this transitional phase and dedicates large amounts of time to cultivating the adolescent male voice" (266).

During her time at the ABS, Kennedy (2004) observed patterns of voice change among the students and witnessed the diligence of instructors to provide individual attention to the boys, in addition to keeping their best interests at heart. For example, one student was not allowed to participate in a concert cycle for the touring choir as a protective measure because of his particular stage of voice change. The music director explained, "Michael could go on the fall tour because he's such a good musician. There's a glorious instrument in there, a tenor voice, but I don't want to push him. He'll definitely go on the December tour" (271).

Students at the ABS recognized the benefits of frequent vocal monitoring, education about good vocal technique, and healthy vocal exploration across the entire vocal range. "I think it was keeping everything alive because if you don't use it, you lose it. Mr. Litton made my voice change a very good experience. I didn't feel bad about losing my treble voice at all" (272). As each voice change experience is unique, special attention to male vocal needs and the provision of an all-male singing environment might be advantageous for male singers during voice change (Kennedy 2004).

An intrinsic case study with her own male choir students allowed Sweet (2010) to examine their perceptions of singing and choral participation in an effort to learn more about her own middle school choral program. "My goal was to gain knowledge of this particular case. I did not conduct research to learn about other cases or about a general problem" (6). A group interview was held with five eighth-grade male choral students who participated in both the daily eighth-grade mixed choir and Choralier Men, an all-male, auditioned, after-school choir. Additional data included informal field notes, concert programs, difficulty level of choral music, and Sweet's personal insights and observations as the boys' teacher and participant observer.

Significant differences existed between student experiences in the daily mixed choir and Choralier Men, especially with regard to peer musical involvement and interactions; the boys consistently preferred Choralier Men. Contrary to Kennedy's (2004) findings, Sweet's male students placed no focus on the single-gender singing environment of Choralier Men, but rather emphasized the importance of teamwork and dedication in a choir or ensemble. Most important to the boys were "opportunities for middle school male singers to work with others who embody similar motivation, goals, and desires regarding singing" (11). As a result of this study, Sweet increased levels of student accountability—both musically and behaviorally—in all ensembles and maintained extracurricular choirs for male and female singers, resulting in a more comprehensive choral program.

5.3.3. Participation with the Music

For his dissertation, Silvey (2002) studied the experiences and perceptions of four high school choral students as they prepared *Rejoice in the Lamb* (Britten), *The Best of All Possible Worlds* (Bernstein, arr. Page), *Magnificent Horses* (arr. Ling-Tam), *La Foi* (Rossini), *Three Flower Songs* (Beach), and *Come Ye Makers of Song* (Henderson). The choral music teacher's role in this process was secondarily examined. Through the frameworks of phenomenology, ethnography, and case study, Silvey collected data through student journals, interviews, observations, and stimulated recall.

The profundity and nature of experience gained by the students was dependent upon a combination of factors: (a) what each participant brought to the experience, (b) the characteristics of the composition itself, and (c) how the potential for understanding was pursued by the individual or fostered in the context of the classroom (Silvey 2002).

> The act of bringing the musical work to the students could be compared to the introduction of two strangers through a mutual friend. The teacher, who already knows the musical work at some level, introduces the work to the student. How the student responds to this initial meeting and subsequent interactions with the piece depends on the piece and the student. (352)

Ultimately, each student had a different multifaceted encounter with each of the choral works; some students' experiences were more musically meaningful than others.

Experiences learning Benjamin Britten's *Rejoice in the Lamb* for three of the aforementioned students were published in a separate article (Silvey 2005). Each of the students reported mixed feelings about learning *Rejoice in the Lamb* that resulted in "varying degrees of meaning in the music they were learning to sing" (115). Silvey suggested that the choir teacher's approach to this specific work, as well as the level of complexity of the composition, may have kept students at a distance from the piece. "Perhaps their teacher could have selected repertoire better suited to student skill levels and therefore allowed the singers to have the heightened perspective that seems to allow for deeper levels of understanding" (116).

Through the framework of phenomenology, Conway and Hodgman (2008) studied the experiences of college and community choir members in a collaborative intergenerational performance project (CIPP). Two questions guided the inquiry: "What were the perceived positive outcomes of the CIPP? What challenges did participants articulate regarding the collaborative performance project?" (221). For the CIPP, the Adrian College Choir and the Lenawee Community Chorus—both under the direction of Hodgman—prepared a performance of the Fauré *Requiem* for Carnegie Hall in New York, as well as a hometown performance in Michigan. Although all participants of each choir participated in the hometown performance, only 51 of the 103-member Adrian College Choir and 42 of the 55-member Lenawee Community Chorus were able to pay for the trip to Carnegie Hall. Research participants were choristers involved in both performances and were selected via intensity sampling.

As the intergenerational chorus prepared the *Requiem*, Conway and Hodgman (2008) gathered chorus members' perspectives during focus group interviews; one interview was conducted with eight members of the community chorus and another was conducted with eight members of the college choir. Participant journals, individual interviews, and the teacher-researcher's personal log contributed additional data.

Chorus members benefited from three overarching positive outcomes (heightened performance experience, a better understanding of others, and no signs of an age barrier) and experienced two primary challenges (importance of preparation for collaboration and issues regarding the placement of singers in the ensemble) (Conway and Hodgman 2008). However, the music itself was identified as the most important positive aspect of the CIPP. In a chorister's words, "People are very different and it can be hard to find common ground. It's the magnitude and value of shared music that made this happen. The love of music was strong. (Molly, final interview)" (227).

Gackle and Fung (2009) documented the four-month process of an American youth choir preparing Chinese choral pieces for a performance in China through a participatory framework. Both researchers collaborated on research aspects of the case study in addition to sharing responsibilities of song selection and teaching the choir. Prior to this study the choir had performed non-English songs in German, Italian, Latin, Spanish, Russian, and French, but never a choral piece in Chinese. Data included documentation of strategies used to teach the intricacies of the choral works, input from choir members throughout the learning process, and evaluations of the youth choir's performance by choral directors in China.

Following the performance, the youth choir was praised for "a superb job in learning and performing the Chinese choral pieces" (Gackle and Fung 2009, 74). Therefore, the teaching strategies used in this study—teaching concepts and skills from parts to whole, the inclusion of both visual and aural demonstration and feedback, and focus on meaning and cultural context of lyrics—proved effective. From this experience, youth choir members benefited from significant musical, pedagogical, cultural, and attitudinal and personal growth (Gackle and Fung 2009). "The music, the language, the travel, the people, and the immersion into another culture was an unimaginable once-in-a-lifetime experience for these students" (76). Further choral research involving an intensive cultural submersion component was highly recommended.

5.3.4. Teacher Participation in the Choral Experience

Research discussed thus far in section 5.3 has focused on the perspective of choir students and participants. In the following studies, the perspective of the choral teacher or choral director is provided.

One of the first qualitative choral music education studies was concentrated on the influence of factors—such as personal biography and classroom role expectations—on the work of secondary choral music teachers (Huff 1989). Using ethnography, Huff observed and interviewed two choral music teachers from different demographics; one teacher taught at an all-black, metropolitan high school and the other worked with small-town, white, middle-class students. Data included observations; interviews; and historical, autobiographical, and program-related documents.

A combination of the choral teacher's personal experiences and past musical participation influenced each teacher's decision-making processes regarding curriculum, methodology, and classroom practice (Huff, 1989). In addition, teaching assignment and school setting impacted curricular and methodological decisions, as details were customized for individual teaching settings. Huff described these findings as problematic when considering that teacher education institutions usually referenced one traditional, professional model of music education based on cultural assumption.

> Programs in teacher preparation in secondary choral music education, through their affirmation of values, processes, and methodologies associated with the professional model of choral singing, may inadvertently perpetuate sets of beliefs and practices that lead teachers to contradictions once they enter the classroom. (287)

As a result of his findings, Huff encouraged choral teacher preparation programs to improve awareness of the influence and importance of biographical, institutional, and societal factors on operational and curricular decisions.

For her dissertation and accompanying article, Grimland (2001, 2005) analyzed teacher-directed modeling, defined as "an important instructional mode in music whereby teachers show students how something is done by doing it themselves as opposed to the mode of verbal instruction in which teachers tell students how something is done" (2001, 214). Secondarily, Grimland questioned whether teachers recognized their own behaviors as modeling. Participants were selected by snowball (or chain) sampling and maximum variation sampling; three choral teachers agreed to take part in the study. Data included observation, field notes, and interviews.

Teachers chose modeling as an instructional strategy for three reasons: (a) to prepare students for a musical task; (b) to demonstrate the correct way to execute a musical task; (c) and to model simultaneously with student singing to guide or reinforce correct performances (2001, 206). In addition, Grimland labeled the three categories of teacher modeling as audible, visible, and process. "Audible models are instructional activities that require the students to listen; visible models rely on students watching the source of the model; process models are those that offer a step-by-step method for completing a musical task" (2001, 207).

Instructional methodology was also the focus of research by Broomhead (2006), who compared three choral teachers' instructional techniques for achieving performance expression. "If students are to develop a well-rounded set of musical skills and understandings, expressiveness, as one of our most valued performance aspects, must be an instructional priority" (7). Choral teachers participants were selected as a result of their "reputations for producing expressive performances" (10).

Instructional strategies utilized by the three teachers did not originate from a formal set of techniques or methods. In fact, instructional techniques regarding performance expression went beyond "verbal" or "nonverbal" cues; most were a unique combination of both.

> The source of the teachers' strategies is unknown, and their behaviors had the feel and appearance of being quite instinctive and spontaneous. The question of instinct versus learned behavior is raised by this finding. If these behaviors were primarily instinctive, the implication is that teacher education has little to do beyond identifying individuals with such inborn talents and propensities. (Broomhead 2006, 17)

From these findings Broomhead identified seven new categories of instructional strategies: student-initiated input, teacher inquiry, referential, demonstration, teacher feedback, detailing, and conducting. "Teachers might use this insight to reevaluate their own practices and become more purposeful in how they choose to teach expressiveness" (18).

Butke's (2003, 2006) dissertation and associated article examined the influence of a reflective process on five choral music teachers' pedagogical and curricular approaches. The research framework was both descriptive and generative:

> As a descriptive study, the intention was to describe the ways in which teachers engage in a reflective process. As a generative study, the goal was to bring to the surface issues that arise in teaching, new ideas for pedagogy and curriculum, and new approaches of reflection. (2006, 57)

Overall, the reflective process allowed the choral teachers to closely examine their belief system by "confirming, denying, and challenging various pedagogical, curricular, personal/professional, and critical topics" (Butke 2006, 66) and five noteworthy findings emerged from data (2003, 2006). First, constructive dialogues proved helpful for choral teachers in reflecting upon teaching practice. Second, perfectionism influenced teacher reflective practice and "tended to manifest through frustration with their effectiveness and level of efficiency" (2006, 66). Third, concerns about time constraints for reflection affected only some participants, not all. The fourth finding exposed emotional fluctuations during the reflective process as teachers reported both pleasure and pain while reflecting on their practice; "Reflection is not neutral, nor without emotional impact" (2003, 275). The fifth finding revealed that reflective practice effectively assisted change in teaching practice.

5.3.5. Conclusion

Within section 5.3 of this chapter, participation and experiences in choir were examined through the perspective of high school and middle school students, as well as choral conductors and directors. Through a variety of research methodologies, from action research (Conway and Borst 2001), grounded theory (Parker 2009), narrative and flow theory (Freer 2009b), and possible selves construct (Freer 2009c) to case study (Carlow 2004, 2006; Gackle and Fung 2009; Silvey 2002, 2005; Sweet 2010), ethnography (Huff 1989; Kennedy 2004; Silvey 2002, 2005), descriptive and generative frameworks (Butke 2003, 2006), philosophical framework (Parker 2011), and phenomenology (Conway and Hodgman 2008; Silvey 2002, 2005), researchers acknowledged that choral singers' varied backgrounds and prior musical experiences dictate an array of musical and social needs that must be recognized and addressed by choral music educators. In addition, the reviewed research centered on positive choral experiences and participation; research did not overtly seek to address negative experiences or focus on reasons people elected to not participate in choir.

Specifically within the final part of section 5.3.4, "Teacher Participation in the Choral Experience," the four studies (Broomhead 2006; Butke 2003, 2006; Grimland 2001, 2005; Huff 1989) addressed a specific approach to teaching or an instructional technique aimed to increase the effectiveness of choral teaching practice. Each of the discussed techniques was found to be most effective when combined with teacher instinct and individual interpretation of a teaching situation.

5.4. Moving Forward

Although it is the nature of qualitative research to not be generalized, broad trends emerged within this review of qualitative choral music education studies. Research revealed that safe spaces are valuable to choral teachers and students, choir members, and directors. In addition, the choral environment and qualities of the teacher have power to positively and/or negatively sway choral participation, regardless of a chorister's stage of life. From this review it is clear that participation in choral music can be a multifaceted experience, as can benefits received from participation.

Because of the small number of published qualitative choral studies, it is understandable that not every cross-section of the choral population is represented. That said, two groupings of people are clearly missing when previously selected participants are considered. The perspectives of adolescent male singers are strongly represented in published research; however, no qualitative research specifically focused on female adolescent choir students, even with urging from researchers such as O'Toole (1994, 2000, 2005). In fact, authors of studies on adolescent male choral students often suggested future research with adolescent female choristers, but nothing has yet been completed and published. Freer (2006) justified his focus on boys versus girls:

> I believe strongly that girls' voices should not be excluded from our conversations, but I argue here that we have not adequately listened to boys' perspectives, and we therefore do not really know what steps might be effective in attracting and retaining boys within school choral music programs. (70)

Also, as discussed in section 5.3, little qualitative research has been conducted with former choral students or non-singers—although it is often recommended for future inquiry. With the exception of Freer (2009a, 2009b, 2009c), former choral members or non-singers are underrepresented in qualitative choral research.

In many ways, research in choral music education is still in its infancy, leaving much for discovery and discussion. Through the work of current researchers, and by cultivating continued growth and interest in the profession, we benefit our educators and singers. As educators, we must continue to expand our music education worldview and endeavor to expand our research in choral music education.

References

Abril, C. 2007. "I Have a Voice but I Just Can't Sing: A Narrative Investigation of Singing and Social Anxiety." *Music Education Research* 9 (1): 1–15.

Adderley, C., M. Kennedy, and W. Berz. 2003. "'A Home Away from Home': The World of the High School Music Classroom." *Journal of Research in Music Education* 51 (3): 190–205.

Borst, J. D. 2002. "The Exploration and Description of the Teaching Life of Two Exemplary Choral Teachers: A Comparative Case Study." PhD diss. ProQuest (Order No. 3064204), Michigan State University.

Broomhead, P. 2006. "A Study of Instructional Strategies for Teaching Expressive Performance in the Choral Rehearsal." *Bulletin of the Council for Research in Music Education* 167: 7–20.

Butke, M. A. 2003. "Reflection on Practice: A Study of Five Choral Educators' Reflective Journeys." PhD diss. ProQuest (Order No. 3093631), The Ohio State University.

Butke, M. A. 2006. "Reflection on Practice: A Study of Five Choral Educators' Reflective Journeys." *Update: Applications of Research in Music Education* 25 (1): 57–69.

Carlow, R. 2004. "Hearing Others' Voices: An Exploration of the Musical Experiences of Immigrant Students Who Sing in High School Choir." PhD diss. ProQuest (Order No. 3152852), University of Maryland.

Carlow, R. 2006. "Diva Irina: An English language Learner in High School Choir." *Bulletin of the Council for Research in Music Education* 170: 63–77.

Conway, C., and J. Borst. 2001. "Action Research in Music Education." *Update: Applications of Research in Music Education* 19 (2): 3–8.

Conway, C., and T. M. Hodgman. 2008. "College and Community Choir Member Experiences in a Collaborative Intergenerational Performance Project." *Journal of Research in Music Education* 56 (3): 220–37.

Fottland, H. 2004. "Memories of a Fledgling Teacher: A Beginning Teacher's Autobiography." *Teachers and Teaching: Theory and Practice* 10 (6): 639–62.

Freer, P. K. 2006. "Hearing the Voices of Adolescent Boys in Choral Music: A Self-Story." *Research Studies in Music Education* 27 (1): 69–81.

Freer, P. K. 2009a. "Boys' Voices: Inside and Outside Choral Music." In *Music Experience throughout Our Lives: Expanding the Boundaries of Music Education*, edited by J. L. Kerchner, and C. Abril, 219–36. Lanham, MD: Rowman and Littlefield Education.

Freer, P. K. 2009b. "Boys' Descriptions of Their Experiences in Choral Music." *Research Studies in Music Education* 31(2): 142–60.

Freer, P. K. 2009c. "'I'll Sing with My Buddies': Fostering the Possible Selves of Male Choral Singers." *International Journal of Music Education* 27 (4): 341–55.

Gackle, L., and C. V. Fung. 2009. "Bringing the East to The West: A Case Study in Teaching Chinese Choral Music to a Youth Choir in the United States." *Bulletin of the Council for Research in Music Education* 182: 65–77.

Grimland, F. H. 2001. "Characteristics of Teacher-Directed Modeling Evidenced in the Practices of Three Experienced High School Choral Directors." PhD diss. ProQuest (Order No. 3073526), University of North Texas.

Grimland, F. 2005. "Characteristics of Teacher-Directed Modeling in High School Choral Rehearsals." *Update: Applications of Research in Music Education* 24 (1): 5–14.

Haywood, J. 2006. "You Can't Be in My Choir if You Can't Stand up: One Journey toward Inclusion." *Music Education Research* 8 (3): 407–16.

Huff, D. M. 1989. "The Impact of Interactions with Students, Community, Colleagues and the Institution of Schooling on the Teaching Practices of Secondary Choral Music Educators: Two Case Studies." PhD diss. ProQuest (Order No. 8923377), University of Wisconsin.

Kennedy, M. A. 2002. "'It's Cool Because We Like to Sing': Junior High School Boys' Experience of Choral Music as an Elective." *Research Studies in Music Education* 18 (1): 26–36.

Kennedy, M. C. 2004. "'It's a Metamorphosis': Guiding the Voice Change at the American Boychoir School." *Journal of Research in Music Education* 52 (3): 264–80.

Krueger, P. J. 1985. "Influences of the Hidden Curriculum upon the Perspectives of Music Student Teachers: An Ethnography." PhD diss. ProQuest (Order No. 8511153), University of Wisconsin.

Markus, H., and P. Nurius. 1986. "Possible Selves." *American Psychologist* 41: 954–69.

Mills, M. M. 2008. "The Effects of Participation in a Community Children's Choir on Participant's Identity: An Ethnographic Case Study." PhD diss. ProQuest (Order No. 3312721), Michigan State University.

Mills, M. 2010. "Being a Musician: Musical Identity and the Adolescent Singer." *Bulletin of the Council for Research in Music Education* 186: 43–54.

O'Toole, P. 1994. "I Sing in a Choir, but I Have 'No Voice!'" *The Quarterly Journal of Music Teaching and Learning* 4–5 (5–1): 65–77.

O'Toole, P. 2000. "Why I Don't Feel Included in These Musics or Matters." *Bulletin of the Council for Research in Music Education* 144: 28–39.

O'Toole, P. 2005. "I Sing in a Choir, But I Have 'No Voice!'" *Visions of Research in Music Education* 6. http://www-usr.rider.edu/~vrme/.

Parker, E. A. C. 2009. "Understanding the Process of Social Identity Development in Adolescent High School Choral Singers: A Grounded Theory." PhD diss. ProQuest (Order No. 3350454), University of Nebraska-Lincoln.

Parker, E. C. 2010. "Exploring Student Experiences of Belonging within an Urban High School Choral Ensemble: An Action Research Study." *Music Education Research* 12 (4): 339–52.

Parker, E. C. 2011. "Uncovering Adolescent Choral Singers' Philosophical Beliefs about Music-Making: A Qualitative Inquiry." *International Journal of Music Education* 29 (4): 305–17.

Silvey, P. E. 2002. "Learning Music from the Inside: The Process of Coming to Know Musical Works as Experienced by Four High School Choral Singers." PhD diss. ProQuest (Order No. 3070436), University of Illinois – Urbana-Champagne.

Silvey, P. E. 2005. "Learning to Perform Benjamin Britten's Rejoice in the Lamb: The Perspectives of Three High School Choral Singers." *Journal of Research in Music Education* 53 (2): 102–119.

Stengel, B. S. 2010. "The Complex Case of Fear and Safe Space." *Studies in Philosophy and Education* 29 (6): 523–40.

Sweet, B. 2008. "Everybody's Somebody in My Class: A Case Study of an Exemplary Middle School Choir Teacher." PhD diss. ProQuest (Order No. 3348226), Michigan State University.

Sweet, B. 2010. "A Case Study: Middle School Boys' Perceptions of Singing and Participation in Choir." *Update: Applications of Research in Music Education* 28 (2): 5–12.

Toraiwa, T. 2009. "Empowerment and Construction of a Safe Space in a Women's Studies Classroom." *Educational Studies in Japan: International Yearbook* 4: 67–78.

CHAPTER 6

A CRITICAL ANALYSIS OF QUALITATIVE RESEARCH ON LEARNING TO TEACH MUSIC IN PRESERVICE MUSIC TEACHER EDUCATION

MARK ROBIN CAMPBELL AND
LINDA K. THOMPSON

IN current scholarship on learning to teach music within preservice music teacher education programs, systematic synthesis or critique of existing studies drawn from the qualitative research paradigm is virtually nonexistent. What does exist are categorical reviews of studies that address music teacher education from a range of topics, including such things as reform-mindedness (Thiessen and Barrett 2002), student teaching (Rideout and Feldman 2002), programmatic structure (Boardman 1990), or instructional and evaluation processes (Verrastro and Leglar 1992).

A syntopical reading of extant studies that draw from the qualitative paradigm, however, indicates several recurrent areas of interest and study contexts. Appearing frequently are (a) the study of preservice teachers' beliefs related to education aspects and phenomena, and (b) the reporting of the perceived effects of various experiential learning activities associated with music teaching or learning. Despite the existence of these studies, much of the work remains uncoordinated, with many aspects of learning to teach music clouded or unclear. Our reading of these studies also indicates a need for the kinds of critique Colwell (2005) advocates for in his appeal to the research community to develop "critical friends." What this plea calls for is a serious and sustained critique of the adequacy and quality of work done, including the breadth and depth of topics within music teacher education, and more particularly an interest in the topic of learning to teach music.

Given the state of knowledge on learning to teach music—particularly within preservice programs—there is vital need for research to illuminate conceptual, empirical, and normative issues. The qualitative perspective—for both programmatic and practical reasons—allows us to focus particularly on the phenomenon in order to describe and analyze what is going on so that relationships between teacher education and teacher learning can be studied. Given also the pressing need for both literature synthesis and critique, this chapter examines qualitative research from 1990 to the present focused on how people learn to teach music in preservice music teacher education programs. Our primary goal is to coordinate and synthesize what is known currently about how people learn to teach music. Our second goal is to provide directions for future research and considerations for improving quality.

6.1. Theoretical Framework

We draw our theoretical perspective regarding research in learning to teach from Carter (1990, 307) in that learning is a matter of framing how one conceives of "what is to be learned and how that learning might take place." We do not define "learning to teach music" or create a specific description of it. Instead we identify incidences in the literature where characterizations have been given, asking the reader to situate the ideas within larger contexts such as program orientations and historic traditions that reflect different assumptions of how learning to teach transpires. Framing our review this way allows us to consider that all research is provisional and dependent upon the perspectives of the individuals involved in the endeavor. In addition, this perspective allows us to include any research within the qualitative paradigm that has the potential to contribute to understanding what learning to teach music means.

Within music teacher education programs, learning to teach music can be said to occur within the specific courses and experiences afforded within a program, along with the specific practices found within them. According to Wideen, Mayer-Smith, and Moon (1998, 132), it is within a programmatic setting that the "action of learning takes place." Thus a program's goals, expectations, orientations, and history also have an important function in characterizing learning to teach music. That current music teacher education programs can be characterized as a complex amalgam of overlapping, contradictory, and even theoretically opposed perspectives would not be an overstatement. Rather than parsing out particular theoretical orientation as a foundation for each study (e.g., positivist, progressive, or critical), we chose to look at study purpose, data selection, methodology, and results. Our look at the literature about learning to teach music was inductive; however, we did identify specific contexts in which each study took place.

6.2. Methodological Framework

6.2.1. Parameters

We approached the review of studies systematically and relied conceptually on the methodological approach designed by Wideen, Mayer-Smith, and Moon (1998) in their critical analysis of the research on learning to teach. As a starting point, we used the list of refereed and tiered journals in music education as constructed by music education research faculty at Northwestern University, based upon survey responses from senior professors at "Big Ten" universities in 2006 (Committee on Institutional Cooperation 2006). Although this list contained both research and professional journals, we examined articles and titles from research journals only. A total of 24 research journals were listed with 8 in tier 1, 6 in tier 2, and 10 in tier 3. To expand our survey, we examined research publications sponsored by the American Educational Research Association and the National Association for Music Education (formerly known as MENC). Dissertations Abstracts and the ERIC databases yielded additional material. From these searches we selected studies that were (a) empirical, that is, data were collected from preservice teachers' experiences, (b) concerned with any aspect of learning to teach music, and (c) designed to capture any aspect of how preservice teachers learn to teach, including evaluative or action-oriented studies using qualitative methods. Using the 1994/1996 qualitative methodologies conferences at the University of Illinois as benchmarks, we set the study inclusion date at 1990, examining studies from that date forward. Our process identified 83 studies.

6.2.2. Procedures

Studies were categorized according to type, using an amalgamation of (a) Creswell's (2008) system for classifying qualitative inquiry and design into phenomenology, ethnography, case study, grounded theory, or historical studies; and (b) Patton's (2002) typology for addressing evaluation and action-oriented research studies. Mixed methods and narrative inquiry were added to our initial classification system as the search progressed. Studies were then classified according to fundamental purpose (or focus/interest). Results of this procedure can be found in Table 6.1. Examination of column 1 of Table 6.1 shows overlap, as many studies had multiple purposes, focuses, interests, or contexts. Specific information regarding participants, methods of gathering data, data analyses procedures, and results for each study was recorded in a working table. In order to illuminate both conceptual and normative issues in learning to teach music, we purposefully chose to present primarily study results in order to preserve the conceptual framework of the review. In a

Table 6.1 Emergent and Analytic Categories of Interest and Research Type*

Purpose/Focus/Interest	n	Type	n
Improvement/Interventions	45	Case Study	33
Perceptions or Attitudes	34	Evaluation	33
Beliefs or Concerns	32	Phenomenology	11
Program Evaluations	7	Action	11
Cooperating Teachers/University Supervisors	7	Ethnography/Grounded Theory	44
		Mixed Methods	3
Mentoring	4	Narrative	2
Conducting	3		
Beginning Teachers	3		

*Note: Column totals do not reflect total number of studies in that typologies and purposes overlapped in some instances.

few instances we did provide pertinent information about participants or data where clarification seemed necessary. Table 6.2 provides participant information. Figure 6.1 shows in aggregate form the kinds of data gathering procedures employed in the studies reviewed.

6.2.3. Analysis

We conducted an inductive analysis of the entire set of studies, looking singularly at each study and then comparatively across all studies for themes, categories, links, and relationships. Analysis suggested three focus areas: (a) beliefs or concerns of preservice music teachers, (b) perceptions or attitudes of preservice music teachers regarding some aspect of learning to teach, and (c) specific course improvements/interventions by music teacher educators for evaluative purposes that would help preservice teachers learn to teach. Additional subcategories within each of these study foci included the arenas in which a study was carried out—student teaching, field experiences, or individual courses (e.g., methods, laboratory experiences, practicums, technology course) (see Table 6.2). Evaluation studies could be further broken into formative or summative orientations, including action-oriented elements or broad program evaluation components.

Both authors read each study in order to develop a common vocabulary and interpretive framework for the entire review and worked from an online-shared document work site that allowed for individual and simultaneous revision of the review. Running notes on different aspects of each study served as a basis for evaluation and critique;

Table 6.2 Studies by Course Specificity*

Course	n
Ensemble	1
Methods	
Instrumental	6
Choral	3
Unspecified Methods	3
General (elementary)	2
Practicum / Lab	
General (elementary)	3
Unspecified Practicum	2
Instrumental Techniques	2
Instrumental Practicum	2
String Project—Practicum	1
Instrumental Teaching Lab	1
Field Experiences	
Band Field Experience	2
Unspecified Field Experiences	2
Early Childhood	1
General (Elementary)	1
Other	
Service Learning	4
Introduction to Music Education	3
Technology	3
Band-Theater Seminar	1
Wind-Band Literature	1
Cultural Immersion Class	1
Student Teaching	18

*Table reflects only those studies specifying a particular course. Some studies involved multiple courses. Some studies involved participants over multiple years.

these notes were kept individually and discussed on an ongoing basis. Discussion was designed to (a) check each author's theoretical perspectives and interpretations of preservice music teacher education research and literature, (b) critique the strengths and weaknesses of the studies, (c) articulate the substantive findings and interpretations of each study, and (d) articulate the major themes to emerge out of the analysis of the entire set of studies.

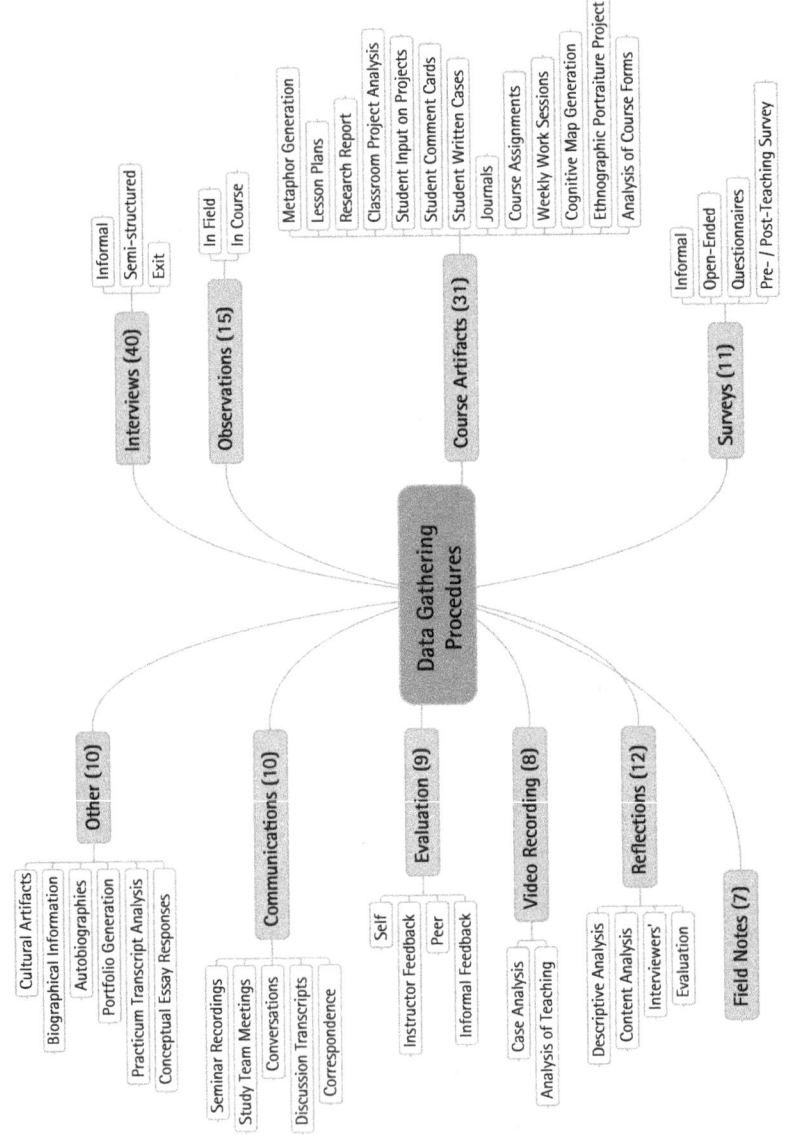

FIGURE 6.1. Aggregate of data gathering procedures.

Note: the parenthetical number refers to studies reporting specific data gathering procedures.

6.3. Mapping the Territory

Figures 6.2, 6.3, and 6.4 present in graphic form the results of our review. Within the three themes to emerge are located subtopics. We realize that we had several options in representing the literature within each theme, but chose to focus on ideas as a structure for portraying how preservice music teachers learn to teach music. Another fruitful and pragmatic approach would be to represent the literature in a temporal structure—such as year one of a program through student teaching. We leave this for future work. Our main goal was to represent the literature in a conceptual way that furthered our understanding of what it means to learn to teach music.

6.4. Results of the Review

6.4.1. Preservice Teachers' Beliefs or Concerns about Learning to Teach Music

Four aspects situated in beliefs or concerns that contribute to understanding how preservice music education teachers learn to teach music are (a) relevance and influence of prior knowledge or experiences; (b) concerns about self, technical, and impact issues; (c) beliefs about teaching linked to images of practice; and (d) reflection on or in teaching that generates self-awareness.

6.4.1.1. *Relevance and Influence of Prior Knowledge or Experiences*

It is clear that preservice music teachers' prior knowledge and experiences play a key role in learning to teach. As Schmidt (1998) noted, experienced-based understandings act as a foundation upon which preservice teachers' build, store, revise, reject, and refine their knowledge about teaching. Derived explicitly from and built upon their own experiences as students, these experiential understandings (supplemented with current learnings within the preparation program) act as "principles of education" (Schmidt 1998, 39) in constructing and evaluating past and existing images of teachers and practices. In addition, performance-related music learning experiences and musical orientations (instrumental or vocal performance) figure into their constructions of learning to teach music (Arostegui 2004; Campbell 1999; Ferguson 2004; Gohlke 1994). Like their experiences as students, these orientations toward subject matter and images of teachers/teaching tend to be potent, robust, and tenacious.

For example, prior experiences working with school-age children, along with personal notions of what constitutes a proper teaching role, affect the extent to which preservice teachers are willing or able to adopt or adapt specific teaching techniques, particularly those related to managing a classroom during student teaching (Schmidt

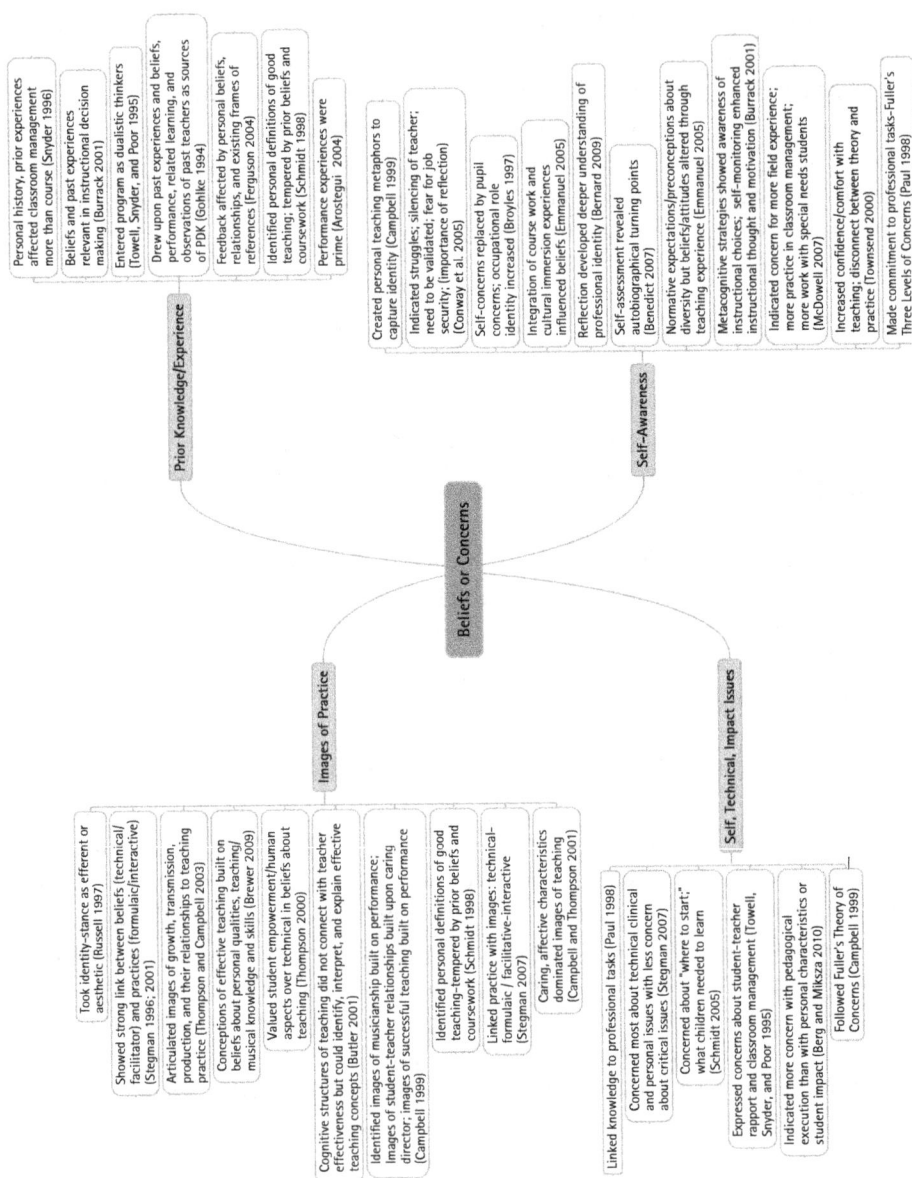

FIGURE 6.2. Preservice teachers' beliefs or concerns about learning to teach music. PDK, Professional Development Knowledge.

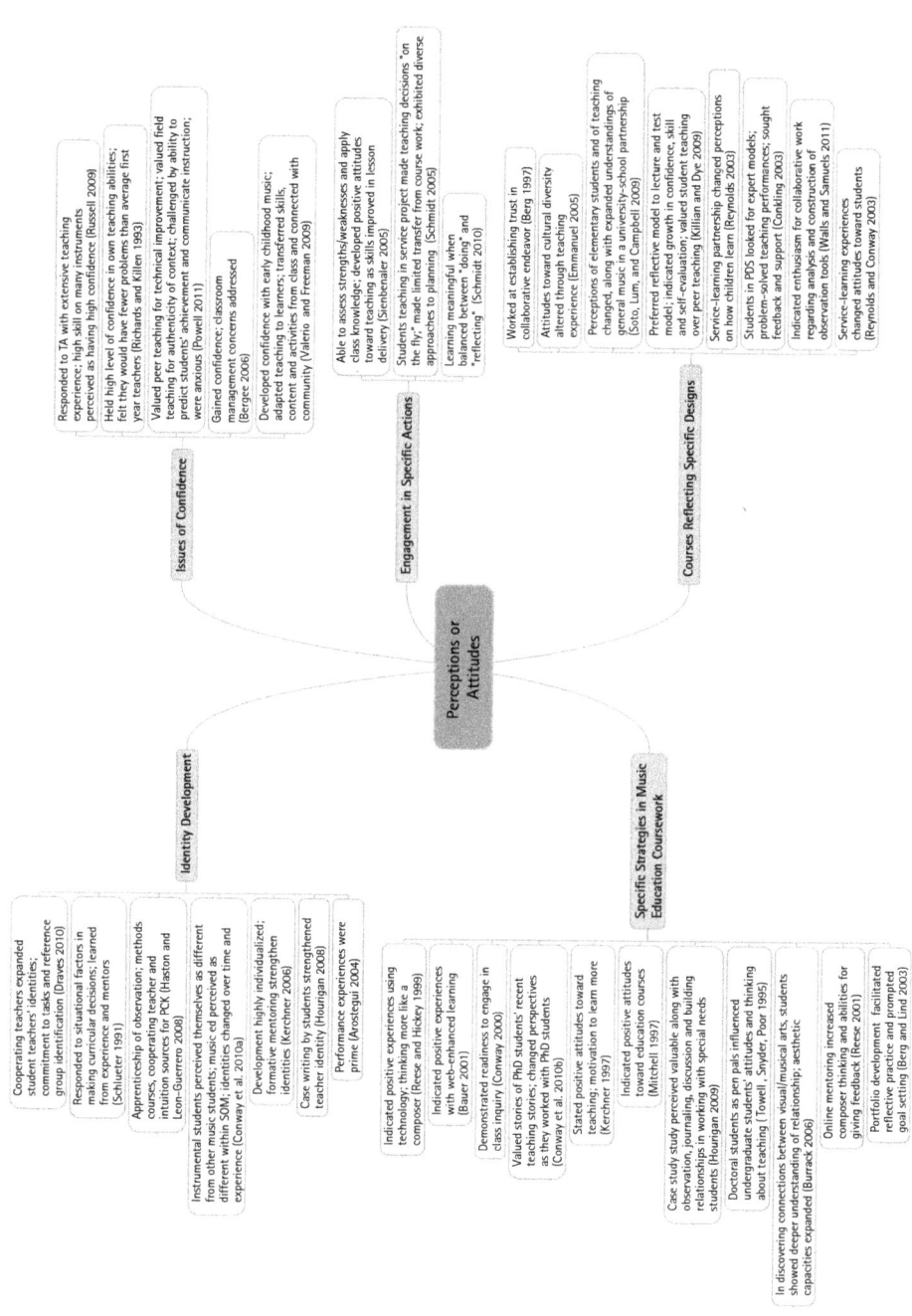

FIGURE 6.3. Perceptions or attitudes regarding learning to teach music.

PCK, Pedagogical Content Knowledge; PDS, Professional Development School; SOM, School of Music.

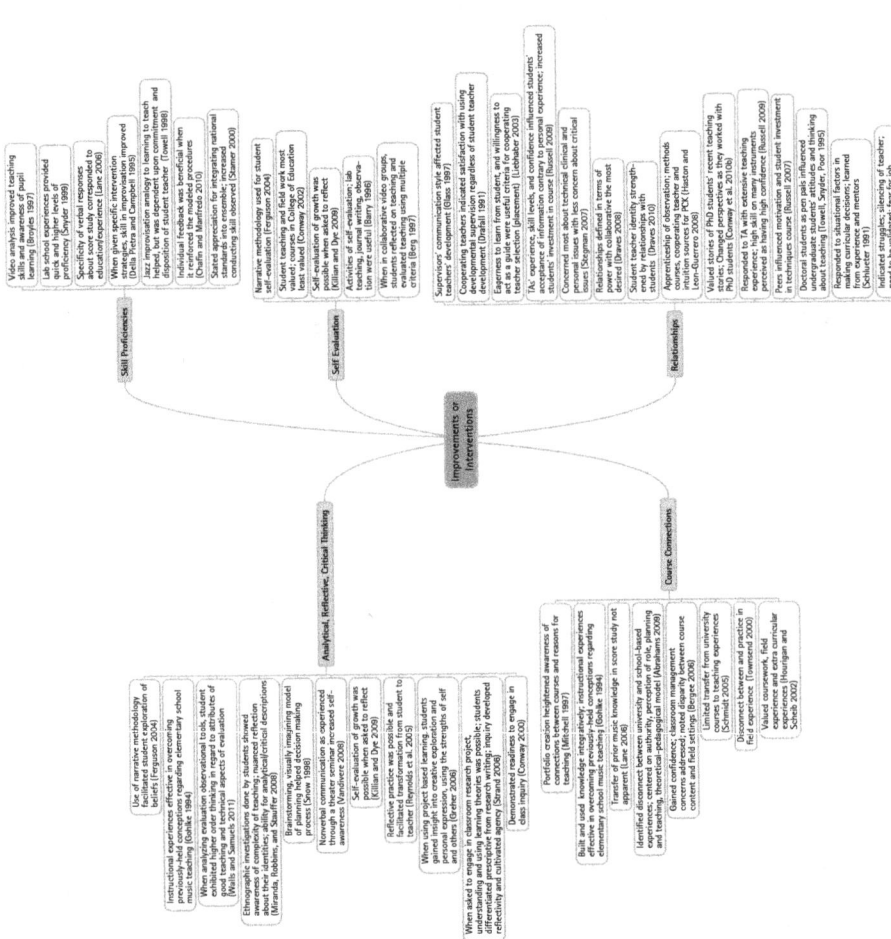

FIGURE 6.4. Improvements/interventions aimed at helping preservice teachers learn to teach music.

PCK, Pedagogical Content Knowledge; TA, Teaching Assistant.

1998; Synder 1999). The ability to articulate, monitor, or refine instructional thought while reflecting on teaching or during teaching has been linked to student teachers' awareness of their own experiences as learners and the role these experiences play in their current thinking about pedagogy (Burrack 2001).

In addition to their observations of teachers, Ferguson (2004) identified how preservice teachers use "personal frames of references" in responding to feedback and the role it plays in guiding future thoughts and actions, including decisions about their own behavior changes and the ways in which they provide feedback to their own students. In their work exploring the role that past experience plays on learning to teach, Towell, Snyder, and Poor (1995) observed that preservice teachers often enter a program with "dualistic" thinking frameworks. That is, teaching is seen as good/bad; specific curricular experiences are seen as right/wrong. Over time and with critical reflection on past experiences, dualistic thinking tends to mitigate.

6.4.1.2. *Concerns about Self, Technical, and Impact Issues*

Studies looking specifically at preservice music teachers' concerns have used several different approaches. Among those drawing upon a priori theoretical frameworks, Fuller's (1969) "concerns" theory of teacher development, symbolic interaction theory, and role conceptualization are prominent. Naturalistic or evaluation frameworks have characterized others. In each of these studies, worry over self, technical, and impact issues related to teaching surfaced among preservice music teachers concerns. Although Paul (1998) and Campbell (1999) found a "weak" yet context-dependent linear path of developmental concerns among the preservice teachers they worked with (i.e., moving from self, to task, and then to student impact—as Fuller proposes), Schmidt (2005) noted a more complex nonlinear relationship among experience and professional knowledge when it came specifically to task skills such as planning. Studies reporting on self-concerns (not derived from Fuller's model) or role identity noted that preservice teachers have a need for developing personal rapport with students (Berg and Miksza 2010; Thompson 2000; Towell, Snyder, and Poor 1995), or a desire to be liked (Campbell 1999), or want to demonstrate a level of confidence or assertiveness (Stegman 2007). "Identifying as a teacher" (as a component of self-concern and/or occupational role identification) appears to be emergent, but is coupled with fears of failure derived from evaluation procedures within program experiences. Commitment to professional tasks and identifying with the profession likewise appear to be emergent and equally dependent upon program experiences (Paul 1998). Studies reporting technical (or job-task) concerns revealed specific worries over classroom management (Campbell 1999; Paul 1998; Stegman 2007; Towell, Snyder, and Poor 1995); lesson planning, including general teaching strategies (Campbell 1999; Paul 1998; Schmidt 2005); making "musical mistakes" (performance errors) (Paul 1998); pacing, time usage, conducting, instrument-/age-appropriate pedagogy, repertoire selection (Berg and Miksza 2010); and sequencing instructional tasks and communicating clearly (Stegman 2007). Studies reporting concern for student learning indicated a focus on preservice teachers' anxieties about or abilities related to diagnosing and evaluating student reactions to instruction (Paul 1998) or motivating students (Berg and Miksza 2010).

Overall, the concerns that seem to characterize preservice students' attentions while learning to teach tend to become more heightened as they use their abilities and knowledge in contexts more similar to those found in professional contexts rather than those found in university classrooms. Furthermore, concerns vary more or less depending upon context.

6.4.1.3. *Beliefs about Teaching Linked to Images of Practice*

Similar to study of preservice teachers' beliefs and images of practices in other areas of education (see Widen, Mayer-Smith, and Moon 1998), preservice music teachers hold a range of images linked to practice. Some studies described beliefs and images in terms of metaphors (Campbell 1999; Stegman 2001; Thompson and Campbell 2003). Others used the idea of stance (Russell 1997), while still others approached preservice teachers' images of teaching through conceptual mapping (Butler 2001) or interactionist frameworks (Brewer 2009), or emergent processes obtained from fieldwork or coursework (Campbell 1999; Schmidt 1998; Stegman 2007; Thompson 2000). Through the use of metaphor analysis, Thompson and Campbell (2003) reported that preservice teachers hold expansive ranges of images about teaching roles and practices. Prominent teaching role images included teacher as transmitter, teacher as facilitator, teacher as collaborator, and teacher as mentor/motivator/leader. Prominent practices images, less frequently discussed, clustered around ideas of direct transfer of information, with "teacher as transmitter" most commonly mentioned. In her study of student teachers' instructional successes/problems, Stegman (1996, 2007) found a strong link between student teachers' images/beliefs about their roles and their actual teaching practices. Those who saw themselves as more technical (i.e., seeing oneself as a skillful musician and possessing aural images of technical perfection) thought about teaching in formulaic ways and assumed teacher-dominated or teacher-centered approaches. Conversely, those who saw themselves as more facilitative (i.e., seeing oneself as a skillful musician and possessing aural images of musical expression) thought about teaching in more interactive teaching ways and assumed student-centered perspectives. Similarly, Russell (1997), in her study of musical conducting stances, found that student conductors situated themselves within either "efferent" (i.e., conveying information) or "aesthetic" (i.e., conveying meaning/expressive qualities) stances.

Other studies looking at preservice teachers' conceptions of effective teaching showed additional role and practice images. Butler (2001, 268), for example, found that preservice teachers' conceptions of teaching effectiveness incorporated elements of role, image, and personality. She noted that students envisioned an effective teacher in terms of a "persona"—that is, "someone who possesses information, personal characteristics, and the ability to carry out specific actions related to teaching." Brewer (2009) found that preservice teachers' conceptions of effective music teaching could be grouped according to skills, characteristics, and knowledge. Music teacher role-identities were seen to develop out of beliefs surrounding personal skills, musical skills, and teaching skills, with individual teacher identity dependent upon occupational goals and interactions with peers and other teachers. Several studies showed that preservice teachers tend to value personal characteristics as "effective teaching," including student empowerment, helping behaviors, developing positive self-concepts (Thompson 2000), caring and friendliness (Campbell 1999), sharing "love of music," and being "personally involved" with students (Campbell and Thompson 2001).

6.4.1.4. *Reflection on or in Teaching That Generates Self-Awareness*

Within the broad frameworks of professional development, occupational identity/role socialization, and reflective thinking, several researchers have examined preservice music teachers' conscious awareness of their own thoughts and actions related to various aspects of learning to teach. A common theme running through these studies is that preservice teachers are more able to articulate their awareness of issues, struggles, concerns, and commitments when they are asked to make differentiations, look for situational relationships, and then "define" or "ascribe" for themselves some kind of (professional) identity. Researchers in music teacher education using occupational identity/role socialization frameworks, for example, contend that professional identity increases when students are placed in learning environments requiring identification and use of specific instructional skills, analysis of teaching tasks and skills, critique (from peers or more knowledgeable others), reflective journaling on practice and its impact on learners (Broyles 1997; Paul 1998). Researchers using developmental or emergent frameworks have painted a more diverse picture. Burrack's (2001) work on the roles that "self-confrontation," metacognitive awareness, and articulation of beliefs/past experiences play in making instructional choices provides information on how self-monitoring and self-motivation contribute to teacher thinking and decision-making. Conway, Micheel-Mays, and Micheel-Mays's (2005) comparison of the experiences of a student teacher and a first-year teacher provides information on how issues of time, job security, "silencing of voice," and having a need for validation are common between the two situations, highlighting the importance of self-reflection in navigating these tensions and struggles. The role reflection plays in developing preservice teachers' intercultural competencies has been studied by Emmanuel (2005), who noted a need for guided field experiences in culturally diverse settings integrated into coursework. Other studies specifically drawing upon reflection (within the context of coursework or fieldwork) noted its importance in developing a deeper understanding of "self as music educator" (Bernard 2009) or identified autobiographical turning points in the stories students construct about themselves as musicians/music teachers (Benedict 2007) or in creating a sense of personal agency (Campbell 1999). A prevalent outcome from reflecting on field experiences prior to student teaching is the awareness of simply needing to know more about "everything" (e.g., classroom management, students, planning instruction, musical skills, repertoire selections, specific methodologies) (see McDowell 2007). Another finding from preservice music teachers' reflections based in field- and course-related work is the notion of developing greater confidence (Townsend 2000), as well as articulating a disconnect between the university/school setting theory and practice (see Abrahams 2009; Townsend 2000).

6.4.2. Perceptions or Attitudes Regarding Learning to Teach Music

Closely related to preservice teachers' beliefs are their perceptions about, and attitudes toward, learning to teach music. An overview of the literature relating to this aspect of music teacher preparation yielded the following themes: (a) issues of confidence, (b) engagement in specific actions, (c) engagement in courses reflecting specific designs, (d) specific strategies in music education coursework, and (e) the development of music teacher identity. While we chose not to categorize studies based solely on context, it is important to note that the majority of studies related to preservice music educators' perceptions and attitudes about learning to teach took place in the context of field experiences, i.e., observations and/or student teaching.

6.4.2.1. *Issues of Confidence*

The development of confidence in one's ability to teach—essentially one's self-efficacy for teaching—has an impact on teacher retention (Carter and Doyle 1995; Skaalvik and Skaalvik 2010), and with this knowledge researchers have increasingly focused on aspects of learning to teach that may encourage the development of this personal sense of confidence in one's teaching. Richards and Killen (1993) explored this idea, discovering that students enter teacher education programs holding a high level of confidence in their own teaching abilities, feeling that they have fewer problems than the "average" first-year teacher. However, no further studies specifically confirm high levels of confidence in preservice music educators entering a teacher education program. Rather, confidence builds from experience, with prolonged opportunities for teaching in authentic contexts providing the greatest prospects for confidence to develop.

Powell (2011) noted that preservice music teachers experiencing both peer teaching and teaching in a field experience context indicate a higher level of nervousness in the field experience setting, with three of the four participants classified in Stage 1 of Fuller's Theory of Concerns (self-concern). The ability to communicate instruction and to predict students' achievement proved challenging. However, these students valued the opportunity for technical improvement in the peer teaching setting, and authenticity of context in field experience teaching. Likewise, Valerio and Freeman (2009) documented that all but one of the preservice teachers in their early childhood music course experienced nervousness teaching in a field experience, but this abated as the children engaged in lesson activities. Feelings of anxiety ran parallel with increased teaching responsibilities, but more teaching opportunities resulted in increased confidence in their teaching abilities. However, Bergee (2006) related that while students in an instrumental field experience context reported an overall increased sense of confidence in their teaching abilities, the limited, brief opportunities for actual teaching did not allow for realistic skill development to occur. Interestingly, Russell (2009) identified that undergraduates' perceptions of high levels of confidence displayed by graduate assistants teaching techniques courses created a greater investment in the course by the undergraduates. Extensive teaching experience and expertise on multiple instruments fostered these perceptions of the graduate assistants as being highly confident, i.e., more effective teachers.

6.4.2.2. *Engagement in Specific Actions*

Shifts in attitudes and perceptions among preservice teachers often occur in relation to specific actions such as engaging in collaborative work (Berg 1997), teaching in service-learning projects (Schmidt 2005; Siebenaler 2005), and teaching in varied settings (Schmidt 2010). While the attitudinal or perceptual shifts reported were predominantly positive, Schmidt (2005) found that students teaching in a String Project held perceptions about teaching differing from those of the other participants and of the professor. These students tended to revert to planning from their own learning styles or perspectives and/or their personal learning experiences. This disconnect between the instruction preparing students for the String Project and the actual teaching was evident for all students, to varying degrees. However, in a later study Schmidt (2010) followed a group of teachers through two years of varied teaching experiences and found that Dewey's principles of interaction, continuity, and learning within community held true for these students as they developed and strengthened their perceptions of teaching through a balance of what Schmidt (2010, 142) referred to as "doing" (action), and "undergoing" (reflection). The opportunity for individual and collaborative reflection was meaningful for these students' development as teachers.

Siebenaler (2005) observed that students teaching in a service-learning project early in their teacher education program developed positive attitudes toward teaching as their skills in planning increased. Students developed the ability to assess their strengths and weaknesses, make connections with the content of their music education courses, and build confidence in their abilities to teach. Yet this early immersion into teaching in an actual classroom challenged these students as they dealt with issues of planning for student engagement, classroom management, and school bureaucracy.

6.4.2.3. *Engagement in Courses Reflecting Specific Designs*

Reflection as the overarching aspect of curricular structure was documented by Killian and Dye (2009) when they introduced their music education students to a reflective model to follow as the students taught in courses (peer teaching) and in authentic contexts (field experiences and student teaching). This model, emphasizing a learner-centered approach, focused on developing students' abilities for self-evaluation (plan/teach/archive/reflect) and the development of a high level of professional responsibility.

Students responded positively to this model, preferring it to a lecture/test model, and expressed increased confidence in their teaching abilities. As with the participants in other studies, these students valued field experiences and student teaching.

The notion of collaborative coursework influenced the development of "professionalism" for student teachers involved in a group analysis of video segments of their teaching episodes (Berg 1997). This analysis, using multiple criteria, promoted trust within the group as they reflected together on their individual teaching experiences. Likewise, preservice music teachers, working in collaboration, experienced a shift in attitudes toward observations when given the opportunity to design their own observation tools (Walls and Samuels 2011). As students made decisions about criteria for observations and had input into the evaluative process, their enthusiasm for, and investment in, the observation process grew. In addition, the instructors noted that students developed deeper understandings about the teaching process as a result of being fully involved in the process of making observations a powerful learning experience rather than a task obligation to complete.

Expanding the idea of collaboration, courses designed as university-school partnerships and service-learning partnerships, allowing preservice music educators greater opportunities to teach in authentic contexts, have shown to have particular impact on students' attitudes and perceptions about learning to teach. Because students believe that it is when they get into the schools that they will learn to teach (Thompson 2000), they find greater meaning in the partnerships that place them in schools for longer periods of time prior to their actual student teaching assignments. Students who participated in a year-long university-school partnership in a culturally distinctive community indicated that their perceptions of elementary students and of teaching changed, as well as their ideas about the role of general music, since the majority of the participants were instrumental majors who had not given much consideration to teaching general music (Soto, Lum, and Campbell 2009). Similar positive shifts in thinking occurred for students involved in a service-learning partnership between a university and a public school where there was no music program, particularly in relation to perceptions about how children learn music (Reynolds 2003; Reynolds and Conway 2003). Being perceived by the children as "the music teachers" added to the growing sense of teacher identity for these preservice music educators. Emmanuel (2005) found that students in a culturally diverse service-learning immersion project entered with predictable attitudes about working with diverse students, but over the course of the project students' attitudes were challenged and changed as their understandings of working in a culturally diverse context expanded.

The Professional Development School (PDS) model provides another perspective on university-school partnerships. Students in a choral methods course regularly met at a public high school (PDS site) where they worked alongside the choral music educator from the school and their university methods professor (Conkling 2003). Over the course of the semester, Conkling sought to uncover students' reflective thinking about their development as educators and their personal ideas and beliefs about pedagogies. Students valued the influence of expert models, and developed increased problem-solving skills. The influence of other practitioners and peers was significant as students sought feedback and support regarding their teaching opportunities.

6.4.2.4. *Specific Strategies in Music Education Coursework*

A variety of instructional strategies have been identified as influencing music education students' perspectives about learning to teach, including aspects of technology (Bauer 2001; Reese 2001; Reese and Hickey 1999), the use of cases prior to observations and journaling in a special needs field experience (Hourigan 2009), doctoral students as "pen-pals" (Towell, Snyder, and Poor 1995), a reflective model course (Killian and Dye 2009), portfolio development (Mitchell 1997), inquiry assignments (Conway 2000), integration of visual arts (Burrack 2006), and the inclusion of PhD candidates' recent teaching stories (Conway et al. 2010b).

Connections between undergraduate and graduate students strengthened preservice music teachers' critical thinking skills as students engaged in a "pen-pal" type correspondence process (Towell, Snyder, and Poor 1995). Although the undergraduate students were found initially to exhibit dualistic thinking (good/bad; right/wrong) about teaching, through correspondence with PhD students a shift from the dualistic thinking to a more reflective analysis of teaching occurred. Students' levels of writing also improved through this experience. Hearing the recent teaching stories of graduate students (Conway et al. 2010) also created a shift in thinking for undergraduate students as they experienced positive interactions with doctoral students. The idea of building relationships was also prominent in a field experience focused on students with special needs, and helped preservice teachers to value their observations in this context (Hourigan 2009). A thorough orientation process, including analysis of cases, led up to the observations, journaling, and reflections on the field experience, resulting in positive perspectives for the preservice music students' thinking about teaching students with special needs.

In studies incorporating strategies emphasizing technology, undergraduate students also indicated positive experiences. When using technology in relation to composing (Reese 2001; Reese and Hickey 1999), preservice teachers showed an increase in their abilities to discuss their musical ideas and compositions in the manner of professional composers. Bauer (2001) asked students in an instrumental methods course to describe their experiences in a Web-enhanced learning environment. He found that overall, students expressed positive attitudes about this strategy, although they expressed concern over occasional time constraints due to Web access. However, the more they worked in an online environment, the feeling of the Web as "impersonal" lessened.

As noted earlier in this chapter, reflective practice prominently factors in preservice teacher development. This idea of reflective practice provides a connective thread between these final studies that look at specific instructional strategies. Conway (2000) sought to promote a mindset of inquiry among preservice music teachers by creating an assignment requiring students to describe action research projects they might envision doing. While students did not actually carry out the action research, the process of considering and reflecting on a research project and possible outcomes revealed that students were very willing to engage in processes of inquiry and to adopt a mindset of inquiry regarding classroom life.

Music education students found portfolio development a positive and useful process (Berg and Lind 2003; Kerchner 1997; Mitchell 1997). As the students collected materials representing their work and growth as music educators, they became motivated to learn more and developed an increased awareness of their teacher education curriculum and the connections among various courses. Reasons for teaching became more explicitly clear for these students through the process of self-assessment and reflection on their cumulative work, and positive attitudes toward teaching were reinforced.

A course connecting music students and visual artists (Burrack 2006) allowed students to reflect on the connections between instrumental music literature and works of visual art, resulting in deeper understandings of the shared principles in these two art forms, and an expanded sense of students' aesthetic capacities.

6.4.2.5. *Development of Music Teacher Identity*

The development of music teacher identity constitutes a critical component in teacher preparation programs (Broyles 1997). This programmatic goal, while not always identified explicitly, necessitates shifts in attitudes and perceptions from that of a student/musician to one of educator/musician. Schleuter (1991) focused on the development of curricular thinking in preservice teachers, observing how music student teachers responded to situational factors in making curricular decisions. She found that this shift from student to teacher identity occurred as student teachers learned from experience and the influence of their mentor teachers. The role of the mentor or cooperating teacher served to expand student teachers' identities (Draves 2010), strengthening their levels of commitment to the tasks of teaching and building a sense of identification with a reference group. Cooperating teachers also influenced the development of pedagogical content knowledge (PCK) as students engage in an "apprenticeship of observation" in methods courses and student teaching (Haston and Leon-Guerrero 2008). While student development throughout the undergraduate program was highly individual, formative mentoring also served to strengthen students' developing teacher identities (Kerchner 2006).

Conway, Eros, Pellegrino, and West (2010a) and Hourigan (2008) specifically examined teacher identity development in instrumental music education students. Conway et al. found that participants perceived themselves as different from other music students and perceived music education students in general to be "different" within the school of music. Conway noted that for these students, their identities as both educators and musicians changed over the course of their experiences in the degree program. Hourigan (2008) noted that case writing by students resulted in stronger music teacher identities. Arostegui (2004), in his study of undergraduate instrumental music education majors enrolled in a Big Ten university, however, noted the primacy of performance in their constructions of being a good music teacher.

6.4.3. Improvements/Interventions Aimed at Helping Preservice Teachers Learn to Teach Music

Five ideas aimed at helping preservice teachers learn to teach music situated in programmatic interventions include (a) analytical, reflective, and critical thinking; (b) self-evaluation; (c) course connections; (d) skill proficiencies; and (e) relationships.

6.4.3.1. *Analytical, Reflective, and Critical Thinking*

Although analytical, reflective, and critical thinking experiences implicitly underpin many of studies in this chapter, several studies explicitly focused on the development of skills within these interrelated areas and showed improvements toward increased skill. For example, higher levels of reflectivity, a greater sense of agency, and differentiation between prescriptive writing from writing research were promoted through inquiry (Conway 2000; Ferguson 2004; Strand 2006). Students' abilities to use higher order thinking skills (Walls and Samuels 2011), to think critically about the complexity of teaching and reflect on their own identities (Miranda, Robbins, and Stauffer 2007), and to transition from student to teacher (Reynolds et al. 2005) were strengthened through analysis and reflection on observation and teaching experience. Project-based learning promoted creative exploration (Greher 2006), while opportunities for planning based on brainstorming and visually imagining helped choral music education students develop decision-making processes (Snow 1998). Vandivere (2008) found that engagement in a theater seminar allowed students to experience increased self-awareness through nonverbal communication. However, in all of these instances, learning directly connected to level of reflection (Gohlke 1994; Killian and Dye 2009; Reynolds et al. 2005).

6.4.3.2. *Self-Evaluation*

Closely tied to analytical and reflective thinking is the process of self-evaluation. Fostering students' abilities for self-evaluation has included use of narrative inquiry methods (Ferguson 2004), journal writing in conjunction with field experiences (Barry 1996), and video analysis (Berg 1997; Broyles 1997). An increase in students' abilities to observe differences in growth resulted. Killian and Dye (2009) saw students' self-evaluation abilities increase as they specifically followed a "plan/teach/archive/reflect" model while teaching in various contexts.

6.4.3.3. *Course Connections*

For university personnel engaged in developing curricular programs, the relationships among courses and between courses and school-based experiences seem apparent, but studies indicate that for many students the connections between theory and practice are not apparent, a discrepancy or disconnect between university- and school-based experiences exists, and the transfer assumed to take place is often absent (Abrahams 2009; Bergee 2006; Lane 2006; Schmidt 2005; Townsend 2000). Students identified field experience and student teaching as having the most value, and courses in colleges of education as being the least valued (Conway 2002). Students valued particular skills, the usefulness of coursework and fieldwork, and the role extracurricular experiences played in the teacher education program (Hourigan and Scheib 2009). Portfolio development (Kerchner 1997; Mitchell 1997) was found to increase students' perceptions of the relationships among courses and across contexts in their undergraduate programs.

6.4.3.4. *Skill Proficiencies*

Although the need to foster a synthesis of course content is essential in developing a holistic picture of learning to teach, several studies have focused on the development of specific skills or the use of specific interventions aimed at improving general teaching skills, many of which focus on the idea of specific feedback for students. For example, Broyles (1997) found that analyzing video recordings of teaching improved specific teaching skills in student teachers, but most importantly brought an increase in awareness of their own pupils' levels of learning. Skills in the integration of national standards, conducting, repertoire selection, and curricular projects improved as students participated in a choral laboratory setting (Stamer 2000). Students teaching in a lab school (Snyder 1996, 1999) with an opportunity for immediate feedback were found to quickly develop higher levels of teaching skills. Individual written feedback, along with modeling that demonstrated and reinforced instructional strategies and procedures, has also been found to be beneficial (Chafin and Manfredo 2010).

Specific instruction in improvisation as a means of understanding improv both as a musician and as a teacher brought about increased sensitivity to the improvisation process, even though students' backgrounds in improv were very different (Della Pietra and Campbell 1995). Using jazz improvisation as an analogy for teaching has had a positive effect on students' processes of learning to teach, but specific skill development is still highly dependent on the commitment and disposition of the student teacher (Towell 1998).

6.4.3.5. *Relationships*

The importance of strong mentoring relationships is a dominant theme in the literature on preservice music teacher development (Draves 2008, 2010; Glass 1997; Haston and Leon 2008; Schleuter 1991; Stegman 2007). Undergraduates look to practicing teachers (Conway 2002; Draves 2010; Haston and Leon 2008), graduate teaching assistants with recent teaching experience (Conway 2010b; Russell 2009; Towell, Snyder, and Poor 1995), and peers (Russell 2007) as "significant others" in their development as teachers, valuing the immediacy of these individuals' experiences. Interestingly, the influence of graduate music education students increased the undergraduates' willingness to accept information that differed from their own personal experiences (Russell 2009). Cooperating teachers also value the relationships with student teachers, displaying an eagerness to learn from them and viewing the cooperating teacher/student teacher dyad as reciprocal (Draves 2010; Liebhaber 2003). Likewise, cooperating teachers expressed positive attitudes about working with university supervisors in using a developmental supervision model (Drafall 1991). Student teachers, however, sometimes struggled with the classroom relationships, feeling their needs for validation were not always met and that their voices were sometimes silenced (Conway, Micheel-Mays, and Micheel-Mays 2005).

6.5. Synthesis

Figure 6.5 presents in graphic form a synthesis of the results of our review of studies. Although we would like to claim that our synthesis illustrates an interdependent ecological perspective and shows how learning to teach music is an ecosystem in and of itself, we cannot. What we can note, however, is the interconnectedness of the themes and the ideas that undergird the three primary themes. There is both overlap in study purposes and enough redundancy in results to suggest that learning to teach music is emergent, contextually sensitive, built on personal beliefs, concern/attitude driven, negotiated, and finally amenable to short-term influences, but tempered by individual historical and biographical experiences. A key connector among the various studies that contributes significantly to our understanding of learning to teach music is the explicit use of the idea of reflection on experience. A common component of many of the studies we examined involved some form of preservice teacher reflection on some aspect of self, teaching, student learning, or context. More frequently, the kind of refection observed was "Deweyan" (reflection *on* experience) rather than "Schön" (reflection *in* experience) in conception (Dewey 1933; Schön 1987). The arrows drawn between different ideas in the themes in Figure 6.5 illustrate how one can make possible connections among the individual studies. For example, reflection generates self-awareness, resulting in more specific reflection on experiences and confidence. This, then, may lead to greater perception of self, learners, and teaching, which can lead to conceptualizing skill proficiencies, bringing the teacher back to a point of reflection. Looking for links among the studies using other "connecters" such as context or perceptual/conceptual change, for example, also produces sets of relational patterns. None of this kind of patterning or synthesizing claims causality, but rather strengthens credibility, dependability, and trustworthiness of assertions offered regarding the processes of learning to teach music while simultaneously reinforcing the transferability of ideas (Lincoln and Guba 1985) into curricular and pedagogical work in the music teacher education program.

A productive way to look synthetically at the body of research as a whole and still retain a sense of uniqueness among the individual studies is to theorize learning to teach music as a process of connecting self-knowledge with social knowledge. Campbell, Thompson, and Barrett (2010, 30), in their articulation of learning to teach music as a matter of personal action, refer to this as developing an awareness of self, learners, subject matter, and the profession while simultaneously cultivating an understanding of the complexity and interrelatedness of school contexts and teaching environments. From this stance, learning to teach music becomes a matter of role negotiation and

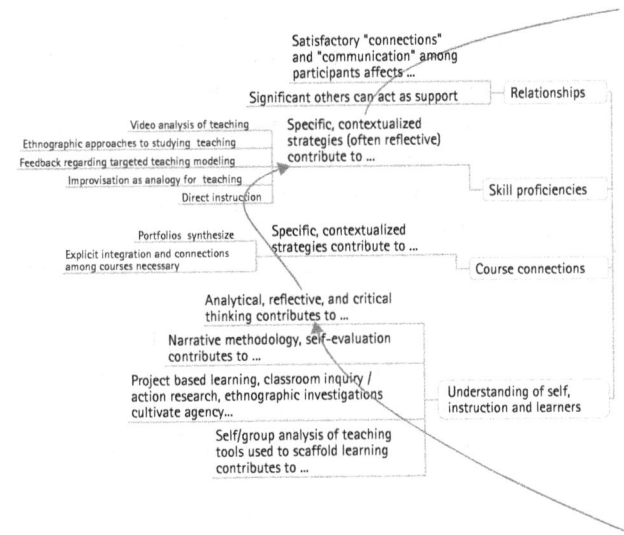

FIGURE 6.5. A synthesis of learning to teach music.

Learning to Teach Music

Beliefs or Concerns

- **Clustered around self, technical and impact issues**
  - Self
    - A need to develop personal rapport
    - Role negotiation / identification
  - Technical
    - concern of classroom management / control
    - Planning, repertoire selection, sequencing
    - Diagnosing learning
  - Impact
    - Pacing, timing, time usage

- **Linked to images of teacher role and practice**
  - Student-centered / Teacher-centered
  - Technical / Facilitative
  - Root metaphors - production, travel, transmission
  - Persona - amalgamation of personality, knowledge and (musical/instructional) skills
  - Affect, caring, fun

- **Reflection generates self-awareness**
  - Immersion in teaching tasks, self-reflection and self-critique creates struggles, concerns and construction opportunity for role socialization
  - Meta-cognition contributes to understanding instructional
  - Context throws into relief issues of time, security and agency
  - Intercultural competence in instructional thinking
  - Disconnect between university / K-12 schools
  - Confidence, self-understanding, agency

- **Based on prior knowledge and affects current thinking and actions**
  - Serves as foundation and acts as "principles of education"
  - Music performance and musical orientations strong influences on identity and career goals
  - Influences ability to articulate and modify instructional thought

Improvements or Interventions

Perceptions or Attitudes

- **Reflection on experience generates confidence**
  - Anxiety, nervousness abated through experience - reflection on action
  - Range and levels of confidence specific to setting, teaching tasks and individuals involved

- **Positive /Altered attitudes emerge out of specific learning opportunities, such as ...**
  - Collaborative work
  - Open-ended /guided Inquiry
  - Service learning projects
  - "Doing"/ "Undergoing" in multiple contexts — Self-assessment of strengths and weakness

- **Positive attitudes emerge out of specific actions**

- **Perception of self, learners, and teaching is modified as a result of specific learning opportunities using ...**
  - Technology
  - Case studying and journalling
  - Reflective modeling
  - Inquiry assignments
  - Story telling

- **Self / Identity is constructed**
  - Changes according to "task demands," course in program, "contexts demands" — Mentors, cooperating teachers, curriculum tasks
  - Shifting and categorical
    - Musician
    - Student
    - Educator

identification, within some notion or cultivated idea of good practice, with perhaps an adumbration of issues related to power and politics (Benedict 2007; Britzman 2003).

6.6. Critique and Conclusion

A key element in our review is a critique of current scholarship in the learning to teach music literature. Although we explored a number of published criteria for determining the "goodness" of a research study (see Creswell 2008; Guba and Lincoln 1994), we ultimately employed what we call a "model of coherence." That is, empirical research in the qualitative arena should be characterized by coherence among its theoretical framework (including argumentation), clarity of purpose, situatedness in relevant literature, purposeful methodology with in-depth data collection, analysis, and reporting procedures. The extent to which the body of literature we examined met the "coherence criterion" is discussed in the following.

6.6.1. Issues of Quality in the Literature

In critiquing each of the studies, we noticed two primary concerns related to design: (a) quality of reporting basic research elements, such as number of or descriptions of participants, or a description of the context; and (b) quality of establishing credibility, such as articulation of criteria used for informing methodological choices or sufficient delineation of procedures used in order to afford assurances that data were carefully handled (e.g., articulation of sources, triangulation, confirming/disconfirming during analysis and pattern/theme generation). A third concern, although related to design, had more to do with classification and type. In the first concern, for some studies it was difficult to match findings to data or data analysis; this resulted in a rather "informal" reporting of results. For studies using a qualitative framework (i.e., phenomenological, ethnography, case study, grounded theory, mixed methods, or narrative), expectations of situating questions, data gathering/analysis, and interpretations within a *well-articulated* conceptual or theoretical framework were often thwarted. In some studies, interpretations and/or conclusions were construed as themes derived from observational or interview data, and not necessarily theoretical perspectives or derived relationships. Where conceptual frameworks were provided (both theoretical and relevant research reviews), situating analysis and interpretations within the framework was uneven (i.e., not all components connected so as to create coherence).

In the second concern, primarily derived from our review of evaluation and action studies where a significant focus of research examined the efficacy or utility of specific approaches or learning experiences, it was difficult to determine the criteria used for assessing both the quality of the study and technical processes used to carry it out (see Patton 2002). In some studies, data appeared to be course assignments—collected somewhat "after the fact," and not always tied into an analysis scheme built upon a systematic pattern analysis. In other studies, information regarding data analysis was either absent or sketchily described or lacked both scope and detail. We believe that all studies built upon a qualitative paradigm (including evaluation studies) should use a set of criteria not only for designing and carrying out research, but also for reporting and finally evaluating its dissemination worth. Ultimately, research must be credible if it is to be trustworthy or have social utility (Lincoln and Guba 1985).

Lastly, we found much difficulty in classifying studies by type, based upon the wide range and actual descriptions provided by the authors to characterize their work. Especially missing was explicit description of the traditions that informed the research undertaken. The notion of study type, we think, is related to both the use and articulation of conceptual frameworks and the criteria used to design and assess quality. Lack of clarity in classification of study type, however, may not be an actual problem, as we do not see the field moving toward clarification or consensus as regards the perspectives that inform research. Rather, the move is likely to trend to more diverse study types, with the need to classify taxonomically considered less important (see Denzin and Lincoln 2011). However, we believe that presence of and clarity in articulating perspectives that inform studies should remain a hallmark of qualitative research and evaluation studies using qualitative methods of inquiry.

6.6.2. Avenues for Future Research

Three avenues for future research that we see as powerful for adding to our understanding of learning to teach music include significant attention to the *personal*, the *relational*, and the *critical*. By the *personal* we mean exploring in greater depth the possibilities of narrative forms of knowing (Bruner 1985, 1990) and the power that narrative inquiry (Clandinin and Connelly 2000) has for making "public" the personal understanding/meaning of "lived experiences." Because of its emphasis on sense—particularity, situation, context, person, and feeling—and its esteem of metaphor, connotation, intention, and agency (Eisner 1998), we think narrative's power to elucidate what it means to learn to teach music from the life experiences of those undergoing the process will yield great utility—not only for music teachers themselves, but for music teacher educators as well. Some of this kind of work has begun already (see Barrett and Stauffer 2009; Conway 2003; Ferguson 2009).

By the *relational* we mean embarking on extended and integrated programs of research from ecosystems-ecological perspectives of inquiry. Here we draw upon Wideen, Mayer-Smith, and Moon's (1998) commentary on the learning to teach research in general education and note the importance of examining the dynamic relationships among individuals (including social institutions and forces) within a specific social situation/organization and the multiple perspectives they offer. Ecosystems-ecological perspectives address the roles that multiple environmental factors play in understanding a phenomenon; the environmental view is as important as the primary participants' view. For example, the learning to teach music story must be told by at least the following: preservice teachers, their peers, and their teachers (including music teacher educators, academic professors in other areas of collegiate study, cooperating teachers, mentors inside/outside the teacher preparation program). Also, these stories require descriptions of the different landscapes in which learning takes place, including, for example, classrooms, practice rooms, buses, lunchrooms, residence halls, homes, etc. Furthermore, people and places cannot be extracted from the cultural and social policies that influence, inform, and operate upon them, including notions of schooling, traditions, and innovations. The embeddedness of ecosystems-ecological perspectives of inquiry, we think, adds valuable information to improving the existing research and existing curriculum and practice within music teacher education programs.

By the *critical* we mean embracing already established and new forms of qualitative research that derive their theoretical foundations from critical and emancipatory traditions with the explicit purpose of helping individuals and groups identify beliefs they have come to accept as "true" that "dis-empower" them and maintain the power of others (Wills 2008, 67). We believe that music education and music (teacher) education research is seriously undertheorized, underdeveloped, and marginally representative of studies within this qualitative research arena. Although our review did not exclude studies from within this tradition, our typology and classification scheme for categorizing study type and purposes did. This "disconnect" highlights the need for recognizing and increasing work within this area. Because our synthesis of studies suggests that one way to theorize learning to teach music is to think of it as a process of connecting self-knowledge with social knowledge, further examination of social knowledge using a critical lens seems particularly productive for displaying the role that authority and power play in the educative process of learning to teach music.

References

Abrahams, F. 2009. "Examining the Preservice Practicum Experience of Undergraduate Music Education Majors: Exploring Connections and Dispositions through Multiple Perspectives a Critical Grounded Theory." *Journal of Music Teacher Education* 19: 80–92. doi:10.1177/1057083709344044.

Arostegui, J. L. 2004. "Much More Than Music: Music Education Instruction at the University of Illinois at Urbana-Champaign." In *The Social Context of Music Education*, edited by J. L. Arostegui 127–210. Champaign, IL: Center for Instructional Research and Curriculum Evaluation.

Barrett, M. S., and S. L. Stauffer, eds. 2009. *Narrative Inquiry in Music Education: Troubling Certainty*. Dordrecht, The Netherlands: Springer. doi:1007/978-1-4020-9862-8.

Barry, N. H. 1996. "Promoting Reflective Practice in an Elementary Music Methods Course." *Journal of Music Teacher Education* 5: 6–13. doi:10.1177/105708379600500203.

Bauer, W. 2001. "Student Attitudes toward Web-Enhanced Learning in a Music Education Methods Class: A Case Study." *Journal of Technology in Music Learning* 1 (1): 20–30.

Benedict, C. 2007. "On the Narrative of Challenged Assumptions." *Research Studies in Music Education* 29: 29–38. doi:10.1177/1321103X07087566.

Bernard, R. 2009. "Uncovering Pre-Service Music Teachers' Assumptions of Teaching, Learning, and Music." *Music Education Research* 11 (1): 111–24.

Berg, M. H. 1997. "Student Teacher Video Cooperatives." *Journal of Music Teacher Education* 7: 16–22. doi:10.1177/105708379700700104.

Berg, M. H., and V. R. Lind. 2003. "Preservice Music Teacher Electronic Portfolios Integrating Reflection and Technology." *Journal of Music Teacher Education* 12: 18–28. doi:10.1177/10570837030120020104.

Berg, M. H., and P. Miksza. 2010. "An Investigation of Preservice Music Teacher Development and Concerns." *Journal of Music Teacher Education* 20: 39–55. doi:10.1177/1057083710363237.

Bergee, M. J. 2006. "Description and Evaluation of Experiences at a New Early Field Site." *Journal of Music Teacher Education* 15: 21–28. doi:10.1177/10570837060150020104

Boardman, E. 1990. "Music Teacher Education." In *Handbook of Research on Teacher Education: A Project of the Association of Teacher Educators*, edited by W. R. Houston, M. Haberman, and J. Sikula, 730–45. New York: Macmillan.

Brewer, W. 2009. "Conceptions of Effective Teaching and Role-Identity Development among Preservice Music Educators." DMA diss., Arizona State University.

Britzman, D. P. 2003. *Practice Makes Practice: A Critical Study of Learning to Teach*. 2nd ed. Albany: State University of New York Press.

Broyles, J. 1997. "Effects of Videotape Analysis on Role Development of Student Teachers in Music." PhD diss., University of Oklahoma.

Bruner, J. 1985. "Narrative and Paradigmatic Modes of Thought." In *Learning and Teaching the Ways of Knowing*, edited by E. Eisner, 97–115. Chicago: NSSE.

Bruner, J. 1990. *Acts of Meaning*. Cambridge, MA: Harvard University Press.

Burrack, F. 2001. "Using Reflection and Video Self-Confrontation to Uncover the Instructional Thought Development of Student Teachers In Instrumental Music." PhD diss., University of Illinois at Urbana-Champaign.

Burrack, F. 2006. "Collaboration within the Arts: A Project Involving a Band Literature Course and Studio Arts." *Journal of Music Teacher Education* 15: 43–48. doi:10.1177/10570837060150020106.

Butler, A. 2001. "Preservice Music Teachers' Conceptions of Teaching Effectiveness, Microteaching Experiences, and Teaching Performance." *Journal of Research in Music Education* 49 (3): 258–72.

Campbell, M. R. 1999. "Learning to Teach: A Collaborative Ethnography." *Bulletin of the Council for Research in Music Education* 139: 12–36.

Campbell, M. R., and L. K. Thompson. 2001. "Preservice Music Educators' Images of Teaching." In *Desert Skies Symposium on Research in Music Education*, edited by D. Hamann, 24–38. Tucson: University of Arizona, School of Music and Dance.

Campbell, M. R., L. K. Thompson, and J. R. Barrett. 2010. *Constructing a Personal Orientation to Music Teaching*. New York: Routledge.

Carter, K. 1990. "Teachers' Knowledge and Learning to Teach." In *Handbook of Research on Teacher Education: A Project of the Association of Teacher Educators*, edited by W. R. Houston, M. Haberman, and J. Sikula, 291–309. New York: Macmillan.

Carter, K., and W. Doyle. 1995. "Preconceptions in Learning to Teach." *The Educational Forum* 59: 186–95.

Chaffin, C., and J. Manfredo. 2010. "Perceptions of Preservice Teachers Regarding Feedback and Guided Reflection in an Instrumental Early Field Experience." *Journal of Music Teacher Education* 19: 57–72. doi:10.1177/1057083709354161.

Clandinin, D. J., and F. M. Connelly. 2000. *Narrative Inquiry: Experience and Story in Qualitative Research*. San Francisco: Jossey-Bass.

Colwell, R. 2005. "Can We Be Friends?" *Bulletin of the Council for Research in Music Education* 166: 75–91.

Committee on Institutional Cooperation. "Referred Journals in Music Education." Unpublished document, 2006.

Conkling, S. W. 2003. "Uncovering Preservice Reflective Thinking: Making Sense of Learning to Teach." *Bulletin of the Council for Research in Music Education* 155: 11–23.

Conway, C. M. 2000. "The Preparation of Teacher-Researchers in Preservice Music Education." *Journal of Music Teacher Education* 9: 22–30, doi:10.1177/105708370000900205.

Conway, C. M. 2002. "Perceptions of Beginning Teachers, Their Mentors, and Administrators Regarding Preservice Music Teacher Preparation." *Journal of Research in Music Education* 50 (1): 20–36.

Conway, C. M. 2003. "Story and Narrative Inquiry in Music Teacher Education Research." *Journal of Music Teacher Education* 12: 29–39. doi: 10.1177/10570837030120020105.

Conway, C. M., J. Eros, K. Pellegrino, and C. West. 2010a. "Instrumental Music Education Students' Perceptions of Tensions Experienced during Their Undergraduate Degree." *Journal of Research in Music Education* 58 (3): 260–75.

Conway, C., J. Eros, K. Pellegrino, and C. West. 2010b. "The Role of Graduate and Undergraduate Interactions in the Development of Preservice Music Teachers and Music Teacher Educators: A Self-Study in Music Teacher Education." *Bulletin of the Council for Research in Music Education* 183: 49–64.

Conway, C., C. Micheel-Mays, and L. Micheel-Mays. 2005. "A Narrative Study of Student Teaching and the First Year of Teaching: Common Issues and Struggles." *Bulletin of the Council for Research in Music Education* 165: 65–77.

Creswell, J. W. 2008. *Educational Research: Planning, Conducting, and Evaluating Quantitative and Qualitative Research*. 3rd ed. Upper Saddle River, NJ: Pearson.

Della Pietra, C. J., and P. C. Campbell. 1995. "An Ethnography of Improvisation Training in a Music Methods Course." *Journal of Research in Music Education* 43 (2): 112–26.

Denzin, N. K., and Y. S. Lincoln, eds. 2011. *The SAGE Handbook of Qualitative Research*. 4th ed. Thousand Oaks, CA: Sage Publications.

Dewey, J. 1933. *How We Think*. New York: D. C. Heath.

Drafall, L. 1991. "The Use of Developmental Clinical Supervision with Student Teachers in Secondary Choral Music: Two Case Studies." EdD diss., University of Illinois at Urbana-Champaign.

Draves, T. J. 2008. "'Firecrackers' and 'Duds': Cooperating Music Teachers' Perspectives on Their Relationships with Student Teachers." *Journal of Music Teacher Education* 18: 6–15. doi:10.1177/1057083708323140.

Draves, T. J. 2010. "Fostering and Sustaining Music Teacher Identity in the Student Teaching Experience." In *Issues of Identity in Music Education: Narratives and Practices*, edited by L. K. Thompson and M. R. Campbell, 15–35. Charlotte, NC: Information Age.

Emmanuel, D. T. 2005. "The Effects of a Music Education Immersion Internship in a Culturally Diverse Setting on the Beliefs and Attitudes of Pre-Service Music Teachers." *International Journal of Music Education* 23: 49–62. doi:10.1177/0255761405050930.

Eisner, E. 1998. "Rethinking Literacy." In E. Eisner, *The Kinds of Schools We Need: Personal Essays*, 9–20. Portsmouth, NH: Heinemann.

Ferguson, K. 2009. "Filtered through the Lenses of Self: Experiences of Two Preservice Music Teachers." In *Narrative Inquiry in Music Education: Troubling Certainty*, edited by M. S. Barrett and S. L. Stauffer, 87–106. Dordrecht, The Netherlands: Springer. doi:1007/978-1-4020-9862-8.

Ferguson, V. K. 2004. "Individual Differences in Responses to Feedback: Case Studies of Two Preservice Music Teachers." DMA diss., Arizona State University.

Fuller, F. F. 1969. "Concerns of Teachers: A Developmental Conceptualization. *American Educational Research Journal* 6: 207–26.

Glass, S. 1997. "The Role of the University Supervisor and Its Influence on the Development of the Music Student Teacher: Two Case Studies." EdD diss., Teachers College, Columbia University.

Greher, G. R. 2006. "Transforming Music Teacher Preparation through the Lens of Video Technology." *Journal of Music Teacher Education* 15: 49–60. doi:10.1177/10570837060150020107.

Gohlke, L. 1994. "The Music Methods Class: Acquisition of Pedagogical Content Knowledge by Preservice Music Teachers." PhD diss., University of Washington.

Guba, E. G., and Y. S. Lincoln. 1994. "Competing Paradigms in Qualitative Research." In *Handbook of Qualitative Research*, edited by N. K. Denzin and Y. S. Lincoln, 105–17. Thousand Oaks, CA: Sage Publications.

Haston, W., and A. Leon-Guerrero. 2008. "Sources of Pedagogical Content Knowledge: Reports by Preservice Instrumental Music Teachers." *Journal of Music Teacher Education* 17: 48–59. doi:10.1177/1057083708317644.

Hourigan, R. 2008. "The Use of Student-Written Cases in Music Teacher Education. *Journal of Music Teacher Education* 17: 19–32. doi:10.1177/1057083708317642.

Hourigan, R. M. 2009. "Preservice Music Teachers' Perceptions of Fieldwork Experiences in a Special Needs Classroom." *Journal of Research in Music Education* 57 (2): 152–68.

Hourigan, R. M., and J. W. Scheib. 2009. "Inside and Outside the Undergraduate Music Education Curriculum: Student Teacher Perceptions of the Value of Skills, Abilities, and Understandings." *Journal of Music Teacher Education* 18: 48–61. doi: 10.1177/1057083708327871.

Kerchner, J. L. 1997. "Portfolio Assessment: Tracking Development." *Journal of Music Teacher Education* 6: 19–22. doi:10.1177/105708379700600207.

Kerchner, J. L. 2006. "Collegiate Metamorphosis: Tracking the Cognitive and Social Transformation of Female Music Education Students." *Bulletin of the Council for Research in Music Education* 169: 7–24.

Killian, J. N., and K. G. Dye. 2009. "Effects of Learner-Centered Activities in Preparation of Music Educators: Finding the Teacher Within." *Journal of Music Teacher Education* 19: 9–24. doi:10.1177/1057083709343904.

Lane, J. S. 2006. "Undergraduate Instrumental Music Education Majors' Approaches to Score Study in Various Musical Contexts." *Journal of Research in Music Education* 54 (3): 215–30.

Liebhaber, B. 2003. "Mentoring in Music Education: The Collaborative Relationship among the Student Teacher, Cooperating Teacher and College Supervisor. A Qualitative Action Research Study." EdD diss., Teachers College, Columbia University.

Lincoln, Y. S., and E. G. Guba. 1985. *Naturalistic Inquiry*. Newbury Park, CA: Sage Publications.

McDowell, C. 2007. "Are They Ready to Student Teach? Reflections from 10 Music Education Majors Concerning Their Three Semesters of Field Experience." *Journal of Music Teacher Education* 16: 45–60. doi:10.1177/10570837070160020106.

Miranda, M., J. Robbins, and S. L. Stauffer. 2007. "Seeing and Hearing Music Teaching and Learning: Transforming Classroom Observations through Ethnography and Portraiture." *Research Studies in Music Education* 28: 3–21. doi:10.1177/1321103X070280010202.

Mitchell, B. 1997. "Using Portfolios in Undergraduate Music Education." *Journal of Music Teacher Education* 7: 23–27. doi:10.1177/105708379700700105.

Patton, M. Q. 2002. *Qualitative Research and Evaluation Methods*. 3rd ed. Thousand Oaks, CA: Sage Publications.

Paul, S. J. 1998. "The Effects of Peer Teaching Experiences on the Professional Teacher Role Development of Undergraduate Instrumental Music Education Majors." *Bulletin of the Council for Research in Music Education* 137: 73–92.

Powell, S. R. 2011. "Examining Preservice Music Teachers' Perceptions of Initial Peer- and Field-Teaching Experiences." *Journal of Music Teacher Education* 21: 11–26. doi: 10.1177/1057083710386751.

Reese, S. 2001. "Integration of On-Line Composition Mentoring into Music Teacher Education." *Contributions to Music Education* 28 (1): 9–26.

Reese, S., and M. Hickey. 1999. "Internet-Based Music Composition and Music Teacher Education." *Journal of Music Teacher Education* 9: 25–32. doi:10.1177/105708379900900105.

Reynolds, A. M. 2003. "Participants in a Service-Learning Partnership: Agents of Change. *Bulletin of the Council for Research in Music Education* 157: 71–81.

Reynolds, A. M., and C. M. Conway. 2003. "Service-Learning in Music Education Methods: Perception of Participants." *Bulletin of the Council for Research in Music Education* 155: 1–10.

Reynolds, A. M., A. Jerome, A. L. Preston, and H. Haynes. 2005. "Service-Learning in Music Education: Participants' Reflections." *Bulletin of the Council for Research in Music Education* 165: 79–91.

Richards, C., and R. Killen. 1993. "Problems of Beginning Teachers: Perceptions of Pre-Service Music Teachers." *Research Studies in Music Education* 1: 40–51. doi:10.1177/1321103X9300100105.

Rideout, R., and A. Feldman. 2002. "Research in Music Student Teaching." In *The New Handbook of Research on Music Teaching and Learning*, edited by R. Colwell and C. Richardson, 874–86. New York: Oxford University Press.

Russell, J. 1997. "Identifying Student Teacher-Conductors' Stances in Practicum Settings." *Bulletin of the Council for Research in Music Education* 131: 39–41.

Russell, J. A. 2007. "I Know What I Need to Know: The Impact of Cognitive and Psycho-Social Development on Undergraduate Music Education Major's Investment in Instrumental Techniques Courses." *Bulletin of the Council for Research in Music Education* 171: 1–66.

Russell, J. A. 2009. "Factors Influencing Undergraduate Music Education Majors' Investment in Instrumental Techniques Courses Taught by Graduate Student Instructors." *Music Education Research* 11 (3): 335–48.

Schleuter, L. 1991. "Student Teachers' Preactive and Postactive Curricular Thinking." *Journal of Research in Music Education* 39 (1): 46–63.

Schmidt, M. 1998. "Defining 'Good' Music Teaching: Four Student Teachers' Beliefs and Practices." *Bulletin of the Council for Research in Music Education* 138: 19–46.

Schmidt, M. 2005. "Preservice String Teachers' Lesson-Planning Processes: An Exploratory Study." *Journal of Research in Music Education* 53 (1): 6–25.

Schmidt, M. 2010. "Learning from Teaching Experience: Dewey's Theory and Preservice Teachers' Learning." *Journal of Research in Music Education* 58 (2): 131–46.

Schön, D. A. 1987. *Educating the Reflective Practitioner*. San Francisco: Jossey-Bass.

Siebenaler, D. 2005. "Music and Service Learning: A Case Study." *Journal of Music Teacher Education* 15: 23–30. doi:10.1177/10570837050150010105.

Skaalvik, E. M., and S. Skaalvik. 2010. "Teacher Self-Efficacy and Teacher Burnout: A Study of Relations." *Teaching and Teacher Education* 26: 1059–69.

Snow, S. 1998. "Rehearsing in the Choral Context: A Qualitative Examination of Undergraduate Conductor/Teacher Planning Processes and Relationships to Emergent Pedagogical Knowledge Evidenced in Teaching." PhD diss., Michigan State University.

Snyder, D. 1996. "Classroom Management and the Music Student Teacher." DME diss., University of Cincinnati.

Snyder, D. W. 1999. "Metcalf Laboratory School: A Report on a Model for Preservice Music Teacher Field Experiences." *Research Studies in Music Education* 12: 1–9. doi:10.1177/1321103X9901200101.

Soto, A. C., C. H. Lum, and P. S. Campbell. 2009. "A University-School Music Partnership for Music Education Majors in a Culturally Distinctive Community." *Journal of Research in Music Education* 56 (4): 338–56.

Stamer, R. A. 2000. "Preparing Future Choral Music Educators to Implement the National Standards." *Journal of Music Teacher Education* 9: 7–13. doi:10.1177/10570837000900203.

Stegman, S. 1996. "An Investigation of Secondary Choral Music Student Teachers' Perceptions of Instructional Successes and Problems as They Reflect on Their Music Teaching." PhD diss., University of Michigan.

Stegman, S. F. 2001. "Perceptions of Student Teachers in Secondary Choral Classrooms." *Journal of Music Teacher Education* 11: 12–20. doi:10.1177/10570837010101100104.

Stegman, S. F. 2007. "An Exploration of Reflective Dialogue between Student Teachers in Music and Their Cooperating Teachers." *Journal of Research in Music Education* 55 (1): 65–82.

Strand, K. 2006. "Learning to Inquire: Teacher Research in Undergraduate Teacher Training." *Journal of Music Teacher Education* 15: 29–42. doi:10.1177/10570837060150020105.

Thiessen, D. L., and J. R. Barrett. 2002. "Reform-Minded Music Teachers: A More Comprehensive Image of Teaching for Music Teacher Education." In *The New Handbook of Research on Music Teaching and Learning*, edited by R. Colwell and C. Richardson, 759–85. New York: Oxford University Press.

Thompson, L. 2000. "Freshmen Music Education Majors' Preconceived Beliefs about the People and Processes Involved in Teaching." PhD diss., University of Arizona.

Thompson, L. K., and M. R. Campbell. 2003. "Gods, Guides and Gardeners: Preservice Music Educators' Personal Teaching Metaphors." *Bulletin of the Council for Research in Music Education* 158: 43–54.

Towell, G. 1998. "Improvisation in Teaching: An Analogy from Jazz Performance." DME diss., University of Cincinnati.

Towell, G. L., D. W. Snyder, and A. Poor. 1995. "Listening to the Past: Using Student Journals in a Music Education Course." *The Quarterly Journal of Music Teaching and Learning* VI (3): 18–29.

Townsend, R. D. 2000. "The Holmes Group: A Private College Plausibility Study." *Journal of Music Teacher Education* 10: 24–31. doi:10.1177/10570837000100105.

Valerio, W. H., and N. K. Freeman. 2009. "Pre-Service Teachers' Perceptions of Early Childhood Music Teaching Experiences." *Bulletin of the Council for Research in Music Education* 181: 51–69.

Vandivere, A. 2008. "An Investigation of the Nonverbal Communication Behaviors and Role Perceptions of Pre-Service Band Teachers Who Participated in Theatre Seminars." PhD diss., University of North Texas.

Verrastro, R., and M. Leglar. 1992. "Music Teacher Education." In *Handbook of Research on Music Teaching and Learning*, edited by R. Colwell, 676–96. New York: Schirmer Books.

Walls, K. C., and S. Samuels. 2011. "Collaborative Design Processes for Authentic Preservice Music Teacher Observations." *Journal of Music Teacher Education* 20: 24–39. doi:10.1177/1057083710371426.

Wideen, M., J. Mayer-Smith, and B. Moon. 1998. "A Critical Analysis of the Research on Learning to Teach: Making the Case for an Ecological Perspective on Inquiry." *Review of Educational Research* 68: 130–78.

Wills, J. W. 2008. *Qualitative Research Methods in Education and Educational Technology*. Charlotte, NC: Information Age.

CHAPTER 7

INSERVICE MUSIC TEACHER PROFESSIONAL DEVELOPMENT

COLLEEN M. CONWAY AND SCOTT N. EDGAR

Music teacher professional development has been a prominent area of discussion for almost two decades.[1] National Association for Music Education (NAfME) President Scott Shuler wrote about the importance of music teacher professional development in 1995:

> The [National] standards reinforce the need for collaboration between universities and state departments of education to encourage and provide avenues for teachers to continue lifelong professional growth.... A teacher who first enters the classroom at the age of twenty-one might spend over forty years in the education profession. Certainly, over the span of a career of this length, there will be many changes in the nature of music, the nature of students, and the nature of schools. Even well prepared teachers must therefore learn to adapt to change. Old dogs must learn new tricks. (10)

Shuler suggested many possibilities that have now become standard practice in education: (a) doing away with lifetime teaching credentials and replacing them with expectations for continued study; (b) development of National Council for Accreditation of Teacher Education (NCATE)[2]-sponsored professional development schools in collaboration with local K–12 school districts; (c) screening processes for teachers at a variety of career points, including admission to the university music school, admission into the teacher preparation program, admission into the teaching profession, and continuation in the teaching profession; and (d) the development of a national system for certifying teachers (10). Although many of these practices are standard, we have limited research that examines these practices and considers ways in which this complex phenomenon may be improved.

Although federal policy has addressed teacher professional development (referred to as PD hereafter) over the past 10–15 years (i.e., No Child Left Behind, Race to the Top), only recently has the research community begun to seriously study the PD of inservice music teachers. Back in 1992, Verrastro and Leglar stated the following in the opening of their comprehensive review of literature on music teacher education:

> Inservice education, including graduate education, inservice conferences, and workshops has received less attention from the research community than the other categories [preservice teacher education]. . . . Although these studies [four studies, none of which was qualitative] offer some insights, they do not provide a sufficient basis for drawing general conclusions and therefore will not be discussed further. (676)

Verrastro and Leglar made this statement in 1992 and it is still true today. Mark Robin Campbell and Linda K. Thompson had many more studies to review when examining qualitative research and preservice teacher education for chapter 6 of this volume than Scott Edgar and I did in preparing this chapter.

7.1. Research on Professional Development

In her chapter in *The New Handbook of Research on Music Teaching and Learning* dedicated to "Professional Development," Hookey (2002, 888) identified four distinct uses of the term "professional development":

- a process of personal professional change
- the set of activities designed to promote personal professional change
- a lifelong project
- an overarching framework for professional change.

Since this source is one of the primary sources on PD in the literature, music education researchers have often used the Hookey definitions of professional development in their work. However, many researchers do not define professional development at all, and this is a weakness within this body of literature.

Hookey included six qualitative studies in her chapter, not presented in this chapter since they were previously reviewed (Dolloff 1996; Duling 1992; Junda 1994; May 1990; Robbins 1994/1995; and Wing 1977). She cited two quantitative studies on teacher PD; one a program evaluation of a specific PD program (Colwell 1996/1997) and the second, Price and Orman's (1999) content analysis of topics of PD offerings at National MENC conferences from 1984–1998. The 14 other empirical studies in Hookey's chapter examine other topics (teacher behaviors, teacher intensity, collaborative partnerships, integrated arts programs, lives of teachers research, and classroom teachers teaching music) somewhat related to PD, but not a part of the scope of our chapter as they will be addressed elsewhere in this *Handbook*.

The acceptance of qualitative research within music education since the late 1990s allowed for more researchers to examine complex topics such as teacher PD. In his introduction to the teacher education section in *The New Handbook of Research on Music Teaching and Learning* (2002), Raths suggested that music teacher education had yet to really discover new research approaches and designs that might facilitate careful study of teacher education. This chapter will highlight the emergence of qualitative research since 1995 and will suggest that the availability of qualitative research has led to more researcher interest and ability to study teacher education and PD. However, we also highlight throughout the chapter the need for researchers to be more transparent in their use of definitions and designs. One can surmise what the context is and which definition fits; however, one real problem with qualitative research papers is that readers are often in the dark about how the design process and analysis process that was in place allowed the researcher(s) to reach their conclusions.

We begin with a presentation of research on the PD of beginning music teachers defined as inservice teachers in the first and/or second year of teaching. Categories in this section include: (a) challenges faced by beginning music teachers; and (b) support for beginning music teachers in mentoring and induction. The second section includes studies of experienced music teacher (third year and beyond) PD presented within the following categories: (a) communities of practice; (b) music-making as PD; (c) graduate school as PD; and (d) action research and teacher research as PD. In the final section of the chapter we review studies examining PD in relation to teacher career cycle. We conclude with a summary and discussion with regard to how qualitative research has been used to study teacher PD and provide suggestions for future research.

7.2. Professional Development of Beginning Music Teachers

7.2.1. Challenges Faced by Beginning Music Teachers

Beginning music teachers can face challenges unique from those experienced by veteran teachers. Krueger (1996) conducted an interview-only study with 16 music teachers for the purpose of documenting teachers' perceptions of problems and challenges faced in the first year. Problems identified in this study (in order from most cited problem) included: student discipline, physical exhaustion, isolation, not teaching in primary area of expertise, scheduling, poor equipment/facilities, budget concerns, left out of decision-making, inadequate materials, and curriculum concerns. This was the first qualitative study in the literature to document the problems that beginning music teachers experience.

Individual case studies have been informative, detailing the challenges beginning music teachers encounter. I (Conway) published a descriptive case study with Mandi Garlock in 2002 (Conway and Garlock 2002) describing the challenges Mandi faced in her first year as an urban K–3 general music teacher. Data included: (a) interviews and observations with/of Mandi, (b) interviews with Mandi's building principals and mentor, and (c) daily journals regarding the first two years of her teaching. Findings were presented in Mandi's own words: "I was not prepared to deal with a student death, an abduction, reporting abuse, a first grader with clinical depression, and so many who had taken on anger as their coping mechanism" (17). "Once I had my own classroom there was no blending into the back of the class when I wasn't feeling well, skipping if I was too tired to get up, or even relaxing when I didn't feel like being on" (18). "If music class is fun, why is everybody crying? It was my daily goal to make it through without someone crying, and a weekly goal to have no one bleed (not to mention wet pants, vomit, or endless trips to the bathroom)" (20).

In another case study (Conway and Zerman 2004), Tavia Zerman and I provided more narrative findings regarding middle school instrumental music needs. Data included: (a) interviews and observations with/of Tavia, (b) interviews with Tavia's building principal and mentor, (c) Tavia's written journal from September to December; and (d) an e-mail log documenting each e-mail communication between Tavia and her mentor for the entire first year. We concluded:

> The music teacher education community must inform policy-makers and program designers that music teachers face challenges that are not faced in other classrooms. Tavia's classes are larger than classroom teachers so classroom management is different for her. She is the only instrumental music teacher in the building so isolation is even more severe. Success for many music teachers (Tavia included) is measured by their communities in terms of public performance and competitions. Choosing concert literature and planning lessons for music courses is driven by content. Generic beginning teacher programs alone do not provide the right kind of support. (82)

In a year-long inquiry in which three university researchers had nine elementary music teachers study their own classrooms, Roulston, Legette, and Lomak (2005) used teacher research (defined and expanded upon later in this chapter) to enhance the practices of participants. Group meetings and individual interviews were used as data sets. Challenges included lack of time, access to participants, lack of research knowledge, and lack of support. Benefits included providing a venue for collaboration, developing a sense of teacher reflection, and developing an identity as a teacher researcher. Conclusions suggest this sort of PD should be developed over a substantial period of time and be structured with specific goals for participants.

In Conway and Christensen (2006), we examined Stephanie Christensen's perceptions as a first-year middle school instrumental music teacher regarding PD, including: (a) in-service programs provided by the school district; (b) programs offered by the state music organizations; (c) programs attended by the teacher; and (d) informal experiences that provided assistance to the teacher. Narrative inquiry was used and data included Stephanie's daily journal, researcher observation and interview, and Stephanie's written reflections regarding beginning teacher PD material. For this final data set, I provided Stephanie with information regarding teacher PD from Danielson's (1996) model for teacher evaluation since this framework is commonly used in organizing PD in Michigan. Stephanie read the material and wrote about how the "generalizations" about teachers either did or did not resonate with her experiences. Findings were presented around the themes of: (a) views of professional development, (b) isolation, and (c) music festivals and competitions. Some of these findings speak to the fact that professional development can be alienating and unhelpful.

Schmidt and Canser (2006) and Schmidt (2008) both present the story of a struggling novice teacher, Jelani (co-author Canser), and his successful improvement through proper mentoring. This study draws from self-study, as Schmidt was one of three mentors, as well as narrative analysis, as the presentation of data is largely Jelani's story and the mentors' story of support. Discussion with mentors about teaching strategies, lesson planning, assessment, classroom management, and pacing helped guide Jelani through his first years and the challenges he faced in these areas. Elements cited for Jelani's improvement included increasing pedagogical content knowledge, addressing his self-confidence and persistence, giving him the opportunity to teach in the university's String Project classes, and the supervisor's mentoring style. Findings included newfound knowledge and skills and increased ability to better describe and assess his own teaching.

In an effort to "contribute to the novice music teacher case literature by studying the prevalent themes in the experience of 5 first year teachers" (64), Barnes (2010) collected electronic journals from teacher participants. Barnes did not report how many of the five teachers sent e-mails, nor how many pages of journals were generated in the study. She also conducted a phone interview with each of the teachers in January of their first year. Themes with the highest frequency counts included: students (behavior); students (musical); administrative; students (personal); self-evaluation (discipline); and self-evaluation (personal). These findings are consistent with past research regarding beginning teachers, further solidifying our empirical base for understanding the experiences of beginning teachers. Table 7.1 presents a summary of the challenges beginning teachers faced, discussed in the preceding.

7.2.2. Supporting Beginning Music Teachers in Mentoring and Induction

Despite the challenges beginning music teachers face, research on PD, mentoring, and induction of beginning music teachers suggests it is possible to aid these novice teachers

Table 7.1 Summary of Findings: Challenges Faced by Beginning Music Teachers

Krueger (1996)	Student discipline, physical exhaustion, isolation, not teaching in primary area of expertise, scheduling, poor equipment/facilities, budget concerns, left out of decision-making, inadequate materials, curriculum concerns
Conway and Garlock (2002)	Student death, an abduction, reporting abuse, a first-grader with clinical depression, student anger as a coping mechanism, too tired to get up
Conway and Zerman (2004)	Large class sizes, isolation, pressure of performance, choosing literature
Roulston et al. (2005)	Lack of time, research access issues, lack of research knowledge, lack of support
Conway and Christensen (2006)	Isolation, music festivals, competitions
Schmidt (2008); Schmidt/Canser (2006)	Teaching strategies, lesson planning, assessment, classroom management, pacing
Barnes (2010)	Students (behavior), students (musical), administrative, students (personal), self-evaluation (discipline), self-evaluation (personal)

in the beginning stage of their career. Programs focusing on the specific needs of those new to the profession may provide music teachers with the assistance they need to grow and learn as new teachers.

Mentoring, specifically, can help in minimizing the feeling of isolation common for beginning music teachers. Krueger (1999) conducted an interview-only study of 20 beginning music teachers to examine beginning music teacher induction and mentor practices. All participants were interviewed during the last month of their first year of teaching and were teaching instrumental, general, choral music, or some combination of the three. She found that new teachers frequently reported feeling isolated from other music teachers and other teachers. Only four of the participants in Krueger's study had been assigned to experienced music teachers as part of a mentor program and these teachers reported feelings of isolation less than the teachers with no mentor program. Four participants (not the same as had experienced mentors) received district-supported release days to observe other music teachers and Krueger reported these observations were also perceived as helpful to them in their first years.

Montague (2000) used collective case study design to examine the mentor and mentee interactions of four pairs of beginning teachers/mentors. Data included 90-minute, semi-structured interviews with each participant. Montague's findings highlight the specific nature of the teaching context in relation to mentoring and are presented in the following categories: mentor and mentee background and influences, early influences, program perceptions, procedure and protocol, mentor, mentoring style, mentor availability, role and relationship, and changing roles. He wrote: "Further analysis revealed the complex interrelated nature of the themes that combined within the novice teachers' communities of practice and situational contexts to define the mentorship" (iv). Although this data set is limited to single interviews, this study represents an early qualitative research study in mentoring (2000).

The presence of a mentoring or induction program was not always successful in diminishing the challenges experienced by beginning music teachers. Conway (2001) examined beginning music teacher perceptions of district-sponsored induction programs. Induction for this study was defined as the PD provided to the teachers outside of or in addition to a mentor program. For most participants these constituted inservice days or release days with other beginning teachers in the school or county. Data included: researcher observations of the beginning teachers, beginning teacher interviews, teacher journals, focus group meetings, mentor interviews, administrator interviews, PD documents provided by the beginning teachers, responses on two beginning teacher questionnaires, and the principal investigator's log. Profiles of the participants revealed inconsistency of induction programs, dissatisfaction with the most extensive induction programs, and the presence of music-specific beginning teacher issues. Suggestions for induction programs for music teachers include: guidance for administrative duties, help in choosing literature and in lesson-planning, observing experienced music teachers, receiving observations from music content specialists, attention to curriculum and assessment in the second year of induction, and involvement of higher education and state music organizations.

Conway (2003) examined beginning music teacher mentor practices in 13 school districts in mid-Michigan. Data included: beginning teacher interviews, teacher journals, focus group meetings, mentor interviews, administrator interviews, and the principal investigator's log. Profiles of the teachers show a lack of consistency in the types of mentor programs in the schools and varying degrees of teacher satisfaction with the programs. The lack of consistency is discussed in relation to the context of school, the teaching responsibility and classroom setting, the type of mentor assigned, and the degree to which that mentor was paid or trained. Teacher perceptions of the value of the program are discussed in relation to the degree and type of contact (i.e., weekly, informal, etc.) with the assigned mentor. The conversations between mentors and mentees often centered on the following issues: administrative duties, classroom management, parent interaction, building and district policies, and personal issues. The paper concludes with general suggestions for mentor practices including: early identification of mentor, scheduling so mentors can observe, and opportunities for getting to know one another informally.

Group mentoring was an alternative explored in Stevanson's (2005) collective case study examining three elementary music teachers in a mentoring program through the lens of three existing frameworks—the Stages of Concern (Hord, Rutherford, Huling-Austin, and Hall 1987), the Hierarchy of Needs (Maslow 1970), and the Categories of Support (Merriam and Simpson 2000). Data included individual and focus group interviews. She found: (a) group mentoring has advantages over individual mentoring; (b) elementary music teachers have unique needs not typically met in generalized mentoring programs; (c) elementary music teachers are often conflicted regarding their roles as teachers and performing musicians; and (d) there is a mismatch between mentoring programs and the novice teachers' needs.

In Jacobs (2007), five first-year high school band directors and their mentors were interviewed over a six-month period concerning their mentor-mentee relationships. Citing Rodwell (1998) and Strauss and Corbin (1998), Jacobs suggested his inquiry used a "constructivist content analysis" (2007, 11) as he analyzed the mentor and mentee data separately. He presented his findings in a "multi-case study narrative" (11). Findings provide insight into mentor-mentee interaction and mentor program structure. Jacobs's findings support the need for observation in mentoring.

When done well, mentoring can help beginning music teachers through their first years in the profession. Blair (2008) examined mentoring experiences of five first-year elementary music teachers in the same district working with her as their mentor. Data included participants e-mail correspondence with the researcher, end-of-the-year reflective journals for each teacher, the mentor/researcher's journal, and a focus group interview at the end of the year. Blair wrote:

> Two key issues arose during the year that profoundly affected the professional self-confidence of these novice teachers: their struggles with classroom management, and issues that arose during their experiences with the district's process of teacher evaluation. Within the context of these common problems, the teachers seemed to value the meetings as an opportunity to give and receive support in a safe, collegial environment, in which all those present understood the parameters of their unique jobs and cared about each other as individuals and music educators. What began as a group of individuals emerged as a community of practice. (99)

Continued investigation into the thoughts of music teachers regarding PD as they progress through their careers offers insight into changing needs and perceptions. Conway (2012) examined reflections of experienced teachers ($N = 7$) on their past perceptions of induction as documented in Conway (2001). Data collected in 2010 included participant e-mail survey responses and individual interviews. Findings suggested: (a) induction practices and professional development are still inconsistent in the field; (b) participants now focus more on students than they did in their early years; (c) participants feel as if they "understood schools" better now than they did as beginning teachers; (d) findings were inconclusive regarding the notion that music content is necessary in induction and professional development.

The purpose of Conway (2013) was to examine the current reflections of experienced teachers ($N = 13$) on their past perceptions of mentoring as documented in Conway (2003). Data included participant e-mail journals and individual interviews. In the e-mail journals, participants were responding to the data gathered 10 years previously (journals, surveys, interviews, mentor and administrator interviews). Findings categories consistent with the 2003 investigation included: (a) lack of consistency in mentor programs and teacher perceptions of their value; (b) curricular concerns; (c) music teachers still need music mentors; (d) time for mentor/mentee interaction.

New insights included: (a) mentoring can be valuable for the mentor; (b) concerns regarding who should mentor; (c) new teachers must be proactive in finding answers to questions. Table 7.2 presents a summary of findings regarding supporting beginning music teachers in mentoring and induction.

7.2.3. Discussion and Suggestions

Within the beginning teacher literature (challenges as well as mentoring and induction), qualitative research has provided the profession with descriptions, stories, and

Table 7.2 Summary of Findings: Supporting Beginning Music Teachers in Mentoring and Induction

Krueger (1999)	Mentoring and induction helped beginning teachers combat loneliness.
Montague (2000)	Background influences, early influences, program perceptions, procedure and protocol, mentor, mentoring style, mentor availability, role relationship changing roles
Conway (2001)	Documentation of induction programs provided, dissatisfaction with the most extensive induction programs, and documentation of what beginning teacher issues may be different for music teachers
Conway (2003)	A lack of consistency in the types of mentor programs in the schools and varying degrees of teacher satisfaction with the program
Stevenson (2005)	Group mentoring has advantages over individual mentoring; elementary music teachers have unique needs that are not typically met in generalized mentoring programs; elementary music teachers are often conflicted regarding their roles as teachers and performing musicians; there is a mismatch between mentoring programs and the novice teachers' needs.
Jacobs (2007)	Mentor-mentee interaction, mentor program structure, and support the need for observation in mentoring
Blair (2008)	Struggles with classroom management and issues that arose during their experiences with the district's process of teacher evaluation affected teacher self-confidence. Teachers valued meetings with mentor music educators.
Conway (2012)	Induction and professional development are still inconsistent in the field, participants now focus more on student; participants feel as if they "understood schools" better now than they did as beginning teachers; findings were inconclusive regarding the notion that music content is necessary in induction and professional development.
Conway (2013)	Lack of consistency in mentor programs and teacher perceptions of value, curricular concerns, music teachers still need music mentors; time for mentor/mentee interaction, mentoring can be valuable for the mentor, concerns regarding who should mentor, new teachers must be proactive in finding answers to questions

narratives of teacher experiences. There is some evidence to suggest that teacher research, mentoring, and induction may provide appropriate support; however, it seems as if we might know more about what does *not* work in supporting beginning teachers than what is useful.

The research does not clearly indicate the value of mentoring and induction. Nor does past research define the different positive or negative influences of mentor-only as opposed to induction-only or combined mentor-induction beginning teaching models. It is also unclear how preservice teaching experiences interact with events in the early years of teaching.

Most of the researchers reported on the beginning teachers' viewpoints, with the exception of Conway (2001, 2002), who included building administrator and mentor perspectives as well as those of teachers. It might be useful for the profession to continue to explore the perspectives of these stakeholders (i.e., administrators, more experienced teachers, mentors, parents, and P–12 students). It would be beneficial for researchers to begin to work to connect a research focus on challenges directly to ways of addressing them through mentoring and induction so we can begin to explore how or if beginning teacher programs can address the issues outlined in the challenges literature.

7.3. Professional Development of Experienced Music Teachers

Studies of experienced teacher PD are presented within the following categories: (a) communities of practice; (b) music-making as PD; (c) graduate school as PD; and (d) action research and teacher research as PD.

7.3.1. Communities of Practice

Music teachers can perceive PD as more valuable if it is conducted in a group of similar stakeholders. Standerfer (2003, 2008) conducted a multiple case study specifically addressing influences of the National Board for Professional Teaching Standards (NBPTS) process on three choral music teachers. Two of the teachers were high school choral directors, and one taught choral and general music at a middle school. Seidman's (1998) three-interview model was used and the teachers were interviewed in their school setting. Each teacher completed the requirements for NBPTS Early Adolescent through Young Adulthood Music Certification during the 2001–2002 school year, and had not received results of their submissions. Cross-case analysis led to themes related to the NBPTS process including motivation, benefits, and learning. All participants reported improvement in their knowledge, skills, and dispositions. Other issues arising for all three music teachers included a high stress level resulting from the intensity and time requirements of the process, as well as the need for personal and professional support systems. Even so, the researcher suggested the NBPTS process as a potential source of effective PD for music teachers.

Gruenhagen (2008) utilized an instrumental case study to explore the role of collaborative conversations among early childhood music teachers as a form of PD. Observing conversations at 11 meetings and conducting individual interviews with the 12 participants provided insight into the growth of the group, individuals, and changes in practice. Findings suggest PD is a process and a journey, and collaboration could help this process.

Although communities of practice can be informal, a more formal arrangement can be beneficial as well. Stanley (2009) examined the experiences of three elementary music teachers and the researcher, in a collaborative teacher study group (CTSG) designed to focus on student collaboration in elementary music. The CTSG met seven times to discuss aspects of student collaboration by analyzing video from each participant's classroom. The study was a social constructivist inquiry based on the researcher's reconstruction and interpretation of participant views throughout the CTSG experience. Using interviews and CTSG meeting transcripts, Stanley investigated ways in which CTSG members' perceptions were affected by their group interactions. She traced the evolution of their socially constructed definitions of elementary music student collaboration. Findings regarding the CTSG's effect on teaching practice include: (a) increased confidence in professional knowledge through the opportunity to verbalize and share teaching expertise; (b) expanded vocabulary to analyze and describe student behavior; (c) more habitual reflective examination of teaching; (d) expanded understanding of the scope of student collaboration; and (e) greater knowledge of the teacher's role in facilitating student collaboration.

All of the studies in this section examined programs in which participants made a choice to participate, and all of the experiences studied in this section were collaborative ventures—not one-shot, isolated PD experiences. Researchers conducting this type of inquiry in the future might consider descriptions of one-shot or isolated PD events as a way of comparing types of PD experiences (Lyndon and King 2009 provide a model within general education). Considering that one-shot and isolated PD experiences are the most common for music teachers, it may be important for qualitative researchers to examine this phenomenon. The Professional Development Area for Strategic Planning with the Society for Music Teacher Education has issued a statement for music teacher professional development that supports this same suggestion (smte.org).

7.3.2. Music-Making as Professional Development

As mentioned earlier in the "Communities of Practice" section (7.3.1), Stanley (2009) studied a collaborative teacher study group (CTSG). The experiences of this group (three elementary music teachers and her) led to transformative PD impacting participants' teaching and the experiences of their students. Stanley suggested centering a future CTSG on chamber music performance. She wrote:

> I would like to reconvene a CTSG around the idea of chamber music collaboration, and have us perform as well as study together to see if the added layer of making music would add further dimension to our interactions. Also, I would like to incorporate some type of musicianship building exercises within a CTSG to see if the experience of being music learners together changes our dialogue. . . . I wonder if getting in touch with each other's music learner identities would give us additional things to talk about. (308–09)

Pellegrino's (2010) phenomenological case study examined the meanings and values of music-making in the lives of four string teachers and explored the intersections of music-making and teaching. Data sets were generated through background surveys, multiple individual interviews, videotaped classroom observations, focus group interviews that included music-making and conversation, researcher's self-interview, and researcher's journals. Participant suggestions regarding the benefits of music-making as PD included learning literature and new genres of music that could be brought back to students, developing strategies for helping students while engaged in music-making, keeping teachers' listening and playing skills at high levels so that they could provide excellent models for students and support their own musician identity, relating to the students as learners, becoming more empathetic to the issues learners are facing, helping teachers' sense of well-being, and combating burn-out.

Pellegrino (2011) suggests:

> My findings point to music-making as a potentially transformative professional development activity. Engaging in music-making was described as being inspirational and bringing a general feeling of excitement back to a teacher who was feeling burned-out as well as helping teachers be more present in the classroom. (85)

Oddly, only one researcher in music education has considered music and music-making as part of PD. There is clearly a need for much more information regarding how (making) music interacts with music education with regard to PD. Pellegrino (chapter 6 in Volume 2 of this *Handbook*) provides additional information regarding music-making as data in qualitative research.

7.3.3. Graduate School as Professional Development

PD can occur beyond the teaching context as well. Continuing education at the tertiary level can be a valuable form of PD. Hanley and King (1995) described a graduate course instructed by co-author Hanley, the aims of which included addressing curriculum issues in music education and the musicianship of the participants. The domains outlined in ArtsPROPEL, which was a collaborative effort between Harvard's Project Zero and the Pittsburgh public schools, guided the class and a domain project assignment. There was little attention to methodology in the empirical description of this course. It could be classified as self-study or teacher research, although there is no discussion of formal data collection or analysis methods. The anecdotal findings suggest that domain projects, originally designed for P–12 students, could be a beneficial learning activity at the university level as well. This activity was found as mutually beneficial for both students and instructors.

The effects of PD on future teaching is a limited area of research; however, Conway, Eros, and Stanley (2009) examined teacher ($N = 9$) perceptions of the effect of the master's degree in music education degree (MM) on teaching practice and teacher perceptions of student (P–12) achievement. Data included an online survey, participant journals, and individual interviews. All data sets were reviewed and coded for common themes. Although it was not an aim of the study to state whether graduate school was, in fact, PD or not for the participants, the researchers did find that some aspects of graduate education can have a transformative effect on music teaching and learning. Participants discuss music performance, connect research with practice, have "re-interaction" with undergraduate content as they make connections between their MM work and teaching practice. Participants believed there was a relationship between the graduate degree and student achievement; however, they were unable to pinpoint the direct link. Additional findings include: (a) the thesis or exam as a powerful connection to teaching practice; (b) the value of the community of learners in a MM program; and (c) questions regarding the development of an identity as a teacher/scholar.

Barrett (2006) pointed to graduate work's potential for creating a productive two-way movement between teaching theory and practice. She wrote that master's degree courses "can be especially strong in their capacities to engage teachers in the study of music and music teaching, which builds disciplinary depth, and also in fostering teacher-directed inquiry" (26); however, we know little about how or if graduate study really accomplishes this. Graduate study as professional development is another area ripe for continued inquiry.

7.3.4. Action Research/Teacher Research as Professional Development

The terms "action research" (and) "teacher research" are often used interchangeably due to shared characteristics. In both action research and teacher research, teachers seek answers to questions or situations they find puzzling (Conway and Jeffers 2004; Robbins, Burbank and Dunkle 2007) and this information is used to alter or transform their practice (Cochran-Smith and Lytle 1999). In a recent review of action research and teacher research methods, West (2011) suggested, "what is valuable about teacher research is one's *personal experience* with the topic rather than reading about another's experience" (90).

Though action research and teacher research share commonalities, for the purpose of this chapter, we differentiate between the two. Lewin (1946) first described action research as a "spiral of steps" composed of "planning, executing, and reconnaissance or fact-finding for the purpose of evaluating the results of the second step, for preparing the rational basis for planning the third step, and for perhaps modifying again the overall plan" (38). Similarly, Glanz (1998) described action research as a four-step process consisting of (1) selecting a focus, (2) collecting data, (3) analyzing and interpreting the data, and (4) taking action. Based on this description, we define *action research* as systematic inquiry, data collection, and analysis that results in a modification of practice, leading to further investigation. Robbins, Burbank, and Dunkle (2007) defined teacher research as "when [teachers'] observations and records of classroom events and experiences are done systematically and intentionally" (42). Thus, we use "action research" to describe a project that includes a "cycle" of data collection and immediate instructional change and the term "teacher research" when teachers are studying their own classrooms without a closed "cycle" of data collection and instructional change.

Most action research germinates from a curiosity or a need to improve one's own teaching and teaching environment. Conway and Jeffers (2004a, 2004b) described a collaborative action research process used in an examination of assessment procedures in a beginning instrumental music class. Jeffers, a veteran elementary instrumental music teacher, wanted to develop and examine various assessment procedures supporting the teaching techniques he had learned in a summer workshop. As the university researcher, I (Conway) searched for past literature on the topic of assessment in beginning instrumental music. Jeffers and I discussed issues of data collection and design and developed research questions. Jeffers developed student and parent questionnaires and made arrangements for another teacher to conduct student interviews. I conducted phone interviews with parents. We both listened to the student and parent interview tapes and examined the student and parent questionnaire data. We published two articles from the study, one on the findings (2004a) and one of the "process" of doing teacher research (2004b).

One of the most interesting findings to emerge from the study concerned PD, described here by Jeffers:

> This research project presented a significant opportunity for my professional development. All of the previous professional development that I had experienced in my teaching career was dictated by administrators. They would choose what we would be studying or learning about. They would set up when we would do it, where we would do it, how long it would be for and what the proposed outcome(s) would or should be. All of the arranged in-services had little or no relevance to music teachers or to most other "special area teachers". . . . When I contrast traditional professional development with the possibilities offered by collaborative action research I find a wide range of opportunities for investigating areas that are interesting /or

problematic to teachers. The teacher can have the opportunity to learn about or improve some aspect of teaching that pertains directly to his/her teaching /or classroom environment. If research is something a teacher is not familiar or comfortable with (most classroom teachers are not) then collaboration with a university professor is a way to initiate professional development that will be applicable to his/her teaching classroom situation. (Conway and Jeffers 2004b, 42)

Combining action research with collaborative PD (discussed earlier) can result in powerful PD experiences. Roulston et al. (2005) were involved in a music teacher-research community designed to contribute to the PD of early-career elementary music teachers. They wanted to investigate how a teacher-research community, involving both university educators and teachers, could be structured around a "practice-based orientation to research" (4) in which group members would design and conduct individual research projects. The group consisted of two university educators, as well as a second-year and third-year elementary music teacher. The group met monthly for three hours to discuss action research models and methods. As the classroom teachers created research questions and collected/analyzed data, the university educators served as research mentors by providing guidance in such areas as locating literature, creating research instruments, and gaining university and district study approval. They performed a group self-study examining "naturally occurring data" (Roulston et al. 2005, 7) related to the experience of being in the research community. All meetings were audiotaped and transcribed, the four group members interviewed one another, "wrote early and often" (8) and shared the writing, so that all group members could look at primary data, as well as read, revise, and check interpretations of the group experience. Analysis of group discussion indicated the elementary teachers learned new ways to consider and reflect on their practice; for example, one teacher was able to analyze group interactions in her classroom based on data collected by a paraprofessional, finding that what was really going on in the classroom was different from her prior perceptions. The group concluded, "teacher research collaborations between university educators and practicing teachers can supplement existing mentoring programs contribute to the development of . . . professional learning communities" (17).

Often action research projects can occur in conjunction with a graduate program, discussed earlier as a valuable form of PD. Robbins, Burbank, and Dunkle (2007) told the story of two teachers engaging in classroom research projects during their master's degrees. This inquiry was largely a self-study between two classroom teachers (Burbank and Dunkle) and a university professor (Robbins) with university collaboration serving as the primary theme. The narrative shares the project design process, the data collection, and the writing process. Experiences of the teacher researchers were also shared (co-authors). The availability of university support and teacher growth are key themes associated with collaborative teacher research.

Due to district-specific requirements for PD, action research may or may not be officially viewed by administrators as part of teachers' continuing education. Conway, Edgar, Hansen, and Palmer (2014) examined experiences of seven music educators who conducted teacher research or action research in their classrooms. Using a comparative case study design, data included: field notes from a project "start-up" meeting; an e-mail survey; an observation of each participant in their classroom; two individual interviews with each participant; two focus group interviews; artifacts from the participant projects; and a co-researchers' log. In this study, participants viewed action research as a positive PD experience, and two of the participants were able to "count" the project toward their "official" professional development requirements. All of the participants valued the collaboration with the university and the opportunity to reflect on their teaching practices.

While action research is a valuable form of PD, projects can be difficult to implement. Conway, Edgar, Hansen, and Palmer (2015) examined experiences of music educators who designed and implemented action or teacher research in their classrooms in relation to adult learning. Participants included seven music teachers who designed an action research or teacher research project in their classrooms during the 2010–2011 school year. Data included: field notes from a project "start-up" meeting; an e-mail survey; an observation of each participant; two individual interviews with each participant; three focus group interviews; artifacts from the teacher projects; and a co-researchers' log. Findings were presented in seven participant profiles and suggest that adult learning motivations to participate included a desire to be a better teacher and an interest in collaborating with the University. Collaboration helped participants stay motivated to continue with their projects, as did their curiosity about the learning of their students. Issues of time hindered some of the participants' ability to spend time and complete their projects.

Chapter 9 in Volume 1 of this *Handbook*, by Janet Robbins, provides a complete discussion of teacher research and action research. We have only addressed the issues related to professional development here.

It is important to note that all studies we present in this section examined PD in which teachers chose to participate in collaborative programs that met over extended periods of time. Participant choice, collaborative interactions, and extended time are critical elements for meaningful PD (Conway 2012). While participants in Conway (2008) (discussed in the next section) refer to typical PD experiences in schools and districts, there has not been comprehensive qualitative research in this area.

7.4. Career Cycle

Research in general education has examined the changing PD needs of teachers as they proceed through what researchers refer to as the career cycle. Some of these researchers have defined career cycle in relation to a particular theory of career development (i.e., Steffy 1989; Steffy Wolfe, Pasch, and Enz 2000), while others have just examined music teachers at various times in their careers.

Conway (2008) used a narrative approach to examine the perceptions of 19 experienced music teachers regarding PD throughout their careers. I did not define a particular theory of career cycle. Data included: mid-career teacher interviews ($n = 13$), veteran teacher interviews ($n = 6$), a focus group with some of the veteran teachers ($n = 4$), and the principal investigator's log. I found that teachers perceived informal interactions with other music teachers as the most powerful form of PD. I also observed that the expressed PD needs of the educators varied according to their career stage. At all points in their professional lives, the teachers valued informal interactions with peers as one of the most beneficial types of PD. As they matured in their careers, the teachers noted that in addition to benefiting through participation in formal PD, they learned from their students, student teachers they supervised, administrators, colleagues, by leading PD inservices, and through presenting sessions at professional conferences. Several educators suggested that early in their careers they relied on their school district for PD experiences, but at some point they realized they had to be proactive about their own professional growth. Veteran teachers reported thinking about PD for new roles, such as teaching collegiate methods classes or supervising student teachers, that they wished to pursue upon retirement.

As was articulated earlier in this chapter, music teachers continue to experience challenges beyond those encountered in their first years. Eros (2009) examined experiences of three second-stage music teachers (using Steffy et al. 2000 as a framework) who taught in urban settings. Recognition of career cycle is a relatively new concept for music education qualitative researchers. In the conclusion of his policy analysis of the use of "second stage" in music education career cycle, Eros (2011) states:

> The second stage is a particularly important place to examine the notion of stage-appropriate professional development. The transition from a first to a second stage has numerous specific markers that can be used to identify it, such as a sense of comfort in classroom management and an increasing interest in pedagogy, as well as passing the five-year mark. Moreover, it signifies the time when teachers no longer face survival but begin to consider career-long development, and as such, is the time when professional development needs are more likely to diverge among teachers.
>
> The stakes are high, considering that second-stage teachers, with the years of experience that they bring, represent a valuable resource that might be at a high risk for attrition. Professional development, and policymakers who design professional development experiences, would be well advised to have knowledge of the career cycle of the second stage in particular. (69)

In Eros's (2009) descriptive case study, data were collected from three teachers using a background survey, journals, interviews, and a focus group discussion. Data were analyzed using Merriam's (2009) constant-comparative model. Relevant to PD was the research question: How do participants perceive their career development from the first into the second stage and how do they discuss their anticipated career trajectory? Analysis of data for this research question revealed that participants: (a) perceived a development over the course of their careers, including transition to a new stage, changes in confidence, and different professional development needs than earlier in their careers; (b) had different perceptions of themselves as second-stage teachers; (c) were unsure of their futures in education; and (d) had concerns about withdrawal from teaching.

Conway and Eros's study (2013) aimed at describing and examining characteristics of the second stage of music teachers' careers. The design was a secondary analysis of survey and interview data previously collected for three studies of teacher views on mentoring, induction, and preservice preparation. Participants ($n = 13$) were previously involved in three studies in which they were asked to reflect on their beginning teaching experiences and discuss their music teaching careers in the last 10 years. Data from the previous studies were then re-examined through the lens of "second stage" theory (as defined by Steffy et al. 2000) and guided by the following research questions: (a) What characteristics distinguish a "second stage" music teacher from a beginning teacher? (b) How do participants describe the transition from "second stage" to what might be coming after? We found that characteristics distinguishing the second stage included: (a) leadership and respect in the school and community; (b) "settled" in to teaching; and (c) new personal life stage. As participants described their second stage transition, they discussed two themes: (a) an unsure future; and (b) a desire for challenge and change. A final theme emerging from the analysis included the apparent power of scheduling and administrator support in dictating career cycle experiences.

Further research on the varied PD needs of teachers at different points in their careers is necessary to ensure that continuing education needs are met throughout music teachers' careers.

7.5. Conclusion

Qualitative research has been used to report on the voice of teachers, both beginning and experienced, regarding PD in music education. Case study has been the most common methodological approach. This may be due to the often-isolated nature of even the longest PD programs. Case study fits well with studying specific programs in a bounded time period. Other qualitative approaches, such as phenomenology (see chapter 7, by Hourigan and Edgar, in Volume 1 of this *Handbook*) and ethnography (see chapter 6, by Krueger, in Volume 1 of this *Handbook* by Krueger) should be used in exploring various aspects of PD. One glaring weakness in the qualitative research regarding PD is that there is a lack of longitudinal research examining PD over any extended time period.

In Hookey's (2002) conclusion she outlined an agenda for future PD research and suggested the following two guiding questions for inquiry:

1. What do teachers and other music education practitioners know, how do they learn it, and how does this knowledge guide their practice?

2. What are the purposes and consequences of professional development experiences, and in what ways are the teachers individually or collectively implicated in their professional development? (898)

The studies reviewed in this chapter seem to focus around the first part of this second question and describe professional development experiences. Few studies have carefully examined teacher knowledge, and fewer studies have tried to determine how teachers are implicated in their PD practice.

The large majority of PD studies have examined teacher perceptions of the value of PD offerings. Researchers may begin to consider perceptions of administrators, parents and P–12 students, and PD facilitators regarding changes in teaching that can be attributed to PD. This body of research often presents unsupported and/or vague use of terminology with regard to methodology (i.e., case), and program-related terms (i.e., collaborative). We suggest that qualitative researchers continue to work to be clear and comprehensive in their definitions of terms. We also invite qualitative researchers to be more transparent to readers in describing the "aha moments" in their analyses when suddenly things become clearer.

It is impossible for music teachers to learn all they need to successfully navigate the profession in undergraduate teacher education or through mentoring and induction activities. Continuous, career-long PD is necessary for music educators to successfully teach in a constantly changing environment. Ensuring that findings from this research are made available to inservice teachers and PD facilitators is essential to improving the quality of music education PD. There is still much to be discovered about how teachers learn throughout their careers.

As was stated in the opening, qualitative approaches are useful for studying complex issues, relationships, and problems. It is our hope that researchers in music education will continue to ponder these complexities in relation to professional development and will continue to develop and devise new and innovative ways to examine them.

Notes

1. We wish to thank the following critical readers for their assistance with this chapter: Mary Hookey, Kristen Pellegrino, Alden Snell and Ann Marie Stanley.
2. NCATE is now part of the Council Accreditation of Educator Preparation (CAEP).

References

Barnes, G. V. 2010. "Teaching Music: The First Year." *Bulletin of the Council for Research in Music Education* 185: 63–76.

Barrett, J. R. 2006. "Recasting Professional Development for Music Teachers in an Era of Reform." *Arts Education Policy Review* 107 (6): 19–30.

Blair, D. V. 2008. "Mentoring Novice Music Teachers: Developing a Community of Practice." *Research Studies in Music Education* 30 (2): 99–117.

Cochran-Smith, M., and S. L. Lytle. 1999. "The Teacher Research Movement: A Decade Later." *Educational Researcher* 28 (7): 15–25.

Colwell, R. 1996/1997. "Professional Development Residency Program." *Quarterly Journal of Music Teaching and Learning* 7 (2–4): 76–90.

Conway, C. M. 2001. "Beginning Music Teacher Perceptions of District-Sponsored Induction Programs." *Bulletin of the Council for Research in Music Education* 151: 1–11.

Conway, C. M. 2003. "An Examination of District-Sponsored Beginning Music Teacher Mentor Practices." *Journal of Research in Music Education* 51 (1): 372–91.

Conway, C. M. 2008. "Experienced Music Teacher Perceptions of Professional Development throughout Their Careers." *Bulletin of the Council for Research in Music* 176: 7–18.

Conway, C. M. 2012. "Experienced Teacher Reflections on 'Beginning Music Teacher Perceptions of District-Sponsored Induction Programs.'" *Bulletin of the Council for Research in Music Education* 193: 63–76.

Conway, C. M. 2014. "Experienced Teacher Reflections on 'An Examination of District-Sponsored Beginning Music Teacher Mentor Practices.'" *Journal of Music Teacher Education*: 88–102, published online December 18, 2013. doi:10.1177/1057083713512837.

Conway, C. M., and S. Christensen. 2006. "Professional Development and the Music Teacher." *Contributions to Music Education* 33 (1): 11–27.

Conway, Colleen, Scott Edgar, Erin Hansen, and C. Michael Palmer. 2013. "Teacher Research as Professional Development for P–12 Music Teachers." *Music Education Research* 16 (4): 404–17. doi:10.1080/14613808.2013.848850.

Conway, C. M., S. Edgar, E. Hansen, and C. M. Palmer. 2015. "Teacher Research in Music Education: Profiles of Teachers." *Learning Landscapes Journal* 8 (2): 135–56.

Conway, C. M., and J. Eros. 2013. "Descriptions of the 'Second-Stage' of Music Teachers' Careers." Paper presented at the American Educational Research Association, San Francisco.

Conway, C. M., J. Eros, and A. M. Stanley. 2009. "Perceptions of Master's Graduates Regarding the Effects of the Master of Music in Music Education Program on P–12 Teaching Practice." *Research Studies in Music Education* 31 (2): 1–13.

Conway, C. M., and A. Garlock. 2002. "Teaching K–3 General Music: A Case Study of Mandi." *Contributions to Music Education* 29: 9–28.

Conway, C. M., and T. Jeffers. 2004a. "Perceptions of Parents, Students, and the Teacher Regarding Assessment Procedures in Beginning Instrumental Music." *Bulletin of the Council for Research in Music Education* 160: 16–25.

Conway, C. M., and T. Jeffers. 2004b. "The Teacher as Researcher in Beginning Instrumental Music." *Update: Applications of Research in Music Education* 22 (2): 35–45.

Conway, C. M., and T. Zerman. 2004. "Perceptions of an Instrumental Music Teacher Regarding Mentoring, Induction, and the First Year of Teaching." *Research Studies in Music Education* 22: 72–83.

Danielson, C. 1996. *Enhancing Professional Practice: A Framework for Teaching*. Alexandria, VA: Association for Supervision and Curriculum Development.

Dolloff, L. A. (1996). "Expertise in Choral Music Education: Implications for Teacher Education." PhD diss., University of Toronto. *Dissertation Abstracts International* 56 (07), 2600.

Duling, E. B. 1992. "The Development of Pedagogical-Content Knowledge: Two Case Studies of Exemplary General Music Teachers." PhD diss., Ohio State University. *Dissertation Abstracts International*, 53 (06), 1835.

Eros, J. 2009. "A Case Study of Three Urban Music Teachers in the Second Stage of Their Teaching Careers." ProQuest Dissertations and Theses database (UMI 3354146), University of Michigan.

Eros, J. 2011. "The Career Cycle and the Second Stage of Teaching: Implications for Policy and Professional Development." *Arts Education Policy Review* 112 (2): 65–70.

Glanz, J. 1998. *Action Research: An Educational Leader's Guide to School Improvement*. Norwood, MA: Christopher-Gordon.

Gruenhagen, L. 2008. "Investigating Professional Development: Early Childhood Music Teacher Learning in a Community of Practice." PhD diss., ProQuest Dissertations and Theses database (UMI 3295323), Eastman School of Music.

Hanley, B., and G. King. 1995. "Peeling the Onion: Arts PROPEL in the University Classroom." *Journal of Music Teacher Education* 5 (1): 15–29.

Hookey, M. 2002. "Professional Development." In *The New Handbook of Research on Music Teaching Learning*, edited by R. Colwell and C. P. Richardson, 887–902. New York: Oxford University Press.

Hord, S. M., W. L. Rutherford, L. L. Huling-Autin, and G. E. Hall. 1987. *Taking Charge of Change*. Alexandria, VA: Association for Supervision Curriculum Development.

Jacobs, J. 2007. "A Qualitative Study of First-Year High School Band Director and Their Mentors." PhD diss., ProQuest Dissertations and Theses database (UMI No. 3271149), University of Florida.

Junda, M. E. 1994. "A Model In-Service Music Teacher Education Program." *Journal of Music Teacher Education* 3 (2): 6–20.

Krueger, P. J. 1996. "Becoming a Music Teacher: Challenges of the First Year." *Dialogue in Instrumental Music* 20 (2): 88–104.

Krueger, P. J. 1999. "New Music Teachers Speak out on Mentoring." *Journal of Music Teacher Education* 8 (2): 7–13.

Lyndon, S., and C. King. 2009. "Can a Single, Short Continuing Professional Development Workshop Cause Change in the Classroom?" *Professional Development in Education* 35: 63–82.

Lewin, K. 1946. "Action Research and Minority Problems." *Journal of Social Issues* 2: 34–46.

Maslow, A. 1970. *Motivation Personality*. 2nd ed. New York: Harper and Row.

Merriam, S. 2009. *Qualitative Research*. San Francisco: Jossey Bass.

Merriam, S., and Simpson, E. L. 2000. *A Guide to Research for Educators and Trainers of Adults*. 2nd ed. Malabar, FL: Krieger.

May, W. T. 1990. *Art/Music Teachers' Curriculum Deliberations*. East Lansing, MI: Center for the Learning Teaching of Elementary Subjects (ERIC Document Reproduction Service No. ED 328512).

Montague, M. G. 2000. "Processes Situatedness: A Collective Case Study of Selected Mentored Music Teachers." PhD diss., ProQuest Dissertations and Theses database (UMI No. 9978591), University of Oregon.

Pellegrino, K. 2010. "The Meanings and Values of Music-Making in the Lives of String Teachers: Exploring the Intersections of Music-Making Teaching." PhD diss., University of Michigan, Ann Arbor. Proquest/UMI (Publication No. AAT 3429263).

Pellegrino, K. 2011. "Exploring the Benefits of Music-Making as Professional Development for Music Teachers." *Arts Education Policy Review* 112 (2): 79–88.

Price, H., and E. Orman. 1999. "MENC National Conferences 1984–1998: A Content Analysis." *Update: Applications of Research in Music Education* 18 (1): 26–32.

Raths, J. 2002. "Introduction: Fuzzy Teacher Education." In *The New Handbook of Research on Music Teaching Learning*, edited by R. Colwell and C. P. Richardson, 757–58. New York: Oxford University Press.

Robbins, J. 1994/1995. "Levels of Learning in Orff SPIEL." *Bulletin of the Council for Research in Music Education* 123: 47–53.

Robbins, J., M. K. Burbank, and H. Dunkle. 2007. "Teacher Research: Tales from the Field." *Journal of Music Teacher Education* 17: 42–55.

Rodwell, M. K. 1998. *Social Work Constructivist Research*. New York: Garl.

Roulston, K., R. Legette, M. DeLoach, C. Bukhalter-Pittman, L. Cory, and R. Grenier. 2005. "Education: Mentoring Community through Research." *Research Studies in Music Education* 25: 1–23.

Roulston, K., R. Legette, and S. T. Womak. 2005. "Beginning Music Teachers' Perceptions of the Transition from University to Teaching in Schools." *Music Education Research* 7 (1): 59–82.

Schmidt, M. 2008. "Mentoring and Being Mentored: The Story of a Novice Music Teacher's Success." *Teaching and Teacher Education* 24: 635–48.

Schmidt, M., and J. Canser. 2006. "Clearing the Fog: Constructing Shared Stories of a Novice Teacher's Journey." *Research Studies in Music Education* 27 (1): 55–68.

Seidman, I. E. 1998. *Interviewing as Qualitative Research*. 2nd ed.å. New York: Teachers College Press.

Shuler, S. C. 1995. "The Impact of the National Standards on the Preparation, in-Service Professional Development, Assessment of Music Teachers." *Arts Education Policy Review* 96 (3): 2–14.

Standerfer, S. L. 2003. "Perceptions and Influences of the National Board For Professional Teacher Certification on Secondary Choral Music Teachers: Three Case Studies." PhD diss., ProQuest Dissertations and Theses database (UMI No. 3083085), University of Virginia.

Standerfer, S. L. 2008. "Learning from the National Board for Professional Teacher Certification (NBPTS) in Music." *Bulletin of the Council for Research in Music Education* 176: 77–88.

Stanley, A. M. 2009. "The Experiences of Elementary Music Teachers in a Collaborative Teacher Study Group." PhD diss., University of Michigan, Ann Arbor. Proquest/UMI. (Publications No. AAT 3354182).

Steffy, B. E. 1989. *Career Stages of Classroom Teachers*. Lancaster, PA: Technomic.

Steffy, B. E., M. P. Wolfe, S. H. Pasch, and B. J. Enz. 2000. *Life Cycle of the Career Teacher*. Thousand Oaks, CA: Corwin Press.

Stevanson, B. A. 2005. "A Study of a Pilot Support Program for First Year Elementary Music Teachers." PhD diss., ProQuest Dissertations and Theses database (UMI No. 3172115), University of Texas.

Strauss, A. S., and J. Corbin. 1998. *Basics of Qualitative Research*. Thousand Oaks, CA: Sage Publications.

Verrastro, R. E., and M. Leglar. 1992. "Music Teacher Education." In *Handbook of Research on Music Teaching Learning*, edited by R. Colwell, 676–96. New York: Schirmer Books.

West, C. 2011. "Action Research as a Professional Development Activity." *Arts Education Policy Review* 112 (2): 89–94.

Wing, Liz A. 1977. "Formative evaluation in the general music classroom." Unpublished doctoral dissertation, University of Illinois at Urbana-Chanpaign.

CHAPTER 8

COMMUNITY MUSIC EDUCATION

NATHAN B. KRUSE AND ERIN M. HANSEN

8.1. INTRODUCTION

THERE is an ongoing, international dialogue regarding the philosophy, structure, and purpose of community music (CM) and its relationship with school music instruction. In the United States, CM is championed by several organizations, including the National Guild for Community Arts Education (NGCAE).[1] In their historical examination of CM in the United States, as well as a survey of current practices, Leglar and Smith (2010) describe three general categories in which CM exists:

> That which exists to carry out specific educational objectives; that which has performance as its chief objective, but also has an education component; and ... that which is carried on solely for cultural transmission and/or for social and entertainment purposes. (348)

Community music also can be an alternative place for students to make music or explore different musical styles that might not be offered in school music programs (Bowman 2009; Byo and Cassidy 2005; Higgins 2007).

American CM often looks different from that of other countries with longer traditions of CM activities, especially in Western Europe and Canada (Coffman 2002; Dabback 2010). The International Society for Music Education (ISME) established its Commission on Community Music Activity (CMA) in 1982 ("Community Music Activity Commission [CMA]" 2012; McCarthy 2007). In their vision statement, the CMA cites several reasons for the involvement and support of CM activities, including musical excellence, personal and communal expression, and community development ("Community Music Activity Commission [CMA]" 2012). Additionally, the commission believes that CM activities can complement and extend ideas presented in formal music education. Although the CMA is an international model, consideration for its guidelines of CM programs in conjunction with the general principals of arts education, as provided by the NGCAE, may offer a possible model of CM activities in the United States.

This chapter presents qualitative research that focuses on community music-making. Qualitative methods are some of the most appropriate platforms for exploring these socially situated areas of music performance and experience. Youths and adults who elect to take part in community-based music activities do so for a multitude of reasons, which can parallel the reflexivity and multiple realities best expressed through qualitative methodology. Similar to the emergent nature of some qualitative designs, CM programs often develop over time, based on the needs of their participants and surrounding communities. Thus, qualitative researchers have worked to illuminate the unique characteristics of community-based music initiatives by conducting studies that recognize contextual relevance, explore phenomena related to active music-making, address the aging process, and capture the essence of music learning beyond P–12 school structures.

This chapter provides a collection of American qualitative studies that exemplify diverse and successful models of community music-making and learning for youths and adults. Guided by the previously mentioned research (Bowman 2009; Byo and Cassidy 2005; Higgins 2007; Leglar and Smith 2010), we categorize these studies as follows: community music programs with (a) performance objectives, (b) educational aims, (c) cultural connections, and (d) a focus on social justice. We illustrate the common musical, social, instructional, and administrative qualities researchers have identified as contributing to the successes of these portrayed models and explore the growing relevancy of community-based music activities in the United States and its relationship to school music education. Additionally, we discuss emerging models of CM, needed areas of research, and the use of qualitative designs in the study of CM programs. Tables of composite findings from these studies complete each major section, and Table 8.A1 (in the Appendix to this chapter) includes additional information on CM organizations and their defined missions. While the intent of this chapter is not to present an exhaustive account of CM education research, we recognize there are stories that do not appear in the following pages but that contribute greatly to the discourse surrounding CM. Our hope is that this chapter serves as a collective foray into the qualitative nature of CM education, and as a platform for sustaining conversation regarding lifelong music learning.

8.2. Community Music Programs with Performance Objectives

American CM research has identified public performance as a common and valued musical activity. Like school music ensembles, community ensembles typically hold regular rehearsals in preparation for scheduled concerts that showcase the performers as well as engage community members in musical experiences. Community ensembles also can reflect some of the formalized instructional qualities depicted in school ensembles, including teacher-led rehearsals and appropriate performance standards through cohesive, collective musicianship. This section looks at community band, orchestra, and choir research that examines the characteristics behind participation in traditional performing ensembles, although special attention will be given to the authors' chosen methodology. In this section, we focus on adult and senior adult performance groups and include the areas of the New Horizons International Music Association, Traditional Performing Ensembles, and Spiritual Connections.

8.2.1. New Horizons International Music Association

One of the most visible crusades in organized musical performance opportunities for adults is that of the New Horizons International Music Association (NHIMA).[2] The New Horizons movement is an American model of formal music instruction that provides entry points for adult learners in instrumental and choral settings, and includes members who have little to no prior experience in music-making as well as those who have been inactive for a period of time (Ernst 2001). Numerous NHIMA bands, orchestras, choruses, and jazz/dance bands emerged since the inception of the first band in 1991, and typically include members from the 50-and-older adult population, although some groups remain open to individuals of any age. To date, over 8,500 adults participate in over 200 NHIMA ensembles in the United States, Canada, Ireland, England, The Netherlands, Italy, and Australia ("New Horizons International Music Association" 2013).

Several qualitative studies and dissertations have documented the non-competitive, supportive, and inclusive environments of NHIMA bands (Dabback 2008; Kruse 2008; Tsugawa 2009), which reportedly are predominant qualities of NHIMA ensembles. The majority of research comprises case studies that illuminate the rewards of identity (i.e., sense of belonging, safety, purpose) and meanings associated with adult music participation, and have highlighted the challenges of cognitive and physical limitations that come with the aging process (i.e., eyesight, hearing, fine motor dexterity). Three such case studies (Dabback 2008; Kruse 2008; Tsugawa 2009) identified some of the rewards and limitations that senior adults experienced in various NHIMA ensembles.

Dabback (2008) examined the social interactions, networks, and identity formations among members of the Rochester (NY) New Horizons band program.[3] Dabback created two separate focus groups within the band; one group contained members with fewer than five years of experience, and one group contained members with five years of experience or more. In keeping with Krueger's (1994) recommendation for enlisting six to nine participants in a focus group, Dabback recruited seven band members for each group and conducted two separate focus group interviews with the participants. Dabback analyzed the transcripts using data-coding procedures. He also employed observations and dialogue journals from three additional participants to situate his findings within identity theory.

Four of Kruse's (2008) 12 case study participants were members of the East Lansing, Michigan, New Horizons band program.[4] Andragogy, or the concept of adult learning principles, was used as the theoretical framework for the study. Because Kruse had rehearsed and assisted with this particular group in the past, he believed a mutual sense of trust had been established that would engender an honest, positive rapport during data collection. One-on-one interview transcripts, participant-observations, and field notes were coded, sorted into themes, and organized within the context of andragogy.

Tsugawa (2009) conducted a collective instrumental case study with the Desert Foothills New Horizons Band[5] in Arizona and the Brigham Young University New Horizons Orchestra[6] in Utah. Two unique facets of this study included dual locations and distinct instrumental settings (band and strings). Tsugawa's overall intent was to explore the concepts of "music learning, motivation, meaning construction, and sense making" (44) as expressed by the participants in the two ensembles. He interviewed 16 participants, who were categorized as either adult beginners or returning musicians, and collected additional data through observations, personal journals, recorded rehearsals, and artifacts, including voluntary participant journals. Interview analysis included coding the initial transcript data, further organizing the codes using NVivo,[7] creating drawings and visual representations to depict relationships and connections, and finally, establishing resultant themes and findings.

NHIMA ensembles[8] continue to serve adult learners in a variety of social, expressive, musical, and intellectual ways. While NHIMA has a widely acclaimed national and international reputation, other independent, non-NHIMA community ensembles also serve adult musicians at the local level; these settings include self-governing, traditional performing ensembles, such as community bands, community orchestras, community choruses, and faith-based ensembles.

8.2.2. Traditional Performing Ensembles

One of the most studied considerations in CM includes understanding the characteristics of continued, voluntary participation in ensembles. Sustained involvement in music often is connected to previous musical experiences, as Shansky (2010) discovered. Shansky's (2010) case study explored the motivations of adult participation in the Bergen Philharmonic Orchestra[9] in Northern New Jersey. Seven orchestra members were selected to participate based on their history and experience with the orchestra, and included three professional musicians and four non-professional musicians. Shansky conducted semi-structured interviews through either a face-to-face or telephone format depending on the participants' availability. The interview questions were e-mailed to two of the participants for whom telephone or in-person interviews were not possible. The open-ended questions were designed in three sections, with 16 total questions. As a flutist in the orchestra, Shansky was also a participant-observer and used historical literature research on the orchestra as a third data source. While Shansky did not share explicit analysis procedures, she stated that the three data sources were triangulated and were consistent in the findings.

In another study, Taylor et al. (2011) adopted a phenomenological stance in order to describe the lived experiences of 16 adult flute players in two long-standing metropolitan flute choirs. Data were collected over the course of eight weeks, which included individual semi-structured interviews with two directors and 14 members, weekly rehearsal observations and recordings, and a mixture of emic and etic perspectives from the researchers. A facet of this study included an examination of the unique characteristics associated with a homogeneous ensemble setting. Interview transcript analysis was consistent with Colaizzi (1978) in that significant statements were extracted from the transcripts, assigned meanings, and then clustered into themes.

Faivre-Ransom (2001) also examined continued musical involvement, but with regard to choral settings. She used theories of participation and music belief systems as theoretical frameworks for investigating the Norfolk Chorale in Norfolk, Virginia.[10] Faivre-Ransom funneled themes from coded interviews and observations and constructed case study findings relating to the participants' previous music experiences. Emergent themes indicated that high school music experiences were influential in determining adult music experiences. The popularity of Western choral traditions has generated numerous vocal music-making opportunities in the United States. One of the most accessible and visible prospects includes faith-based ensembles, which are discussed in the next subsection.

8.2.3. Spiritual Connections

Spirituality, faith, and service are some of the personal sentiments and topics of discussion found in faith-based ensembles, in particular, choirs. Church vocal groups typically are expected to meet performance objectives as well as service roles within the context of worship. Although the community chorus tradition stems from faith-based choral traditions, additional moral or theological philosophies might be present for those who participate in religious vocal ensembles. Research has suggested that vocal ensembles connected to worship and spirituality can afford participants unique rewards.

Dabback (2012) observed the inner workings and spiritual focus of a Mennonite high school choir in Virginia. This case study was grounded in the four-part singing tradition of the Mennonite community and explored the roles of faith and religion in the formation of musical identity among its singers. Dabback conducted interviews and focus group interviews with Mennonite singers and their director, and analyzed transcripts and field notes using data-coding procedures. In doing so, Dabback examined the underpinnings of both individual and group identity within the context of religious music-making.

Rohwer (2009) conducted semi-structured interviews with 22 choral musicians from three different denominations, including Congregational Christian, Lutheran, and Methodist choir members. In an effort to examine the ways in which church music might represent additional aspects of CM, Rohwer sought to describe the participants' musical backgrounds and their perceptions regarding church music participation. The individual interviews contained 18 open-ended questions. Following transcript member checks, her categorized findings were corroborated using peer review and reflected the notions of group cohesion, connections between music and God, and differences between church music and school music education.

8.2.4. Section Summary

This section has reviewed research devoted to community bands, orchestras, and choirs. Speaking through mostly case studies or phenomenological designs, participants elucidated the rewards and challenges of CM participation as well as the appeal of a lifelong commitment to music-making endeavors. Table 8.1 reflects additional findings from the studies discussed in this section. The methodological design choices were appropriate for capturing the voices of the participants, recreating their stories, and providing lessons learned from their experiences. As mentioned earlier, many CM programs often include performance objectives, although this is not always the case. Additional forums for CM activities are available that include varied teaching styles, diverse structures, and breadth of scope. These models are chronicled in the next section.

Table 8.1 Summary of Findings: Community Music with Performance Objectives	
Dabback (2008)	Positive social networks created in the band setting mitigated identity crises often experienced by senior adults; several considerations associated with identity and older adulthood were reported.
Dabback (2012)	Four-part singing reflected the participants' identity within a Mennonite community tradition; singing was integral to the broader connections to Mennonite values.
Faivre-Ransom (2001)	Participants noted that high school music experiences, church choir, family, and private lessons were influential in determining adult music experiences; the choir, its mission, and the music contributed to continued involvement.
Kruse (2008)	Devotion to the collective, reciprocity within the group, and appropriate repertoire difficulty were integral aspects of the learning process, despite physical challenges that periodically interrupted participants' involvement.
Rohwer (2010)	The act of worship instilled a sense of service and duty rather than a sense of leisure or aesthetic motivation; group prayer and the sharing of joys and concerns were essential for many.
Shansky (2010)	The love of music and the challenges it presented were no different between professional and amateur musicians; overall, musical aspects were more important than social aspects.
Taylor et al. (2011)	Serendipity, non-competitive atmospheres, part rotation, and positive director leadership styles were distinct rewards; fatigue and the aging process became challenges.
Tsugawa (2009)	Members found meaning in the self-directed learning process, the benefits of making music, camaraderie, humor, and conductor-teacher effectiveness; changing identity roles among adults were addressed.

8.3. Community Music Programs with Educational Aims

Most, if not all, community music activities have an educational element, be it explicitly stated or tacitly inferred. This section describes community music programs that are designed to achieve specific educational aims and that offer instruction in a more traditionally perceived form, such as through lessons and classes. In this category, we include community music schools, collaborative music programs, and summer music programs and camps.

8.3.1. Community Music Schools

Several types of CM programs are structured around educational objectives, the most common being community music schools. Often, community music schools are associated with a particular pedagogical philosophy or method.[11] It also is common for community music schools to offer programs in a variety of methods and styles, as does The Neighborhood Music School (Baranski 2010). Additionally, the populations of community music schools often are diverse, and consequently, the schools can serve as a "come one, come all" type of gathering place, as presented in Palmer's (2010) study of a New York community music school. The following two case studies explore the characteristics that contributed to the longevity of two successful yet different community music schools.

The Neighborhood Music School (NMS),[12] located in New Haven, Connecticut, is a centennial community music school that endeavors to increase public participation in the arts. Using a case study methodology (Stake 1995), Baranski (2010) explored (a) participants' reasons for their involvement in the NMS, (b) factors that contributed to prolonged participation in the NMS, and (c) the meanings of the NMS in the lives of its members. Baranski conducted in-depth and casual interviews of teachers, students, administrators, parents, and board members, as well as class and concert observations four days a week over the course of a year. Additional data were collected through analysis of historical and current documents. Baranski provided detailed descriptions of the NMS programs based on participants' descriptions including policy, procedural, and financial information, as well as program particulars such as Early Childhood, Suzuki, Music Theory, and the Music Performance Certificate Program.

A different community music school, the David Hochstein Memorial Music School, was founded in 1920 (now called the Hochstein School of Music and Dance).[13] Its founding principles were to provide music instruction to an ethnically diverse group of students from all musical and socioeconomic backgrounds. By means of a historical case study design, Palmer (2010) sought to determine whether the Hochstein School preserved its original principles over time and to enumerate attributes of the school that may be replicated by other community music programs. Palmer examined historical documents over three historical time points (1920–1928, 1960–1970, and 1970–1980) and conducted interviews with previous executive directors of the Hochstein School. Use of past board minutes, director's reports, concert programs, brochures, fliers, and newspaper articles contributed to Palmer's reconstruction of a historical record, from which he formed his analysis.

Both Baranski and Palmer examined particular community music schools as cases, for which the inspection of historical documents provided important context. Additionally, Baranski offered another view of the school by vividly retelling the stories of three students of the Hochstein School. The students' experiences were presented as three case studies. He felt the use of case study method was important and stated:

> The lack of critically in-depth case studies is problematic because although continuous participation in community music school programs demonstrates a clear need for an interest in these offerings, we have too little insight into what brings people into these community music programs or what keeps them engaged in them. (70)

Interviews are important tools for capturing the voices and experiences of participants. For example, Baranski and Palmer discovered the importance of strong, visionary leadership and understanding of the surrounding community through interviews. Different research methodologies that also draw on the interpretation and analysis of interviews, such as phenomenology and ethnography, can be especially successful in illustrating the lived experiences of participants as demonstrated in the next two subsections on collaborative music programs and summer music programs.

8.3.2. Collaborative Music Programs

Other educationally structured music programs are formed as partnership initiatives, often where both the members of the organization (e.g., professional music organizations, universities or colleges, or paid performing ensembles) and CM students learn and benefit from the collaboration. The following studies highlight two collaborative music projects for both youth and adult community members.

Drawing from heuristic phenomenological inquiry, Conway and Hodgman (2008) examined an intergenerational, collaborative performance project (CIPP) of Fauré's *Requiem* between community and university chorus members. Participants included eight members of a small liberal arts college choir and eight members of a community chorus, and were selected using intensity and purposeful case sampling (Patton 2002). To explore their participants' experiences of the CIPP, Conway and Hodgman examined data through the perspectives of college students, community-choir members, and teacher-researchers, while Hodgman occupied the roles of co-researcher and conductor of the project's choir. After each researcher individually analyzed individual participant interviews, focus group interviews, and journal entries, they compared analyses and jointly developed codes and categories. In addition to the findings presented in Table 8.2 at the end of this section, the authors discovered that performers were positive toward intergenerational musical collaborations.

Davis (2011) explored the experiences of those involved with the University of South Carolina String Project (USCSP),[14] which included students and faculty from the University of South Carolina (USC),[15] faculty from the USCSP, and members from the community. The USCSP openly supported the local school music programs by requiring all students who participated in one of the program's orchestras to also participate in their school orchestra programs. Using a case study design, Davis gathered data through archival documents, field notes, participant observations and interviews, pictures and video recordings, and participant journals over the course of 14 months. Thirty-three participants were interviewed, including 13 USCSP students (6 teenage and 7 adult) and 11 USC undergraduate students who taught in the string program. Data collection and analysis were conducted concurrently following Creswell's "data analysis spiral" (2007, 55) and were organized and coded within the software HyperRESEARCH.[16]

Table 8.2 Summary of Findings: Community Music with Educational Aims

Baranski (2010)	Students were intrinsically motivated to participate and continued membership in the community music school due to their interactions with applied music faculty.
Conway and Hodgman (2008)	Participants felt they experienced an enhanced performance, an improved understanding of others, and a blurring of age barriers; participants had an overall positive opinion of intergenerational musical collaborations.
Dabczynski (1994)	Beginning fiddle students valued being able to learn music with faculty and peers of varying abilities; participants were intrinsically motivated to learn new repertoire and interact with like-minded musicians; Dabczynski discussed the differences between fiddle and classical music and possible ways in which fiddle music can be incorporated into school string programs.
Davis (2011)	USCSP students valued opportunities such as learning and creating music with others, affordable instruction, and weekly participation; undergraduates valued development of teacher identities and teaching abilities, relationships with mentors, and learning to balance responsibilities as teachers, musicians, and students; USCSP and university faculty valued furthering the mission of USC, helping undergraduates become successful teachers, and providing opportunities for the community to become lifelong musicians.
Fetter (2011)	Fetter discussed the development of a living curriculum and the need for school music teachers to engage with community musicians and students; identity development, fostering musical exploration, diversity of music styles, and school music teachers making music within the community were also discussed.
Palmer (2010)	Success of the Hochstein School attributed to: (a) consistency of mission, (b) visionary leadership, (c) innovative programming, (d) connections with surrounding community.

Conway and Hodgman (2008) and Davis (2011) sought to explore their participants' experiences during collaborative music-making projects. Both studies employed participant journal writing as a data collection method, though their method of employment and usage during analysis varied. Despite their potential for rich data, researchers like Conway and Hodgman and Davis have found that participant journals can be an inconsistent data source, as the degree of contribution varied among participants.

Collaborative models of CM are increasing, perhaps due to proclamations stating the need for more music education opportunities, as made by the American String Teachers Association[17] and the League of American Orchestras.[18] More research is needed with regard to collaborative community music projects as to the experiences of their participants and surrounding community members. The next subsection will present a different version of collaborative music-making, that of summer music programs.

8.3.3. Summer Music Programs

Though not traditionally perceived as "community music," summer music programs, workshops, and camps can provide a sense of community among attendees in a relatively short amount of time. Some programs are organized around a genre of music, such as the Ashokan Fiddle and Dance Camp,[19] which offers instruction in Cajun, Zydeco, Country, Swing, and Hardingfele styles, to name a few. Other programs may be organized around an instrument type, geographic location, or guest artists. Similar to other CM programs, summer camps and workshops often gear their programs to clientele with widely divergent abilities and experiences (Fetter 2011). The difficulty in categorizing summer music programs is similar to the challenge researchers have faced in defining CM; however, it is important to acknowledge their role in this conversation. The following studies (Dabczynski 1994; Fetter 2011) provide two perspectives related to summer music programs and the possible methods used to study them.

Dabczynski (1994) conducted an ethnographic study of the 1991 Northern Week session of Jay Ungar and Molly Mason's Ashokan Fiddle and Dance Camp. One purpose of the study was to describe the characteristics of the teaching and learning processes Dabczynski observed at the camp and to hypothesize the viability of incorporating such characteristics in a public school string program. Dabczynski gathered data from an initial questionnaire, audio and video recordings of music lessons, observations, and document analysis. Of note, Dabczynski analyzed the recordings of teachers and their interactions with students using a self-modified "Observation Form" from *The Master Teacher Profile* created by Robert Culver (1989). Additionally, Dabczynski described the effect of the camp experiences through cases of four students (including himself as a participant-observer) based on his analysis of interview transcripts using Dienske's (1990) five-cycle analysis model. Dabczynski maintained a phenomenological outlook during and after his camp attendance so that "the individual participant at *Northern*

Week was viewed with openness, so as to allow commentary to reflect his or her concepts of reality" (14).

A more recent study of an alternative styles program was conducted by the director of the summer camp, String Jam[20] (Fetter 2011). Fetter employed facets of postmodern curriculum design (Doll 1993; Slattery 2006) to assemble curricular goals for the camp. To explore aspects of "alternative" music in string music education, Fetter investigated (a) whether "postmodern curriculum design align(s) with major curricular ideas in an alternative styles string experience" (11), (b) the experiences of two students who had participated in String Jam for three or more consecutive years, and (c) the possible influences of alternative music-making and learning on students' current and future musical identities. The study is presented in two parts: first, Fetter examined the curriculum of String Jam using postmodern curriculum design theory and compared this alternative string music education curriculum to Green's (2008) popular music project, Musical Futures; second, he explored the identity development of two cases (Merriam 2009) using criterion-based sampling (LeCompte and Preissle 1993). Data were obtained from single interviews that took place in each participant's home. The home settings allowed Fetter to observe and take field notes of such things as practice spaces, instruments, computers, music play lists, and wall decorations.

Dabczynski's and Fetter's roles as participant-observers allowed them to gain a more comprehensive understanding of the camps' settings, to select participants, and to explore the phenomena of attending an alternative summer music program. Furthermore, Dabczynski and Fetter explored "alternative" curricula (i.e., non-classical) and their intersections with school music string programs. More study is needed as to the relationships of CM and school music programs, especially studies that consider educationally based CM programs of nontraditional musical genres and pedagogical styles and the experiences of students who participate in both contexts. The next section will further explore nontraditional CM programs, both in subject and format.

8.4. Community Music with Cultural Connections

The majority of CM models presented thus far have been formal in nature. The balance between formal and informal music education, however, has been a recurring theme in CM research. Qualitative researchers have begun to capture the holistic and ethnographic traditions of informal music-making in society by examining indigenous, folk, roots, and rock music as alternatives to the kinds of music typically performed by some school and community ensembles. Often, students are drawn to these genres because of their connection to popular or vernacular culture. Although Canadian and European music education researchers have been exploring these ideas with greater frequency and for a longer period of time, it is important to highlight American models of informal music-making with cultural connections. This section includes several studies on music-making in the rock, steel band, and folk genres (Dabback 2010; Haskett 2009; Jaffurs 2004; Kruse 2012; Thornton 2010) and in online music communities (Bryant 1995; Kruse 2013).

8.4.1. Vernacular Community Music

A common thread among CM research is learning how individuals engage in informal music-making and transmission. One of the most popular and recognized forms of informal CM is the garage band phenomenon. Jaffurs's (2004) ethnographic study on the formation of a five-member (two girls and three boys) teenage garage band included two rehearsal observations, recorded rehearsal segments, field notes, interviews, and think-aloud interviews at the second rehearsal observation. She also conducted "spontaneous discussion interviews" (192) with the parents, which included three separate families across the five students, some of whom were siblings. While no specific account was given regarding analysis procedures, Jaffurs did acknowledge the triangulation between the video observation, interviews, and think-aloud protocol, and situated the findings within preexisting theories of informal learning and sociology.

Another cultural connection in CM includes steel bands. Haskett (2009) conducted a case study of the Desert Winds Community Steel Orchestra (DWCSO)[21] in Arizona to explore the motivations behind adult beginners' participation in steelpan drumming. Haskett interviewed eight participants, maintained field notes, observed rehearsals and performances, and collected artifacts to support the findings of his study. He organized interview transcripts and field notes chronologically and assigned thematic codes to the data using Creswell (1998) and Glesne (1999) as models. Haskett further supported rigor through trustworthiness, which included prolonged engagement and the confirming and disconfirming of evidence.

Jaffurs (2004) and Haskett (2009) suggested that there could be a noticeable gap between the kind of music that is learned in schools and the kind of music that actually exists in community settings. Thornton (2010) examined this disparity by exploring the musical engagement of three adults whose voluntary music activity did not necessarily reflect a typical school music curriculum. He looked at the independent musicianship of an avid music listener, a member of a church praise team, and a Bluegrass guitarist/singer to identify ways that music learning occurred throughout their lifetime. Data sources included observations and four one-on-one interviews with each participant. Thornton used interpretive phenomenological analysis as well as cross-case analysis of the transcript data to situate the findings within the context of music learning, and triangulated the data to increase trustworthiness.

As some of the findings in Table 8.3 suggest, independent musicianship and self-directed learning have been common factors in the CM studies reviewed thus far.

These concepts also play a role in the historical and social attributes of American folk (or roots) music, a subject that has garnered increasing attention from CM researchers. As such, cultural connections have been explored through North American Old Time and Bluegrass music in the Shenandoah Valley of Virginia (Dabback 2010) and the Blue Ridge Mountains of North Carolina (Kruse 2012). Specifically, Dabback's (2010) study centered on four participants' expressed meanings of various teaching and learning practices found in CM traditions in the Shenandoah Valley. The contexts from which the participants came included organized community ensembles, informal music-making, educational institutions, and faith communities. As a way to examine these communities of practice, Dabback employed a phenomenological design, "which explores participant meanings that emerge from the interactions of people within a given context" (215). Transcripts from a focus group interview, observation notes, and

Table 8.3 Summary of Findings: Community Music with Cultural Connections

Bryant (1995)	Five elements of a cultural system were revealed; the listserv owner wielded some level of implicit power through maintaining the software program; members ranked below him but did not appear to compete for social status, despite occasional attempts at outdoing each other musically online; members constructed identities from musicians in the real world.
Dabback (2010)	Findings reflected the importance and value placed on intergenerational music groups, the relationship between musicians and audience members in the music-making process, and the tension between recreational musical standards and performance standards.
Haskett (2009)	Participants attributed steel band membership to genuine curiosity and a positive association toward the steelpan due to their children's experiences in the school steel band program; group leaders should take into account the level of inclusiveness or exclusiveness that a selected curriculum/methodology might convey to participants.
Jaffurs (2004)	Students experienced social constructivism, enculturation, and relevant music-making; students created a distinct separation between school music and garage band; the ways in which people learn are not necessarily the ways people are taught to learn.
Kruse (2012)	Participants identified a connection to history and acknowledged their place and responsibility in carrying on Appalachian folk music traditions; they believed folk music will endure in modern society.
Kruse (2013)	Enculturation to the online community and the abundance of tutorials were important in the learning process; insider-outsider role conflict and a sense of isolation emerged as challenges; online communities can be just as meaningful as offline communities.
Thornton (2010)	Participants expressed a sense of fulfillment, a connection to humanity through expression, and free choice in selecting a musical niche; they found their own paths toward becoming musically engaged and constructed their own meaning of music over time.

photographs served as main data sources and captured the essence of the participants' musical heritage. Analysis was ongoing during data collection and included creating meaning from an inductive procedure, such as identifying actors, activities, ideas, and settings, which was posited by Lofland and Lofland (1984).

Kruse (2012) used narrative inquiry as a way to depict the perspectives of three North Carolina mountain musicians with regard to the folk music idiom and its continued transmission in a modern society. Participants included an Appalachian music icon, an Iraq War veteran, and a bowed dulcimer luthier. Data sources included transcripts from individual participant interviews, field notes, recorded jam sessions, and photographs from various locales across North Carolina. Kruse then combined these sources to create one metaphorical "town" that served as a singular entity for representing these multiple settings. There is only a passing mention of data analysis and trustworthiness procedures in the method section, however, which lies between narrative scenes.

8.4.2. Online Community Music

The aforementioned studies have illustrated, in part, the intermingling of formal and informal music learning and the various cultural settings that have appealed to learners. A concluding, more recent faction of CM education, examined through qualitative methods, includes online music communities. For many consumers who want to learn and share music, online settings have become attractive options because of their accessible and ubiquitous nature. Additionally, online music-making has reflected the growing realization that both music and community can be established in offline (in-person) as well as online communities.

The ways in which individuals interact and engage in online music-making activities has grown considerably over the past 20 years. In a groundbreaking study with an ethnomusicological stance, Bryant (1995) examined an early virtual community, Folk-Music,[22] which was based on the music of contemporary American singers and songwriters. Applying a theoretical model of music as a cultural system and drawing on ethnomusicological works, Bryant sought to understand Folk-Music members' perceptions of their online cultural system. She monitored listserv message activity for eight months and conducted interviews with community members and industry experts via e-mail, phone, and in-person formats. Bryant analyzed Folk-Music communications and interview transcripts through coding procedures in order to understand how this particular online community functioned as a microcosm within a much larger, offline American folk music subculture.

In another example, Kruse (2013) constructed an autoethnography that described his experiences in learning to play mandolin solely through online resources over the course of nine months. Data sources included online instructional video observations, weekly practice logs, recorded practice sessions, personal journal entries (formal), and personal memos (informal). Analysis included extracting codes from the journal data and sorting them into appropriate themes. During the triangulation of the multiple data sources, Kruse relied on peer review to corroborate said themes as well as to mitigate a potentially narrow or self-serving focus.

8.4.3. Section Summary

This section has reviewed research that described the cultural connections made through informal music-making online and offline. By adopting mostly ethnographic lenses, researchers found that participants achieved a sense of community through aligning with a particular musical genre, negotiating its construction, and perpetuating its history. Ethnographic techniques were one of the most advantageous means for capturing the essence of these cultural phenomena, as the nature of the participants' contexts was paramount for extrapolating social and musical meaning. As demonstrated by the design choices in this section, researchers discovered that community musicians became engaged, self-directed learners who independently acquired the language and skills necessary to thrive in a particular music culture. There are others for whom these choices are not as accessible, however. Examples of these instances are included in the following section on CM and social justice.

8.5. Community Music Programs with a Focus on Social Justice

As discussed in aforementioned studies (Dabback 2012; Palmer 2010), some CM organizations declare service to groups in need or to under-serviced peoples as a fundamental aim of their mission. The premise of using musical activities as a vehicle for social justice is becoming more common among community-based music programs. The next three studies discuss ways in which music performance has been used in correctional facilities (Brewster 2010; Cohen 2008, 2010; Warfield 2010), and are outlined in Table 8.4.

Cohen's (2008) multiple case study documented prison choir conductors' views of teaching practices and served as an impetus for compiling information to assist other prison choir directors. She interviewed nine prison choir conductors in an effort to gather their perspectives on the past and current practices of six prison choir programs in Kansas. Research questions included: "a) When and how did each chorus begin? b) What are the unique characteristics of conducting a choir in a prison? c) How do conductors perceive their respective programs? d) In what ways do data from this investigation support or require revision of prison choir participation?" (320). To answer the first three research questions, data collection included questionnaires, follow-up interviews, and "material culture" (320). For the fourth research question, Cohen

Table 8.4 Summary of Findings: Community Music with a Focus on Social Justice

Brewster (2010)	AIC was essential in assisting inmates reintegrate into society; AIC helped the participants discover self-worth and self-improvement, reconnect with family members and children, bridge racial gaps, and work at their art purposefully.
Cohen (2008)	Inmates entered the choir with limited vocal skills and attention spans, but consistent rehearsal attendance yielded improved focus, expanded singing, and a community of trust; conductors noted an increase in inmates' group responsibility and their capacity to interact with others, including audience members.
Warfield (2010)	Orchestra members benefited socially as well as musically, and gained personal confidence through successes related to playing opportunities.

applied pattern matching to compare established theories with operational or observed data (Trochim 1989) and to strengthen the case (Yin 1994).

Brewster (2010) conducted a study with formerly incarcerated men who participated in a California-based prison arts program, Arts-in-Corrections (AIC).[23] This particular program was nearly 30 years old at the time of the study and had helped reform thousands of inmates, many of whom had re-entered society. AIC provided numerous arts outlets to the incarcerated, including ceramics, painting, writing, sculpting, and music. Brewster led in-depth interviews with six former AIC inmates who participated in its various music programs. Of particular concern was ascertaining whether the program positively influenced former inmates' lives and if they continued to explore the arts following incarceration. Brewster organized his findings by themes that emerged from the interview transcripts, although a specific analysis procedure was not reported.

From an instrumental perspective, Warfield (2010) examined the underpinnings of the women's string orchestra program at the Hiland Mountain Correctional Center (HMCC).[24] Set in Alaska, this 400-bed correctional facility houses adult female offenders as well as a unique string program that was founded in 2003. At the time of the study, two orchestras with 22 total members performed twice annually and were deemed a rarity, as most prisons typically do not allow string instruments onto the grounds since they could be viewed as "contraband" (108). Primary data sources in the case study included interviews with one orchestra volunteer and one orchestra conductor. Like Brewster (2010), data analysis procedures were not explicitly stated, although Warfield chronicled the characteristics of the orchestra program based on the two interviews, and advocated for future implementation of music programs like the HMCC within correctional facilities. He also suggested that conducting a longitudinal collective case study with the HMCC would provide richer information regarding the impact that orchestra participation has on inmates' lives.

8.5.1. Section Summary

This section has reviewed research related to CM initiatives within the context of social justice. Case studies have been a common research design in illuminating the social and musical needs of participants as well as the missions and outcomes of particular music programs. As society becomes increasingly aware of the roles that music plays in the lives of individuals, there is a growing need for more studies that depict the unique characteristics of CM programs that serve underrepresented groups of people. As suggested (Warfield 2010), longitudinal studies, especially comparative case studies, are needed to document the effects of such programs on its members and surrounding community members. Additional studies that focus on underserved populations are reviewed in chapters 9, 10, and 11 of this volume.

8.6. Discussion and Future Directions

The qualitative studies discussed in this chapter represent a variety of CM models in the United States. Though the focus of this *Handbook* is on the use of qualitative methods in music education, it is nevertheless important to discuss their overall findings, particularly those characteristics that might have contributed to the perceived successes of these highlighted programs. Examination of the literature revealed common musical, social, instructional, and administrative qualities, which will be discussed in the following as a complement to the findings illustrated in Tables 8.1–8.4.

Study participants often discussed their appreciation for having a variety of opportunities to make music, learn new ideas, grow as musicians, and share their music through performance (Dabczynski 1994; Davis 2011; Faivre-Ransom 2001; Tsugawa 2009). Especially among the adult population, CM participants appreciated having multiple entry points from which to begin new musical experiences and valued acquiring the tools needed for lifelong music learning beyond their CM experiences (Davis 2011; Palmer 2010).

The CM organizations that provided opportunities for participants to engage in fun and social experiences with their peers and instructors succeeded most in creating a genuine sense of "community" (Baranski 2010; Dabback 2008, 2012; Dabczynski 1994; Kruse 2008, 2009; Tsugawa 2009). When participants believed they were accepted and supported by others, regardless of differences, they felt more confident, capable, and valued as musicians and as individuals, as if they were a part of something larger than themselves (Brewster 2010; Cohen 2008; Taylor et al. 2011; Thornton 2010; Warfield 2010). Though not commonly noted, some CM program participants discussed their increased support for local school music programs and their wish to give back to the greater surrounding community (Conway and Hodgman 2008; Davis 2011; Fetter 2011; Kruse 2012; Palmer 2010; Rohwer 2010).

Additionally, participants valued music instructors who were not only musically competent but also interpersonally competent (Baranski 2010; Shansky 2010; Taylor et al. 2011; Tsuwaga 2009). Teachers who were sensitive to their students' musical goals, interests, and unique learning styles (i.e., cognitive, emotional, physical), and who demonstrated their commitment to the musical community were highly respected (Baranski 2010; Dabczynski 1994; Palmer 2010; Tsugawa 2009). Other participants discussed the importance of affordable instruction and financial assistance, which often allowed musical experiences and instruction for people who otherwise would not be able to participate (Davis 2011; Palmer 2010).

A discussion of this nature would not be complete, however, without considering the following question: Why is qualitative research an appropriate methodology for exploring CM? As seen in the reviewed studies, the reflexive character of qualitative research complements the diversity of CM activities in society. Because many, if not all, of these activities were in socially situated venues of music performance and experience, a qualitative lens was useful for depicting the particular context in which the music learning occurred. The descriptive features of qualitative research allow readers to better understand the community and social context of various CM programs. As in ethnography, context is intricately linked to the interactions between community musicians, teachers, and audiences. Contextual knowledge is an important gateway for understanding and embracing the purpose and longevity of CM programs, and for gauging the success of those programs. In addition, a qualitative design highlights the views and perspectives of individual participants by not generalizing findings to the point where social and community context is lost. Building relationships and connections among CM participants is crucial, and qualitative inquiry values the voice of the researcher as well as the relationships that are forged between the participants and researcher. Because these exchanges are difficult to quantify, qualitative methodologies are useful for capturing the essence of such interactions, as Dabczynski (1994), Davis (2011), and Shansky (2010) demonstrated.

As the profession looks outward and enters the next stage of qualitative inquiry, it would be irresponsible to discount the value that CM holds in the lives of students of any age, and how the precepts of lifelong music activity might align with current and future music education philosophies and pedagogical trajectories. As suggested by the research presented in this chapter, school music and community music can be separate yet intertwined, independent yet reliant. Recognizing and honoring this relationship might assist the profession in discovering and applying new musical possibilities that emerge from their intersection. Educational models in public, private, charter, and professional development school settings, including homeschool groups, present unique sets of challenges and possibilities for music educators, students, and communities (Clements 2010; Veblen, Messenger, Silverman and Elliott 2013; Yarbrough 2000). These could include issues of funding, staffing, certification, access to music, and musical-political landscapes. In addition, technology (e.g., the Internet, Skype, YouTube, computer-meditated instruction) and its role as a conduit in teaching, learning, and disseminating music are becoming increasingly visible (Bryant 1995; Kruse 2013; Veblen et al. 2013); although its use might be regional and dependent on local resources. Consequently, many of the aforementioned factors associated with school music instruction could impact how CM is perceived and supported in the community. A more compelling notion, perhaps, is considering the ways in which CM might impact school music instruction.

Another factor in looking ahead at CM education research includes considering international partnerships. As previously mentioned, there are numerous Canadian and European CM models that stem from the literature base, especially with regard to informal and technology-mediated music learning. It is possible that the sociological differences in American, Canadian, and European perspectives might be linked to the respective public/private school music structures, which, at times, are inextricably reflected in the degree of societal music participation. Nonetheless, the profession can look to international CM research for alternate approaches to music participation and issues related to cultural authenticity. If one of the goals of music education and CM is to look outward, as a sociological perspective might suggest, then partnering with international programs or research initiatives might provide a comprehensive understanding of CM as definitions of music participation are extended.

The profession also can look to cross-disciplinary research that has been conducted with regard to community music-making. Disciplines outside music education, such as sociology, psychology, anthropology, computer technology, and communications, have examined musical phenomena throughout various layers of society. Consequently, learning how other fields perceive music engagement might inform how music educators approach music teaching and learning from a community perspective.

As suggested by the literature in this chapter, future directions in qualitative CM research could include longitudinal research of CM programs and effects; comparisons between different CM populations; examinations of learning styles in comparison to teaching styles; alternative, informal, and vernacular music in school settings; CM programs associated with music methods or associations (e.g., Suzuki, Orff, Kodaly, ASTA); and teachers who cross borders (i.e., they teach for both CM and school music programs). Researchers might also explore and implement a variety of design choices beyond case studies so as to expand the multiplicity of qualitative methodologies employed in CM research. If current trends persist, the appeal of examining the phenomenon of CM will no doubt increase as community musicians' stories are conveyed persuasively through the qualitative research paradigm.

Appendix

Table 8.A1 Community Music Organizations

Organizations and Affiliations	Premises/Functions
National Guild for Community Arts Education (NGCAE), founded 1937 http://www.nationalguild.org/Home.aspx	Advances and supports access to lifelong learning arts opportunities; fosters the creation and development of community arts education programs; provides information and research resources; promotes professional development and networking; provides funding opportunities.
Commission on Community Music Activity (CMA) (ISME), founded 1982 http://www.isme.org	Encourages debate and dialogue regarding international CM practices and collaborations; promotes empowerment of participants; endeavors to complement, interface with, and extend formal music education; facilitates and promotes the dissemination of research and information across numerous CM fields.
Adult and Community Music Education Special Research Interest Group (ACME SRIG) (NAfME), founded 2003 http://www.acmesrig.org/	Works to collect and disseminate national and international models of CM activities and methodologies; maintains a blog for posting and publicizing CM initiatives; organizes bi-annual research symposia.
North American Coalition for Community Music (NACCM) (ACME SRIG), founded 2008 http://naccm.info/	Initiates innovative practices and programs; broadens the base of CM practitioners; promotes the exchange of information; builds partnerships; raises awareness of the power and possibilities of CM; works to transform the culture of institutions and organizations, as well as inform and influence policymakers.

Notes

1. The National Guild for Community Arts Education (NGCAE) was founded in 1937 and is dedicated to the promotion of lifelong learning opportunities in the arts for all ("About" 2011).
2. http://www.newhorizonsmusic.org/.
3. http://www.esm.rochester.edu/community/newhorizons/.
4. http://www.cms.msu.edu/el/adults/horizonsBand.php.
5. http://www.dfnhb.org/.
6. http://ce.byu.edu/cw/newhorizons/.
7. http://www.qsrinternational.com/products_nvivo.aspx.

8. Readers interested in additional qualitative and quantitative research in this area can consult the NHIMA archive section at http://www.newhorizonsmusic.org.
9. http://www.bergenphilharmonic.org/.
10. http://www.vachorale.org/.
11. Suzuki (e.g., www.communitysuzuki.org) or Music Learning Theory (e.g., www.overturekids.com).
12. http://neighborhoodmusicschool.org.
13. http://hochstein.org.
14. http://www.music.sc.edu/special_programs/stringproject/index.html.
15. http://www.sc.edu/.
16. http://www.researchware.com/products/hyperresearch.html.
17. http://www.stringprojects.org.
18. http://www.americanorchestras.org/advocacy_and_government/music_ed_advocates.html.
19. http://www.ashokan.org.
20. String Jam is run through the Hochstein School of Music and Dance, http://hochstein.org.
21. http://www.steelesoundarizona.com/index.html.
22. http://www.folkmusic.org/fmfaq.html.
23. http://www.williamjamesassociation.org/prison_arts.html.
24. http://www.artsontheedge.org/index.html.

REFERENCES

"About." Nationalguild.com. http://www.nationalguild.org/About.aspx.

Baranski, S. M. 2010. "In the Settlement House Spirit: A Case Study of a Community Music School." PhD diss., New York University. *ProQuest Dissertations and Theses* (UMI No. 3439404).

Bowman, W. 2009. "The Community in Music." *International Journal of Community Music* 2 (2–3): 109–28.

Brewster, L. 2010. "The California Arts-in-Corrections Music Programme: A Qualitative Study." *International Journal of Community Music* 3 (1): 33–46. doi:10.1386/ijcm.3.1.33/1.

Bryant, W. 1995. *Virtual Music Communities: The Folk-Music Internet Discussion Group as a Cultural System.* http://proquest.umi.com/pqdweb?did=742875051&sid=1&Fmt=2&clientId=7935 6&RQT=309&VName=PQD.

Byo, J. L., and J. W. Cassidy. 2005. "The Role of the String Project in Teacher Training and Community Music Education." *Journal of Research in Music Education* 53 (4): 332.

Clements, A. 2010. *Alternative Approaches to Music Education: Case Studies from the Field.* Lanham, MD: Rowman and Littlefield.

Coffman, D. D. 2002. "Adult Education." In *The New Handbook of Research on Music Teaching and Learning*, edited by R. Colwell and C. Richardson, 199–209). New York: Oxford University Press.

Cohen, M. L. 2008. "Conductors' Perspectives of Kansas Prison Choirs." *International Journal of Community Music* 1 (3): 319–33. doi:10.1386/ijcm.1.3.319_1.

Cohen, M. L. 2010. "Risk Taker Extraordinaire: An Interview with Elvera Voth." *International Journal of Community Music* 3 (1): 151–56. doi:10.1386/ijcm.3.1.151/7.

Colaizzi, P. F. 1978. "Psychological Research as the Phenomenologist Views It." In *Existential Phenomenological Alternatives in Psychology*, edited by R. Valle and M. King, 48–71. New York: Oxford University Press.

"Community Music Activity Commission (CMA)." 2012. http://www.isme.org/index.php?option=com_content&view=article&id=41:community-music-activity-commission-cma&catid=20:cma&Itemid=14.

Conway, C., and T. M. Hodgman. 2008. "College and Community Choir Member Experiences in a Collaborative Intergenerational Performance Project." *Journal of Research in Music Education* 56 (3): 220–37.

Culver, R. 1989. "The Master Teacher Profile: 'Elements of Delivery at Work in the Classroom'" (Manual for accompanying videotapes). Madison: University of Wisconsin–Madison, Division of University Outreach, Department of Continuing Education in the Arts: 24, 63–66.

Creswell, J. W. 1998. *Qualitative Inquiry and Research Design: Choosing among Five Traditions*. Thousand Oaks, CA: Sage Publications.

Creswell, J. W. 2007. *Qualitative Inquiry and Research Design: Choosing among Five Approaches*. 2nd ed. Thousand Oaks, CA: Sage Publications.

Dabback, W. M. 2008. "Identity Formation through Participation in the Rochester New Horizons Band Programme." *International Journal of Community Music* 1 (2): 267–86. doi:10.1386/ijcm.1.2.267_1.

Dabback, W. M. 2010. "Exploring Communities of Music in Virginia's Shenandoah Valley." *International Journal of Community Music* 3 (2): 213–27.

Dabback, W. M. 2012. "Breathing Together: Community Connections in a Mennonite School Choir Program." Presentation for the Music and Lifelong Learning Conference, Harrisonburg, VA.

Dabczynski, A. H. 1994. "Northern Week at Ashokan, 1991: Fiddle Tunes, Motivation and Community at a Fiddle and Dance Camp." PhD diss., University of Michigan, Ann Arbor. *ProQuest Dissertations and Theses* (UMI No. 9423169).

Davis, S. A. 2011. "Acts of Hospitality: A Case Study of the University of South Carolina String Project." PhD diss., New York University. *ProQuest Dissertations and Theses* (UMI No. 3454465).

Dienske, Ten. 1990. "Vijf analysecycli in het interpretatieproces van het narratieve interview." Translated, adapted, and summarized by Ton Beekman in *Coursepack: Education 725*, School of Education, University of Michigan. Ann Arbor, MI: Dollar Bill Copying.

Doll, W. 1993. *A Post-Modern Perspective on Curriculum*. New York: Teachers College Press.

Ernst, R. 2001. "Music for Life." *Music Educators Journal* 88 (1): 47–51. doi:10.2307/3399777.

Faivre-Ransom, J. L. 2001. "An Investigation of Factors That Influence Adult Participation in Music Ensembles Based on Various Behavioral Theories: A Case Study of the Norfolk Chorale." DMA diss., Shenandoah University, Winchester, VA. *ProQuest Dissertations and Theses* (UMI No. 3091192).

Fetter, J. P. 2011. "Alternative Styles in String Music Education: Identity Development and Curriculum Design in the Postmodern Era." PhD thesis, University of Rochester. *ProQuest Dissertations and Theses* (UMI No. 3478288).

Glesne, C. 1999. *Becoming Qualitative Researchers*. New York: Longman.

Green, L. 2008. *Music, Informal Learning and the School: A New Classroom Pedagogy*. Aldershot, UK: Ashgate.

Haskett, B. L. 2009. "A Case Study on the Importance and Value of the Desert Winds Steelpan Programs." PhD diss., Arizona State University, Tempe. *ProQuest Dissertations and Theses* (UMI No. 3361302).

Higgins, L. 2007. "Acts of Hospitality: The Community in Community Music." *Music Education Research* 9 (2): 281–92.

Jaffurs, S. E. 2004. "The Impact of Informal Music Learning Practices in the Classroom, or How I Learned How to Teach from a Garage Band." *International Journal of Music Education* 22 (3): 189–200. doi:10.1177/0255761404047401.

Krueger, R. A. 1994. *Focus Groups: A Practical Guide for Applied Research*. 2nd ed. Thousand Oaks, CA: Sage Publications.

Kruse, N. B. 2008. *Andragogy and Music: Canadian and American Models of Music Learning among Adults*. Saarbrücken, Germany: VDM Verlag Dr. Müller Aktiengesellschaft and Co. KG.

Kruse, N. B. 2009. "'An Elusive Bird': Perceptions of Music Learning among Canadian and American Adults." *International Journal of Community Music* 2 (2–3): 215–25. doi:10.1386/ijcm.2.2-3.215_1.

Kruse, N. B. 2012. "'Sheer Spine': Evoking Past and Present in the Southern Highlands." In *Narrative Soundings: An Anthology of Narrative Inquiry in Music Education*, edited by S. Stauffer and M. Barrett, 79–94. New York: Springer.

Kruse, N. B. 2013. "Locating *The Road to Lisdoonvarna* via Cyber Autoethnography: Pathways, Blockades, and Detours in Self-Directed Online Music Learning." *Journal of Music, Technology, and Education* 5 (3): 293–308. doi:10.1386/jmte.5.3.293_1.

LeCompte, M., and J. Preissle. 1993. *Ethnography and Qualitative Design in Educational Research*. 2nd ed. San Diego: Academic Press.

Leglar, M. A., and D. S. Smith. 2010. "Community Music in the United States: An Overview of Origins and Evolution." *International Journal of Community Music* 3 (3): 343–53.

Lofland, J., and L. Lofland. 1984. *Analyzing Social Settings: A Guide to Qualitative Observation*. 2nd ed. Belmont, CA: Wadsworth.

McCarthy, M. 2007. "The Community Music Activity Commission of ISME, 1982–2007: A Forum for Global Dialogue and Institutional Formation." *International Journal of Community Music* 1 (1): 39–48.

Merriam, S. 2009. *Qualitative Research: A Guide to Design and Implementation*. San Francisco: Jossey-Bass.

"New Horizons International Music Association." 2013. http://www.newhorizonsmusic.org.

Palmer, G. L. 2010. "The Hochstein School of Music and Dance: History, Mission, and Vision." PhD thesis., University of Rochester. *ProQuest Dissertations and Theses* (UMI No. 664010480).

Patton, M. Q. 2002. *Qualitative Research and Evaluation Methods*. 2nd ed. Thousand Oaks, CA: Sage Publications.

Rohwer, D. 2009. "Church Musicians' Participation Perceptions: Applications to Community Music." *Research and Issues in Music Education* 8 (1). http://www.stthomas.edu/rimeonline/vol8/Rohwer.htm.

Shansky. 2010. "Adult Motivations in Community Orchestra Participation: A Pilot Case Study of the Bergen Philharmonic Orchestra (New Jersey)." *Research and Issues in Music Education* 8 (1). http://www.stthomas.edu/rimeonline/vol8/shansky.htm.

Slattery, P. 2006. *Curriculum Development in the Postmodern Era*. 2nd ed. New York: Routledge.

Stake, R. E. 1995. *The Art of Case Study Research*. Thousand Oaks, CA: Sage Publications.

Taylor, D. M., N. B. Kruse, B. J. Nickel, B. B. Lee, and T. N. Bowen. 2011. "Adults' Experiences in Homogeneous Ensemble Settings." *Contributions to Music Education* 38 (1): 11–26.

Thornton, D. H. 2010. "Adult Music Engagement: Perspectives from Three Musically Engaged Cases." PhD diss., The Pennsylvania State University, State College. *ProQuest Dissertations and Theses* (UMI No. 3442897).

Trochim, W. 1989. "Outcome Pattern Matching and Program Theory." *Evaluation and Program Planning* 12: 355–66.

Tsugawa, S. 2009. "Senior Adult Music Learning, Motivation, and Meaning Construction in Two New Horizons Ensembles." PhD diss., Arizona State University, Tempe. *ProQuest Dissertations and Theses* (UMI No. 3392131).

Veblen, K. K., S. J. Messenger, M. Silverman, and D. J. Elliott, eds. 2013. *Community Music Today*. Lanham, MD: Rowman and Littlefield.

Warfield, D. 2010. "Bowing in the Right Direction: Hiland Mountain Correctional Center Women's String Orchestra Programme." *International Journal of Community Music* 3 (1): 103–10.

Yarbrough, C. 2000. "What Should Be the Relationship between Schools and Other Sources of Music Learning?" In *Vision 20/20: The Housewright Symposium on the Future of Music Education*, edited by C. Madsen, 191–208. Reston, VA: Music Educators National Conference.

Yin, R. 1994. *Case Study Research: Design and Methods*. 2nd ed. Thousand Oaks, CA: Sage Publications.

CHAPTER 9

QUALITATIVE RESEARCH EXAMINING STUDENTS WITH EXCEPTIONALITIES IN MUSIC EDUCATION

RYAN M. HOURIGAN

According to the National Center for Educational Statistics, 5.9 million students ages 6–21 are served under the Individuals with Disabilities Education Act (National Center for Educational Statistics 2011). For music educators, the continued push for inclusion has highlighted the importance of being able to teach music to students with a wide variety of learning differences. Qualitative investigations of phenomena surrounding students with special needs in music education settings have provided insight in understanding the plight of students with learning challenges from the perspective of all stakeholders in a deep, reflective, multilayered viewpoint. Merriam (1998)[1] explains that "In fact I believe that research focused on discovery, insight, and understanding from the perspective of those being studied offers the greatest promise of making significant contributions to the knowledge base and practice of education" (1). Examining music students with disabilities, through the eyes of the participants, has and will continue to heighten our awareness of effective inclusion of students with exceptionalities as well as professional development and music teacher preparation.

There are terms that are interchanged throughout the literature that should be clarified before further examination. First, the term *inclusion* is used to describe the process of including school-aged students with disabilities in regular education classrooms to learn along with their peers. This is typically done with the students' educational challenges in mind, and, if possible, in their home schools. This leads to another widely used term, *mainstreaming*. This is an older term used to describe placing students with disabilities in select parts of the regular education curriculum. This is typically done in accordance with where they can be the most successful (Florida State University Center for Prevention and Early Intervention Policy, 2012). Sometimes these terms are used interchangeably within the literature. *Special learner* is also a term used in the literature. The preferred way to refer to a person who is challenged with a disability is to use "person-first" language. "Students" or "children" with special needs (or exceptionalities, disabilities) is the acceptable terminology used within the special education community. Another term that appears often in the literature is *IEP*. This term is short for *Individualized Education Program,* which is a federally mandated document that defines the goals, needs, accommodations, and services that each child with special needs requires in order to be successful. This plan is developed in partnership between the student (if applicable), the parents or guardians, educators, service providers, and administration, and must be followed once implemented.

Qualitative inquiries into students with exceptionalities have become a part of the fabric of the literature in music education. After an extensive search of databases and reference lists it became clear that much of the qualitative research in this area (students with special needs) could be categorized into three main areas. This chapter will focus on the following areas of qualitative research and children with disabilities: (a) qualitative examinations of inclusion strategies in music education; (b) qualitative studies of specific diagnoses in music education; and (c) qualitative studies in music teacher education and students with special needs. Only qualitative research in music education research was examined. Music therapy research was only included if the studies were qualitative in nature, had curricular or educational goals as the focus (not therapy interventions for non-musical skills or understandings), and addressed the aforementioned goals and topics of research.

9.1. Qualitative Examinations of Inclusion Strategies in Music Education

As inclusion becomes more of a standard practice in music education, inclusive pedagogies in music education are becoming more important for our profession to understand. Jellison and Flowers (1991) conducted one of the earliest qualitative studies in music education that examined children with special needs. The purpose of this study was to describe, categorize, and compare data concerning music preferences, experiences, and skills obtained from interviews with 228 students labeled "disabled" ($n = 73$) or "nondisabled" ($n = 155$). The research design was described as "naturalistic inquiry" in which a structured assessment interview was used by university student proctors to collect information from the students in four age groups. Their respective schools identified certain students as eligible for special education services, and this constituted the group labeled "disabled." The same questions were also asked of students who did not receive special education services.

The questions that were developed for the interview focused on listening preferences and experiences, musical instrument preferences and performance, and singing and clapping (steady beat) performance. Findings suggested that there are similarities in responses from the two groups ("disabled" and "nondisabled") regarding how they learn and respond to music. This early study laid the groundwork for research to be conducted in music education looking at students with disabilities in self-contained and in what were then called mainstreamed settings. This study also shows how far we have come as a profession in labeling students. Jellison and Flowers used the term "disabled" and "nondisabled" in their descriptions of the participants. More recent studies have moved to a person-first use of labels.

Lapka (2005) studied the inclusive practices of an Illinois high school band that included eight students with severe disabilities. Although vague, the researcher used the following research questions to guide this study: "1) how was the process initiated; 2) how was the process implemented; 3) how was the process sustained, and 4) to what degree have the students with disabilities established relationships with their peers" (iii). "This process" is assumed to mean the process of including high school students into instrumental music education programs.

The participants included band students, special education teachers, an instrumental music teacher, and members of the "Advantage" class, which consisted of eight students with disabilities who were included in the percussion section of an instrumental music class (band). Lapka examined this phenomenon through the use of observations, individual interviews, and focus group interviews over a three-month period. Observations were done in full-group band classes and small-group lessons. Formal individual interviews were conducted with students and teachers (band and special education). At the conclusion of this inclusive experience, students (non-Advantage Class students) were allowed to choose one of three focus group interviews. Parents of the students enrolled in the Advantage Class also participated in one focus group interview. These interviews were videotaped for analysis.

All interviews were transcribed and field notes were taken for all observation events. Detailed transcripts and field notes are included in the manuscript. Lapka's findings suggest the following elements for successful inclusion of students in instrumental music: "1) teachers from special education and general education embracing the cause without mandates from the administration, 2) implementation that was gradual, 3) efficient time management exhibited by teachers who used technology and less formal means of teaming, 4) teachers who adopted the proper philosophy that encouraged them to solve problems, 5) inservice teachers learning from mentors, 6) teachers advocating the program, 7) parent and peer support, 8) flexibility and creativity as key components for solving problems, 9) curriculum that was based on student abilities which required modifications of the general curriculum and creation of an alternative curriculum, 10) teachers who understood how to adapt teaching methods to accommodate learners, 11) recruitment, education and supervision of peer tutors, 12) the staff coming out of isolation to work together in and outside of the classroom, 13) true collaboration based on mutual respect, communication, and shared responsibilities, and

14) social, personal, and curricular goals" (iii). Many of the preceding findings are consistent with other studies, described in the following, that examine similar populations in music education.

Haywood (2007) examined, through a single case study, the possibilities and potential benefits of including a child with special needs in a choral music setting. This study was phenomenological in design, with the aim of focusing on the participants' lived experience in choir. The researcher used semi-structured interviews that were "open-ended" and "conversational." Follow-up interviews were conducted not only with the participants, but also with other family members, to obtain a complete picture of the phenomenon. These interviews were triangulated with observations and historical documentation.

Deborah (pseudonym) was the main focus of a single case study and the researcher sought to capture the essence of her experience in choral music through examination of what "this individual is experiencing through inclusion in a choral setting" (Haywood 2007, 411). Deborah was chosen purposefully because of her past exclusion from choral music programs. Haywood found that Deborah had experienced many barriers that excluded her from participation in choral music because of the lack of accessibility of performance venues. Deborah also expressed that music teachers should advocate for inclusion of students with exceptionalities. Findings also suggested that coming together and building relationships among all of the students, teachers, and administrators will allow for successful inclusion of a student with special needs in music.

Bell (2008) examined the process of playing, improvising, composing, and digitally recording music with an adolescent with special needs. Specifically, the researcher was interested in responses to participation in a music program and how the teaching process develops in response to the participants' needs and desires. This study took place over 12 music sessions with a single participant. The participant was an 18-year-old student named Tim who was diagnosed with Down's syndrome.

A case study design was used and video transcriptions of the sessions, along with interviews and meta-analysis of incidents between the researcher and the participant, were analyzed. Bell states that the design of this study "took an emergent design as the study progressed" (6). In addition, Bell states that this design borrowed design strategies from other studies in music education. However, there was a lack of explanation of what was borrowed and how this study is indeed an emergent qualitative study.

The findings suggest that when working with an adolescent with special needs, the following conditions need to be present in order for the student to be creative: (a) the student must have an opportunity to explore music; (b) a student's perceptions of what making music is may be different than those of the teacher; (c) musical age and emotional age may vary by participant; and (d) music teachers should focus on the abilities of the student rather than the challenges.

Meier (2009) examined a single student's experiences in a high school instrumental music ensemble (band). The purpose of this study was to examine, using a case study design, the experiences of a student with special needs as he progressed through the high school band experience. The research questions that guided this study included: "(1) What are a student's perceptions of his inclusive band experiences? (2) What are the parent's perceptions of their child's experiences? (3) What are the band director's descriptions of his experiences teaching a student in his inclusive band classroom? (4) What are the paraprofessional's descriptions about his interactions and relationships with the student? (5) What are special educator's descriptions of the student's inclusive musical learning experience? (6) What considerations should be given for students with special needs in band settings?" (10–11).

Meier used a single case study design (Merriam 1998) and the data-collection site was a medium-sized high school located in the Midwest. The participants included a band director, a student with special needs, Steven (pseudonym), a parent of the child with special needs, the school psychologist, and Steven's paraprofessional. The participants were chosen purposefully because of prior knowledge of the student, ease of obtaining appropriate consent, and an "already established relationship between the program, the director, the student, and the university the researcher was attending" (35).

Data included semi-structured interviews with all of the participants and observations of Steven's instrumental music classes (band). All field notes and interviews were transcribed for analysis. Materials were coded for emerging themes and then were organized into the case record (Merriam 1988).

Findings suggested paraprofessionals are a key component of a successful inclusion experience in band for a child with special needs. In addition, instrumental music teachers help a student like Steven see the importance of social networking. Contrarily, Steven stressed the importance of being treated just like every other *regular* student and expressed the difficulties and challenges that arise when working in an inclusive learning environment. Other students were shown to benefit from working with Steven and some students were more accepting than others.

Analysis of the qualitative examinations described in the preceding uncovered common themes across all of the findings. First, including students with special needs in music is a collaborative effort among teachers, parents, students, and paraprofessionals. Specifically, peer tutors and paraprofessionals are critical liaisons between the teacher, student, and other stakeholders. Second, in-service music educators should collaborate with other providers and educators, and are in need of mentorship. This is probably due to the lack of special education preparation in university music education programs.

The most important part of the qualitative body of research is the in-depth look into the plight of individuals who are included in our music programs. The case studies revealed that students with special needs have had a variety of experiences, from getting messages of discouragement about participation to receiving an outpouring of support. Further research should investigate the factors as to why this wide range exists in our profession.

9.2. Qualitative Studies of Specific Disabilities in Music Education

In attempting to see the perspective of a student who is challenged by a specific diagnosis or disability, qualitative tools provide unique insight into the music education of students with special needs. Often students with various disabilities can have similar challenges. Qualitative investigations into specific populations of music students are important in that strategies can apply to a multitude of circumstances.

Learning disabilities are one of the largest known categories of special needs. According to the National Centers for Disease Control and Prevention (2011), 13.87 percent of all children ages 3–17 have a developmental disability (the term used to cover both learning disabilities and attention deficit hyperactivity disorder). McCord (1999) examined students with learning disabilities and composition. Specifically the researcher's main purpose was to observe, describe, and analyze the behaviors that children with learning disabilities use as they compose music and to discover adaptations for children who had learning disabilities that interfered with their ability to understand and create music using a Music Instrument Digital Interface (MIDI) keyboard synthesizer and computer.

This examination included four participants aged seven, eight, and nine who spent six sessions in a MIDI classroom exploring composition ideas using MIDI synthesizers with a custom-designed computer software program (*Music Mania*: http://www.musicmania.co.nz). This software guided them through the composition process. As the participants explored musical ideas and worked toward the final task of creating a musical composition, all of the music they played on their synthesizers was unknowingly recorded. The recorded data was used to examine the participant's musical thinking processes.

Data included MIDI files, transcriptions from videotaped sessions, and observation notes. The data was charted for each participant using qualitative descriptors (general descriptors, process styles, composition emergence, recurring musical patterns, and distractibility). Findings suggested all four participants were categorized in low creativity groups, which meant that the participant either did exactly what *Music Mania* told him to do, or did not show any imagination at all in his playing. Only one participant went beyond experimentation and developed his composition.

Findings revealed that learning disabilities did interfere with learning and understanding music. In most instances the data correlated with information already known from the child's IEP, and each participant progressed through *Music Mania* very differently. In some cases the hardware and software adapted well for the disability, and in other cases adaptations were not possible.

Intellectually gifted students are often left out of the special needs conversation (Hammel and Hourigan 2011). Often in the literature students with learning challenges that are below the norm are considered "special needs." There is also a large population of gifted students who excel in music when given the appropriate learning environment. Qualitative inquiries into the experiences of gifted students in music education provide a unique insight into their needs in the music classroom.

Fredstrom (1999) examined musically gifted students' perceptions about their school music experience. Fredstrom identified 21 musically gifted students using Renzulli's Three-Ring Conception of Giftedness (Renzulli 1988). This model identifies giftedness as the intersection of above-average ability, creativity, and task commitment.

Data was gathered using semi-structured interviews of the gifted students. Participants were asked to describe the following: (a) their musical life, (b) things that motivated them in school music, (c) things that frustrated them in school music, and (d) their ideas about what would make a perfect school music experience for them. It was not clear how the researcher triangulated the data. However, the informants' responses were transcribed and analyzed using "grounded theory analysis procedures."

Findings suggested that the participants' perspectives of their school music experience was influenced by four categories of musical characteristics: (a) musical commitment, (b) musical success, (c) musical passion, and (d) musical awareness. The participants described their musical beginnings as happening in both in-school music classes and out-of-school musical involvement. There was a point in the informants' life, in about middle school, when they became vigorously involved in music, again taking place both in school music classes and in out-of-school musical involvement. The informants moved between describing their in-school experiences and their out-of-school experiences with great fluidity as they told their stories. Further, their musical characteristics influenced their perceptions of these experiences.

The researcher reported that it was clear that the informants' satisfaction in school music was greatest where rigor was promoted, and conversely their satisfaction was decreased when vigor was impeded. This was the central phenomenon of the study. The students described aspects of their experiences that they perceived to effect vigorous musical involvement that included: (a) their teachers, (b) the instruction they received, (c) the opportunities available to them, (d) musical excellence, and (e) their relationships with other students in school music classes.

Williams syndrome (WS), or Williams Beuren syndrome, was discovered in the 1960s and has been identified as a distinctive, genetic, neurological condition. It is estimated that 1 out of 20,000 to 50,000 births result in a diagnosis of WS. Although students that are affected by this disorder have many challenges, it has been noted that they have a high interest and ability in music in relationship to other academic areas.

Milne (2001) examined eight female and eight male participants with WS between the ages of 8 and 18 in a 10-day intensive music program entitled "Music and Minds: A Talent Development Model." Although the study was not labeled mixed method, Milne used a combination of qualitative and quantitative data-collection techniques.

Data was collected in four phases. In phase one, the participants and their guardians completed a questionnaire as part of their application process. This questionnaire included questions about basic demographic information, historical and health information, and interest. Phase two consisted of semi-structured telephone interviews with parents of the participants. Phase three involved observations at the research site, and phase four consisted of "follow-up data collection, designed to further elaborate, confirm, or explore issues that arose during the previous phases" (Milne 2001, 51).

In addition, the School-Wide Enrichment Model (SEM) (Renzulli and Reiss 1997) was used to analyze the experiences of the students involved in this study. The SEM is a series of reform ideas for schools that center around three types of curricula: Type I enrichment (general exploratory experiences); Type II enrichment (group training activities);

and Type III enrichment (individual and small group investigations of real problems) and enrichment teaching and learning (enrichment clusters).

Results included two in-depth case studies of students with WS involved in the "Music and Minds." Findings suggested that all of the students were well aware of their disability and knew that they were treated differently as a result. In fact, a common concern among the participants is how they may overcome their disability to realize their potential in music. In addition, Milne found that students had a varying degree of experiences in music and that their parents mostly supported their participation in music. However, the mother-child dyadic relationship can affect the nurturing of musical abilities among persons with WS. Participants also reported a wide range of support for music from teachers and families because of their disability.

A common challenge among students in early childhood special education is in the area of communication development. In addition, communication disorders can affect development in other domains such as cognition and social interaction. Frick (2000) examined four children with special needs as part of an early childhood class. The researcher was also a participant. The central focus of the study was how a musically rich early childhood special education classroom may contribute to the ways children with disabilities learn to communicate.

This study was designed to (a) describe the classroom music activities and communication patterns of four young children with communication disabilities in an early childhood special education classroom; and (b) explore how types of music, methods of music inclusion, and children's individual differences may contribute to the process of communication development. Data included researcher audiotaped and videotaped observations (38 total school days for three hours a day); artifact analysis of the participants' IEPs; and observational field notes, as well as a personal journal. Interviews with the designated children's parents were conducted.

Results suggested: (a) music that was routine and supported instruction resulted in more vocalization; (b) music created a social context for child-to-child interaction; and (c) all four children increased vocalizations in different ways.

Moss (2009) examined students who were visually impaired and were mainstreamed into instrumental music education. Specifically, Moss was interested in what motivated students to be involved in instrumental music and how their learning challenges affected their overall experience. Also, Moss was interested in how interventions assisted with the students' experience and how their social connection was enhanced. Specifically, his research questions were: "How do the motivations for participation in instrumental music of blind and visually impaired students compare to what is known from research about sighted students' motivations for participation in these classes? To what extent, if any, does the ability to develop their own strategies for learning affect the quality of secondary school blind or visually impaired students' experiences in instrumental music classes? To what extent is the quality of secondary school blind or visually impaired students' experiences in instrumental music related to the intervention or assistance of other people? To what extent do blind or visually impaired secondary school students' perceptions of social connectedness determine the quality of their experiences in instrumental music classes?" (91).

Moss used a series of phone interviews with 11 participants that he became acquainted with through various national organizations. Moss centered his interview questions around the following themes: (a) their motivations for participation in band or orchestra; (b) their strategies for participation; (c) the extent to which other people assist them in their participation; and (d) the extent to which feelings of social connectedness contribute to their instrumental music experience.

Moss coded the data into categories that corresponded to the research questions. Findings suggested the following: (a) memorizing was the most common tool used in participation in band and orchestra; (b) participants also used Braille and enlarged print music notation as "mediation means"; (c) peer assistants, parents, and instructors were also seen as crucial to success in participation in instrumental music education.

Because there are so many different types of disabilities, researchers may find it difficult to generalize findings. Even within one diagnosis, there may be a wide spectrum of challenges. However, a common theme that arose from all of the findings in this section (Qualitative Studies of Specific Disabilities in Music Education) was that the perceived quality of the students' music education experience is connected to the ability of the music teacher to adapt and be resourceful to meet their needs, and that students have had a wide variety of music experiences. The qualitative perspective on these studies has shed light into the length (or lack of length) at which music educators must go to accommodate students. In addition, music students with disabilities can be very descriptive about their needs.

9.3. Qualitative Studies in Music Teacher Education and Students with Special Needs

Music teacher preparation to teach music to students with special needs has been a growing area of research in music education. Specifically, researchers have chosen to focus on how to best prepare music teachers to individualize instruction within diverse and inclusive teaching environments. Using qualitative means to examine the participants' view (i.e., teacher educators, preservice music teachers, cooperating teachers, and students with special needs) has been shown to provide unique insight into the process of preparing music teachers for challenging, inclusive teaching contexts.

Hammel (1999) examined a proposed unit of study for undergraduate music education students regarding the inclusion of special learners in music classrooms. The proposed unit of study was designed in accordance with the following research problems: (a) to identify teacher competencies used by practicing elementary music teachers when including special learners in classrooms, (b) to determine how college and university music education faculty use undergraduate elementary music education methods classes and field experiences to instruct undergraduate elementary music education students regarding the inclusion of special learners, (c) to identify teacher competencies essential for undergraduate elementary music education students relevant to the inclusion of special learners, and (d) to design a unit of study that focuses on the inclusion of special learners and is appropriate for undergraduate elementary music education students.

This study was qualitative and ethnographic and included an examination of 26 teacher competencies identified by Williams (1988). Data included surveys of elementary music educators as well as college and university faculty members who teach undergraduate elementary music education methods courses; interviews with practicing elementary music educators; observations of students with special needs who were included in elementary music classrooms; and artifact analysis that included syllabi from college and university faculty members who teach undergraduate courses that focus on inclusion.

The results of this study concluded that 13 of the 26 teacher competencies examined were considered necessary for elementary music educators when including special learners in their classrooms. The study concluded that teachers should be acquainted with or have knowledge of: various conditions; the Individuals with Disabilities Education Act (IDEA); the music teacher's role on the evaluation team. In addition, teachers should be able to: develop and use informal assessment procedures; monitor the learning process of all students; evaluate program effectiveness for special learners; modify, if necessary, the instructional program to accommodate special learners; encourage appropriate social interactions among all students; adapt materials to provide for individual differences; adapt material to provide for individual differences. Also teachers should have knowledge of how to modify the physical environment of a classroom for special learners; effective classroom management techniques; appropriate materials for diverse learning abilities and styles. As a result of this study, Hammel developed an in-depth unit of study for undergraduate music majors.

Hourigan (2007) examined the process of preservice music teachers providing one-on-one assistance to a single student with special needs in an instrumental music classroom (band). This process was examined from the perspective of two music education majors, a student with special needs, a music teacher, a parent, and the researcher. Research questions included: (a) What were the preservice music teachers' perceptions of assisting a student with special needs as part of their fieldwork experience in an instrumental music methods class? (b) What were the music teacher educator's perceptions of coordinating music majors to teach students with special needs? (c) What were the challenges faced by a student with special needs (and the student's family) in a junior high band class?

A case study design (Merriam 1998) was used in this investigation. Data included journals by the music majors, interviews of the participants, and observations. The participants concluded that this experience was an important part of their fieldwork in music methods classes. Findings suggested that this experience enhanced music majors' perspective on issues of teaching and learning. In addition, this experience helped music majors develop sensitivities and confidence in working with students with special needs. Results of this study also indicated that preservice students have much anxiety upon entering the field, especially with an unfamiliar population, and that preservice teachers need some sort of orientation to a special needs placement.

Hourigan (2009) examined preservice music teachers' perceptions of working with students with special needs. The purpose of this study was to examine phenomenologically a special needs fieldwork experience through the perceptions of seven participants. All of the participants were part of a long-term field experience as part of their student teaching. The research question was: How was this experience assisting and teaching students with special needs in an elementary general music context perceived and constructed by the participants individually and as they collaborated and interacted with one another, as indicated by journals, semi-structured interviews, case writing, and field observations?

This phenomenological investigation utilized a qualitative case study design to explore preservice music teachers' experiences. Student teacher journals and case-writing, participant interviews, and observations were used as data.

Findings suggested that orientation to working with special needs students was beneficial for the preservice teachers before entering this experience. This included field observation, introduction to terminology, and a basic understanding of classroom expectations. In addition, serving as one-on-one assistants while the cooperating teacher delivered the lesson was also crucial to the preservice music teachers' confidence in teaching students with special needs. Also, team-teaching in pairs to start, as well as completing reflective journals about these lessons, was shown to be a positive influence on the preservice music teachers' ability to teach students with special needs. Finally, the act of participating in the study (observation, journaling, and discussion) was beneficial.

Preparation of in-service music teachers and students with special needs is equally important. Blair (2009) used narrative inquiry as a tool to study the perceived experiences of students with special needs in music education classrooms through the eyes of graduate music education students. This was done through a *Teaching Music to Learners with Special Needs* course. Each in-service general music teacher was required to not only write narratives of their experiences in working with children with disabilities but also attempt to describe what they thought the experiences were like for students with special needs in their music classrooms. This data was triangulated with field notes from class discussion and a group interview. When in class, discussion of the narratives was woven into the curriculum, along with readings and projects. In addition, guest speakers listened to their narratives and gave advice to changing teacher practice in assisting students with special needs.

The report focused on a participant named Sonja (pseudonym) because of the unique way she presented her narratives about working with a student named Tyler. Findings suggested that having in-service music teachers write about their own experiences as well as what they think the experience might be for students with special needs proved to be valuable. In fact, Blair states: "Sonja was becoming less concerned about herself and becoming more 'wakeful' to the circumstances around her (15)." This allowed for teachers like Sonja to envision better learning environments for their students.

This particular study examined at length the use of narrative inquiry as a tool for qualitative research. Blair suggests that narrative inquiry can be used not only as a tool for inquiry, but also as a curricular tool for graduate courses. In addition, she suggests using music teacher stories as a conversation starter because of the unique and complex situations that in-service music teachers face, especially working with students with special needs.

The findings in this section (Qualitative Studies in Music Teacher Education and Students with Special Needs) suggest some commonalities for successful music teacher preparation in working with students with special needs. Undergraduate students need to be acclimated to the unique needs of special education students and the learning environment by which some students learn. Serving as one-on-one assistants, team teaching with a peer or mentor, and observing are seen to be an important part of the process. In addition, as seen in the list of teacher competencies provided by Hammel (1999), pre-service music teachers must have the ability to individualize, accommodate, and adapt their technique in order to be successful in an inclusive classroom. It is hoped that because of the continued focus on inclusion, our methods sequence in music education will continue to include an individualized focus.

9.3.1. Conclusion: Suggestions for Future Research

It is through a qualitative view of the human experience that researchers develop theory to enhance the experience of a student (especially a student with special needs) in the music classroom. Van Manen (1999) explains:

> [N]atural science studies "objects of nature," "things," "natural events," and the way objects behave. Human science, in contrast, studies "persons," or beings that have "consciousness" and that "act purposefully" in and on the world by creating objects of "meaning" that are "expressions" of how human beings exist in the world. (4)

As human scientists, researchers are directed to study the experiences existing within the phenomena of the teaching and learning relationship. Therefore, it is imperative for qualitative examinations of students with special needs in music education to continue to exist within the context of the music education literature.

Since inclusion is the aim for many students who receive special education, qualitative research such as Haywood (2006), Lapka (2005), Bell (2008), and Meier (2009) allows for music educators to build theoretical understandings behind successful inclusion. This includes the structures or relationships that exist between all of the participants in the phenomenon. In addition, comparative, multiple, or cross-case-study examinations allow our field to further understand the viewpoint of music teachers and music students (Bell 2008; Meier 2009) within an inclusive environment.

It is hoped that future research will include longitudinal research that examines the experiences of students in music throughout their P–12 experience. There are many "snapshot" studies of students at various levels and of various types (i.e., performance experiences vs. general music experiences); however, it is tough to make the case that these experiences characterize the totality of the participants' experience in P–12 music. In fact, as pointed out by Haywood (2006), there is a wide variety of experiences in music for children with disabilities.

As our inclusion literature in music education continues to grow, it will be important to have multiple examples of case studies of specific diagnosis that incorporate all age groups within music education settings, such as Moss (2009), Frick (2000), Milne (2001), Fredstrom (1999), and McCord (1999). Music teachers and music teacher educators must have case study research from which to generalize potential strategies for these disabilities or that might be generalized for all children within an inclusive music classroom.

P–12 students with special needs will have an enhanced learning environment and have a better chance of acquiring skills and understandings if researchers are able to inform practice for music teacher preparation. More qualitative research, such as Hourigan (2007, 2009) and Hammel (1999), are needed to understand the types of experiences and teaching techniques that are needed for preservice music educators to better prepare them for teaching students with special needs.

Often music teachers are not prepared as undergraduates to work with students who have learning challenges. Therefore, more research into professional development and in-service music teacher preparation, such as Blair (2009), should be further investigated. In addition, further inquiries into graduate coursework and the competencies teachers should have in working with students with disabilities, such as Hammel (1999), is important to further our understanding of what it takes to prepare teachers for students who have unique learning challenges.

After reviewing the research discussed in the preceding, there are a few voices that are missing or that have received little attention. For example, the voice of in-service music teachers and their successful teaching pedagogies, though often included, are not the central focus of a study. Blair (2009) examined this voice; however, there is still a large potential body of research that includes the voice of performance-based music teachers as well as classroom music teachers. Also, continuing to find students with special needs who can articulate their own plight is critical to understanding the music teaching and learning environment for children who are included.

In relationship to the quantitative research and music therapy research on music and students with special needs, the volume of qualitative students in music education is rather small; however, as shown in this chapter, the last decade has seen a substantial increase in qualitative research on this topic. It is hoped that this trend will continue and that thick, rich descriptions will provide a unique perspective of the experiences of this unique population of music students.

Note

1. Newer edition of Merriam (2009) is available.

References

Bell, A. P. 2008. "The Heart of the Matter: Composing Music with an Adolescent with Special Needs." *International Journal of Education and the Arts* 9 (9): 2–36.

Blair, D. V. 2009. "Fostering Wakefulness: Narrative as a Curricular Tool in Teacher Education." *International Journal of Education and the Arts* 10 (19): 2–13.

Fredstrom, T. C. 1999. "Musically Gifted Students and Promoted Vigor: A Grounded Theory Guiding Instructional Practices for Teachers of Musically Gifted Students in School Music." PhD diss., University of Nebraska–Lincoln.

Frick, J. W. 2000. "A Qualitative Study of Music and Communication in a Musically Rich Early Childhood Special Education Classroom." PhD diss., George Mason University.

Hammel, A. M. 1999. "A Study of Teacher Competencies Necessary When Including Special Learners in Elementary Music Classrooms: The Development of a Unit of Study for Use with Undergraduate Music Education Students." DMA diss., Shenandoah University,.

Hammel, A. M., and R. H. Hourigan. 2011. *Teaching Music to Students with Special Needs: A Label-Free Approach.* New York: Oxford University Press.

Haywood, J. S. 2006. "You Can't Be in My Choir if You Can't Stand Up: One Journey Toward Inclusion." *Music Education Research* 8 (3): 407–16.

Hourigan, R. M. 2007. "Music Majors as Paraprofessionals: A Study in Special Needs Field Experience for Preservice Music Educators." *Contributions to Music Education* 34: 19–34.

Hourigan, R. M. 2009. "Preservice Music Teachers' Perceptions of a Fieldwork Experience in a Special Needs Classroom." *Journal of Research in Music Education* 57 (2): 152–68.

Jellison, J. A., and P. J. Flowers. 1991. "Talking about Music: Interviews with Disabled and Nondisabled Children." *Journal of Research in Music Education* 39: 322–33.

Lapka, C. M. 2005. "A Case Study of the Integration of Students with Disabilities in a Secondary Music Ensemble." PhD diss., University of Illinois at Urbana-Champaign.

McCord, K. A. 1999. "Music Composition Using Music Technology by Elementary Children with Learning Disabilities: An Exploratory Case Study." DME diss., University of Northern Colorado.

Meier, K. A. 2009. "The Musical Experience of a Band Student with Special Needs." Master's thesis, University of Michigan.

Merriam, S. B. 1998. *Qualitative Research and Case Study Applications in Education.* San Francisco: Jossey-Bass.

Milne, H. L. O. 2001. "A Comparative Case Study of Persons with Williams Syndrome and Musical Interests." PhD diss., University of Connecticut.

Moss, F., Jr. 2009. "Quality of Experience in Mainstreaming and Full Inclusion of Blind and Visually Impaired High School Instrumental Music Students." PhD diss., University of Michigan,.

National Centers for Disease Control and Prevention. 2011. "Developmental Disabilities Increasing in US." http://www.cdc.gov/Features/dsDev_Disabilities.

National Center for Educational Statistics. 2011. "Status Trends in the Education of Racial Ethnic Minorities." http://nces.ed.gov/pubs2010/2010015/indicator1_8.asp.

Renzulli, Joseph S. 1988. "A Decade of Dialogue on the Three-Ring Conception of Giftedness." *A Journal on Gifted Education* 11 (1): 18–25.

Renzulli, J. S., and S. M. Reiss 1997. *The Schoolwide Enrichment Model: A How-to Guide for Educational Excellence*. 2nd ed. Mansfield Center, CT: Creative Learning Press.

Van Manen, M. 1999. *Researching Lived Experience*. Albany: State University of New York Press.

Williams, D. 1988. "Regular Classroom Teachers' Perceptions of Their Preparedness to Work with Mainstreamed Students as a Result of Preservice Coursework." PhD diss., Indiana University.

CHAPTER 10

INTERSECTIONALITIES

Exploring Qualitative Research, Music Education, and Diversity

BRUCE CARTER

THE purpose of this chapter is to broadly explore several aspects of the social world and music education as investigated through qualitative methodologies. Specifically, this chapter will examine topics of LGBT2QI (lesbian, gay, bisexual, transgender, queer, questioning, and intersexed) studies, gender studies, and feminist studies within music education research. After reviewing these areas and providing suggestions for future qualitative research, I end the chapter with a call for an "intersectionalities" approach to understanding marginalized communities.

What will become clear to reader as the chapter unfolds, is that to label, classify, or define the LGBT2QI studies, gender studies, and feminist studies is a troublesome endeavor. They exist in contested spaces, and within categories like *social justice, equity, marginalized,* and *identity*, to name a few. I recognize the inherent problems associated with established social categories yet acknowledge the relevance of utilizing the categories to begin the process of examining our complex Western social ecology.

Simply stated, the issues associated with accounting for the multiple axis of oppression and their labels are numerous. As a brief example, I could point readers to the current debate occurring between queer theorists and LGBT2QI scholars. More specifically, even within LGBT2QI research, disagreements exists among scholars concerning the proper order of the letters, in addition to the inclusion of 2QI, which refers to queer, questioning, or intersexed. In the late 1980s, the term "GLBT" was prevalent in both academic writing and in the press. However, feminist scholars noted that the "L" for lesbian should be placed before the "G" for gay for numerous political reasons but most notably to refrain from the inference that women are submissive or given a subordinate position within our heteronormative patriarchal society. The newest acronym for some academicians is LGBTQQCSI which stands for lesbian, gay, transgender, queer, questioning, confused, supportive, or intersexed. This example provides an illustration of how labels, even acronyms utilized within social research, are often met with confusion and scrutiny. Within the social sciences other examples of contested labels or categories include *multiculturalism, social justice*, and *culturally relevant pedagogy*, to name a few. Categories presented in this chapter act as a means of organizing literature for the reader, recognizing that social inequalities felt within these groups exist beyond the bounds of a singular label. Finally, the term "underrepresented" describes the broad landscape examined in this chapter while communicating an underlying belief that more research is needed to address these communities within music education.

The tangle of labels and their meanings can be seen in the most recent *Sage Handbook of Qualitative Research* (Denzin and Lincoln 2011), more specifically, within the appendix section. In this vast text encompassing overviews of qualitative research there is one reference to "gay, lesbian, and transgender" (745) while numerous citations are given for "queer" (751) topics of identity, theories, methods, etc. Within the queer category, gender is cross-referenced and within the gender category topics of feminism/feminists research are mentioned as "see also." This cross-referencing and mixing of labels demonstrates a common blurring of these critical lenses. What is paramount to highlight, regardless of critical approach, is the *exceptional* way qualitative research explicates the human experience, specifically in areas of social justice. Denzin and Lincoln (2011) write:

> It is time to open up new spaces, time to explore new discourses. We need to find new ways of connecting persons and their personal troubles with social justice methodologies. We need to become better accomplished in linking these interventions to those institutional sites where troubles are turned into public issues and public issues transformed into social policy. (ix)

For music education researchers, utilizing qualitative methodologies to examine musical experiences of underrepresented populations can inform curricula, public issues, and the educational institution in evocative and nuanced ways. In this way, researchers can invite contestation, contradiction, and philosophical tension into the music education discourse, not to haphazardly invite discord, but instead to promote a critical dialogue for growth and development for *all* members of the educative community.

10.1. Benefits and Losses of Entering at the Recapitulation

The most recent edition of the *Handbook for Research in Music Education*, published in 2002, included a chapter titled "Feminism, Feminist Research, and Gender

Research in Music Education" (Lamb, Dolloff, and Howe). Within this chapter the authors state:

> Music education has not yet been influenced by third wave feminism, gender studies, studies of masculinity, or queer theory, although third wave kinds of research are beginning to be published, particularly outside of traditional music education venues. There is not space in this chapter to present an analysis as to why music education has been so isolated from these theories while the same theories have had an impact on education as a discipline and music as a discipline.
>
> This is an important topic that deserves critical exploration and thorough analysis. (648)

It is clear in these words that the authors are confounded by the lack of research being published that addresses underrepresented communities. In the nearly two decades since the *Handbook for Research in Music Education* was published, there have been some strides in publishing work in these areas. These breakthroughs have largely been made possible within the music education milieu by conferences such as G.R.I.M.E. (Gender Research in Music Education), a professional organization founded in 1991 at the first Feminist Theory and Music Conference; the Music Education Studies Research Group within the American Educational Research Association, and the first LGBT Research Symposium held May 23 through 26, 2010 titled: *Establishing Identity: LGBT Studies and Music Education*.

As Lamb, Dolloff, and Howe (2002) state, with few exceptions, music education researchers were tacit during the emergent sociological research that meaningfully informed the academy in the 1980s and 1990s. Borrowing from a musical example, music educators might consider that much of the work on race, class, gender, ethnicity, and LGBT2QI studies has been introduced and vetted within an extended exposition and development section but out of the purview of the music education research. Therefore, for music education researchers, it might be prudent to consider these topics from the perspective of beginning at the recapitulation. In doing so, music education researchers entering late into the field of social justice or any form of critical sociological studies would be encouraged to meaningfully investigate the historical and theoretical underpinnings surrounding the evolution of each topic. Because music education research concerning underrepresented communities is sparse and newly developed, much of the literature required to scaffold an author's research should be retrieved from areas outside of music education. Finally, readers should be aware that while a brief historical backdrop is presented for each category, this chapter, like the research it addresses, begins at recapitulation. In other words, the emphasis in this chapter is placed on critical differences, postmodernity, multiple perspectives, education theory, research, and practice. At the end of each section selected readings are provided to help guide researchers who plan to pursue any form of future research in this field.

10.2. LGBT2QI Studies in Music Education

At the first conference to address LGBT studies: *Establishing Identities: Lesbian, Gay, Bisexual, and Transgender Studies and Music Education,* held May 23–26, 2010 at the University of Illinois, two keynote addresses by Nadine Hubbs and Nelson Rodriguez highlighted the duality and dissonance surrounding current LGBT2Q studies. Both keynote addresses were published in the *Bulletin for the Council of Research in Music Education* (*CRME*) and provide an excellent starting point to consider LGBT2Q studies in music education since both experienced researchers addressed the field of music education from the perspective of beginning at the recapitulation.

In broadest terms, LGBT2QI or LGBT studies is the largest umbrella or moniker for research pertaining to gender and sexuality studies. Most scholarship labeled within this genre is related to topics of activism, visibility, rights, stereotypes, and community. Researchers utilizing the label of LGBT studies often connote an inclusivity with an intentionality toward similarities of non-heteronormative discourse. Hubbs (2011) cautioned music education researchers who investigate LGBT people to avoid the pitfalls of previous academicians who, since the 1980s, have institutionalized LGBT studies. She states that while broader acceptance of LGBT community members within the academy and American society as a whole should obviously be welcomed, placing LGBT people within a static frame can be unintentionally oppressive. This critique or pushback of a now mainstreamed conceptualization of LGBT studies or people has led to a new term, *homonormativity*.[1] In her description of homonormativity, Hubbs writes:

> The term carries with it a critique of recently mainstreamed LGBT identities and politics that uphold the institutions and assumptions of heteronormativity. "Homonormativity" points to the normalization, naturalization, and capitalist commodification of a certain, narrowed set of homosexual practices and identities that leave intact the social, sexual, political, and economic status quo rather than pursuing the potential of same-sex relations to call into question so many sociocultural assumptions, prescripts, and inequalities. (9)

In other words, Hubbs calls into question the concept of the conference, the notion of establishing an identity with an institutionalized framework that maintains "sociocultural assumptions." She cautions music education researchers to avoid the pitfall of institutionalization and singularity of an LGBT identity, arguing for a non-monolithic view of LGBT expression. Next, Hubbs stated that the most significant contribution of LGBT studies that began in the 1970s "is its revelation of what we know as 'sexuality' as culturally specific and constructed rather than natural or given" (10). The concept of sexuality as a culturally constructed, non-binary hetero-homo behavior, identity, or politic has been central to much of the sociological work thus far and largely agreed upon by scholars across the academy. Furthermore, Hubbs notes an important trend occurring within LGBT studies, the concept of sexuality as being not only binary, or easily labeled within an ever-expanding acronym of acceptance, but the concept of sexuality as an ever-fluid, dynamic part of one's life. She notes a trend for researchers drawing upon LGBT studies across disciplines to ignore static notions of sexuality that are easily labeled, objectified, and stereotyped and to consider sexuality in new, more progressive, non-traditional frameworks.

Nelson Rodriguez, the other keynote speaker of the conference, provided insight into another lens by which topics of sexuality and gender are often investigated—queer theory. Queer theory, like most other forms of post-structural sociological inquiry, has evolved substantially since its inception. Queer theory emerged from the collision of LGBT political and cultural activism in the late 1980s, as feminist cultural studies and identity politics were reframed within the academy. Though conceived within a political milieu, queer theory quickly became a lens to actively question tropes across numerous areas of the academy. Led by women scholars, primarily the texts of Judith Butler (1990), *Gender Trouble*, and Eve Kosofsky Sedgwick (1990), *Epistemology of the Closet*, queer theory not only contested preconceived notions of sexuality and gender, their work codified a means of questioning meaning in broader epistemological and ontological traditions. One of the most prolific and cited queer theory scholars, David Halperin (1997) defines the current state of queer theory as "at odds with whatever is at odds with the normal, the legitimate, the dominant." There is nothing in particular to which it necessarily refers. It is an identity without an essence. "Queer" then, "demarcates not a positivity but a positionality vis-à-vis the normative" (62). Queer theory became synonymous with the deconstruction of any normative value, labeled by Turner as radical deconstructionism (2000). Turner (2000) writes:

> If queer theorists have anything in common, it might be that they consistently celebrate the unformed, inchoate, provisional character of the field, and they look with suspicion on the possibility that, after a tumultuous, boisterous, and unfocused adolescence, queer theory will settle into an adulthood of traditional disciplinarity, with a clearly defined field of inquiry, a journal or two, and a few doctoral programs at the more advanced universities. (84)

Lastly, Rodriguez suggests another model for examining topics related to sexuality—*critical sexuality studies*. Beasley (2005) codified critical sexuality studies by identifying five areas of study: (1) emancipatory or liberationist; (2) sexuality difference or gay and lesbian identity; (3) multiple differences; (4) social constructivism; and (5) postmodern sexuality studies. These categories, thoroughly explained within Rodriguez's text, help provide researchers with meaningful entry points and methods of categorization. The emphasis within all classifications is the "critical" approach to sexuality studies, "the analyses of the existing organization and social meaning of sexuality and sexual studies, rather than merely descriptive accounts of doing sex" (Beasley 2005, 117). Rodriguez encourages the use of critical sexuality studies as a framework for emergent music education research, and the lens provides substantial breadth for meaningful inquiry while allowing authors to circumnavigate troublesome identity politics associated with other modes of inquiry.

Music education researchers considering work within LGBT studies are tasked with situating studies within frameworks laden with historical meaning. It is imperative for authors to understand the political landscapes that shaped various modes of inquiry. To state that one's work is situated within a frame of *LGBT studies, queer theory*, or *critical sexuality studies* greatly influences the reader's perception and understanding of authorial intent.

The publication of articles presented at the conference in *CRME*, edited by Greg DeNardo, served as an important beachhead for LGBT studies in music education. Of the 10 published articles published in *CRME*, most could be classified within the first category of Beasley's critical sexuality studies—emancipatory or liberationists. The authors describe topics of anti-discrimination and assimilation, often with the intent of furthering the notion of rights and equality within schools and society at large.

Furman (2011) and Duling (2011) both describe the lived experience of being an openly gay or lesbian faculty member within a school environment. Furman's qualitative work describes the life of "Pamela" both personally and professionally, focusing on her experiences teaching in K–12 and university settings in the Midwest and Southern states. In this case study, Furman describes the difficulties surrounding Pamela's life as an instrumental music educator. Utilizing Seidman's interviewing technique (2006), Furman adopted a phenomenological approach to identifying the educator's experience. The data was expressed through narrative that emerged from three interviews in addition to classroom observations of Pamela's teaching. Although being an "out" lesbian presented numerous difficulties, most of Pamela's feelings of professional isolation stemmed from her feeling of isolation due to gender. For Pamela, events where band directors gathered reinforced her belief of loneliness, as the instrumental music educators were almost all male and she felt excluded socially. Duling (2011) describes the isolation of being the lone "out" LGBT person within a faculty. Duling provides a phenomenological autoethnographic account of the pressures being the "go-to" faculty member when students or other faculty members have questions pertaining to LGBT topics. Duling addresses six scenarios that he often encounters as the "go-to" professor, including: (a) addressing the awkwardness of being asked if gay; (b) working with LGBT students who use the gay experience to sometimes inappropriately make excuses for poor behavior or work; (c) helping students navigate social pressures; (d) the ever-present topic of coming out; (e) the demands of being the "go-to" faculty member but lacking proper training and information. While Duling expresses his willingness to provide consultation, he concurrently addresses the stresses involved with providing information and guidance beyond his scope of training. In sum, Duling addresses the problems surrounding the assumption that the lone LGBT person is capable of offering appropriate advice simply because they identify as non-heterosexual.

Haywood (2011) investigated the lived experiences of four self-identified LGBT music educators. Data was collected in a series of open-ended, semi-structured interview protocols over a four-month period. Utilizing a phenomenological lens, Haywood constructed four narratives detailing the lived experience of four LGBT teachers. Primary themes that emerged from the across-case analysis of the participants included: personal identification (i.e., I am transgender); coming out as an ever-present event; pedagogical implications; self-awareness as model for students; and student empowerment. Additionally, for each of the four participants the importance of visibility was primary in what they considered a responsibility in advocating a positive model for their students. Cavicchia (2011) interviewed three gay male choral professors teaching at the university level over a six-week period. Utilizing domain questions informed by Cass's Model of Sexual Identity (Cass 1979), data was collected, transcribed, and coded using inductive coding procedures and processes. Each successive interview protocol was informed by directions discerned during the data analysis process. Peer debriefing occurred with music education faculty familiar with qualitative research procedures. Thick description of participants, contents, and interview responses were provided to ensure that the emic voice was most prominent. In the case study, Cavicchia examined the career paths of the music educators and the ways being gay may have influenced their professional identities. The primary theme that emerged from Cavicchia's research included negotiating "the closet," and the constant burden of worry concerning student and peer reaction to their sexual orientation. Each of the participants described being bullied throughout their lives due to their sexual orientation and effeminate qualities. Participants stated that their primary reason for coming out to peers and students was to serve as a role model for undergraduates who might be struggling with their own sexuality.

Sweet and Paparo (2011) investigated the role of the academy, specifically teacher training programs, in providing meaningful preparation for addressing LGBT issues in the music classroom. By reviewing previous research in preservice education they sought to determine: (a) What do music teachers need to know about sexual identity and orientation? (b) What are the implications of this knowledge? (c) How are these issues relevant to teaching? Primary themes that emerged from their investigation included the importance and difficulty of starting a conversation about LGBT topics, allowing for safe classrooms where critical questions and conversation can occur, and, finally, the importance of a personal identity statement for LGBT people. Abramo (2011) also addressed the role of a personal identity statement, but from the perspective of a gay male who chose to never come out during his tenure as a K–12 teacher. Using a post-structural framework (Foucault 1980; Weedon 1997), this study investigated how music teacher identity is constructed through practice and influenced by the discourses that surround instrumental music teachers' work in classrooms (Britzman 2003; Zemblyas 2003). Data was collected through in-depth interviews, field notes from non-participant observations, and participant journal entries. Using narrative analysis to analyze these data, Abramo identified themes through participant stories of dilemmas and successes in practice (Riessman 1993). In her case study she interviewed "Chris," a veteran music educator who chose to hide his sexual identity from his colleagues and students. He described his life as a music educator as chameleon, as he changed his behaviors in ways that allowed him to fit into his surroundings. He described his mannerisms outside of the classroom as substantially different from those he showed while in the educative community. For Chris, the importance of "passing" was paramount in his life and to his educational identity. In other words, he placed tremendous merit on his ability to act in a way that others would not perceive as effeminate or as a marker for a gay person. Abramo suggests that the ability to pass as straight can be seen as a commodity for teachers who chose to hide their personal lives from students. In contrast, a teacher's ability to "not pass" or to be seen as effeminate or gay can be viewed as a liability that is potentially damaging when teaching in communities less tolerant of LGBT people.

10.3. Summation of LGBT Research in Music Education

In sum, the majority of research in music education and LGBT topics thus far has focused on issues of equality and visibility. As researchers continue this trajectory of inquiry it is important for authors to look beyond equity and investigate Beasley's more critical lenses of multiple differences, social constructivism, and postmodern sexuality studies. The examination of the lived experiences of LGBT music educators has revealed topics of coming out, serving as an LGBT ally for the educative community, and the role of passing, among others. Future research is needed to compare and contrast ways in which *music* educators' experiences differ from those teaching in other subject areas. While it may seem commonsensical or anecdotal to believe that music educators, or arts educators in general, are more aware of the needs of the LGBT community, few examples of empirical research exist specifically examining these connections. Lastly, researchers should attend to the complexities of multiple identities (e.g., LGBT and religion, LGBT and race, LGBT and socioeconomic status) and how these relate to the music education experience.

10.4. Gender and All of Its Forms

Although the underrepresented communities discussed in this chapter vary in numerous ways, they all share one confounding commonality: a definition. Within qualitative research, gender is no exception. Gender has been examined in relation to androgyny, binary construction, cultural traditions, equity, empowerment, conformity to cultural traditions, femininity, masculinity, sexuality, ands dysphoria, to name a few. Similar to studies concerning the LGBT community, qualitative researchers must carefully position and articulate the way gender is being expressed in their work.

Much of the work concerning gender thus far in music education research, especially in quantitative analyses, has centered on a binary consideration of gender as it relates to instrument choice or selection (Abeles 2009; Delzell and Leppla 1992). Lastly, researchers must grapple with the difficulties surrounding the labels of "sex" and "gender" as they are presented within research literature. While it is common practice in current sociological research to understand gender as socially constructed or performative and sex as biological, previous research often utilized the terms interchangeably. O'Neill (1997) and Sinsel and Dixon and Blades-Zeller (1997) discuss the evolution of gender vs. sex terminology within sociological studies in great detail and provide a great starting point for music education researchers.

Numerous qualitative researchers have also investigated music educators' role in forming gendered identities in music within educative environments. In a cornerstone of sociological music education research, Green (1997) examined gender roles through students' musical participation, beliefs, and preferences in a public school setting. Over a six-month period, students and teachers were observed and interviewed at a suburban school outside of London. Green observed meaningful differences in the ways teachers and students described their musical experiences. For example, teachers portrayed girls as more musically expressive and eloquent than boys. Furthermore, teachers described the girls as better singers and more enjoyable to teach in the classroom. Similarly, the girls stated that they were more active in the classroom and demonstrated more sophisticated musical skills than the boys. However, with regard to music composition, girls described their abilities and interests as inferior to the boys. Similarly, while the boys described their singing as substandard to girls, they bragged about their abilities as composers. Green asserts that for girls, taking risks and playing out of turn in the classroom during composition exercises was not considered fun or appropriate. Meanwhile, the boys described composition activities as exciting and rewarding. In summarizing the ways girls were defined as better performers and boys as composers, Green states, "girls and boys experience their own music as a reflection and legitimization of their own gender identities" (151). For Green, gender roles were evident in the classroom; passive musical activities were favored by girls, while more individual, risk-taking activities were preferred by the boys.

Similarly, Abramo (2011) observed music practices of adolescent students examining the role of gender in their own music-making. Abramo collected data throughout the course of a year at a school where he served as music instructor. Data collection included observations of rehearsals and individual interviews, which were documented through field notes and audio recordings. In describing the theoretical framework of the study, Abramo rejects the identity of a male or female as fixed or static sexed identity. He positions gender as an identity that is fluid and changes depending on the social situation of the individual. This study is one of the few in music education research journals that embraced gender as performative and dynamic, looking beyond binary representations. He determined that girls and boys rehearsed and composed music in different ways. Boys concurrently utilized musical gestures and nonverbal cues to create a seamless sonic soundscape, while girls separated talk and music production. In mixed gender groupings, tensions were noted due to participants' different learning styles that were misunderstood by members of the opposite gender.

Although I detail the need for research like Abramo's that looks beyond a simplistic view of gender, in music education research the topic of gender and music instrument selection has been extensively investigated and merits review. As early as the 1970s, researchers were investigating why males or females preferred certain musical instruments. The negative influence of gender in music instrument selection has been further identified by quantitative researchers (Bruce and Kemp 1993; Delzell and Leppla 1992; Fortney, Boyle, and DeCarbo 1993; Tarnoski 1993). Research has also demonstrated that the negative of gender stereotyping has a greater impact on boys (Delzell and Leppla 1992; Sinsabaugh 2005). Quantitative researchers have detailed the ways in which individuals mark or describe instruments, leaving a meaningful space for qualitative researchers to question *why* gender associations exist.

Another large body of research in music education related to gender is found within the performance practice of choral music that is addressed specifically in chapter 5 of this volume. Specifically, a common topic relates to the issues surrounding boys' participation in choir. Many articles concern the dissonance boys feel participating in choir when singing is often considered effeminate. Kennedy (2004) examined the way teaching choral music differs when student were placed in single-sex environments. He found that while teaching in single-sex environments was beneficial, it was not a panacea for the problems that boys encounter. He states that the single most important part of teaching boys relates to the special needs of each individual student. Sweet (2010) explored middle school boys' perceptions of singing and participation in choir. In her case study approach, she found that the boys' participation in choir was predicated largely on the esprit de corps felt among the choral members. Similarly, Freer (2010) found that male involvement in middle school choir is subject to fluctuation as a result of influential factors including desire to sing, allure of other activities, and scheduling conflicts. Demorest (2000) determined that the difficulties boys encounter during their vocal change is often so traumatic and embarrassing that they discontinue singing within public spaces like the school choir. While articles concerning the experiences of boys in choir are numerous, no articles were found detailing the perspective of choir from a girl's perspective.

Although elliptic to the K–12 experience, there are numerous qualitative studies in music education utilizing a gender studies lens. For example, Denora (2000) examined the way gender is marked by adolescent girls by preferring mainstream and acoustic styles, while boys chose subversive forms of musical expression like rock, punk, heavy metal, and emo. More broadly, Moisala and Diamond (2000) suggest that popular music practices are largely male-centered and dissuade women from pursuing or prospering in popular music professions. Furthermore, research has also examined the way gender influences the musical approach of instrumental study (Clawson 1993; Green 1997) and the way the physical body informs musical practice (Bayton 1997).

10.5. Feminist Studies

"The webs of feminism in music education have been spinning since Roberta Lamb completed her dissertation at Teachers College, Columbia, in 1987, more than 20 years ago" (Lamb 2009). Since Lamb's dissertation, which served as a beachhead for not only feminist scholarship, but also critical sociological writings as a whole, numerous academicians have meaningfully influenced the music education dialogue from feminist approaches. However, in the years since the publication of the second edition of the *Handbook for Research in Music Education* (2002), in which Lamb reviewed feminist writings and called for more study, few qualitative research articles have been published in North American peer reviewed journals. Moreover, the few academic feminist writings have largely addressed philosophical underpinnings. For example, in the text *Nomadic Turns: Epistemology, Experience, and Women University Band Directors* (2005), Gould articulates a definition of feminism that invites music academicians to question the climate of the profession, specifically instrumental music education. Drawing upon the metaphor of the nomad, Gould details the experience of women university band directors as similar to the exotic Western interpretation of a nomad that is isolated, feared, and misunderstood. Gould's work examines the professional climate that women band directors face, and meaningfully questions issues of power within the academe. Koza (2005) responded to Gould's work, not to refute her philosophical findings, but to present a clarification to what she sees as current feminist understandings. She writes:

> Feminism is a constellation of dynamic political positions, which addresses an attempt to change the unequal power relation and material conditions that are produced and supported by a normative regulatory ideal called sex. . . . I acknowledge the existence of a multiplicity of modern and post-modern feminisms, and by calling these positions dynamic, I acknowledge their fluidity. (188)

Lamb (2009), Gould (2005), and Koza (2005) address the ways feminist approaches inform our understanding of the music experience. To date, however, the lack of qualitative research drawing upon their attentive explanation of feminist inquiry is disheartening. When questioning why feminist lenses are largely silent, one must question the field of music education. What underpinnings either in music education doctoral programs or parameters for journal acceptance provide barriers of entry for this line of inquiry? After articulating and diagnosing these "underpinnings," how can researchers interested in feminist studies politic in ways that move feminist studies into mainstream music education dialogues?

10.6. Summary

While research that addresses gender is more prevalent than other areas of the social justice spectrum, much of the work relates to binary considerations of gender. The clarion call for research proposed by Lamb, Dolloff, and Howe (2002) calling for poststructural approaches to gender studies remains largely unanswered. For qualitative researchers the prospect to meaningfully investigate the musical experiences from an LGBT or gender lens remains largely unexplored and rich with opportunity. Although these research areas present complications due to their fluid and multifaceted nature, the music education landscape would be deeply enhanced by their addition.

There is a tremendous need for qualitative articles in music education journals that meaningfully explore topics related to underserved communities. Due to the small size of the music education research community, few articles exist to help scaffold sociological work. Additionally, qualitative research, especially as it relates to areas of race, gender, class, and LGBT studies, are dynamic and constantly evolving and being redefined. Consequently, for music educators, current work exploring the underserved is best supported by researching sociological work from various arenas of the academy seeking intersections with up-to-date qualitative lenses.

The inclusion of the word "intersectionalities" in the title was meaningful in setting the tone for this chapter and grappling with the difficult proposition of reviewing literature that exists within an ever-changing and dynamic world. Intersectionality is a methodology of studying "the relationships among multiple dimensions and modalities of social relationships and subject formations" (McCall 2005, 13). Emerging from Black feminism, the term "intersectionality theory" was codified by Kimberlé Crenshaw in 1989 while investigating complexities surrounding the oppression of Black women. Intersectionality theory asserts that oppression acting upon members of all marginalized groups does not occur in singular or uniform methods. Social inequalities experienced by these groups occur in complex systems of subjugation that require comprehensive and critical interrogation by social scientists.

In this way, there is also a need for music education research to look beyond one-dimensional description of an underserved population. Life is too messy and complicated to simply state that being a member of one group denotes a single type of representation. Returning to the title of the chapter, I look forward to qualitative research that examines the constellation of life and musical experiences of people who identify themselves in multifaceted ways. For example, how does growing up as both lesbian and a minority impact the musical identity formation of a young person? Qualitative research continues to offer insightful ways to examine the musical experience of underrepresented groups in nuanced ways.

Note

1. The term originates in Lisa Duggan, *The Twilight of Equality? Neoliberalism, Cultural Politics, and the Attack on Democracy* (Boston: Beacon Press, 2003).

References

Abeles, Hal. 2009. "Are Music Instrument Gender Associations Changing?" *Journal of Research in Music Education* 57 (2): 127–139.

Abramo, Natalie. 2011. "Sexuality and the Construction of Instrumental Music Teacher Identity." *Bulletin of the Council for Research in Music Education* 188: 41–44.

Bayton, Michael. 1997. "Women and the Electric Guitar." In *Sexing the Groove*, edited by S. Whiteley, 7–49. London: Routledge.

Beasley, Chris. 2005. *Gender and Sexuality: Critical Theories, Critical Thinkers.* London: Sage Publications.

Britzman, Deborah. P. 2003. *Practice Makes Practice: A Critical Study of Learning to Teach.* Albany: State University of New York Press.

Bruce, Rosemary, and Anthony Kemp. 1993. "Sex-Stereotyping in Children's Preferences in Music Instruments." *British Journal of Music Education* 10 (3): 213–17.

Butler, Judith. 1990. *Gender Trouble: Feminism and the Subversion of Identity.* New York: Routledge.

Cass, Vivienne C. (1979). "Homosexual Identity Formation: A Theoretical Model." *Journal of Homosexuality* 4 (3): 219–35.

Cavicchia, John. 2011. "Queer Path and Career Path: A Phenomenological Study." *Bulletin of the Council for Research in Music Education* 188: 30–33.

Clawson, Mary Ann. 1993. "'Not Just a Girl Singer:' Women and Voice in Rock Bands." In *Negotiating at the Margins: The Gendered Discourses of Power and Resistance*, edited by S. Fischer and K. David, 235–54. New Brunswick, NJ: Rutgers University Press.

Conway, Colleen. 2000. "Gender and Music Instrument Choice: A Phenomenological Investigation." *Bulletin of the Council for Research in Music Education* 146: 1–17.

Delzell, Judith, and David Leppla. 1992. "Gender Associations of Musical Instruments and Preferences of Fourth-Grade Students for Selected Musical Instruments." *Journal of Research in Music Education* 4 (1): 68–74.

Demorest, S. M. 2000. "Encouraging Male Participation in Chorus: A Carefully Planned Workshop for Adolescent Boys can Motivate Them with Stimulating Rehearsals, a Chance to Hear Male Choruses, and a Final Performance Opportunity." *Music Educators Journal* 86 (4): 38–41. doi:10.2307/3399604.

DeNora, Tia. 2000. *Music in Everyday Life.* Cambridge, UK: Cambridge University Press.

Denzin, Norman, and Yvonna S. Lincoln. 2011. *The Sage Handbook of Qualitative Research.* 4th ed. Thousand Oaks, CA: Sage Publications.

Duling, Edward. 2011. "The Go-to-Guy." *Bulletin of the Council for Research in Music Education* 188: 15–17.

Eros, John. 2008. "Instrument Selection and Gender Stereotypes." *Update: Application of Research in Music Education* 27 (1): 57–64.

Fortney, Patrick, David Boyle, and Nicholas DeCarbo. 1993. "A Study of Middle School Band Students' Instrument Choices." *Journal of Research in Music Education* 41 (1): 28–39.

Foucault, Michel. 1980. *Power/knowledge: Selected Interviews and Other Writings 1972–1977.* New York: Pantheon Books.

Freer, Patrick. 2010. "Two Decades of Research on Possible Selves and the 'Missing Males' Problem in Choral Music." *International Journal of Music Education* 30 (2): 17–30.

Furman, Lisa. 2011. "The Lived Experience of a Lesbian Instrumental Music Educator." *Bulletin of the Council for Research in Music Education* 188: 13–15.

Green, Lucy. 1997. *Music, Gender, Education.* Cambridge, MA: Cambridge University Press.

Gould, Elizabeth. 2005. "Nomadic Turns: Epistemology Experience, and Women University Band Directors." *Philosophy of Music Education Review* 13 (2): 147–64.

Halperin, David. 1997. *Saint = Foucault: Towards a Gay Hagiography.* New York: Oxford University Press.

Haywood, Jennifer. 2011. "LGBT Self-Identity and Implications in the Emerging Music Education." *Bulletin of the Council for Research in Music Education* 188: 24–28.

Hubbs, Nadine. 2011. "Visibility and Ambivalence: Thoughts on Queer Institutionalization." *Bulletin of the Council for Research in Music Education* 188: 9–13.

Kennedy, Mary. 2004. "'It's a Metamorphosis': Guiding the Voice Change at the American Boychoir School." *Journal of Research in Music Education* 52 (3): 264–80.

Koza, Julia. "In Response to Elizabeth Gould, Nomadic Turns: Epistemology Experience, and Women University Band Directors." *Philosophy of Music Education Review* 13 (2): 164–73.

Lamb, Roberta. 2009. "Music as Sociocultural Phenomenon: Interactions with Music Education." In *Critical Issues in Music Education: Contemporary Theory and Practice*, edited by H. Abeles and L. Custodero, 22–36. New York: Oxford University Press.

Lamb, Roberta, Lori-Anne Dolloff,, and Sondra W. Howe. 2002. "Feminism, Feminist Research, and Gender Research in Music Education." In *The New Handbook of Research on Music Teaching and Learning*, edited by R. J. Colwell and C. Richardson, 648–74. New York: Oxford University Press.

McCall, Leslie. 2005. "The Complexity of Intersectionality." *Signs* 30 (3): 1771–800.

Moisala, Pirkko, and Beverley Diamond. 2000. *Music and Gender.* Chicago: University of Illinois Press.

O'Neill, Susan. 1997. "The Social in Music Performance." In *The Social Psychology of Music*, edited by D. J. Hargreaves and A. C. North, 193–201. New York: Oxford University Press.

Riessman, Catherine. K. 1993. *Narrative Analysis.* Thousand Oaks, CA: Sage Publications.

Sedgwick, Eve Kosofsky. 1990. *Epistemology of the Closet.* Berkeley: University of California Press.

Sinsel, Tiffany, Wallace E. Dixon Jr., and Elizabeth Blades-Zeller. 1997. "Psychological Sex Type and Preferences for Musical Instruments in Fourth and Fifth Graders." *Journal of Research in Music Education* 45 (3): 48–65.

Sinsabaugh, Katherine. 2005. "Understanding Students Who Cross over Gender Stereotypes in Musical Instrument Selection." PhD diss., Teachers College, Columbia University.

Sweet, Bridget, and Stephen Paparo. 2011. "Starting the Conversation in Music Education Programs." *Bulletin of the Council for Research in Music Education* 188: 36–38.

Turner, William. 2000. *A Genealogy of Queer Theory.* Philadelphia, PA: Temple University Press.

Weedon, Christine. 1997. *Feminist Practice and Poststructuralist Theory.* 4th ed. Malden, MA: Blackwell.

Wych, Gina. 2012. "Gender and Instrument Associations, Stereotypes, and Stratification: A Literature Review." *Update: Application of Research in Music Education* 30 (2): 31–54.

Zemblyas, Michalinos. 2003. "Interrogating 'Teacher Identity': Emotion, Resistance and Self-Formation." *Educational Theory* 53 (1): 107–27.

CHAPTER 11

WORLD MUSICS AND CULTURAL DIVERSITY IN THE MUSIC CLASSROOM AND THE COMMUNITY

YIANNIS MIRALIS

THE music classroom has always been a place where thoughts and ideas from various local and faraway cultures have found their way in the schools. This is especially so since the second half of the twentieth century, during which one can observe a tremendous increase of interest and publications on music from various cultures and styles that divert from the "canon" of Euro-American music education. Most of these materials have been in the form of position papers in support of the inclusion of world musics in the curriculum, with those papers offering practical recommendations for its inclusion as well. Nevertheless, this area within music education has not been extensively studied by the music education research community. As various researchers indicated, the amount of research focusing on issues relating to world musics was limited (Campbell 1991; Chin 1996a; Edwards 1998; Jordan 1992; Miralis 2002; Okun 1994). Specifically, Chin (1996a) supported that "little is known about the actual state of multicultural music education in American schools" (5), whereas Okun (1998) concluded that "there is little research about multicultural music in music teacher education" (28). Furthermore, Jordan (1992) noted that "research has yet to answer the questions regarding the effects of cross-cultural exposure on musical perception, the developmental readiness of various ages for the study of world musics, the effectiveness of various approaches, and the question of bimusical and multimusical capacity" (744). This is even more so when one considers qualitative research in this area. As Edwards (1998) stated, "limited qualitative research regarding instruction in American Indian music or other multicultural music exists. No qualitative studies were found that addressed achievement resulting from instruction in multicultural music" (62). A few years later, though, a big shift was observed. According to Kantorski and Stegman (2006), the most researched topic (i.e.,

13 percent) in qualitative research dissertations in music education during the period of 1998–2002 was that of multiculturalism.

This chapter explores qualitative studies from 1980 to 2011 that focus on the teaching of world musics and cultural diversity in the United States or Canada. It does not aim to include every qualitative study with such emphasis. Instead, the chapter concentrates on selected studies that follow a clear qualitative methodology with an educational focus or implications. In studies that follow a mixed design, attention is given only to the qualitative part. For a broader examination of the literature, the interested reader is referred to other related studies (i.e., Feay-Shaw 2000; Jordan 1992; Lundquist 2002).

From the 38 studies included in this chapter, 23 were doctoral dissertations, three were masters' thesis, nine were journal articles, two were book chapters, and one was an unpublished paper. Studies are presented chronologically and alphabetically within the following six categories: studies conducted in (a) elementary school (Gr. 1–5); (b) middle school (Gr. 6–8); (c) high school (Gr. 9–12); (d) higher education; (e) an unclear or combined educational level (elementary to university); and (f) a community context. Most studies occurred in elementary school ($n = 10$) and in higher education ($n = 9$), followed by studies in the community ($n = 6$), in middle school ($n = 5$), and in an unclear or combined educational level ($n = 5$). Only three studies were found that focused on high school.

11.1. STUDIES IN ELEMENTARY SCHOOL (GR. 1–5)

Most of the studies in this chapter occurred in elementary school. Stellaccio (1995) conducted the first qualitative study in elementary general music in which she sought to examine the effect of mandates on elementary curricula, to explore teachers' attitudes and beliefs about the teaching of music from a multicultural perspective, and to examine how music education can accommodate expectations for social action. Data for this ethnographic analysis of multicultural curriculum and pedagogy were collected through interviews with supervisors, teachers, and coincidental subjects, as well as through document analysis and teaching observations. Findings illustrated the existence of three distinct ideologies in general music education, those being the common elements approach, infusion, and dynamic multiculturalism. The dynamic multicultural curriculum was found to be one that included strategies for best addressing learning styles, values education, cross-curricular connections, and thinking skills. Nevertheless, music educators were found to be inadequately prepared to address the complexity of multicultural music teaching.

The following year, Klinger (1996a) investigated the attempts of a suburban school district in the Pacific Northwest to enrich and diversify its elementary curriculum with the addition of world musics. This ethnographic study examined the formed partnership with a regional folk arts council that brought artists-in-residence to elementary schools through programs that focused on the music and culture of West Africa and Puget Sound Native Americans. The researcher looked at teacher perceptions regarding the role of music in multicultural education, the necessary musical skills and knowledge of the teacher, issues of musical and cultural authenticity, and the manifestation of cultural and historical contextualization in the classroom. Data were collected over an extended two-year span and included document collection; interviews with teachers, artists, administrators, and leaders; and observations of classes, residencies, and workshops. Findings showed a shared value and respect for musical diversity and a preference for the inclusion of culture-bearers. Nevertheless, residencies were not found to be of long-term value.

In a journal publication from the same study, Klinger (1996b) provided an account of the practical struggles and problems experienced by "Angela," one of the teachers involved, who prepared the whole fifth grade for an evening conmprising African music, dances, and folk tales. Data were gathered through open- and close-ended interviews with "Angela," the fifth-grade teachers, and other teachers in the district, and from examination of music curricula and district documents. Findings pointed to the problematic nature of limited teacher knowledge and expertise, Eurocentric musical training, the limitations posed by musical notation, and the limited availability and inappropriateness of existing materials; findings documented "Angela's" struggles to "do the best she can, given the limited resources and time" (35). Nevertheless, they also revealed the fundamental role that music can play in introducing children to other cultural groups.

Edwards (1998) investigated the musical or nonmusical student achievement from four different instructional approaches in American Indian music in fourth grade. Each approach was assigned randomly to four intact general music classes, whereas an additional class received traditional music instruction. Data were collected through open-ended student-written paragraphs focusing on content knowledge and skill acquisition. Coded analysis revealed a wide range of intergroup differences, not only in content and skill but also in intercultural sensitivity. These differences "can be transformed into response patterns representing various levels or depths of multicultural sensitization and perception" (77). The author proposed a working instructional theory in regards to the multicultural achievement of fourth-grade students.

Four years later, Meidinger (2002) sought to determine the attitudes and practices of six selected expert general music teachers from Oregon regarding the implementation of multicultural music. It further attempted to establish connections between teacher attitudes, experiences, and training. Data were collected through on-site observations, personal interviews, and a survey of 354 fourth-graders and were analyzed using a constant comparison approach. Findings showed the important role that multicultural music played in the curriculum and the positive feelings of students for music of various cultures. It was further revealed that the greatest influence on student response toward multicultural music was the attitude and classroom practices of the teacher. Teachers were catalysts in dealing with the challenges encountered in multicultural music education.

Abril (2006) examined the effect of multicultural music instruction on the learning outcomes of 170 white, middle-class students from four suburban public schools in a large Midwestern city. Two intact fifth-grade classes at each school were randomly assigned to two groups that followed a teaching approach focusing on music concepts or sociocultural context. Treatment during the six lessons included songs from various non-Western cultures. Data were collected through two writing prompts which asked students questions about newly acquired knowledge, understanding, and skill. Analysis of data revealed that instructional approach significantly affected children's descriptions of knowledge, suggesting that educators should engage students in discussions regarding sociocultural issues if they want to teach them about tolerance and acceptance.

In her study, Chen-Hafteck (2007)[1] investigated the effects of an interdisciplinary program based on a sociocultural approach, with Chinese music and culture, which was introduced to 250 fifth- and sixth-grade students from three public elementary schools. The study followed a multiple case methodology, and data were collected through teacher reports and questionnaires, field observations, discussion with teachers, and examples of students' work. It was found that the success of this project balanced on (a) its sociocultural approach, (b) a student-centered and flexible curriculum, (c) a performance-based method, (d) live demonstrations by native Chinese musicians, and (e) the positive attitude and the collaborative effort of the teachers involved.

In a mixed methods study, Lehmberg (2008) examined the perceptions of six effective, urban, elementary general music teachers in regard to preservice teacher preparation for, and effective teaching in, urban elementary general music classrooms. Culturally responsive teaching and effective teaching were the two theoretical frameworks that guided the design of the study. The researcher followed a nested, collective case study research design in which participants with high levels of cross-cultural adaptability were identified from the survey sample of experienced, effective teachers. Data were gathered through individual, semi-structured phone interviews. Content analysis revealed 100 common emerging themes and four common meta-themes: (a) flexibility, (b) cultural knowledge and skills, (c) caring and responsive attitude, and (d) musical knowledge and music teaching skills. Through these findings the author generated a model for effective, urban, elementary general music teaching.

Kelly-McHale (2011) examined the relationship between the musical identities of four second-generation Mexican American students and the beliefs and practices of their general music teacher at a Midwestern suburban elementary school. Following a collective case study design, Kelly-McHale explored the interaction between music instruction, cultural responsiveness, and musical identity. Data were collected through semi-structured group interviews, observations, journal entries, and artifact collection. Findings support the development of nontypical musical experiences that legitimize and value the music role of students and their families, thus breaking down borders between the school and the community and the formal and informal ways of learning. They also point to the importance of culturally responsive curricula that take into consideration the identity, background, and life experiences of students, instead of a Eurocentric, notation-oriented, "color-blind" approach to music education.

The same year, Stafford-Davis (2011) sought to understand the multicultural teaching experiences of music teachers in two public school districts in Arkansas, focusing specifically on issues of definition, methods, and motives and challenges for implementation of multicultural music education. Eight elementary schools were purposefully selected and data were gathered through document collection, semi-structured interviews, and classroom observations. Findings led to the production of a working definition for multicultural music education and revealed that most participants justified its inclusion on the grounds of the diversity found in their communities and classrooms. The study also showed that implementation was based on thematic units and holidays from around the globe and through the use of foreign language songs, ethnic instruments, and dances.

Overall, studies in elementary school explored a wide variety of areas ranging from teacher attitudes toward and experiences with world musics (Stellacio 1995; Klinger 1996a; Meidinger 2002; Stafford-Davis 2011) to the interaction between music instruction, cultural responsiveness, and student's musical identities (Kelly-McHale 2011). They also examined issues relating to the effectiveness of various teaching approaches (Edwards 1998) and of multicultural music instruction (Abril 2006), cultural contextualization (Klinger 1996a), the effects of an interdisciplinary program based on Chinese music and culture (Chen-Hafteck 2007), how music education can accommodate expectations for social action (Stellacio 1995), and music teacher preparation and effective teaching (Lehmberg 2008).

11.2. Studies in Middle-School (Gr. 6–8)

Studies focusing on middle school are much more recent and fewer in number. The first qualitative study on world musics in middle school was by Withers-Ross (1999), who sought to examine "how the use of folk songs as text influence students' perceptions and attitudes of other cultures as well as their own" (14). Participants included sixth-grade students from four social studies classes at a middle school in South Carolina. Through a nontraditional constructivist method focusing on multiple intelligence centers of interest and the use of an integrated curriculum, lyrics from folk songs from three different cultures (i.e., Native American, Caribbean, and African American) served as topics for discussions, with the overall aim of promoting cultural awareness and respect. Data were gathered through observations, field notes, interviews, audio recordings, and informal discussions, as well as through student reflection pages and portfolios. The study illustrated that students became more aware of their self-worth, felt empowered, and exhibited self-growth and thoughtfulness about social conditions. It is unclear, however, whether these positive changes occurred due to the use of multicultural folk songs or the method of instruction.

Ten years later, in a case study with extreme case sampling, Abril (2009) investigated how Nancy, a middle school instrumental music teacher, responded to culture through the curriculum. The study examined how several events and circumstances affected the curriculum and informed Nancy's culturally responsive teaching. Data included extensive observations, informal dialogues with Nancy, formal interviews, journal reflections, field notes, and document analysis of lesson plans and other related material. The study revealed the crucial impact that a recent summer trip to Mexico had on Nancy and the importance of professional development through enrollment in a graduate music education program. These personal and professional experiences inspired her to come closer to Mexican culture and to pursue change at her school by establishing a mariachi ensemble. Through this ensemble Nancy followed a sociocultural approach to teaching music and developed a heightened cultural awareness and empathy toward her students. The study brought attention to the potential importance of an immersion experience in unfamiliar cultural communities for preservice teachers, questioned admission criteria in music teacher education programs, addressed issues regarding the nature of school-based ensembles in American music education, and illustrated that "educators have the potential to make music programmes more relevant to the lives of their students" (89).

In a case study of an urban middle school, Calloway (2009) sought to investigate issues of educational equity in regards to music and urban education. He specifically examined whether students were receiving an equitable, culturally and socially relevant music education. Data were collected primarily through interviews with the principal, counselor, music teachers, and two student focus groups, as well as through the document collection, field notes, and class observations. The study found that the school failed to provide an equitable music education for all students and that there was a lack of culturally relevant content and pedagogy. It also revealed the importance of having successful models of urban music education, as well as stability, consistency, expertise, and training in the music faculty.

A year after his previous study, Abril (2010) examined ". . . how Nancy's pedagogical and curricular decisions [were] imparted [to] a particularly thoughtful, political, and articulate student in her class, a fourteen-year-old girl named Juli" (6) and pointed to the tensions that occurred in the mariachi program. Data analysis from the three interviews with Juli revealed three major areas of tension that centered on problems regarding the selection of "inappropriate" repertoire and the superficial approach toward cultural content knowledge. The author suggested that music educators should (a) carefully choose their repertoire, (b) help students make connection between music, society, history, and politics, and (c) encourage students to engage in meaningful discussions about the music.

Finally, Ryan (2011) examined the effectiveness of world music pedagogy in a middle school general music classroom in developing students' understanding of Andean musical practice. Specifically, this action research study compared the effectiveness of Western transmission techniques to a transmission process used by indigenous Andean *altiplano* musicians. Students in two sixth-grade general music classes engaged in learning Andean music through singing, performing, and composing Andean-styled music. Data were gathered through pre- and post-instruction questionnaires, student and teacher journals, performance assessments, and group interviews. Results revealed that students in the Andean class were able to replicate Andean musical characteristics with a higher degree of authentically, to create music communally and voluntarily built on Andean music-making skills. Overall, this study showed that learning to make music through a world music pedagogy that focuses on listening, moving, singing, and playing instruments can be educationally beneficial. As Ryan indicated, "the experience, hybrid in the sense that it combines elements of cultural musicking and classroom musicking, is one that brings students as close as possible to authentic musicking while in the general music classroom" (216).

Overall, the small number of qualitative world music studies in middle school explored students' attitudes (Withers-Ross 1999; Abril 2010), teacher's experiences (Abril 2009), pedagogical issues focusing on culturally relevant music education (Abril 2009; Calloway 2009) and the effectiveness of different teaching approaches (Ryan 2011).

11.3. Studies in High School (Gr. 9–12)

Johnson (1997) conducted the first qualitative world music study in a Canadian high school. She explored the views of three music teachers selected through maximum variation sampling. The study followed an emergent research design, starting as three separate case studies and later synthesizing its findings in a single study. Data were gathered through focused and open interviews, participant observations, and document collection, and their analysis included case and cross-case analysis. Of importance in this study was the researcher's role of observer-participant and her own struggles with the teaching of world musics. Results indicated that the most influential factors for the teaching of world musics were (a) exposure to diverse musical genres and styles, (b) experience of a broad-based music program in high school, and (c) personal interest and contact with diverse musics. The study also revealed that three factors that negatively affect the teaching of world musics were (a) the limited available literature and research on the teaching of world musics, (b) the limited communication among practitioners about the issues encountered when teaching world musics, and (c) the limited preservice training for the teaching of world musics.

In one of the few qualitative studies focusing on school instrumental ensembles that perform "multicultural music," Oare (2008) examined and analyzed the operation of the Chelsea House Orchestra (CHO), an afterschool Celtic string ensemble in Michigan. This case study aimed "to describe how a high school orchestra program balances the need for a more diverse repertoire of music with the limitations and requirements inherent to traditional instrumental music programs" (64). Data were gathered through interviews with the ensemble director, a focus group interview with four members, and rehearsal observations. Data analysis revealed four emerging themes: (a) social music-making with an emphasis on democratic learning processes, creativity, and enjoyment; (b) a balance between classical and folk music education, exhibiting an emphasis on classical Western European tradition with a sincere respect for other musics;

(c) evolving authenticity and the need to make creative compromises; and (d) creolization of musical transmission, in which aspects of both traditional school pedagogy and traditional folk methods are incorporated and fused. The study further addressed the need for identification and description of a specific model of a successful multicultural ensemble.

In a study that sought to understand the high school music experience, Countryman (2010) examined music at a Canadian high school. Using a narrative inquiry and following Charmaz's "interpretive, constructivist grounded theory" approach, she sought to document and understand the views and experiences of 32 former high school music students and seven experienced music educators. Even though her study does not focus on the use of world musics, it is, nevertheless, included in this chapter since one of the fundamental questions it addressed was "whose music do we teach." Data were gathered through interviews, focus group discussions, and follow-up conversations and were analyzed based on the theoretical frameworks of figured world and communities of practice. Overall, the study found that there were enormous challenges in assessing quality and professional growth experiences in music teaching in high school. Countryman provided recommendations for high school music practice and emphasized the importance of teacher professional development through the formation of "real communities of practice among small groups of self-initiated music educators" (279). She concluded that what was needed in order to transform practice was empowered and affirmed music educators.

The three qualitative world music studies in high school explored teachers' views and experiences (Johnson 1997), the operation of world music ensembles (Oare 2008), and the lived musical experience of students and teachers (Countryman 2010). It is interesting to note that two of the three studies were conducted in Canadian high schools, which might indicate that the focus of American high school music education is predominantly placed on various types of large performing ensembles (i.e., bands, orchestras, and choirs) and not on world musics or on issues of diversity and multiculturalism. Nevertheless, despite the small number of studies conducted, these three studies have shed significant light on high school music education and will pave the way for more in-depth studies in the future.

11.4. Studies in Higher Education

Montague (1988) conducted the first qualitative world music study in higher education. She examined preservice teacher training in multicultural music education in selected colleges in the United States and the effect of state legislation and policies on university curricula. Data were collected through a questionnaire and through 23 interviews with music education and ethnomusicology faculty members. Visits to music classes provided additional data. The study led to a representative sample of multicultural music courses and pointed to the crucial importance of undergraduate music training.

Eight years later, Barry (1996) examined the level of comfort for diversity of 45 predominantly white preservice teachers and the effects of special training and field experience on their comfort level with multicultural situations. Subjects were enrolled at a Southeastern university and received the same special training in multicultural music education. They were also placed for six weeks in two general music classes (K–6), one predominantly black and the other predominantly white. The study followed a mixed design methodology, with data collected through journals, instructor's observations, and a two-part questionnaire. Results indicated that subjects were not able to adequately apply what they had learned during field experiences and felt anxiety and uncertainty about multicultural issues in education.

Chin's (1996) dissertation focused on the status of multicultural music training in higher education. She followed a two-phase design, with the qualitative part being a case study of two exemplary music programs, one at a private small liberal arts college and the other at a large public research university. Data were collected through semi-structured interviews with students, faculty, and administration members, as well as class observations, interaction with students, and document collection.

Okun's (1998) bi-part study investigated how undergraduate music teacher education programs responded to the demands of cultural diversity and multicultural education. Data for the first part of the study were collected through phone interviews with four selected leaders in multicultural music education, focusing on the identification of their philosophies, goals, and implementation strategies. The second part of the study was a case study of the exemplary music education program at the University of Washington. Data included university document collection, on-campus observational fieldwork, and interviews with six music professors. The study attempted to synthesize data regarding "an ideal" and "a real" program concerning multicultural music teacher education. Findings led to the construction of seven long-term assessment guidelines for music teacher education programs.

The same year Zaretti (1998) conducted a case study on the experiences of student-participants of the International Vocal Ensemble (IVE), a vocal ensemble at Indiana University that focuses on the re-creation of music from outside the Western art tradition. Zaretti indicated that she wanted to "examine the ways in which multicultural music education is being 'lived' in an American university ... through an understanding of instructional methods and student responses" (8–9). Data were collected through fieldwork as participant-observer, interviews with IVE participants, formal and informal interviews with the ensemble's director and with guest conductors, observations of videotaped rehearsals, and research on relevant data. The study provides insights into the function of one of many possible models of world music ensembles in higher education and explores "experience-based educational paradigms."

Emmanuel's (2002) doctoral dissertation focused on the beliefs and attitudes of five female preservice music educators engaged in a short-term immersion field experience in a public elementary school in Detroit. This type of immersion experience in a culturally diverse setting was framed around the theory of intercultural competence and was part of a broader university course at Michigan State University. The study followed a phenomenological research paradigm and used an instrumental descriptive case study methodology. Data were collected through course assignments and classroom discussions, field notes, teaching observations, focused and informal group discussions, individual interviews, and daily journals kept by the five participants and the participant-observer. Results indicated that "... immersion experiences combined with coursework with opportunities for guided reflection under the supervision of an informed instructor would likely have dramatic effects on the attitudes and beliefs of pre-service music teachers" (283). A summative article from the dissertation appeared in the *International Journal of Music Education* (Emmanuel 2005).

The purpose of Miralis's (2002) bi-part dissertation was to examine the availability of multicultural courses at the Big Ten universities and explore the perceptions of music faculty regarding multicultural–world music education and undergraduate music teacher education. A descriptive content analysis of available courses appeared in an *Update* article (Miralis 2003). Data for the second part of the study were collected through 33 semi-structured interviews with purposefully selected music education and ethnomusicology professors. Analysis of data revealed nine themes in regard to the problematic implementation of multicultural–world music education and provided 15 suggestions for improvement. The study concluded with recommendations for overall change in music education and aimed to contribute to the construction of a grounded theory on music teacher education regarding the teaching of world musics.

In a study that examined the content and process of implementing an internationalized course on general music education, Addo (2009) focused on the experiences of 23 undergraduate music education students at a large Midwestern university. Students were enrolled in an innovative course that encouraged the integration of international perspectives and study abroad experiences and included modeled lessons, field observations, teaching experiences, and collaborative assignments. Data were collected through student reflective papers, observations, and small group instructional delivery. Findings focused on enablers and constraints of internationalizing on preservice teacher education. Content analysis revealed four major challenges in internationalizing and pointed to the importance of access, equity, and quality, as well as the acknowledgment of the experiences, cultures, and communities of the students. The study further brought attention to issues of civic responsibility, the broadening of interdisciplinary and institutional relationships, the integration of music and cultural skills, and the expansion of music education toward global relevance.

In one of the few studies focusing on popular music, Powell (2011) examined the perspectives and experiences of participants in three popular music ensembles from two higher education institutions in the Northeastern United States. Following a multiple case study design, data for this ethnographic study were collected through formal and semi-structured interviews with the two ensemble directors and with music administrators and student members; informal conversations with alumni members; classroom observations; document collection; and audio and video recordings of rehearsals, activities, and performances. Data analysis revealed six challenges regarding the implementation of popular music ensembles in higher education and provided suggestions regarding music education. The study proposed a model for the incorporation of popular music ensembles into music education.

Generally speaking, studies in high school were numerous and diverse, with most of them focusing on preservice teacher training in multicultural music education (Addo 2009; Chin 1996; Emannuel 2002; Miralis 2002; Montague 1988; Okun 1998). Others examined the views and experiences of preservice teachers (Addo 2009; Barry 1996; Emannuel 2002) and of music faculty (Chin 1996; Miralis 2002; Okun 1998). Some were case studies of exemplary music programs (Chin 1996; Okun 1998), whereas others focused on world music ensembles (Powell 2011; Zaretti 1998) and the teaching of popular music (Powell 2011). A couple of studies concentrated on the value of an immersion field experience (Emmanuel 2002) and of an internationalization and study abroad program (Addo 2009).

11.5. Studies in an Unclear or Combined Educational Level (Elementary to University)

Five of the studies included in this chapter did not fall under any of the preceding categories or focused on a combined educational level and are, therefore, presented in a separate category. Gilchrist (1980) was the author of the oldest study included in this chapter. The overall purpose of his mixed method study was to assess the preparation of vocal teachers from North Carolina's public schools in performance practices of black gospel music. In addition to survey data collected from 60 vocal music teachers, the researcher interviewed 10 of them with regard to the performance practices used in three audiotaped excerpts of gospel arrangements. Analysis of data revealed that most of the teachers were not adequately prepared to teach black gospel music, were not aware of distinctions between traditional and contemporary forms of black gospel music, and did not perceive this music genre to be as significant as others.

Norman (1994) sought to investigate the perceptions of selected participants regarding multicultural music education. Participants included music faculty and doctoral students from three American universities, as well as music supervisors and music teachers from suburban and urban school districts. They were equally associated with vocal and instrumental music and exhibited diversity in regard to their racial background and teaching experience. Data were collected primarily through serial interviews, focused group interviews, and participant observation. Findings from the study provided an extensive range of 15 issues, with a fundamental issue being that of a "... critical lack of a philosophy to support multicultural music education, and especially a philosophy that emphasizes equal opportunity in the classroom, school, community, and society at large" (434). Norman concluded that there is a need for a change in focus away from musical products to pedagogical and musical processes. A summative article from the dissertation appeared in the *Council for Research in Music Education* (Norman 1999).

In her study, Young (1996) examined the attitudes, philosophies, and approaches toward multicultural education of elementary and middle school music teachers in suburban and urban schools in Ohio. Data were gathered through teacher surveys, interviews, classroom observations, and document collection. Findings indicated an overall agreement in regard to the value and importance of multicultural education. Teachers considered music to be a major expression of cultural identity and felt that the diversity of the world's music should be included in the curriculum regardless of the minority background of the students in the classroom. Nevertheless, the study also revealed an absence of a shared definition and understanding of multicultural education, a lack of teacher training, and ineffective implementation.

In a case study of the Kamehameha Schools (K–12) in Hawaii, Szego (1999) investigated the history and practice of this unique intercultural educational setting in which native Hawaiians were educated in Hawaiian and Western musical styles. Through an existentialist phenomenological approach, the study explored issues of power between colonial education and native Hawaiian musical traditions. Data were gathered during extensive fieldwork and through document collection and formal and informal interviews with students, teachers, parents, and alumni. Analysis of the students' diverse experiences with a broad range of musics and through "various kinds of practice, e.g., the singing, chanting, moving, dancing, perceiving and interpreting" (261), led to the development of the concept of "travel" and illustrated the complexity of sound perception, especially in regard to text-based music. According to Szego, "it may be wise to set our sights on charting an 'aesthetics of incomprehensibility' or at least an aesthetics of partial linguistic comprehensibility" (265).

Hess (2009) interviewed nine fourth- to eighth-grade students of diverse backgrounds from a public school in Toronto with regard to their experiences from participating in the school's Sankofa Drum and Dance Ensemble. The ensemble, initiated and taught by the researcher, focused on the study and performance of music and dances from the Ewe tradition in Ghana. Results revealed the students' preference for learning music aurally and a valuing for both the visual and aural aspects of aural transmission. Results also illuminated the students' feelings of enjoyment for the social aspect of the aural learning process, pointed to the importance of learning music "authentically," and brought attention to the need for expansion and enrichment of the music repertoire used in public school music education.

Overall, the foci of these five studies were previously addressed in other studies described earlier. These ranged from examination of music teacher preparation for world musics (Gilchrist 1980), exploration of the views and experiences of administrators and teachers (Norman 1994; Young 1996), and specific examples of intercultural education and issues of power in music and culture (Szego 1999). One of the studies focused on student perceptions with regard to participation in world music ensembles (Hess 2009).

11.6. Studies in a Community Context

Studies under this category occurred in the community, in a setting outside the confines of a school. The first such study was an ethnography by Gaines (1989), who investigated the educational role of Patakin/Carambu, an ensemble of eight professional musicians and dancers in New York City. The group presented lecture-demonstrations focusing on Afro-Cuban and Afro–Puerto Rican music and dances, providing cross-cultural education for a bilingual community. The study examined the role, function, and relevancy of music in the community. Data were gathered through participant observations, informal interviews, field notes, and analysis of recorded performance events. Results pointed at the critical role of music in cross-cultural education and illuminated music's significant contribution toward the development of ethnic and cultural identity.

Fourteen years later, Powell (2003) studied the social and cultural organization of learning within the context of San Jose Taiko, a nonprofit professional ensemble dedicated to the practice of Japanese American drumming. The group balances between its Japanese musical and cultural tradition and its desire for innovation and is involved in the cultural preservation and promotion of Japanese aesthetics and empowerment of community members. The study followed a sociocultural theoretical framework and also drew from theories of artistic and aesthetic knowledge and phenomenological theories of place. Data from this ethnographic study included participant observation over an extensive four-year period, interviews with many of its members and the artistic and managing director, document collection, descriptive field notes, and transcription and analysis of videotaped sessions. Findings were organized into six thematics regarding the quality of learning experiences and further included six broad implications for education.

In an ethnographic study of Latino music culture in Toledo, Ohio, O'Hagin and Harnish (2006) sought to better understand Latino communities and educate public and school institutions about this distinct musical culture. Data were gathered through observations and interviews in the form of a free-flowing dialogue with community leaders and musicians from 12 different Latino bands, focusing on the histories, influences, perceptions, and effects of music-making in their lives. Findings focused on the nature and function of Latino music ensembles, the musical styles they perform, and their role as direct connections with the value of music for identity formation. The authors proposed that community migrant musicians be incorporated in the design of culturally sensitive, socially responsible curricula for school music education. They further supported that music educators and their students should acknowledge and understand the meaning of music in the lives of their students and community members and advocated for the value of field music experiences of university students. The study could serve as a model for fieldwork in preservice teacher education programs.

Bradley (2008) investigated how world music (global song), anti-racism pedagogy, and multicultural choral music education can contribute to the development of a grounded theory of multicultural human subjectivity. Data for this ethnographic study were collected through individual and focus group interviews with members of a community youth choir in the racially and ethnically diverse Canadian city of Mississauga, as well as through analysis of videotaped performances and a reflexive journal kept by the researcher. Results pointed to the need ". . . to move away from music education practices that ignore context in their overemphasis on musical technique, to pedagogies that situate music within the local habitus, and in doing so conscientize (Freire 1970) the power relationships that reiterate oppressions and reproduce biases" (132). It was further supported that the teacher's role today is to explicate issues of power, engage ethically with music, promote anti-racial pedagogies, and foster students' self-understanding.

In another ethnographic study of a mariachi nonprofit, community-based arts association in Houston, Dodd (2001) examined the value of the experience of playing one's own ethnic music and its impact on personal life and academic success. This case study of a specific successful model of multicultural education followed a participant observation methodology in which the researcher participated in rehearsals and concerts and held informal interviews with parents and semi-structured interviews with students and staff members. Analysis of data revealed that participation in the ensemble contributed significantly to the life of students in the areas of music, ethnic identity, and education; helped develop and enrich confidence, self-esteem, and interpersonal cooperation; enhanced students' ethnic heritage and sense of belonging in a community; promoted cooperative learning and creativity; advanced musical skills; strengthened the linkage between public schools and community centers; and positively affected their academic achievement.

Finally, in an ethnographic study, Montague (2011) sought to identify and document commonalities among pedagogical approaches, values, and beliefs of three master Ghanaian musicians and teachers who have extensive teaching experience in a wide range of classes, workshops, residencies, and ensembles in the United States. Participants were purposefully selected and data were gathered through participant observations of rehearsals and performances, semi-structured interviews, and collection of a wide range of documents. Results were presented in a descriptive narrative and focused on the identification of similar pedagogical approaches and the emergence of seven major themes. The study illuminated that the three master Ghanaian teachers successfully combined teaching and learning techniques from Ghana and the United States, leading to the development of innovative pedagogical approaches that take into consideration their own background and training as well as the background of their American students.

Most of the studies in this category examined the development of ethnic and cultural identity through the richness of musical experiences available within the community (Dodd 2001; Gaines 1989; O'Hagin and Harnish 2006; Powell 2003). Some focused on the experiences within and the role of specific ethnic ensembles performing Afro-Cuban (Gaines 1989), mariachi (Dodd 2001), Japanese-American (Powell 2003), and multicultural choral music (Bradley 2008), whereas others investigated the role of music within a local Latino culture (O'Hagin and Harnish 2006). One study explored the specific experiences and pedagogies of non-American expert music teachers (Montague 2011) and others dealt with broader issues such as cross-cultural and bilingual education (Gaines 1989) and anti-racial pedagogy (Bradley 2008).

11.7. Conclusion

As this chapter has illustrated, qualitative research has been significantly used for investigating complex and multifaceted issues regarding cultural diversity and the use of world musics in the school and the community. Most of the studies were identified as case studies and ethnographies of selected students, teachers, music programs, and ensembles. A significant number of the studies followed a mixed method design. Almost two-thirds of the studies were dissertations, and only a quarter of them were journal articles. One interesting observation is the publication gap under each type of source. Specifically, even though the first articles were written at the end of the 1990s, it was not until a decade later that other articles were published, with most of them published during the three-year period of 2006–2009. Such a gap is also observed in the publication of master's theses and dissertations, with nine dissertations written during the seven-year period of 1996–2002 and another five during 2011. As indicated in the beginning of this chapter, this trend in dissertations was first observed by Kantorski and Stegman (2006). This might indicate that researchers are lately more inclined to take advantage of the benefits offered through qualitative research, as exemplified through ethnographic, phenomenological, action research, and case studies, for better understanding complex issues pertaining to music, culture, education, and pedagogy.

Overall, the 38 studies included in this chapter focused on the rich and diverse views and experiences of teachers, students, and administrators with regard to cultural diversity and the teaching of world musics; examined exemplary teaching approaches, ensembles, and programs; explored innovative approaches in music teacher education; and brought attention to issues of cultural identity, culturally responsive teaching, and anti-racial pedagogy. Even though it is difficult to categorize each study under a single thematic umbrella, most of the studies ($n = 8$, or 21 percent) investigated teacher attitudes toward and experiences with world musics, as well as preservice teacher training in multicultural music education ($n = 7$, or 18 percent).

Researchers and music educators should continue to further investigate the important issues described in the preceding. At the same time, they should also turn their attention to other areas that have not been adequately examined and have to do with the teaching of world musics and cultural diversity. Such areas include, but are not limited to, the views and experiences of students and parents; the necessary skills, knowledge, and competences for future music educators; the breadth and depth of preservice and in-service music training; the value of nontypical and informal music experiences; the obstacles faced by practicing teachers; the quality and experiences provided by world music ensembles in the schools and the community; and broader issues such as the role and function of music, admission, and graduation criteria for music educators, and the issue of teaching for democracy and social change. The profession would also benefit from longitudinal and historical research on the teaching of world musics and from action research conducted by practicing teachers in their individual classrooms. Qualitative research has a lot to offer toward a better understanding of the complexities of teaching, performing, and experiencing a wide range of world musics in the school and the community.

NOTE

1. Even though the study is focusing on Grades 5-6, it is nevertheless included in this category because the three schools were identified as elementary schools.

REFERENCES

Abril, C. R. 2006. "Learning Outcomes of Two Approaches to Multicultural Music Education." *International Journal of Music Education* 24 (1): 30–42.

Abril, C. R. 2009. "Responding to Culture in the Instrumental Music Program: A Teacher's Journey." *Music Education Research* 11 (1): 77–91.

Abril, C. R. 2010. "Opening Spaces in the Instrumental Music Classroom." In *Alternative Approaches in Music Education: Case Studies from the Field*, edited by A. C. Clemens, 3–14. Lanham, MD: Rowman and Littlefield.

Addo, A. O. 2009. "Towards Internationalizing General Music Teacher Education in a U.S. Context." *Journal of Research in International Education* 8 (3): 305–25.

Barry, N. H. 1996. "The Effects of Special Training and Field Experiences upon Preservice Teachers' Level of Comfort with Multicultural Music Teaching Situations." Paper presented at the annual meeting of the American Educational Research Association, New York (ERIC Document Reproduction Service No. ED397035).

Bradley, D. 2008. "Teaching in an Unforgiving Present for the Unknowable Future: Multicultural Human Subjectivity, Antiracism Pedagogy and Music Education." In *Diverse Methodologies in the Study of Music and Learning*, edited by L. Thompson and M. R. Campbell, 111–35. Charlotte, NC: Information Age.

Calloway, J. 2009. "In Search of Music Equity in an Urban Middle School." PhD diss., University of San Francisco.

Campbell, P. S. 1991. "What's Wrong with This Picture? Cries for Research in Multicultural Music Education." Paper presented at the American Orff-Schulwerk Association, San Diego, California.

Campbell, P. S. 2003. "Ethnomusicology and Music Education: Crossroads for Knowing, Music, Education, and Culture." *Research Studies In Music Education* 21: 16–30.

Chen-Hafteck, L. 2007. "Contextual Analyses of Children's Responses to an Integrated Chinese Music and Culture Experience." *Music Education Research* 9 (3): 337–53.

Chin, L. 1996. "Multicultural Music in Higher Education." PhD diss., University of Oregon.

Clemens, A. C., ed. 2010. *Alternative Approaches In Music Education: Case Studies from the Field*. Lanham, MD: Rowman & Littlefield.

Countryman, J. 2010. "Missing Voices in Music Education: Music Students and Music Teachers Explore the Nature of High School Music Experience." PhD diss., University of Toronto.

Dodd, J. C. 2001. "Playing Mariachi Music: Its Influence in Students' Lives. An Ethnographic Study of Mariachi MECA." MM thesis, University of Houston.

Edwards, K. L. 1998. "Multicultural Music Instruction in the Elementary School: What Can Be Achieved?" *Bulletin of the Council for Research in Music Education* 138: 62–82.

Emmanuel, D. T. 2002. "A Music Education Immersion Internship: Pre-Service Teachers' Beliefs Concerning Teaching Music in a Culturally Diverse Setting." PhD diss., Michigan State University.

Feay-Shaw, S. 2000. "Multicultural Perspectives on Research in Music Education." *Bulletin of the Council for Research in Music Education* 145: 15–26.

Freire, P. 1970. *Pedagogy of the Oppressed*. New York: Seabury Press.

Gaines, J. H. 1989. "Music as Socio-Cultural Behavior: Implications for Cross-Cultural Education—A Case Study." PhD diss., Columbia University.

Gilchrist, C. H. 1980. "An Assessment of the Preparation of North Carolina Public School Music Teachers in Performance Practices of Black Gospel Music: Implications for Curriculum Revisions in Higher Education." PhD diss., University of North Carolina.

Hess, J. 2009. "The Aural Tradition in the Sankofa Drum and Dance Ensemble: Student Perceptions." *Music Education Research* 11 (1): 57–75.

Johnson, S. 1997. "High-School Music Teachers' Meanings of Teaching World Music." MM thesis, Queen's University.

Jordan, J. 1992. "Multicultural Music Education in a Pluralistic Society." In *The Handbook of Research on Music Teaching and Learning*, edited by R. Colwell, 735–48. New York: Schirmer.

Kantorski, V. J., and S. F. Stegman. 2006. "A Content Analysis of Qualitative Research Dissertations in Music Education, 1998–2002." *Bulletin of the Council for Research in Music Education* 168: 63–73.

Kelly-McHale, J. L. 2011. "The Relationship between Children's Musical Identities and Music Teacher Beliefs and Practices in an Elementary General Music Classroom." PhD diss., Northwestern University.

Klinger, R. 1996a. "Matters of Compromise: An Ethnographic Study of Culture-Bearers in Elementary Music Education." PhD diss., University of Washington.

Klinger, R. 1996b. "From Glockenspiel to Mbira: An Ethnography of Multicultural Practice in Music Education." *Bulletin of the Council for Research in Music Education* 129: 29–36.

Lehmberg, L. J. 2008. "Perceptions of Effective Teaching and Pre-Service Preparation for Urban Elementary General Music Classrooms: A Study of Teachers of Different Cultural Backgrounds in Various Cultural Settings." PhD diss., University of South Florida.

Lundquist, B. R. 2002. "Music, Culture, Curriculum and Instruction." In *The New Handbook of Research on Music Teaching and Learning*, edited by R. Colwell and C. Richardson, 626–47. New York: Oxford University Press.

Meidinger, V. F. 2002. "Multicultural Music: Attitudes and Practices of Expert General Music Teachers in Oregon." PhD diss., University of Oregon.

Miralis, Y. 2002. "Multicultural–World Music Education and Music Teacher Education at the Big Ten Schools: Identified Problems and Suggestions." PhD diss., Michigan State University.

Montague, M. J. 1988. "An Investigation of Teacher Training in Multicultural Music Education in Selected Universities and Colleges." PhD diss., University of Michigan.

Montague, D. M. 2011. "Traditional Ghanaian Music Pedagogy and Philosophy: An Overview of Teaching and Learning Techniques of Three Ghanaian Master Musicians Teaching in the United States." PhD diss., Boston University.

Norman, K. N. 1994. "Multicultural Music Education: Perceptions of Current and Prospective Music Education Faculty, Music Supervisors, and Music Teachers." PhD diss., University of Michigan.

Norman, K. 1999. "Music Faculty Perceptions of Multicultural Music Education." *Bulletin of the Council for Research in Music Education* 139: 37–49.

Oare, S. 2008. "The Chelsea House Orchestra: A Case Study of a Non-Traditional School Instrumental Ensemble." *Bulletin of the Council for Research in Music Education* 177: 63–78.

O'Hagin, I. B., and D. Harnish. 2006. "Music as a Cultural Identity: A Case Study of Latino Musicians Negotiating Tradition and Innovation in Northwest Ohio." *International Journal of Music Education* 24 (1): 56–70.

Okun, M. J. 1998. "Multicultural Perspectives in Undergraduate Music Teacher Education Programs." PhD diss., University of New Mexico.

Powell, K. A. 2003. "Learning Together: Practice, Pleasure and Identity in a Taiko Drumming World." PhD diss., Stanford University.

Powell, R. J. 2011. "Popular Music Ensembles in Post-Secondary Contexts: A Case-Study of Two College Music Ensembles." PhD diss., Boston University.

Ryan, C. B. 2011. "World Music Pedagogy in the United States Middle School: A Comparison of Western and Indigenous Teaching of Andean Music." PhD diss., Boston University.

Stafford-Davis, C. 2011. "Multicultural Education in The Music Classroom: Definitions, Methods, and Motives." PhD diss., University of Arkansas.

Stellaccio, C. K. 1995. "Theory to Practice: An Ethnographic Analysis of Multicultural Curriculum and Pedagogy in Elementary General Music." PhD diss., University of Maryland.

Szego, C. S. 1999. "Musical Meaning-Making in an Intercultural Environment: The Case of Kamehameha Schools." PhD diss., University of Washington.

Withers-Ross, H. K. 1999. "Multicultural Folksongs in Presenting Cultures in a Sixth-Grade Social Studies Classroom." PhD diss., University of South Carolina.

Young, S. M. 1996. "Music Teachers' Attitudes, Classroom Environments and Music Activities in Multicultural Music Education." PhD diss., Ohio State University.

Zaretti, J. L. 1998. "Multicultural Music Education: An Ethnography of Process in Teaching and Learning." MM thesis, Indiana University.

CHAPTER 12

TEACHING QUALITATIVE RESEARCH EXPERIENTIALLY AND AESTHETICALLY

LIORA BRESLER

THE past 20 years have seen a tremendous increase in qualitative research in music education.[1] This fine volume is a testimony of this growth. The increased use of qualitative research implies a corresponding need for qualitative research education. In reflecting on relevant contents and pedagogies, it is important to recognize that the conduct of fieldwork, interpretation, and writing involve more than theoretical knowledge and scripted procedures. Theories are essential to the teaching of research and the induction into a scholarly community. Yet, they are not enough. The goals, characteristics, and methods of qualitative research, reflecting the basic assumptions of a postmodern paradigm underlying this methodology, require the cultivation of corresponding dispositions.

The postmodern assumption of the multiplicity of social reality (as discussed, for example, in chapter 1 of Volume 1 of this *Handbook*) implies that researchers aim to capture multiple perspectives, rather than one objective truth. The related recognition that the researcher is the main instrument requires that researcher's subjectivity be attended to and articulated throughout the process of inquiry. The qualitative goal of understanding personal and cultural lived experience aims at depth in capturing complexity within a small number of contextualized cases and concepts.[2] Because researchers learn about what is most worthwhile to study *as* they study it, research questions identified at the outset need to be complemented by those that emerge through increasing understanding of the specific cases and concepts. Conceptualizations and interpretations are ongoing. Accordingly, data analysis, concurrent with data collection, requires agility in traversing between the concrete and abstract, identifying additional themes as they emerge through the research process. The emergent nature of data means that methods must be flexible and adaptable. Indeed, the terms for the key qualitative methods—*unstructured* observations and *open-ended* or *semi-structured* interviews—designate their open-endedness. Unlike quantitative research methodologies, where the initial design determines the research procedures, qualitative research requires responsiveness to unfolding data, manifested, for example, through probing interviews, and following promising directions in observations. In preliminary data analysis, which shapes the next cycle of data collection, a priori categories and codes are complemented with emergent ones. Scholarly literature that has served the researcher in the planning stage needs to be revisited and expanded to respond to evolving questions, themes, and issues. While thorough preparation, including knowledge of methodological and conceptual frameworks and the development of specific skills before embarking on the study, is critical, the cultivation of heightened perception and the ability to respond in data collection and analysis are equally crucial.

Attentive presence is a prerequisite to fresh perception and connection, which in turn enable responsiveness to what is encountered. Being a researcher, I argue, involves not "merely the sensation of knowledge in the making" but "a sensing of our selves in the making" (Ellsworth 2005, 1). That is true for veteran researchers, and is particularly true for graduate students. But is the ability to perceive richness and complexity teachable? How do we teach responsiveness? Agreeing with Etienne Wenger (1998/2003) that we can't design learning but can design situations and experiences conducive to learning, this chapter addresses the teaching and learning of qualitative methodology within a research course.

Dance educator Sue Stinson has commented that the music we listen to during our high school and college years is the music that most resonates with us throughout our lifespan (Stinson 2010). This lasting resonance, I believe, is equally applicable to the research experiences and dispositions gained in graduate studies. The qualitative dispositions described earlier include intensified perception, responsiveness, and improvisation; awareness of subjectivities (Peshkin 1988, 1994) alerting researchers to the values that shape their perception; and the capacity for an ongoing interplay between the concrete case and the abstract theorizing toward conceptualizations that transfer broadly and deeply. It requires the ability to "zoom in," move closer, and "zoom out," gain a broader perspective on what is studied, as well as on one's own stances and values.

This chapter is part of the growing area of the scholarship of teaching and learning (SOTL). Ernst Boyer, then president of the Carnegie Foundation for the Advancement of Teaching, identified the scholarship of teaching along with the scholarship of discovery, integration, and application as "four separate, yet overlapping functions" of the professoriate (Boyer 1990, 16). By going public with their work, scholars of teaching and learning aim to create a new space for pedagogical exchange, a space in which communities of educators committed to pedagogical inquiry and innovation come together to exchange ideas about teaching and learning, share literature, and add a new body of knowledge derived from inquiry and innovation in situations of practice (Boyer 1990, 2).[3] Given the exponential growth in the conduct of qualitative research in music education, I offer my perspective and reflections based on years of experience as a catalyst for research educators and their students to engage in this conversation.

12.1. The Power of Experiential Learning: Lessons from the Arts

It was consideration of what knowledge, skills, and dispositions students need in order to conduct qualitative research and be able to function as members of the research community that sharpened my understanding of qualitative research as experiential processes. It is all too common to focus on what is easy to teach, relying on carefully organized knowledge outlined by textbooks. However, cultivating qualitative dispositions is fundamentally different from teaching a defined body of knowledge and skills. Building on the theoretical understandings of postmodern assumptions and qualitative scholarship, my courses aim to cultivate research skills through a series of experiential exercises, supported by an intellectual community that works together in "interpretive zones" (Bresler, Wasser, Hertzog, and Lemons 1996). A sample syllabus for my course appears in the Appendix.

Intensified perception and responsiveness to what is encountered during data collection require going beyond the surface and the conventional. In this intellectual endeavor, existing theories are starting points, guiding perception but not determining it. More than reporting of observational and interview data and matching them with existing theories, qualitative research includes the ability to generate innovative perceptions and interpretations, enhancing theories and developing concepts. Responsiveness entails the ability to note and pursue the emergent, rather than stick with the a priori; to deepen the conventional and established ways of seeing things. These dispositions call for experiential, improvised pedagogies where research is experienced as a dynamic practice.

Experiential learning theory, introduced by John Dewey (1938), is based on the demonstrated value of active, personal, and direct experiences as opposed to reading about the subject or the vicarious experience of observing others (Kolb 1984). The literature on experiential learning focuses on the dialectical move between action and reflection (Schon 1983). This interplay of doing and thinking allows musicians, artists, educators, scientists, nurses, and physicians, among others, to interpret the outcome of their actions and learn from them.

Underlying my teaching is the assumption that music in particular, and the arts in general, can teach us valuable lessons for qualitative research methodology (Bresler 2009). Fundamental to the power of the arts is their ability to engage us experientially, juxtaposing affect and cognition rather than dichotomizing them. The arts, as psychiatrist Daniel Stern has argued, manifest vitality in a relatively purified form, pure in the sense that the dynamic features of arts performances have usually been amplified, refined, and rehearsed repeatedly (Stern 2010, 75). It is the vitality of the arts and the amplification of their dynamic features that help us pay attention.

In aiming to cultivate qualitative dispositions, I draw on encounters with artworks and musical performances as rich spaces to pay attention, wonder, contextualize, and interpret. Lessons from the arts address its capacity to evoke resonance, fostering empathic, interpretive understanding. The arts engage us in exploring personal and cultural lived experience through interplay between the concrete (sounds, textures, colors, rhythm) and the abstract (moods, conceptualizations, ideas). Engagement with the arts requires an embodied presence that is cognitive and affective, creating a heightened perception. The very engagement with qualitative research, I suggest, parallels the engagement with the arts in the focus on attentive presence, heightened perception, interpretation, and quest for empathic understanding. Encounters with the arts require a commitment and ability to be fully present to what emerges "out there," as well as to connect with our own subjectivities "in here." This commitment and ability are also essential to qualitative research.

The focal assignment described in this chapter involves fieldwork in music performances. The assignment aims to cultivate an aesthetic disposition to scholarship, drawing on the interdependent qualities of the holistic and the analytic, the concrete and the abstract, the temporal and the stable, the embodied and the conceptual. The aesthetics of scholarship, I suggest, is created through the juxtaposition of two types of distances—connectedness and detachment. Connectedness involves closeness and intimacy. It allows us to discern nuances, subtleties, and variations. Detachment involves distancing, allowing us a broader view. The juxtaposition of moving closer and farther enables fresh perception and conceptualization.

When I first embarked on qualitative research, I turned to musical lenses to provide structures and conceptual organizers for meaning-making. These lenses can capture qualities of lived experience, highlighting attention to form, rhythm, dynamics, texture, and orchestration (Bresler and Stake 1992/2006; Bresler 2003). Perceptions of the fluid, evanescent quality of music and sound can sensitize us to the fleeting quality of lived experience. The ephemeral quality of music can heighten our attention to the temporal as a source of knowledge and understanding (Bresler 2005). Other arts-related aspects that prove directly relevant to the conduct of qualitative studies include the use of the body to perceive and communicate (Bresler 2006) and a dialogic, improvisatory style (Bresler 2009).

12.2. Detached Connection toward Intensified Perception and Conceptualization

Intensified, fresh perception is not commonplace. All too often, as Dewey insightfully observed, recognition can be a hindrance to perception. "Recognition," Dewey wrote, "is perception arrested before it has the chance to develop freely" (1934, 52).[4] While useful in daily life, when the ordinary does not need special attention, recognition hinders attentive perception. Indeed, the ordinary, British philosopher Peter de Bolla observes, is often too close for attention, extraordinary in its ability to go unremarked. The everyday has an "uncanniness of... proximity," to slip *behind* attention (de Bolla 2001, 64). It is as if in order to survive we need to construct a mode of inattention, creating a domain too close for the reach of attention (de Bolla 2001).

The adage "making the strange familiar and the familiar strange" addresses this very process of fresh seeing. Adopted in anthropological writing in the twentieth century, the familiar/strange interplay has actually been coined in the context of the art worlds in the late eighteenth century. It was not a coincidence, I believe, that this concept was generated within the time period that the concept of aesthetic distance emerged and gained momentum. The disposition involved in aesthetic distance (Bullough 1912/1956) juxtaposes intimacy of perception with detachment from action, allowing us an expanded perception. This juxtaposition of distances, I argue, is at the core of the participant-observation stance in qualitative research.

A second hindrance to exploratory perception is judgment. Like recognition, judgment is useful to our everyday functioning. However, it limits us when we aspire to go beyond, closing wonderment and further inquiry. The culture of trained musicianship can promote judgment to the point of glorification as the mark of expertise and professionalism, a proof of one's refined taste. Detachment from readymade judgment creates a space, an opening for further exploration, suspending habitual ways of seeing in order to perceive in depth. While we cannot (and don't want to) give up our expertise, convictions, and established criteria of excellence—essential parts of being insiders to our musical communities and genres—we aspire as qualitative researchers to expand our expertise by seeking to understand before we evaluate. Experimenting with physical and mental distances allows us to question things taken for granted by incorporating additional perspectives. Like the distancing involved in aesthetic perception, it enables a broader view.

Theorists of art since Aristotle have sought to capture the peculiar blend of closeness and distance in aesthetic experience. However, within the context of research methodology the issue of the right distance between the researcher and the researched is contentious. Distance is often marked as the distinguishing line between the worldviews of positivist "hard" sciences communities on the one hand versus post-positivist "soft" sciences communities on the other. The former is based on objectivity and detachment. The latter claims subjectivity and connection. Both communities regard distanced connection as an oxymoron.

It is useful to acknowledge the historical meaning of distances as part of a worldview and their significance in the "paradigms wars" (Gage 1989) of the 1980s as well as in contemporary research. Within a Cartesian research culture that has highlighted objectivity and distance as part of the enlightenment's quest to reduce religious dogma, connectedness to participants and to settings is a breach. Avoiding connectedness was relatively easy to follow in the field of laboratory psychology given its setting, structures, and participants (mostly rats). It was harder to maintain in disciplines that required prolonged engagement in social settings and extensive interaction with human participants. The discipline of anthropology was a pioneer in deconstructing distance in research; it discovered that distance was difficult to maintain through prolonged engagement in a remote setting when researchers were dependent on their participants, as Bronislaw Malinowski experienced nearly a century ago. Interpretive, empathic understanding came to distinguish the aims and processes of the human sciences (van Manen 1990), including educational research, from other forms of research.

In the social sciences, to various degrees and following different paces, the pendulum swung in the last 40 years from a demand for objectivity to the acknowledgment of situated subjectivity (Peshkin 1988, 1994). The rejection of the notion of objectivity (e.g., Lincoln and Guba 1995) meant for many the rejection of detachment, a concept that has come under fierce attack by postmodernists. In class preparation for the experiential, arts-based assignments, I suggest that it is precisely the juxtaposition of connectedness within detachment that is most generative for perception in qualitative research, allowing expansion of perspectives and new conceptualizations.

How is detachment distinguished from the positivist objectivity? Detachment is a situational rather than an epistemological state. Spinosa, Flores, and Dreyfus (1997, 6–7) contend that detachment enables us to obtain a wider view by extracting ourselves from the immediate pressures of the moment and to see what is before us in terms of its relationship to other matters. Spinosa et al. point to the two-sidedness of detachment, detachment *from* passion and detachment *in order to see* all the relevant interconnections. The former facilitates the latter. These two types, they maintain, support a third type that is related to distance in both the arts and qualitative research methodology—detachment from habitual and practical forms of seeing. I suggest that detachment from habitual seeing combined with intense engagement is characteristic of the practice of qualitative researchers, enabling them to go beyond recognition of the familiar, toward heightened, fresh perception, to "make the familiar strange."

How do we create learning opportunities in moving students beyond the dichotomy of detachment versus connectedness to a productive interplay between them? The challenge of qualitative research is maintaining an interested connectedness to what we study and to our participants, as well as detachment from our habitual forms of seeing and judging, upholding the necessary distance involved in disciplined scholarship. In striving toward this precariously balanced disposition, I find it useful to distinguish between connectedness and *attachment*, which I regard as the "near enemy"[5] of connection. Experiential learning is key here. To that end, course assignments require students to perceive and examine their values and attachments, part of their "subjectivities," not in order to get rid of them, but to be able to name and own them through reflective distancing. Physical distance, for example, in observations of performances, determines what researchers see and hear from their location. Similarly, an *aesthetic*, or intellectual distance applies to the ability to perceive the outside world. It also applies to perception of the inner self.

How do we create this interplay of distances in teaching research? Course readings of anthropological and ethno-musicological literature, disciplines with a tradition of exploring "strange" settings, provide productive models for investigation and inspiration. Making sense when one is not able to "recognize" facilitates seeing afresh (Gottlieb and Graham 1995; Nathan, 2005; Sæther 2003; Stoller 1989). De-familiarization can be useful in observing one's home culture (Nettl 1995; Tobin et al. 2009). In fieldwork assignment I draw on the aesthetic distance inherent in settings such as museums and performing arts centers, settings that invite both engagement and contemplation, to cultivate the interplay between the strange and the familiar. Other mechanisms for de-familiarization include the use of theoretical frameworks in writing organized by conceptualizations. Course assignments highlight communication with both teacher and peers in forming interpretive zones. Communication facilitates distancing. As important is the listening to the multiplicity of credible perspectives, driving home the realization that the same situation can be perceived and comprehended in diverse ways, á la *Rashomon*.[6] This comprehension of multiple perspectives, a core goal of qualitative research, is basic to communication, enabling us to hear each other in dialogue rather than mere self-affirmation.

Another strategy for intensified perception and conceptualization entails the explorations of dissonance and of themes and variations. The clash of dissonance jolts us into attention. Theme and variation activate a gentler discernment. In research, the theme is typically an identified concept; the variations are the manifestation of the phenomenon in diverse situations and contexts. Looking for variations cultivates nuanced perception through recognition of differences, allowing us to perceive subtlety and complexity. Underlying both dissonance and variation is comparison.[7] Because qualitative research seeks to portray the uniqueness of the case and targets a small number of cases, statistical comparison and generalization are impossible. It is informal comparisons that are at play here. Informal comparisons are humble in that they have no aspiration to generalize, yet essential in providing a frame of reference as tools for perception. Comparisons enable the perception of variations, and of dissonance. Detached connection supports a comparison driven by wonderment and exploration rather than by readymade preferences of like/dislike.

Fundamental to perception and discernment, comparison and contrast are present in the different genres of qualitative research including ethnography (Heath and Street 2005; Tobin et al. 2009); case study and evaluation (Eisner 1991; Stake 2010); variation theory (Marton and Booth 1997); phenomenology (van Manen 1990); and the constant comparative method (Charmaz 2006).

12.3. A Course as an Occasion for Cultivating Qualitative Dispositions

The course on which this chapter focuses is semester-long, structured around weekly three-hour meetings and additional attendance of performances. The 21 students who took this class came from diverse units, including Curriculum and Instruction, Educational Policy and Organizational Leadership, Special Education, Music

Education, and Art Education. My role as a teacher includes selection of reading materials, designing educational experiences and planning activities, lecturing, facilitating discussions, and evaluating. Scholarly readings, an essential aspect of the course, provide a foundational support for the experiential activities. I select course materials for their potential to illuminate significant theoretical and practical issues.

In the first course session I present the core assumption of the postmodern paradigm: the multiplicity of perspectives on social realities, including that of the researcher, shaped by viewpoint and contexts. We discuss the goals of interpretive, empathic understanding of personal and cultural lived experience; the characteristics of qualitative research (e.g., case and issue oriented, descriptive/interpretive, prolonged engagement, emic/etic perspectives), its methods and criteria. These discussions continue, stretto-like, throughout the course, as we address the multiplicity of realities in ethnographies and case studies and in our own observations, examining in each case how the multiplicity contributes to understanding the phenomena studied. We attend to the different types of realities (Lincoln and Guba 1985), from the tangible, "objective reality," acknowledging the physical position from which we perceive and what it enables us to see, hear, and experience; to the "constructed realities," centering on shared social and cultural values, and our personal "created realities" evoked in the process of interpretation. Drawing on qualitative books and dissertations as well as our own writing, we discuss the appropriate trustworthiness criteria compatible with the qualitative research worldviews, including a range of process criteria (e.g., prolonged engagement, persistent observations, triangulation, peer debriefing, member checking) and product criteria (e.g., transferability).

The first assignment takes these ideas and concepts to the experiential level. I structure a museum activity aimed to support students in forming intensified relationships with a "bounded system," a case, moving beyond habitual ways of seeing and hearing. To highlight the role of values in interpretation, students are asked to choose two artworks, one that appeals to them and another that evokes aversion or neutrality, and to stay with each for at least 30 minutes. Targeting the skills of observations, conceptualizations, and generation of further inquiries, students are assigned to describe in detailed field notes what they observe; to identify themes, issues, and curiosities; and to locate relevant contexts, including archival and Web-based information (Bresler 2012).

The next assignment, described in the following, widens perception to a temporal bounded system, one that extends visual observations to listening and drawing on other senses. The temporal, ever-moving world of music brings a different level of complexity compared with the relative stability of qualities of artworks. Students are placed further in the methodological continuum of participant-observation toward increased participation. Music performances, I have found, make rich cases, evoking a mix of insider/outsider musical and social identities, deep-seated subjectivities and values. Closely tied with identities, music performances are generative spaces to discern dissonances and consonances. Settings for the music performance vary, from community concerts in libraries to concerts in performing arts centers. Whenever possible, I choose events that present a wide array of musical styles, venues, audiences, and etiquettes, to facilitate a variety of choices and relationships. The ELLNORA Guitar Festival at Krannert Center was such an event. It served as the site for fieldwork and an occasion to cultivate intensified perception through detached connection. The task called for unstructured, improvised observations; contextualization; development of conceptualizations; identification of wonderments; and generation of questions to hypothetical participants to expand perspectives. It also required dialogical connections to scholarly literature, and the ability to reflect on their processes of inquiry.

12.3.1. Musical Performances as Learning Opportunities: Seeing, Hearing, and Conceptualizing

Assignment for Paper #2

Based on your attendance of two concerts at the ELLNORA Guitar Festival:

1. Describe in detail what you observed in the concerts, attending to sights, sounds, smell, and touch. Note time every 5–10 minutes.
2. Identify themes and issues.
3. What are you curious about? Generate a list of questions to:
    a. One of the musicians.
    b. Two other audience members (address explicitly your purposive sampling).
    c. A person of your choice.
4. Identify contextual (including archival) information.
5. Reflect on how your observations followed the Emerson, Fretz, and Shaw's guidelines on observations. If you were to write your own guidelines on observations, would you add anything to these suggestions? Relate your experience of observations to other course readings.
6. Reflect on your experience as a researcher.

12.3.2. Scaffolding the Assignment

Qualitative sampling of events or interviewees is purposeful, never random. Sampling targets productive learning opportunities, ranging from best cases through ordinary to worse (as is the choice of an artwork that elicits aversion). In the guitar festival, the wide range of musical styles, settings, and etiquettes meant that class members could select the events they attended. Reflecting on their selections, they consider their choices (and its complement, what they did *not* choose), including settings and informants. In discussing emerging issues and contexts, we discussed which contexts are initially useful for the conduct of the study; which contexts emerged as being useful once the study is underway; which contexts were only minimally or not at all useful.

The writing of paper #2 was scaffolded through several steps. Following the performance, students were asked to bring their field notes of the performances to class. They shared their field notes with each other, and we discussed the various lenses and subjectivities that contributed to the individual observations, distinguishing between those objective aspects (e.g., facts relating to venues, time of day, ensemble makeup) and the created ones, shaped (but not determined by) their personal musical and artistic background and experiences, familiarity with the venue, ethnicity and age, among other influences.

Below are excerpts[8] from papers submitted by Christopher Dye and Stephanie Cronenberg, two doctoral students who took this research course in Fall 2011. Christopher was a second year EdD student in Music Education at the University of Illinois. Previously a middle school and high school band director in Texas, Christopher's degrees are in music education and instrumental conducting from Texas Lutheran University and Columbus State University. Christopher's position as an insider to the setting meant that he brought relevant musical experience and attention to nuances. His researcher's role and the task of writing aiming to enhance others' understanding and perception created a distancing.

Musical Borders and Boundaries

Christopher Dye

Coming to Krannert from New Perspectives

My arrival at the ELLNORA Guitar Festival feels strange and impersonal. I spend a great deal of time in the Krannert Center for the Performing Arts as a teacher, conductor, and performer. I know the concrete slab floors and cinderblock walls of the production level by heart. The rehearsal rooms, the loading dock, the dressing rooms, and the percussion storage rooms: they all provide the context for the Krannert I am familiar with that is in contrast to the serenity of stepping on the stage of Foellinger Great Hall or slipping in through a side entrance.

I buy my ticket to see Calexico the night before from the Krannert website. It is the first time I have paid to see a performance at Krannert. On the afternoon of Saturday, September 10, I ascend the concrete stairs to the main Krannert entrance, thinking, "This is what it's like for the 'regular' people." I feel as if I am ascending a monument, like a Mayan temple. At the top, I see that the area in front of the lobby and amphitheater is populated with short white tents. Vendors are selling food and drinks in the tents closest to the entrance, and the air smells of barbecue and the oil from a deep fryer.

The lobby is alive. A wide spectrum of Champaign-Urbana society is milling about the open space, negotiating arced paths around small bistro tables laden with long, vibrantly colored cloths. . . . We descend a staircase, and I enter door number 4, prepared to take my seat at the back of the hall in row AB, seat 4. My comfort and expectations are jarred when an usher checks my ticket and points at the stage, saying, "Front row, even seats on the right," close enough to the stage to be aglow in the performance lights. My anticipated distance for quiet note taking had suddenly transformed into immediacy to the performers that profoundly impacted the way I reflected on the concert.

Traveling with Calexico

The ELLNORA website describes Calexico in terms of geography, referring to how they have "meandered through landscapes," "off into the horizon," and are now "scouring the terrain" for further inspirations. Their performance indicated even broader travels, jet setting between American, Latin, and South American styles as well as time travelling to eras of classic country and West Coast surfer rock.

4:42 The performance begins. A group of four white males, roughly in their forties, enter the stage and immediately initiates an undulating two-chord progression that builds throughout the first piece. They are joined by the rest of the ensemble, four men of Spanish or Hispanic background, before their second song. At this point, the music flows outside of the boundaries of any genre I can label. The combination of steel guitar, vibraphone, trumpet, synthesizer, maracas, and timpani mallets on the drumset produces a soundscape that is reminiscent of 1960s psychedelic rock shows. This is visually supported by a sudden shift in the lighting from blue to pink.

4:50 Each player in the group externalizes the pulse of the music in a different way. The drummer rocks back and forth between the heel and toe of his left foot on the hi-hat pedal. The lead singer and guitarist stomps his hard-soled black shoes aggressively to assert tempo. The lead trumpet player flexes his knees slightly on each beat, while the other trumpeter shows no externalization of the pulse. The bassist taps his toes, while the steel guitarist subdivides the beat with his right heel . . . .

5:15 The southern geographic swing has resulted in a palpable change in the audience. What began as polite applause after each song has transitioned to performer-modeled backbeat clapping, and is now moving down to the feet of the listeners. The current song is a Bossa Nova in the key of A major, taking us below the equator, and the audience is responding with unprompted foot tapping that is vibrating the floor under my red cloth seat.

Christopher's second concert is Noveller at the outdoor amphitheater, the very last event of the festival. Christopher notes the variations created by the time of day, venue, ensemble, musical styles, and etiquette. His interpretive descriptions relate to the music, attending to textures, rhythm, and form, and the setting, for example, describing the amphitheater as transitional space rather than judging audience's behavior.

10:16 Silence is not an essential part of this music. Loops of sound continue without pause, and it is difficult to discern what is being played live, what is being looped, and what is being created through filters and other effects. A lull in the sound elicits applause from some audience members seeking to identify the periodic breaks between pieces that are normal in most performances. The performer briefly nods her head as she continues with the next composition, reaching for a violin bow to create new effects with her guitar.

10:23 The amphitheater becomes a transitional space. A crew begins to break down the speakers and amplifiers set up from previous concerts, signaling the impending end of the festival. A crew of festival workers passes through the crowd, creating a visual distraction with their florescent green vests and iridescent orange hats, presumably heading to the street to guide post-concert traffic. The crowd on the terraces of the amphitheater has gradually changed and is now populated mostly by couples sitting close to each other, looking toward the tents.

10:37 I move from the amphitheater down to the small steps directly behind the café tables. From this vantage, I can now see various leafy plants casting shadows under the tents to the right and left of the performance stage. The sense of the organic meant literally in the name Sonic Garden also provides an apt metaphor for Noveller's music. Each soundscape grows from a single motif and shifts of style and tonality happen gradually, almost imperceptibly. The combination of the dark shadows and her deep focus makes the performance feel deeply serious.

10:57 I move to the very top of the amphitheater. From this height, the performance in the tent is placed in the context of a larger campus. There are lights on in several offices across the street. In the distance, I can see the carillon on the south quad and the peak of Foellinger Auditorium. At the tents farthest from the stage, concertgoers are buying drinks and socializing, as oblivious to Noveller's performance as the late night workers across the street. The top of the performance tent obscures my view of the performer, and I am struck by the complexity of the music. Without witnessing the mechanics of the performance, it is hard to imagine that the sound is all emanating from one woman with a guitar.

Following narrative descriptions and questions incorporating explicit and implicit issues, Christopher's subsequent discussion (not included here because of space limitation) was organized by issues. The theme and variations strategy is developed through consideration of a swap of venues and its impact on the experience. Self-observations are an essential aspect of the assignment, including relating one's conduct of fieldwork in relation to course readings, and to other students' sharing in class discussions, recognizing the multiplicity of experiences and perspectives. Christopher continued:

Reflecting on the Processes in the Field

In the process of taking field notes at ELLNORA, I found myself getting wrapped up in observations. I had a difficult time pausing to consider my participation in the performances. I was concerned throughout that if I stopped taking notes for two or three minutes I would miss or misrepresent the details of what happened in those moments.

David Howes (2003) asserts a historical tendency towards the primacy of visual perception, while I find myself drawn to give auditory stimuli the most focus. I made concerted efforts to include visual information in my encoding of musical performances. I found this particularly challenging when trying to describe kinesthetic actions that lead to sonic consequences, such as the motion of a drummer's arm producing a particular tone quality. My initial instinct is to write "wide trumpet vibrato," and I had to make myself pause and add "from embouchure/jaw movement."

Considering the advice on data collection in our course discussion and readings (specifically Emerson et al. 1995), I constantly fought a desire to analyze and thematize on the spot. As I took notes at Calexico, I started making columns of skilled/unskilled instrumental techniques and traditional/Mariachi trumpeting indicators. I am concerned that I have a tendency, especially in a field where I bring a high level of expertise, to focus in on specific areas but exclude many other details from my perception. In the classroom, this is usually an asset, allowing me to focus my pedagogy on targeted issues. This diagnostic skill is great for quickly individualizing instruction, but it may be a limiting habit for the qualitative researcher. As Emerson describes it, I have difficulty separating my "writing" and "reading" modes.

My experiences as a researcher and audience member at ELLNORA were revealing. It gave me the opportunity to encounter the experiences of Krannert performances from the other side of the stage. From our classroom discussions, I am aware that there are still elements of that experience that are foreign to me, especially feelings of "otherness" and concerns about belonging. In my future planning of musical experiences and my participations in musical happenings, I will be more attuned to the dynamics of the setting and the organic and stylistic processes that take the performers and audience from one place to another.

We note Christopher's processes of "making strange," of establishing distances. Distancing involves an inner mental state, but also actions like purchasing a ticket and exploring diverse physical viewpoints. We also note his awareness of his multiple roles: as a musician, as a teacher, and as a researcher. Christopher's themes include the affordances and constraints of the different venues, and performers' physical responses to the music.

The second paper is by Stephanie Cronenberg. Stephanie's degrees include Music Education, Arts Education, and Ethnomusicology from the University of Maryland and Harvard. Her teaching experiences encompass fourth- through eighth-grade general music, and directorship of education and community programs for the Choral Arts Society of Washington (DC). In Fall 2011 she was a first-year PhD student in the Aesthetic Education program at the College of Education, University of Illinois. Stephanie organizes her paper around three themes and issues, illustrating them using short (indented) vignettes taken from her field notes.

What's My Role? Performer Identities, Audience Behavior, and Researcher Synthesis

Stephanie Cronenberg

Themes:

1. *Observing everyday events to understand rituals (acquiring tickets or not; positionality of artists).*
2. *Narrowing and widening the zoom (the music/artists versus the wider contexts, including audience).*
3. *Description and interpretation, including emerging themes, identified in the immersion in the setting.*

At 3:50 pm on Friday, September 9th, 2011, I made my way across campus to Krannert Performing Arts Center for the ELLNORA Guitar Festival. . . . The Colwell Playhouse event required a purchased ticket, a requirement that automatically created an altered atmosphere from that of the crowded lobby. During my observations throughout the evening, I altered my role as participant/observer and attempted to attend to the environment with all of my senses. The crowded lobby at 4:00 pm prevented me from finding a seat, so I chose to move throughout the lobby during the performance to capture the experience of audience members from multiple perspectives. Given that the 6:30 pm event was ticketed, I was assigned a vantage point in a theatre, in the middle of the last row near the lightboard and soundboard, from which to experience the performance.

As a trained musician, I can easily tune out all external distractions and focus solely on the musical performance. However, in this case, I challenged myself to not exclusively tune into the musical performances forsaking all other external "interference" as I might regularly do during a performance. In what follows, I attempt to describe three themes and the resulting issues I identified from my field notes, and I attempt to illustrate those themes and issues using short vignettes taken from my field notes. Within each section, I identify questions regarding the theme or issue that I would like to ask of the artists, audience members, or commissioners, as well as additional contextual information I would ideally like to obtain. In the final section of this paper, I conclude with a section referencing course readings.

Stephanie's first section, titled "Look at Me: Performer Identity," is a rich description of artists and audience behavior, focusing on the role of vision in the concert in both the lobby and the hall. In the second section, presented in the following, the focus is on physical response to the music. Stephanie starts with a broad overview of audience responses to concerts, as a framework and conceptual organizer to this specific event.

Feel the Beat: Physical Response to Music

For many concert attendees or avid music listeners, music has the power to evoke physical responses in the listeners. In both churches and rock concerts, listeners moved by the music sing along and raise their hands high in the air. Although the purposes for hand-raising are different, both are physical responses evoked by music. Students learning a new instrument or receiving instruction in music appreciation are often taught to clap or tap their foot along to the beat of the music as a means for keeping time. At other times, the sound vibrations, whether amplified electronically or acoustically, can create physical responses in the ear or chest of the listener. Audience members love to respond physically to the beat of the music.

The fourth song in the set performed by Luther Dickson and Alvin Youngblood Hart features a drone under the melody, all performed on one guitar. The lights on the brick wall serving as the back of the stage have changed and are now alternating blue, pink, and green. The lights are also shifting across the wall while alternating to accompany the beat of the song. Audience members, moved by the beat of the music, move their bodies in synchronization with the lights on the wall. Although unplanned, all move together. An older man lifts his cane up and down, people standing at the back bob their heads or tap their feet, a woman dances with a baby, and another woman fans herself with a piece of paper.

If the audience were observed with the sound muted, it would appear as if many audience members were controlled by an invisible marionette string. Though parts of their bodies move in unison, the invisible force is not authoritarian; the musical beat simply invites them into the experience of the music with its own unique force.

Much like the performance of "Sweet Home Alabama" at a social gathering in Mobile, the playing of "Georgia on My Mind" at Stone Mountain, or the singing of "Deep in the Heart of Texas" at the fourth of July in Dallas, the meaning of some songs is culturally constructed based on time and place. The physical reaction of the crowd led me to conclude that the final song played by Luther Dickson and Alvin Youngblood Hart was a song of this nature. As a geographical and musical outsider, I did not understand the reaction, but the audience reaction was unmistakable. There are cheers from the crowd as the final song in the set begins at 4:46 pm. I do not recognize the song, but it is clear from the cheers that even the opening cadence is recognizable to many people in the audience. In unison, the audience begins clapping on the beat as the song leaves the introduction and moves into the first verse. This is the first song that moves nearly the entire audience to respond physically to the beat. Long after much of the audience abandons the clapping to the beat, a young boy around age 10 continues clapping. He is standing approximately eight feet from me near the chair of a man I assume is his father. As he claps, he shifts his feet and turns half toward the stage and half toward his father while continuing to clap. It is as if he knows that everyone else in the audience has stopped clapping and therefore feels he should too, but he is unable to contain his physical response to the song. Eventually his clapping lessens and fades away, but he is still unable to stand still as the song progresses.

Stephanie's third section, titled "One Person's Music, Another Person's Noise: Musical Tastes," is organized around the preferences of the audience of the performances accompanying the two silent films, one favorable, another unfavorable, preferences contrasting with her own. Stephanie's substantiates with detailed descriptions (*a woman in the audience yells "turn it down!" A man in the audience yells "NO!" Another male voice yells "put your ear plugs in." The girl next to me mutters, "didn't know we'd need them." The two guys at the light board chuckle and say something like, "early show and already everyone's drunk."*), including her own responses (*While I found these two moments of musical contrast most powerful, I do not believe I shared this reaction with much of the audience, who seemed to become uncomfortable in these moments.*)

It is only after the performance, while reflecting on the two dramatically contrasting interpretations of the appropriate music for a silent movie that I consider my preferences in relationship to the preferences of the audience. While the audience physically responded in a variety of ways to the Luther Dickson and Alvin Youngblood Hart performance, I remained rather neutral to the music. Both Lee Ranaldo and Marc Ribot elicited dramatic reactions from the majority of audience members, including me, but my reactions differed from those I could sense around me. Had I not experienced all three events and reflected on them as a collective experience, I would not have seen the dichotomies between audience reactions in different performances or the insider/outsider dichotomy (Bresler 2006, 25) of my own experience relative to that of the audience.

Having read the Emerson, Fretz, and Shaw (1995) chapters prior to my field research, I wanted to attempt to write jottings rather than my usual more detailed notes. In keeping with this goal, instead of using my iPad to make detailed notes, I chose a small notepad and pen. Unlike in an art museum, the light from the iPad would be culturally unacceptable in a musical performance, especially one inside a theatre. I also primarily wrote phrases or sentence fragments throughout my observation in attempt to adhere to the instructions of Emerson, Fretz, and Shaw (1995, 20). Despite anticipating this challenge, I had to balance my compulsion to continually write, with focusing on the most salient details that would help me construct a full picture of the important incidents later, when I fleshed out my field notes. Further, I was faced with determining how and when to write without disrupting the cultural construction of a quiet darkened theatre, a construction that I am sure impacted my field notes.

Typically, my notes are quite messy and are composed in a manner unintelligible to anyone but me when I complete a final writing such as this paper. However, knowing that my classmates and professor would potentially see the messy way in which my brain operates led me "to include more details of background and context to make fieldnotes more accessible" (Emerson, Fretz, and Shaw, 1995, 44). Although I wanted my field notes to be comprehensible if I were called upon in class, the more natural position of "maintain[ing] a loose, flowing, and shifting approach, not [writing] with consistency of voice and style" eventually won out (Emerson, Fretz, and Shaw, 1995, 44).

While Emerson, Fretz, and Shaw provide strong guidance and excellent tips for jotting notes in the field and later constructing field notes, I feel the need to add to their tips and guidelines. In rereading their writing, though they acknowledge that field research might be conducted at night—"as soon as possible after the day's (or night's) research is done" (Emerson, Fretz, and Shaw, 1995, 40)—they do not provide any guidance in creating jottings during nighttime research or in darkened venues. I would add tips to provide guidelines for conducting research in circumstances where jottings or field notes cannot easily be seen during the act of writing. While I feel that I was fairly successful, my notes were scrambled, spread out, and on a few occasions, written over each other. One tip I might offer is to place a finger of the non-writing hand on the page where the previous jotting ceased so that the writer can easily know where to begin jotting again. Another tip would be, should notes be written over one another, to later, out of the field, take two different colored pens and attempt to trace letters in order to discover the words or phrases of one jotting hidden under another jotting.

When I asked Stephanie what she saw as relevant to music educators, she wrote:

Perhaps most relevant to this paper is the opening mindset of musicians who are trained to listen and observe in a way that is necessary for qualitative research. I think that, for me, the course made the processes of qualitative research easier to grasp because we used art forms as our research sites. But specifically related to the musical performance at ELLNORA, I found that trying to think about the performance as a qualitative researcher first rather than as how I was trained, as an ethno-musicological qualitative researcher, both liberating and challenging. In my own training,[9] the emphasis was always on the music or potentially on the accompanying dancing/ritual. There was an expectation that as an ethnomusicologist the goal would be to "capture" the music whether by recording or transcription. I realized going into ELLNORA that you didn't want a musical transcription for the assignment, which left me challenged by what I should focus on, but also liberated to observe whatever I found most important. For me, taking this class allowed me to begin thinking about what I thought was important (without the control of someone else) to observe and note during participant observation. It made me think about what I was observing and why and whether or not those things were ok to be observing, given whatever questions I might have as a researcher. This particular performance at ELLNORA also confirmed for me the importance of emergence, because if I hadn't been thinking about what to observe outside of the musical performance, I might have dismissed the audience's reaction to the performances and thus lost one of the most interesting aspects of the performance.

Stephanie's comments illustrate how the strengths of musicians—the ability to focus on the music—can also be a liability in music education research. The need to transfer the focused connection exemplified in musical engagement to a broader arena needs to be addressed explicitly and systematically. Here it is the sensibilities of our teaching persona that support researchers in identifying and exploring educational issues. Teaching involves the ability to attend to multiple sources of information simultaneously, to respond to the unexpected dynamics and interactions of the classroom. The sensitivities of musicians and educators complement each other. If music teaches us to zoom-in, teaching requires the capacity to zoom-out.

Another key movement of relationships is researchers' agility in moving back and forth from attending to "out there" when doing fieldwork to "in here," which is their values and commitments. The latter is typically conducted in the private space of data analysis and writing. Both of these movements often draw on dissonance as a useful tool for heightened perception. We noted the outside dissonance in Stephanie's observations of the audience's discomfort with the music accompanying the film. An example of an "inner dissonance" is the discrepancy between Stephanie's own responses to the music as compared with other audience members' responses, or Christopher's disappointment in his allocated seat, clashing with his expectations of his researcher role. Dissonances usually announce themselves loudly. They often signal the presence of meaningful issues, alerting the researchers to underlying personal and cultural expectations and values. Because of their jarring quality and our tendency to shy away from discomfort, we often avoid dissonances or turn them into judgment, closing off exploration. The disposition of detached interest facilitates closer scrutiny, conducive to greater understanding.

Another, gentler strategy to cultivate intensified perception is the identification of theme and variations within and across events. Theme and variations attend to the nuances of educational phenomena. The identification of themes is a process akin to Karl Popper's notion of conjectures (Popper 1963). It involves a conceptual leap, to be developed and substantiated systematically. Christopher's theme of performers' expressions of musicality is developed through detailed observations of the two trumpeters, focusing on the variations in their technique and posture, speculating about their background and education. Stephanie's theme on audience responses contextualizes it through descriptions of the varied use of music and the artists' presentations of self in the lobby, at the concert, and in the films. She includes the disparity between her own responses and the rest of the (audible and observable) audience. These "thick descriptions" become part of a larger conceptualization, for example, musical and verbal actions of musicians and audiences as reflecting traditions of specific genres and styles, or audiences' enculturation and musical preferences.

Improvisation is practiced in identifying promising directions and foci in observations; in generating and pursuing emerging questions to various key participants; and in seeking relevant contexts and theoretical frameworks. Fieldwork can be regarded as choreography, where students move closer and farther from specific events, situations, and foci, exploring how a change of distance contributes to their perception. We discuss qualitative works by master researchers in diverse fields (Barone 2001; Myerhoff 1978; Peshkin 1986) that exemplify this choreography of intimacy and detachment, the concrete and the abstract. Drawing on the wide array of course readings, the final course assignment calls for an elaborate discussion of related methodological issues.

12.4. Learning as Experiencing, Doing, Belonging, and Becoming

Wenger (1998/2003, 5) pinpoints four constituents of communities of practice: learning as experience; learning as doing; learning as belonging to a community; and learning as becoming, shaping one's identity. I regard these components as central aspects of teaching qualitative research.

Learning as experience is fundamental to fieldwork. Since experience is elusive to teach and evaluate, course assignments interlink experiencing with doing, for example, requiring a continuous note taking through fieldwork observations. Note taking is essential in fieldwork. Just as music is "phenomenally evanescent, relentlessly moving, ever changing" (Burrows 1990, 21), social life, too, is constantly changing. The personal experience of settings, sights, and sounds assumes another dimension when writing. The private experience is rendered public in the act of communication.

In aiming to cultivate learning as belonging to a community, I construct the class setting as an "interpretive zone" (Bresler, Wasser, Hertzog, and Lemon 1996; Wasser and Bresler 1996). Drawing on Vygotsky's "zone of proximal development" (1986), among other uses of zone, the concept highlights the social and contextual aspects of interpretation. Zone, more than interpretation, forces us away from the image of the lone researcher working in isolation. The notion of zone implies dynamic processes, exchange, transaction, and intensity. Indeed, exchanging perspectives is an integral aspect of the course, including the sharing of foci, wonderments, relationships to the settings, descriptions and interpretations, and writing styles. Students become aware of the diversity of themes and respective variations identified by their peers, reflecting their background, areas of commitment, and expertise. Class discussions broaden and deepen understanding of the case, exemplifying the contributions of multiple perspectives of the event. They also manifest that not all perspectives are equal, countering a relativistic stance. Some issues, interpretations, and writing are better substantiated, generating new and meaningful understanding; others are more surface-level, thinner, easily refuted. The sense of belonging to the class (cemented, I am often told, by the experiential qualities of the course, including the performances, sharing food, and dynamics of the conversations) facilitates, I believe, a sense of belonging to the larger scholarly community.

Learning as becoming is at the core of research education. Elsewhere (Bresler 2008), I referred to Parker Palmer's famous saying that "we teach who we are" (Palmer 1998, 2), making a case that teachers' inner landscapes are central to what they do. I argued that other occupations to various extents are shaped by those who "occupy" them, referring in particular to the profession of researchers, musicians, and artists. This shaping, I believe, is established through the connection to, and exploration of, what we study, the craft and skills we develop, and the voice and communication style we acquire through these processes. These processes move recursively. Supported by a space for prolonged engagement[10] with both setting and data, inquiry is inspired by the deep wish to understand and communicate to our audiences—fellow researchers and students. Ultimately, conducting research and, as I have found, the teaching of research intensify the process of becoming.

Appendix Sample Syllabus

C and I 509 QRM

Fall 2011
Thursdays, 9:00–11:50 a.m.
Room 385 Education
CURRICULUM RESEARCH:
QUALITATIVE METHODS RESEARCH

Instructor:	Liora Bresler
Office Hours:	393 Education Bldg.
	Mondays 1–4:00 PM (These and other times by appointment)
Telephone:	244-0734, 244-8286
E-mail:	liora@illinois.edu

Purpose: This course is designed for people who wish to gain a general understanding of qualitative research and who want to conduct studies using qualitative methods. We will examine the nature of qualitative research in various research "genres" and intellectual traditions; will practice the tools and methods of qualitative research; and will discuss quality in qualitative research.

Acknowledging the multiplicity of perspectives involved in qualitative research, we will explore ways of engaging in fieldwork and data analysis—procedures and techniques, as well as ways of connecting and improvising, exploring the continuous process of mutual discovery. We will examine the ways in which our identities and roles as fieldworkers, individuals, and members of our own communities shape the questions we ask and the answers we receive. Fundamental to qualitative research is the interplay between the concrete and the abstract. This experiential course will provide a space to explore the dynamic relationship between theory and method in diversity of settings.

Format will be a mix of lecture, laboratory, and seminar. We will spend time doing intensive observations (of so-called "static" as well as "real time" events,) and interviewing, identifying research themes and issues, and using these for group reflections/interpretations, creating a space for an interpretive zone.

Seeing, Hearing, Sensing, and Conceptualizing—the Foundations of Qualitative Research
8/25   Topic: The Journey, and a Map
         Overview of Course: Goals, assignments, and grading.
         Overview of Qualitative Methodology: Epistemology, characteristics, and methods.
9/01   Lingering observations towards empathic understanding.

Assignments:

- Read Liora Bresler's article: "Experiential Pedagogies in Research Education."
- Read Bogdan and Biklen's Chapter 1 in *Qualitative Research for Education*.

Prior to September 1st:

- *Choose 2 artworks* in the Krannert Art Museum, one that you find appealing, and one that evokes negativity (or leaves you neutral). Spend at least 30–40 minutes with each artwork. Keep notes of your perceptions and observations.
1. Describe in detail what you see (note how long you stayed with each of the artworks).
2. Reflect and interpret. Identify themes and issues.
3. What are you curious about? Generate a list of questions to:
   a. The artist
   b. The person who first bought it
   c. The curator
4. Identify contextual (including archival) information: What else would you like to know to better understand and relate with the artwork? Where will you search for this information?
5. Reflect on the way that lingering caress and mutual absorption (to draw on Armstrong's aspects described in Bresler's work) lent themselves to empathy (search for existing definitions and add your own understanding of the term). Following Armstrong, reflect on the ways in which these five aspects were manifested (or not) in your own interaction with the artwork. You are invited to identify other aspects and relationships that emerge through your encounter of the artworks, as relevant.

- Submit electronically paper no. 1 reflecting on these by Saturday, September 3rd, at 2:00 pm.

  9/08 Topic: Observations

Assignments:

- Read Emerson, Fretz, and Shaw's Chapters 1–3 in *Writing Ethnographic Field Notes*.
- Read Powell's Chapter 2: "Inside-out and Outside-in: Participant Observation in Taiko Drumming" in G. Spindler and L. Hammond's *Innovations in Educational Ethnography*.
- Read Graham and Gottlieb's article: "Tasting Culture, Writing Rhythm, Dreaming Worlds."

9/08–10 Concerts at Krannert Performing Center: ELLNORA Guitar Festival. ******

- *Attend two concerts* at two different times from the festival www.ellnoraguitarfestival.com/
- Take notes for each concert for 60 minutes describing what you see, hear, touch, and smell. Reflect on the values (explicit and implicit) enacted in this setting.
- *Be prepared to share 2–3 pages of the field notes with class members on 9/15.*

  9/15 Topic: Multiplicity of Descriptions and Interpretations

Assignments:

- *Bring to class* 2–3 pages of your field record (use large [18–20] fonts) to share with other class members.
- Read Constance Classen's article: "Foundations for an Anthropology of the Senses."
- Read David Howes's Fore-Taste and Chapter 1 in *Sensual Relations: Engaging the Senses in Culture and Social Theory*.
- Read the first 6–10 pages from Bresler's Danville Chapter 3 in Stake, Bresler, and Mabry's *Custom and Cherishing*.
- *Reflect on how your observations fit and diverge from these readings.*

Paper #2: (10+ pages.) To be submitted by September 29, both electronically and hard copy.

1. Describe in detail what you observed in the concerts, attending to sights, sounds, smell, and touch. Note time every 5–10 minutes (e.g., 11:30; 11:35).
2. Identify themes and possible issues. Include (at least 5) themes identified by other class members on September 15.
3. What are you curious about? Generate a list of questions to:
   a. One of the artists
   b. Two other audience members
   c. A person of your choice

4. Identify contextual (including archival) information:
   a. What else would you like to know to better understand the event from any perspective that is of interest?
   b. Where will you search for this information?
5. Reflect on how your observations followed Emerson's guidelines on observations. If you were to write your own guidelines on observations, will you add anything to their suggestions? Relate your experience of observations to Howes and Classen (this part of the assignment should be addressed at the end of your paper, and is worth 20 percent of this paper's grade).

9/22 Topic: Initial Data Analysis and Interpretation.

Assignments:

- Read Miles and Huberman's Chapter 3 in *Qualitative Data Analysis*.
- Read Bernard and Ryan's Chapters 1, 3, and 4 in *Analyzing Qualitative Data*.
- *Bring to class* 2–3 pages of your one-page Contact Summary Sheet.

9/29 Topic: Educational Connoisseurship and Criticism: identifying areas of expertise and lack of.

Assignments:

- Read Elliott Eisner's Chapters 4 and 5 in *The Enlightened Eye*.
- Read Tom Barone's Chapters 1 and 2 in *Touching Eternity*.
- If you were to cultivate connoisseurship that would help you in the observations, what would it be? Address Eisner's categories, as well as other relevant course readings.
- *Paper #2: 10 pages. To be submitted as a hard copy in class and electronically.*

10/6 Topic: Multiple Perspectives and Multiple Narratives.

Assignments:

- Read Akutagawa's chapter, "In the Grove."
- *Watch (in class)* Kurosawa's movie, *Rashomon*.

1. In small groups (of 3–5) discuss the multiple perspectives presented.
2. Address objective realities and created/constructed realities.
3. In 1–3 pages, discuss the different versions of the event, and the self and other presentations in each of the stories.
4. What is Kurosawa's film about? (if multiple views of Kurosawa's themes, please list all views).

- *Submit group notes* on *Rashomon* (*one per group*) on Oct. 13th.

10/13 Topic: Cultural and historical contexts in research.

Assignments:

- Read Tobin, Hsueh, and Karasawa's book *Preschool in Three Cultures Revised: China, Japan, and the United States*.
- Reflect on methods, methodological issues, contexts, and themes.

  10/20 Topic: Continuation of Preschools
  10/27 Topic: Interpretive Zones

Assignments:

- Read Wasser and Bresler's article, "Working in the Interpretive Zones."
- *Watch* the Japanese and American segments of the "Preschool in Three Cultures Revisited."
- In small groups of four people discuss:
1. What you have observed in the DVD that adds a dimension to the book, on any level.
2. A-priori themes based on your reading of the book, watching the Japanese section and classroom discussion (please come to class with three identified themes).
3. Emergent themes (2) based on the Chinese and American segments.
4. After sharing these themes, discuss how Tobin et al. build and develop their themes, including use of contexts and scholarly literature.
- Please submit group notes in class on Nov. 3rd.
- Discuss in your small group the different types of interpretive zones of your discussion, focusing on the post-DVD discussion but when relevant include class discussions of the ELLNORA, museum visit and readings.

  11/03 Topic: Interviews.

Assignments:

- Read van Manen's Chapter 1 in *Researching Lived Experience*.
- Read Steinar Kvale's Chapters 1, 4, and 5 in *InterViews*.
- Read Janet Cape and Jeananne Nichols' chapter, "Engaging Stories: Co-constructing Narratives of Women's Military Bands."

Guest Presentation: Professor Jeananne Nichols.

Optional: Professor Philip Graham's visit at 4 pm. (Philip's two chapters are on e-reserve for this class).

  11/10 Topic: Participant/Observation and Interviewing Examined Closely.
  11/17 Topic: The Use of Theory in Qualitative Research.

Assignments:

- Be prepared to discuss Myerhoff's Chapters 1 and 2 in *Number Our Days*, drawing on the questions sent a couple of weeks ago.

- Reflect on methods, methodological issues (including insider-outsider), contexts, themes, and the ways in which the two chapters reflect (or not) Kvale's ideas of interviewing.
- Read Paul Prior's Appendix A and Chapter 4 in *Writing/Disciplinarity: A Socio-Historic Account of Literature Activity in the Academy*.
1. Reflect on the research questions, design and data gathered in both studies.
2. Discuss methodological issues presented in the data of both studies.
3. Reflect on the multiplicity of perspectives and interpretations in each study.

Guest Presentation: Professor Paul Prior

12/1 Criteria in Qualitative Research: Ethics, Trustworthiness and Usefulness.

Assignments:

- Read Lincoln and Guba's Chapter 11 in *Naturalistic Inquiry*.
- Read Wolcott's Chapter 11 in *Transforming Qualitative Data*.
- *Submit paper #3 by Friday, December 9th, at 9:00 a.m.*[a]

GRADING PROCEDURES

Participation in all sessions and activities; careful, thorough reading of all course materials required; and timely submission of all three papers and the two group assignments.

1. Paper 1: Museum Paper. 6–7 pages.   *20 percent* Due date: 9/03
2. Paper 2: Observations and Issues. 10+ pages.   *35 percent* Due date: 9/29
3. Group Notes: *2 sets, 5 percent each*
       A.   Rashomon   05 percent Due date: 10/13
       B.   Interpretive Zones   05 percent Due date: 11/03
5. Paper 3: Methodology Paper of 7+ pages. 35 percent Due date: 12/09

   REQUIRED TEXTS (*Textbooks are available in the library on reserve for two-hour loans.*)
   Tobin, J., Hsueh Y. and Karasawa, M. (2009). *Preschool in Three Cultures Revisited: China, Japan, and the United States*. Chicago: The University of Chicago Press.

   [a] For those who would like to have an extension on this paper, the final due date is January 18th, 2011.

REFERENCES (*Readings are available online.*)

Students can access e-reserve lists through the library online catalog reserve module at: http://library.uiuc.edu/ereserves/querycourse.asp
Akutagawa, R. (1964). In the Grove, from *Rashomon*. Tokyo. (pp. 19–33)
Barone, T. (2001). *Touching eternity*. New York: Teachers College Press. (Part 1: pp. 11–32; Part 2: pp. 34–102)
Bogdan, R., and S. Biklen (2003). *Qualitative research for education: An introduction to theories and methods* (fourth edition preferred but not required). New York: Allyn and Bacon. (Ch. 1: pp. 1–48; Ch. 3: pp. 73–108; Ch. 4: pp. 109–146)

Bernard, H., and G. Ryan. (2010). *Analyzing qualitative data: systematic approaches.* Los Angeles: Sage. (Ch. 1: pp. 03–16; Ch.3: pp. 53–73; Ch. 4: pp. 75–105)

Bresler, L. (2013). Experiential pedagogies in research education: Drawing on engagement with artworks. In C. Stout (Ed.), *Teaching and learning emergent research methodologies in art education.* Reston: NAEA.

Bresler, L. (1991). Ch. 3: Washington and Prairie Elementary Schools, Danville, Illinois. In Stake, R., L. Bresler, and L. Mabry (Eds.). *Custom and cherishing: Arts education in the United States.* CRME, Urbana: University of Illinois. (Ch. 3: pp. 55–61)

Cape, J. and J. Nichols (2012). "Engaging Stories: Co-constructing Narratives of Women's Military Bands" in M. Barrett and S. Stauffer (Eds.) *Narrative Soundings,* xx–xx. Dordrecht, The Netherlands: Springer.

Classen, C. (1997). Foundations for an anthropology of the senses. *International Social Science Journal* 153, 401–412.

Eisner, E. (1991). *The enlightened eye: Qualitative inquiry and the enhancement of educational practice.* New York: Macmillan. (Ch. 4: pp. 63–83; Ch. 5: pp. 85–106)

Emerson, R., R. Fretz, and L. Shaw (1995). *Writing ethnographic fieldnotes.* Chicago: University of Chicago Press. (Ch. 1: pp. 1–16; Ch. 3: pp. 39–65)

Geertz, C. (1973). *The interpretation of cultures.* New York: Basic Books. (Ch. 1: pp. 3–30)

Graham, P., A. Gottlieb. (2011, May). Tasting Culture, writing rhythm, dreaming worlds. In L. Bresler and W. Gershon (co-chair), *The intersection of qualitative inquiry and the senses.* Panel conducted at the 7th International Congress of Qualitative Inquiry, University of Illinois, Urbana-Champaign.

Howes, D. (2003). *Sensual relations: Engaging the senses in culture and social theory.* Ann Arbor: University of Michigan Press. (Foretaste pp. xi–xxiii; Ch 1; pp. 3–28)

Kvale, S. (1996). *InterViews.* Thousand Oaks, CA: Sage. (Ch. 1: pp. 3–18; Ch. 2: pp. 19–37; Ch. 5: pp. 83–108)

Lincoln, Y. and E. Guba. (1995). *Naturalistic inquiry.* Thousand Oaks, CA: Sage. (Ch. 11: pp. 289–331)

Miles, M. B., and A. Huberman. (1984). *Qualitative data analysis.* Beverly Hills, CA: Sage. (Ch. 3: pp. 49–78)

Myerhoff, B. (1978). *Number our days.* New York: Simon and Schuster. (Ch. 1: pp. 01–39; Ch. 2: pp. 40–78)

Myerhoff, B. (1988). Surviving stories; Reflections on *Number Our Days.* In J. Busch (Ed.) *Between two worlds; ethnographic essays on American Jewry,* Chapter 11 (pp. 265–295). Ithaca, NY: Cornell University Press.

Neumann, A. (2009). *Professing to learn: Creating tenured lives and careers in the American research university.* Baltimore: John Hopkins University Press. (Ch. 1: pp. 16–42)

Powell, K. (2006). Ch. 2: Inside-out and outside-in: Participant observation in taiko drumming. In G. Spindler and L. Hammond (Eds.), *Innovations in educational ethnography: Theory, methods, and results.* Mahwah, NJ: Lawrence Erlbaum Associates. (Ch. 2: pp. 33–64)

Prior, P. (1998). *Writing/Disciplinarity: A Sociohistoric Account of Literate Activity in the Academy.* Mahwah, NJ: Lawrence Erlbaum Associates. (Ch. 4: pp. 99–134; Appendix A: pp. 288–311).

Udvarhelyi, E. (2011). Reflections on a Politics of Research for the Right to the city. *International Review of Qualitative Research,* 3, (4), 383–401.

van Manen, M. (1990). *Researching lived experience*. The State University of New York. (Ch. 1: pp. 1–34)

Wasser, J., and Bresler, L. (1996). Working in the Interpretive Zone. *Educational Researcher*, 25, (5), 5–15.

Wolcott, H. (1994). *Transforming qualitative data* (second edition). Thousand Oaks, CA: Sage. (Ch. 11: pp. 337–373).

Class Assignments
Paper #1: Observations
Electronic Paper is due by September 3rd.
Paper #2: Observations of two concerts in the ELLNORA The Guitar Festival, Krannert Performing Center.
Paper is due by September 29th.
Group Notes #1: Rashomon.
Summary is due by October 6th.
Group Notes #2: Creating and Working in Interpretive Zones
Summary is due by November 3rd.
   Paper #3: methodological reflections.
   In the methodological paper, address the issues below in relation to the Krannert observations. Whenever you can, connect the issues with course readings as well as on classroom discussions (including references to individual class-members contributions). Drawing on course readings, program notes, and the interpretive zones/peer debriefing, respond to the methodological issues below.

Paper is due on December 12th.

I. Axioms

   1. Truth.

   What are my assumptions on the nature of the realities of this event? Did I attempt to portray multiple realities, if so, how?

   2. The Researcher instrument.

   What do I bring to these observations? Reflect on my "subjectivities," lenses, and values as part of my background. When am I connoisseur and when am I an "outsider"?

II. Titles, Contexts, and Criteria

   1. Provide a list of titles for your field-notes (I suggest between three and four titles) and discuss the extent to which they reflect the evolution of your thinking.
   2. Contexts.

   Which contexts did I provide for my case? Which contexts would I want to provide in a "best of all best worlds," with more time for this study?

   3. What criteria was I able to apply for my case? Did the class discussion following the performances contribute to the quality of the micro-case? Which criteria discussed in Lincoln and Guba and in Wolcott did I not apply?

III. Coping with Emergence

1. What themes did I anticipate before going to the Krannert Center (if any)?
2. What themes emerged?
3. What did I learn from doing these observations in terms of contents? In terms of methodology? Did I learn anything that surprised me?
4. What aspects of the research activity were most difficult? Most frustrating? Most rewarding?
5. What else do I need to learn to improve my perceptions and skills as a qualitative researcher?

I suggest 6–10 pages for the methodology paper (these are only suggestions, papers can be longer). In the methodology paper, criteria for evaluation include the depth of thinking, the ability to relate meaningfully to a wide range (suggested five to nine readings) of course readings, the ability to reflect on your choices and values, and the substantiation of your responses with concrete examples.

Notes

1. I am grateful to my doctoral students who have collaborated with me in the exploration of pedagogies and beliefs, with a special thanks to Stephanie Cronenberg and Christopher Dye for allowing me to share their papers and insights. I am indebted to Diana Dummit, Eve Harwood, Betsy Hearne, Koji Matsunobu, and Philip Silvey for reading this paper and for their insightful comments.
2. That is, rather than generalizable causal relationships of prespecified variables across large samples.
3. This is related but different from the genre of methodological books based on rich experience of teaching qualitative research, for example, Robert Stake's *Qualitative Research* (2010) or Elliot Eisner's *The Enlightened Eye* (1991). In music education, Janet Barrett's pedagogical action research study, focusing on data analysis and the refinement of interpretive perspectives (2007), is a compelling example of SOTL in music education.
4. For a brilliant elaboration of this point, see Higgins 2007.
5. In the Buddhist discussion of the four highest Attitudes/Emotions and sublime abodes, the far enemy is the opposite quality, whereas the near enemy is a quality that can masquerade as the original, but is not the original. For example, the far enemy of compassion is cruelty, whereas its near enemy is pity (Insight Meditation Center, n.d.).
6. Akira Kurosawa's 1950 classic film that conveys that the same event can be genuinely perceived, interpreted, and communicated in diverse ways.
7. Heath and Street (2005, 37) suggest that contrast calls for more observations of qualities as compared to comparison that is guided by beliefs of what *should be*.
8. The original papers, about 16–20 pages each, were shortened for space limitations.
9. This is not generalizable for all ethno-musicology education.
10. This refers to experience in the processes of early research and dissertation, rather than the shorter one-shot course assignments.

REFERENCES

Barone, Tom. 2001. *Touching Eternity*. New York: Teachers College Press.

Barrett, Janet. 2007. "The Researcher as Instrument: Learning to Conduct Qualitative Research through Analyzing and Interpreting a Choral Rehearsal." *Music Education Research* 9 (3): 417–33.

Boyer, Ernst 1990. *Scholarship Reconsidered: Priorities of the Professoriate*. Princeton, NJ: The Carnegie Foundation for the Advancement of Teaching.

Bresler, Liora. 2003. "Out of the Trenches: The Joys (and Risks) of Cross-Disciplinary Collaborations." *Council of Research in Music Education* 152: 17–39.

Bresler, Liora. 2005. "What Musicianship Can Teach Educational Research." *Music Education Research* 7 (2): 169–83.

Bresler, Liora. 2006. "Embodied Narrative Inquiry: Methodology of Connection." *Research Studies in Music Education* 27: 21–43.

Bresler, Liora. 2008. "Research as Experience and the Experience of Research: Mutual Shaping in the Arts and in Qualitative Inquiry." *LEARNing Landscapes* 2 (1): 267–79.

Bresler, L. 2009. "Research Education Shaped by Musical Sensibilities." *British Journal of Music Education* 26 (1): 7–25.

Bresler, Liora. 2012. "Experiential Pedagogies in Research Education: Drawing on Engagement with Artworks." In *Teaching and Learning Emergent Research Methodologies in Art Education*, edited by C. Stout. Reston: NAEA.

Bresler, Liora, and Robert E. Stake. 1992/2006. "Qualitative Research Methodology in Music Education." In *MENC Handbook of Research Methodologies*, edited by R. Colwell, 270–311. New York: Oxford University Press.

Bresler, Liora, Judy Wasser, Nancy Hertzog, and Mary Lemons. 1996. "Beyond the Lone Ranger Researcher: Teamwork in Qualitative Research." *Research Studies in Music Education* 7: 15–30.

Bullough, Edward. 1953/1912. "Psychical Distance as a Factor in Art and an Aesthetic Principle." In *The Problems of Aesthetics*, edited by E. Vivas and M. Krieger, 396–405. New York: Rinehart.

Burrows, David. 1990. *Sound, Speech, and Music*. Amherst: University of Massachusetts Press.

Charmaz, Kathy. 2006. *Constructing Grounded Theory: A Practical Guide Through Qualitative Analysis*. Thousand Oaks, CA: Sage Publications.

Dewey, John. 1938/1997. *Experience and Education*. New York: Touchstone.

Eisner, Elliot. 1991. *The Enlightened Eye: Qualitative Inquiry and the Enhancement of Educational Practice*. New York: Macmillan.

Ellsworth, Elizabeth. 2005. *Places of Learning: Media, Architecture, Pedagogy*. New York: Routledge.

Emerson, Robert, Rachel Fretz, and Linda Shaw. 1995. *Writing Ethnographic Fieldnotes*. Chicago: University of Chicago Press.

Gage, Nathaniel. 1989. "The Paradigm Wars and Their Aftermath. A 'Historical' Sketch of Research on Teaching." *Educational Researcher* 18: 4–10.

Gottlieb, Alma, and Philip Graham. 1995. *Parallel Worlds*. Chicago: University of Chicago Press.

Heath, Shirley Brice, and Brian Street, with Molly Mills. 2005. *On Ethnography*. New York: Teachers College Press.

Higgins, Chris. 2007. "Interlude: Reflections on a Line from Dewey." In *International Handbook in Research for Art Education*, edited by L. Bresler, 389–94. Dordrecht, The Netherlands: Springer.

Howes, David. 2003. *Sensual Relations: Engaging the Senses in Culture and Social Theory*. Ann Arbor: University of Michigan Press.

Insight Meditation Center. (n.d.). Dhamma Lists. http://www.insightmeditationcenter.org/books-articles/dhamma-lists/

Kolb, David. A. 1984. *Experiential Learning: Experience as the Source of Learning and Development*. Englewood Cliffs, NJ: Prentice Hall.

Lincoln, Yvonna, and Egon Guba. 1985. *Naturalistic Inquiry*. Thousand Oaks, CA: Sage Publications.

Marton, Ference, and Shirley Booth. 1997. *Learning and Awareness*. Mahwah, NJ: Lawrence Erlbaum Associates.

Nathan, Rebekah. 2005. *My Freshman Year: What a Professor Learned by Becoming a Student*. Ithaca, NY: Cornell University Press.

Palmer, Parker J. 1998. *The Courage to Teach: Exploring the Inner Landscape of a Teacher's Life*. San Francisco: Jossey-Bass Publishers.

Peshkin, Alan. 1986. *God's Choice: The Total World of a Fundamentalist Christian School*. Chicago: University of Chicago Press.

Peshkin, Alan. 1988. "In Search of Subjectivity—One's Own." *Educational Researcher* 17 (7): 17–21.

Peshkin, Alan. 1994. "The Presence of Self: Subjectivity in the Conduct of Qualitative Research." *Bulletin of the Council for Research in Music Education* 122: 45–57.

Popper, Karl. 1963. *Conjectures and Refutations*. London: Routledge.

Sæther, Eva. 2003. *The Oral University. Attitudes to Music Teaching and Learning in the Gambia*. Malmö: Malmö Academy of Music.

Schon, Donald A. 1983. *The Reflective Practitioner: How Professionals Think in Action*. New York: Basic Books.

Spinosa, Charles, Fernando Flores, and Hubert. L. Dreyfus. 1997. *Disclosing New Worlds: Entrepreneurship, Democratic Action, and the Cultivation of Solidarity*. Cambridge, MA: MIT Press.

Stake, Robert. E. 2010. *Qualitative Research: Studying How Things Work*. New York: Guilford.

Stern, Daniel. N. 2010. *Forms of Vitality: Exploring Dynamic Experience in Psychology, the Arts, Psychotherapy, and Development*. New York: Oxford University Press.

Stinson, Susan. W. 2010. "Music and Theory: Reflecting on Outcomes-Based Assessment." In *Proceedings of the Congress on Research in Dance 2009, Special Conference, 25–27 June 2009, DeMontfort University, Leicester, UK*, edited by T. Randall, 194–98. Champaign: University of Illinois Press.

Stoller, Paul. 1989. *The Taste of Ethnographic Things: The Senses in Anthropology*. Philadelphia: University of Philadelphia Press.

Tobin, Joseph, Yeh Hsueh, and Mayumi Karasawa. 2009. *Preschool in Three Cultures Revisited: China, Japan, and the United States*. Chicago: The University of Chicago Press.

van Manen, Max. 1990. *Researching Lived Experience*. Albany: State University of New York Press.

Vygotsky, Lev. 1986. *Thought and Language*. Edited and translated by A. Kouzolin. Cambridge, MA: MIT Press.

Wasser, Judy, and Liora Bresler. 1996. "Working in the Interpretive Zone." *Educational Researcher* 25 (5): 5–15.

Wenger, Etienne. 1998/2003. *Communities of Practice: Learning, Meaning and Identity*. London: Cambridge University Press.

Index

Figures, tables and boxes are indicated by *f, t* and *b* following the page number. Numbers followed by "n" indicate notes

ABS (American Boychoir School) (Princeton, NJ), 98
Academic research. *See* Research
Action research
   band studies, 56, 63–65, 64*t*
   definition of, 151–152
   naturalistic, 32
   preservice music teacher education studies, 109, 110*t*
   as professional development, 151–154
   spiral of steps, 151–152
Adolescents with special needs, 188
Adrian College Choir, 100
Adult and Community Music Education Special Research Interest Group (ACME SRIG) (NAfME), 180*t*
Adult learners, 60
AERA (American Educational Research Association), 109, 202
Aesthetics, 236, 238
Afro-Cuban music, 226, 226, 228
Afro-Puerto Rican music, 226
Age-appropriate pedagogy, 44
AIC (Arts-in-Corrections), 175–176, 176*t*
Alternative styles programs and curriculum, 82–86, 170–171
Altiplano musicians, 219–220
Amateur performers, 77–78
American Boychoir School (ABS) (Princeton, NJ), 98
American Educational Research Association (AERA), 109, 202
American music education. *See* Music education
American String Teachers Association (ASTA), 68, 170

Analytical thinking, 116*f*, 125
Andean music, 219–220
Andragogy, 164
Anger, Darol, 77
Anthropology, 236–237
Anti-racism pedagogy, 226–227, 228
Applying Research to Teaching and Playing Stringed Instruments (Barnes, ed.), 68
The arts, 234–235
arts education policy, viii–ix
Arts Education Policy Review (AEPR), ix
Arts-in-Corrections (AIC), 176–177, 176*t*
ArtsPROPEL, 151
Ashokan Fiddle and Dance Camp, 82–83, 170–171
ASTA (American String Teachers Association), 68, 170
Attachment, 237
Attention hyperactivity development disorder, 190
Auburn University, 62
Audience behavior, 244–248

Band
   action research studies, 55–56, 63–65, 64*t*
   adult learners in, 60
   composition in, 55
   concert band, 52
   documentation of teaching practices in, 50–52
   future directions for research, 64–65
   gender discrimination in, 59–60
   high school band, 57, 188–189
   high school jazz band programs, 52–53
   jazz band, 52–54
   Journal of Band Research, 49

Band (*Cont.*)
　middle school band, 56–57
　middle school jazz band, 53
　qualitative research studies, 62–65, 64*t*
　school jazz band, 52–54
　school programs, 49
　social aspects of, 58–59
　student motivation for participating in, 57
　student perspectives, 56–58
　students with special needs in, 54
　suggestions for fostering inclusive social atmosphere, 54–55
　teaching, 50–58
Band directors, 59, 60–62
Barrett, Janet, 258n2
BCRME. See *Bulletin of the Council for Research in Music Education*
Beginning music teachers
　challenges faced by, 141–143, 144*t*
　induction of, 143–147, 147*t*
　mentoring for, 143–147, 147*t*
　professional development of, 141–148
　support for, 143–147, 147*t*
Bergen Philharmonic Orchestra, 164
The Best of All Possible Worlds (Bernstein, arr. Page), 99
Bias, 42–43
Bisexual studies. *See* Lesbian, gay, bisexual, transgender, queer, questioning, and intersexed (LGBT2QI) studies
Black feminism, 211
Black gospel music, 224
Borton, Deb, 91
Boyer, Ernst, 233
Brass music, 49–67
Brigham Young University New Horizons Orchestra, 164
Britten, Benjamin, 99
Buddhism, 258n4
Bulletin of the Council for Research in Music Education (BCRME or CRME), 49, 205, 224
　qualitative band research studies, 63, 64*t*
Butler, Judith, 204

CAEP (Council Accreditation of Educator Preparation), 157n2

Calexico, 243–244
Campbell, Mark Robin, 140
Career cycle, 154–156
Caregiving theory, 14
Carey, Tanya, 70
Carnegie Hall (New York), 100
Case studies, 238
　preservice music teacher education studies, 109, 110*t*
　qualitative band research studies, 63–65, 64*t*
Catalytic validity, 43
Cavani String Quartet, 73
Celtic music, 81–82
Center for Music Learning, 71
Chamber music performance, 149
Chamber music programs, 73, 79–80
Chelsea House Orchestra (CHO), 81–82, 220–221
Children. *See also* Early childhood
　adults as co-researchers with, 11
　definition of, 10–11
　preschool, 7
　primary age, 7
Chinese music, 100, 101, 218
CHO (Chelsea House Orchestra), 81–82, 220–221
Choi, Irina, 96–97
Choir(s)
　church choirs, 165–166
　Concert Choir, 94
　high school choir, 94–97
　inclusion in, 188
　middle school choir, 97–99
　participation in, 93–103
　as safe place, 89–93
Choralier Men, 99
Choral music, 88, 99–103, 165, 188
Choral music education
　future directions, 103–104
　instructional strategies, 101–102
　multicultural, 225, 226–227
Choral music research, qualitative, 88–106
Choral teachers, 101–103
Christensen, Stephanie, 142–143
Church choirs, 165–166
Church music, 165–166

CIPP (collaborative intergenerational
    performance project), 100, 188–189
Classroom music, 26
Classrooms
    as interpretive zone, 249
    learner-centered, 72–73
CM. *See* Community music
CMA (Commission on Community Music
    Activity) (ISME), 161–162, 180*t*
CME (Contributions to Music Education),
    49, 64*t*
Collaborative intergenerational performance
    project (CIPP), 100, 168–169
Collaborative music programs, 168–169
Collaborative teacher study groups (CTSGs),
    36, 149
Collegiate-level string instrument
    students, 78–80
Columbia University, 210
Colwell Playhouse, 245
Come Ye Makers of Song (Henderson), 99
Commission on Community Music Activity
    (CMA) (ISME), 161–162, 180*t*
Committee on Critical Issues, 4
Communities of practice, 14, 148–149
Community music, 161, 176–179
    American, 161–162
    categories of, 161
    with cultural connections, 171–175, 173*t*
    with educational aims, 167–171, 169*t*
    with focus on social justice, 175–176, 176*t*
    future directions, 178–179
    online, 174–175
    with performance objectives, 162–166, 166*t*
    spiritual connections, 165–166
    vernacular, 172–174
    world music, 226–228
Community music education, 161–184
Community music organizations, 180*t*
Community music schools, 165–168
Composition, 55
Concert band, 52
Concert Choir, 94
Concert experiences, 80–81
Confidence issues, 115*f*, 120–121
Congregational Christian singers, 165–166
Conjectures, 248

Connectedness, 238
Constant comparative method, 239
Constructivist studies, 41
Contemporary Music Project on
    Creativity, 5
Contributions to Music Education (CME),
    49, 64*t*
"Cool" instruments, 209
Council Accreditation of Educator
    Preparation (CAEP), 157n2
"Creating Positive Discipline and
    Management" workshops, 37–38
Creativity, 188
Crenshaw, Kimberlé, 211
Critical friends, 107
Critical sexuality studies, 204–205
Critical thinking, 116*f*, 125
CRME. *See Bulletin of the Council for Research
    in Music Education*
Cronenberg, Stephanie, 244–248
CTSGs (Collaborative teacher study groups),
    36, 149
Cultural connections, community music with,
    171–175, 173*t*
Cultural diversity, 214–229
Culturally relevant pedagogy, 201
Culturally responsive teaching, 44, 218,
    219–220
Cultural relevance, 201
Culture shock, 97
Culver, Robert, 82, 170
"Curriculum Research: Qualitative Methods
    Research" course, 238–250, 250*b*–258*b*
    Assignment for Paper # 2, 240
    student paper excerpts, 241–249

Daily Observation Notes, 5
DAP (developmentally appropriate
    practice), 14, 29
The David Hochstein Memorial Music School,
    167–168
"Death and the Maiden" (Schubert), 80
De Bolla, Peter, 235–236
Defence mechanisms, 70
DeLay, Dorothy, 70
DeNardo, Greg, 205
Descriptive studies, 40–41

Desert Foothills New Horizons Band, 164
Desert Winds Community Steel Orchestra (DWCSO), 172
Detachment, 235–238
Developmentally appropriate practice (DAP), 14, 29
Developmental niche framework, 14
Development, manipulative, 4
Dewey, John, 234, 235–236
Dickson, Luther, 245, 246
Disabilities, 190–193
Discourse analysis, 63–65, 64t
Discrimination, gender, 59–60
Diversity
　cultural, 215–231
　and music education, 200–214
Documentation, 50–52
Down syndrome, 188
DWCSO (Desert Winds Community Steel Orchestra), 172
Dye, Christopher, 241–244, 248

Early childhood
　as adult construction, 10
　age parameters, 7, 8, 16
　concept of, 10
　definition of, 10, 15
Early childhood music education
　definition of, 8, 10
　history of, 2–9
　stakeholders in, 9–11
Early childhood music education qualitative research, 1–23
　21st-century approaches, 14–15
　considerations for, 9–11
　contemporary, 12
　definition of, 8
　future directions, 15–16
　interest in, 5–7
　reporting on, 8–9
Early Childhood Special Research Interest Group (EC SRIG) (MENC), 6
East Lansing, Michigan, New Horizons band program, 164
EC SRIG (Early Childhood Special Research Interest Group) (MENC), 6

Education
　community music with educational aims, 169t
　music education (see Music education)
　music teacher education (see Music teacher education)
　in qualitative research, 232–260
Education Research Information Center (ERIC), 109
Elementary general music, 26
　outsider observation of students, 28
　outsider observation of teaching practice, 28–29
　panorama of activities, 27–35
Elementary school
　string instrument students in, 74–75
　world music studies in, 215–218
ELLNORA Guitar Festival, 239–240, 241–248
Emerson, Ralph Waldo, vii
Engagement
　in music teacher education, 114f, 121–122
　preservice music teacher, 114f, 120–122
Ensembles, 26
　instrumental, 188–189, 220–221
　students with special needs in, 188–189
　that perform multicultural music, 220–221
　traditional performing ensembles, 164–165
Epistemology of the Closet (Sedgwick), 204
Equity, 200
ERIC (Education Research Information Center), 109
Establishing Identities: Lesbian, Gay, Bisexual, and Transgender Studies and Music Education, 203
Establishing Identity: LGBT Studies and Music Education, 202
Ethnography, 238
　preservice music teacher education studies, 109, 110t
　qualitative band research studies, 63–65, 64t
　world music studies, 227
Ewe tradition, 225
Exceptionalities, 185–199
Experiential learning, 234–235, 249–250
Experiential qualitative research education, 232–260
Exploratory perception, 236

Facilitators, 41
Faith-based ensembles, 165–166
Fauré's *Requiem*, 100, 168–169
Feminism, 201–202, 200–211
Feminist studies, 200, 209–210
Feminist Theory and Music Conference, 202
Field notes, 246–247, 249
   Daily Observation Notes, 5
   reflections, 243–244
Fieldwork, 249
Flanders' Interaction Analysis System, 72
Flow theory, 95
Focus groups, four-student, 32
Folk-Music (virtual community), 174
Folk songs, 228
Four-student focus groups, 32
Future directions
   for band research, 64–65
   for choral music education research, 3104–104
   for community music, 177–179
   for early childhood music education qualitative research, 15–16
   for preservice music teacher education research, 131–132
   for professional development research, 156–157
   recommendations for, 43–45
   suggestions for future research, 196–198
   for teaching students with special needs, 196–198

Gay studies. *See* Lesbian, gay, bisexual, transgender, queer, questioning, and intersexed (LGBT2QI) studies
Gender
   definition of, 207–208
   forms of, 207–210
   and instrument choice, 59–60, 209
"Gender" (label), 208
Gender discrimination, 59–60, 209
Gender roles, 208, 209
Gender studies, 200, 202, 209–210
Gender Trouble (Butler), 204
General music, 24–25
   definition of, 25–27
   elementary, 26, 27–35
   secondary, 26
General music education, 24–48
General music teachers
   research on, 36–38
   support for, 36
Ghanaian music, 225, 227
Giftedness, 191
Gifted students, 190–191
"GLBT" term, 200–201
Global song, 226–227
Goodness criteria, 42
Gospel music, 224
Graduate school, 150–151
G.R.I.M.E. (Gender Research in Music Education), 202
Group interviews, 32
Group mentoring, 145–146
Guitar teaching, 73

Halperin, David, 204
Handbook of Research in Music Education (Colwell), 202, 210
Hart, Alvin Youngblood, 235, 236
Harvard University, 150
Hawaiian music, 225
Head Start, 3–4
Higher education
   collegiate-level string instrument students, 75–77
   graduate school, 150–151
   world music studies in, 221–224
High school band
   jazz band programs, 52–53
   student perspectives on, 57
   students with special needs in, 188–189
High school choir, 94–97
High school jazz programs, 52–53
High school string instrument students, 75–77
High school world music studies, 220–221
Hiland Mountain Correctional Center (HMCC), 179
History
   of early childhood music education, 2–9
   of qualitative research, 2–9

HMCC (Hiland Mountain Correctional Center), 176
Hochstein School of Music and Dance, 167–168, 181n13, 181n20
Homonormativity, 203
Howes, David, 243
Hubbs, Nadine, 203–204
Hurst, Lawrence, 70
HyperRESEARCH, 170

IDEA (Individuals with Disabilities Education Act), 185, 194
Identity, 200
  Establishing Identity: LGBT Studies and Music Education, 202
  music teacher, 115f, 124
  performer, 244–245
IEPs (Individualized Education Programs), 186
Improvisation, 249
Inclusion, 185–186
  in choral music, 188
  elements for success, 187
  in instrumental music, 187
  strategies in music education, 186–189
  suggestions for fostering inclusive social atmosphere, 54–55
Individual interviews, 32
Individualized Education Programs (IEPs), 186
Individuals with Disabilities Education Act (IDEA), 185, 194
Induction, 143–146, 147t
Inquiry. *See* Research
Inservice music teacher professional development, 139–160
Insider observation, 31–33
Insider-outsider hybrid observation, 34–35
Insider/outsider observation, 29–30
Instructional strategies, 101
Instrumental ensembles
  students with special needs in, 188–189
  that perform multicultural music, 220–221
Instrumental music
  inclusion of students in, 187
  strings, 68–87
  winds, brass, percussion, 49–67

Instrument choice, 59, 209
Intellectually gifted students, 190–191
International Club, 97
International Journal of Music Education, 223
International Night, 97
International Society for Music Education (ISME), 161–162
International Vocal Ensemble (IVE), 222
Internet, 174–175
Interpretive zones, 234
Intersectionalities, 211
Intersectionality theory, 211
Interviews
  individual, 32
  open-ended, 232–233
  semi-structured, 232–233
  small-group, 32
iPads, 13, 246–247
iPhones, 13
iPods, 13
ISME (International Society for Music Education), 161–162
IVE (International Vocal Ensemble), 222

Japanese American drumming, 225, 226
Japanese-American music, 227
Jazz band, 52–54
  high school programs, 52–53
  middle school, 53
  themes, 53
Journal of Band Research (JBR), 49, 64t
Journal of Research in Music Education (JRME), 49, 64t
Journal of String Research, 68

Kamehameha Schools (Hawaii), 225
Knowledge, teacher, 36–37, 113–116
Krannert Center, 239–240, 241–248
Kurosawa, Akira, 258n5

La Foi (Rossini), 99
Lamb, Roberta, 210–211
Language acquisition, 14
Lassiter High School, 62
Latino music, 226, 227
League of American Orchestras, 170

Learner-centered classroom
    environments, 72–73
Learning
    as becoming, 250
    as experience, 249–250
    experiential, 234–235
    scholarship of teaching and learning
        (SOTL), 233
Learning disabilities, 190
Learning to teach music, 127, 128–129f
    perceptions or attitudes regarding, 113, 115f,
        120–124
    preservice teacher beliefs or concerns
        about, 113, 114f, 115–119
Lenawee Community Chorus, 100
Lesbian, gay, bisexual, and transgender
    (LGBT) studies, 202–207, 211
Lesbian, gay, bisexual, transgender, queer and
    questioning (LGBT2Q) studies, 202–207
Lesbian, gay, bisexual, transgender, queer,
    questioning, and intersexed (LGBT2QI)
    studies, 200–201, 203–204
Lewis, Brian, 70
LGBT2QI (lesbian, gay, bisexual, transgender,
    queer, questioning, and intersexed)
    studies, 200–201, 203–204
LGBT2Q (lesbian, gay, bisexual,
    transgender, queer and questioning)
    studies, 202–207
LGBTQQCSI acronym, 200
LGBT Research Symposium, 202
LGBT (lesbian, gay, bisexual, and transgender)
    studies, 202–207, 211
Lived experience, 69–70
Lutheran choir singers, 165–164

Magnificent Horses (arr. Ling-Tam), 99
Mainstreaming, 185–186
Manhattanville Music Curriculum Program, 5
Manipulative development, 4
Marginalization, 200
Mariachi music, 219, 225, 227
Masculinity, 202
Mason, James, 24
Mason, Molly, 170
Master Teacher Profile observation form,
    83, 170

McInnes, Donald, 70
Meaningful investigations, 44–45
Media Educators Journal (MEJ), 64t
MENC. *See* Music Educators National
    Conference
Mennonite singers, 165
Mentoring, 143–147, 147t
Methodist choir singers, 165–166
Methodological frameworks, 109–110
Michigan State University, 222–223
Middle school
    jazz themes in, 53
    string instrument students in, 74–75, 81
    world music studies in, 218–220
Middle school band, 56–57
Middle school choir, 98–99
Middle school jazz band, 53
Middle school orchestra, 80
MIDI (musical instrument digital interface)
    synthesizers, 190
Mixed Choir, 95
Mixed methods research
    preservice music teacher education studies,
        109, 110t
    qualitative band research studies, 63–65, 64t
MMR. *See* Mixed methods research
Modeling
    teacher-directed, 101–102
    teaching models, 70–73
Model of coherence, 129
Model of Exemplary Elementary Teachers'
    Instructional Knowledge, 36
Motivation
    for participating in band, 57
    proximal theory of, 95
Multicultural choral music education, 225,
    226–227
Multiculturalism, 201
Multicultural music
    in elementary school, 217
    in music teacher education, 214–215
    school instrumental ensembles that
        perform, 220–221
Music. *See also specific types, instruments*
    Afro-Cuban, 225, 226
    Afro-Puerto Rican, 226
    chamber, 73, 79–80

Music (*Cont.*)
  Chinese, 217
  choral, 101–103
  church, 165–166
  classroom, 26
  collaborative, 168–169
  community, 161–166
  general, 24–27
  Hawaiian, 225
  instrumental, 187
  instrumental (strings), 68–87
  instrumental (winds, brass, percussion), 49–67
  instrument choice, 59, 209
  Latino, 226
  Mariachi, 219, 225, 227
  multicultural, 214–215, 217, 220–221
  participation with, 99–101
  physical response to, 245–245
  selection of, 219
  teacher participation in, 101–103
  vocal, 26
  vocal-general, 26
  world, 214–231
Music acquisition, 14
Musical Futures, 171
Musical instrument digital interface (MIDI) synthesizers, 190
Musical performance
  chamber music performance, 149
  collaborative intergenerational performance project (CIPP), 100, 168–169
  community music with performance objectives, 162–166, 166*t*
  as learning opportunity, 240–249
  traditional performing ensembles, 164–165
Musical taste, 246
Music and arts education policy, viii–ix
"Music and Minds: A Talent Development Model" program, 191, 192
Music Atelieristas, 12
Music education
  choral music, 88–106, 225, 226–227
  community, 161–184
  cultural diversity in, 214–231
  disabilities in, 190–193
  diversity in, 200–213
  early childhood, 1–23
  elementary school, 215–2218
  feminism in, 209–210
  general, 24–48
  higher education, 222–223
  inclusion strategies in, 186–189
  inservice music teacher professional development, 139–160
  instrumental (winds, brass, percussion), 49–67
  LGBT2Q studies in, 203–206
  middle school, 218–220
  multicultural, 217, 225, 226–227
  personal experience method, 3
  strategies in coursework, 114*f*, 122–123
  students with exceptionalities in, 185–119
  world music, 214–231
Music education career cycle, 154–156
Music education journals. *See specific journals by title*
Music education research. *See also* Qualitative research
  choral music, 88–106
  early childhood, 1–23
  feminist studies, 209–210
  gender studies, 208–209
  LGBT2Q studies, 203–207
  LGBT studies, 205, 207
  qualitative, vii, 200–204
Music Education Research Council (MERC), 3
Music Education Studies Research Group (AERA), 202
Music Educators Journal (MEJ), 49
Music Educators National Conference (MENC), 4, 5, 16n5
  Archives, 5
  Early Childhood Special Research Interest Group (EC SRIG), 6
  music standards for children 2-4 years old, 8
  music standards for students k-12th grade, 8
  National Council for Elementary General Music, 24
Music for Early Childhood, 4
Musicians
  performer identity, 244–245
  string instrument performers, 77–78
Music Learning Theory, 167
Music Learning Theory for Newborn and Young Children (Gordon), 14

Music makers, 77–78
Music making, 149–150
Music Mania (software program), 190
Music of Young Children (Wilson), 5
Music Pedagogues or *Music Atelieristas*, 12
Music Standards (NAfME), 9
Music teacher education, 140
  engagement in, 114f, 121–122
  multicultural music in, 214–215
  preservice, 107–138
  strategies in coursework, 114f, 122–123
  and students with special
    needs, 193–198
  suggestions for future research, 196–197
Music teachers. *See also* Teachers
  beginning, 141–148
  career cycle, 154–156
  experienced, 148–154
  general music teachers, 36–38
  identity development for, 114f, 124
  inservice, 139–160
  preservice, 107–138
  professional development of, 141–154
  second-stage, 155–156
  support for, 36
Music teaching. *See* Teaching

NACCM (North American Coalition for Community Music), 180t
NAEYC (National Association for the Education of Young Children), 7, 8–9
NAfME. *See* National Association for Music Education
Narrative inquiry, 109, 110t
National Association for Music Education (NAfME), 16n5, 45n1, 109, 139
  Adult and Community Music Education Special Research Interest Group (ACME SRIG), 180t
  call for musically rich environments for all children, 9
  Music Standards, 9
National Association for the Education of Young Children (NAEYC), 7, 8–9
National Board for Professional Teaching Standards (NBPTS), 148–149
National Council for Accreditation of Teacher Education (NCATE), 139, 157n2

National Council for Elementary General Music, 24
National Education Association, 2
National Guild for Community Arts Education (NGCAE), 161, 162, 180t, 180n1
Naturalistic action research, 32
Naturalistic observation, 29
Naturalistic research, 58
Naturalistic study, 28
NBPTS (National Board for Professional Teaching Standards), 148–149
NCATE (National Council for Accreditation of Teacher Education), 139, 157n2
The Neighborhood Music School (NMS), 167
The New Handbook of Research on Music Teaching and Learning (Colwell and Richardson), 8
New Horizons International Music Association (NHIMA), 57, 163–164, 181n8
NGCAE (National Guild for Community Arts Education), 161, 162, 180t, 180n1
NHIMA (New Horizons International Music Association), 57, 163–164, 181n8
NMS (The Neighborhood Music School), 167
No Child Left Behind Act, 140
Norfolk Chorale, 165
North American Coalition for Community Music (NACCM), 180t
North American Old Time and Bluegrass music, 173–174
North Carolina, 174
Northern Week (Ashokan), 82–83, 170–171
Northridge Children's Choir, 90, 93
Northwestern University, 109
Notes
  Daily Observation Notes, 5
  field notes, 246–247, 249
  reflections, 243–244

Objectivity, 237
Observation
  apprenticeships of, 123
  Daily Observation Notes, 5
  effects on subjects, 41–42
  insider, 31–33
  insider/outsider, 29–30
  insider-outsider hybrid, 34–35

Observation (*Cont.*)
  naturalistic, 29
  outsider, 28–29, 33–34
  teacher, 29–30
  unstructured, 232–233
Online community music, 174–175
Open-ended interviews, 232–233
Orchestra programs and curriculum, 79–83
Orff-Schulwerk teacher training, 36
OrffSPIEL collaborative, 36
Outsider observation, 33–34
  insider-outsider hybrid observation, 34–35
  insider/outsider observation, 29–30
  of students, 28
  of teaching practice, 28–29

Palmer, Parker, 250
Paradigm wars, 236–237
Paraprofessionals, 189
Participation
  in choir, 93–103
  motivation for participating in band, 57
  with music, 99–101
  observer/observer-participants, 41
  research participants, 43
Patakin/Carambu, 226
Pedagogical content knowledge (PCK), 36, 124
Pedagogy
  anti-racism, 226–227, 228
  culturally relevant, 200
  culturally responsive, age-appropriate, 44
  world music, 219–220
Peer tutors, 80
Peery, J. C., 7, 8
Pen-pals, 123
Perception, 236
Percussion
  Japanese American drumming, 225, 226
  winds, brass, percussion (instrumental music), 49–70
Performance
  chamber music performance, 149
  collaborative intergenerational performance project (CIPP), 100, 168–169
  community music with performance objectives, 162–166, 166*t*
  as learning opportunity, 240–249
  traditional performing ensembles, 164–165
Performers
  identity of, 245–245
  string instrument performers, 77–78
Personal experience method, 3
Phenomenological research
  in preservice music teacher education, 109, 110*t*
  qualitative band research studies, 63–65, 64*t*
Phenomenology, 238
Philadelphia Orchestra, 77
Philosophical inquiry, 14
Physical response to music, 245–248
The Pillsbury Foundation for the Advancement of Music Education, 1, 3, 5
The Pillsbury Foundation School, 1, 6, 11
The Pillsbury Foundation Studies (The Studies), 1, 3, 8, 11, 14, 15
Pioneers, 64
Pittsburgh public schools, 150
Play theory, 14
Plummer, Kathryn, 70
policy, viii–ix
Popper, Karl, 248
Positivist objectivity, 237
Possible Selves Program in Music, 96
Practice-based orientation, 152–153
Prairie View Interscholastic League (PVIL), 62
Preschool children, 7
Preservice band directors, 61
Preservice music teacher education research
  categories of interest, 109, 110*t*
  critique and conclusion, 130–132
  future directions, 131–132
  literature quality, 130–131
  literature review, 109–126, 110*t*, 111*t*, 112*f*, 114*f*, 115*f*, 116*f*, 128*f*–129*f*
  methodological framework for, 109–110
  qualitative, 107–138
  results, 126–129, 127*f*–128*f*
  studies, 109, 110*t*
  theoretical framework for, 108
  types of studies, 108, 110*t*
Preservice music teachers
  analytical, reflective, and critical thinking, 116*f*, 125

beliefs about learning to teach music, 113, 114*f*, 115–119
beliefs about teaching, 118–119
concerns about self, technical, and impact issues, 114*f*, 117–118
confidence issues, 115*f*, 120–121
course connections, 116*f*, 125
engagement in courses, 115*f*, 121–122
engagement in specific actions, 115*f*, 121
identity development of, 115*f*, 124
improvements/interventions aimed at, 113, 116*f*, 124–126
perceptions or attitudes regarding learning to teach music, 113, 115*f*, 120–124
prior knowledge or experiences, 113–117, 114*f*
reflection that generates self-awareness, 114*f*, 119
relationships, 116*f*, 126
self-evaluation, 116*f*, 125
skill proficiencies, 116*f*, 126
strategies in coursework, 114*f*, 122–124
Primary age children, 7
Prior knowledge or experiences, 117*f*, 120
Professional development
action research/teacher research as, 151–154
of beginning music teachers, 145–152
continued, 32
definition of, 144
of experienced music teachers, 152–158
graduate school as, 154–151
inservice, 143–164
music making as, 153–154
research on, 144–145, 160–161
Professional Development Area for Strategic Planning (Society for Music Teacher Education), 153
Professional Development School (PDS), 126
Professional performers, 80–81
Progressive Education movement, 3
Projects, 11, 12
Project Zero, 12, 154
Proximal theory of motivation, 99
PVIL (Prairie View Interscholastic League), 62

Qualitative research
21st-century approaches for, 14–15
in American school band programs, 49
band studies, 52, 62–65, 64*t*
in choral music education, 92–110
in community music education, 165–188
considerations for, 9–10
"Curriculum Research: Qualitative Methods Research" course, 243–254, 255*b*–262*b*
detachment and, 240–243
in diversity, 204–218
in early childhood music education, 1–23
in general music education, 24–48
history of, 2–9
on inclusion strategies in music education, 190–193
in inservice music teacher professional development, 143–164
in instrumental music (winds, brass, percussion), 49–70
key methods, 237–238
in learning to teach, 112
model of coherence for, 133
in music education, vii, 204–218
in music teacher education and students with special needs, 197–202
in preservice music teacher education, 111–142
requirements for, 240–243
on specific disabilities in music education, 194–197
on students with exceptionalities, 189–203
suggestions for future research, 200–201
teaching, 237–265
world music studies, 220–230
Qualitative sampling, 245
Quality, literature, 134–135
Queer studies. *See* Lesbian, gay, bisexual, transgender, queer, questioning, and intersexed (LGBT2QI) studies
Queer theory, 206, 208, 209
Questioning studies. *See* Lesbian, gay, bisexual, transgender, queer, questioning, and intersexed (LGBT2QI) studies

Race To The Top, 144
Radical deconstructionism, 208
Ranaldo, Lee, 251

Rashomon, 243, 255n5
Reflection that generates self-awareness, 118f, 123
Reflective thinking, 120f, 129
Reggio Emilia philosophy, 11, 12
Reggio Emilia projects, 11, 12
Rehearsal, 75
Rehearsal Priorities Analysis Form, 75
Reid, Rufus, 81
Rejoice in the Lamb (Britten), 103, 104
Renzulli's Three-Ring Conception of Giftedness, 195
Reporting, 8–9
Requiem (Fauré), 104, 172–173
Research. *See also* Qualitative research
    action research, 32, 56, 63–65, 64t, 151–154
    choral music, 92–110
    in community music education, 165–188
    constructivist studies, 41
    critical sexuality studies, 208–209
    descriptive studies, 40–41
    in early childhood music education, 1–23
    effects on participants, 42–43
    feminist studies, 204, 214–215
    in general music education, 24–48
    LGBT2Q studies, 207–211
    meaningful investigations, 44–45
    mixed methods, 63–65, 64t
    naturalistic, 32
    phenomenological, 63–65, 64t
    practice-based orientation to, 156–157
    in preservice music teacher education, 111–142
    as professional development, 151–158
    on professional development, 144–145, 160–161
    recommendations for, 43–45
    on students with exceptionalities, 189–203
    teacher, 151–158
    world music studies, 220–230, 231–233
Researchers
    as adult visitors, 10
    as co-researchers with children, 11
    as facilitators, 41
    influences on subjects, 41–42
    as insider-outsiders, 40
    as insider/outsiders, 43
    as insiders, 39
    as instruments, 37
    as "least adult," 40
    as *Music Pedagogues* or *Music Atelieristas*, 12
    as observer/observer-participants, 41
    as observers, 38–39
    on-site roles, 10
    as outside experts, 41
    as outsiders, 41
    perspectives of, 38–41
    pioneers, 64
    positioning of, 40–41
    visibility-invisibility of, 40
Research interviews. *See* Interviews
Research journals. *See specific journals by title*
Research participants, 43
Research subjects. *See* Research participants
Responses
    culturally responsive teaching, 43, 222, 223–224
    to music, 250–253
    physical, 250–253
Ribot, Marc, 251
Ritchie, William, 73
Rochester (NY) New Horizons band program, 167
Rodriguez, Nelson, 207, 208

"Safe Place" concept, 95
Safety
    in choir, 93–97
    less safe places, 96–97
Sage Handbook of Qualitative Research (Denzin and Lincoln), 205
Sampling, qualitative, 245
San Jose Taiko, 231
Sankofa Drum and Dance Ensemble, 230
Scaffolding, 245–254
Scholarship. *See also* Research
    aesthetics of, 240
    of teaching, 238
Scholarship of teaching and learning (SOTL), 238
School band programs, 49
    high school band, 57, 192–193
    high school jazz band, 52–53
    jazz band, 52–54

middle school band, 56–57
middle school jazz band, 53
School instrumental ensembles, 225–226
School orchestra programs, 82–86
Schools
    community music schools, 171–172
    teaching models and approaches in, 74–76
School-Wide Enrichment Model (SEM), 196
SEC (Southeastern Conference), 62
Secondary general music, 26
Second-stage music teachers, 159–160
Sedgwick, Eve Kosofsky, 208
Seelman, Marilyn, 73
Self-awareness, 118f, 123
Self-concern, 117–121, 118f
Self-confrontation, 122–123
Self-efficacy, 79–80
Self-evaluation, 119f, 129
Self-image, 93–97, 99
Self-studies, 63–65, 64t
SEM (School-Wide Enrichment Model), 196
Semi-structured interviews, 237–238
Sengstack Educational Foundation, 16n7
"Sex" (label), 212
Sexuality, 207–208
Shelley, Shirley, 5
Shenandoah Valley, 177–178
Shipps, Stephen, 73
Shuler, Scott, 143
Small-group interviews, 32
Social interactions/connections, 58–59
Socialization, teacher, 72–73
Social justice, 179–180, 186t, 204, 205
Society for Music Teacher Education, 153
Solow, Jeffrey, 73
SOTL (scholarship of teaching and
    learning), 238
Southeastern Conference (SEC), 62
Special learners, 190
Special needs
    adolescents with, 192
    band students with, 54–55, 192–193
    intellectually gifted students, 194–195
    preparation for teaching students with,
        197–202
Spiritual connections, 169–170
Stern, Daniel, 239

Stinson, Sue, 238
Stokowski, Leopold, 1
String Jam, 85, 175, 184n20
String Research Journal, 71
Strings (instrumental music), 71–91
"Strings Attached: The Reality Show," 84
Student-directed teaching, 52
Students. *See also* Preservice music teachers
    band students, 54, 56–58, 192–193
    choir students, 97–107
    collegiate-level, 78–80
    elementary school, 77–78
    with exceptionalities, 189–203
    four-student focus groups, 32
    gifted, 194–195
    high school, 78–80, 97–107
    insider observation of, 31–33
    insider/outsider observation of, 29–30
    in instrumental music ensembles, 192–193
    intellectually gifted, 194–195
    middle school, 77–78, 101–103
    outsider observation of, 28
    qualitative research on, 189–203
    special learners, 190
    with special needs, 54–55, 192–193, 197–202
    string instrument students, 77–80
    teacher observation of, 29–30
Studio settings, 73–74
Study groups, collaborative teacher (CTSGs),
    36, 153
Subjectivity, 242
Summer camp, 85
Summer music programs, 174–175
Support
    for beginning music teachers, 147–151
    for general music teachers, 36
Suzuki Method instruction, 73–74, 171

Tanglewood Symposium, 4
Teacher-directed modeling, 105
Teacher knowledge, 36–37
Teacher research
    definition of, 151–156
    as professional development, 151–158
Teachers. *See also* Music teachers
    choral, 105–107
    lived experience of, 72–73

Teachers (*Cont.*)
  observation of students by, 29–30
  preservice, 111–142
  rehearsal priorities, 75
  socialization of, 72–73
  teacher study by, 37–38
Teachers College, Columbia, 214
Teacher study groups, collaborative (CTSGs), 36, 153
Teaching. *See also* Education
  band, 50–58
  beliefs about, 122–123
  in chamber music settings, 76
  guitar, 76
  models and approaches for, 73–76
  outsider observation of, 28–29
  qualitative band literature on, 52
  qualitative research, 237–265
  scholarship of, 238
  scholarship of teaching and learning (SOTL), 238
  in school settings, 74–76
  student-directed, 52
  in studio settings, 73–74
Teaching Music to Learners with Special Needs course, 199
Technical issues, 118f, 121–122
Terminology, 212
Texas band programs, 61
Theoretical frameworks, 112, 239
Think-aloud interviews, 34
Thompson, Linda K., 144
Three Flower Songs (Beach), 103
Three-Ring Conception of Giftedness (Renzulli), 195
Traditional performing ensembles, 168–169
Transgender studies. *See* Lesbian, gay, bisexual, transgender, queer, questioning, and intersexed (LGBT2QI) studies
"Twinkle, Twinkle Little Star," 82

Ungar, Jay, 174
University of Maryland, 5
University of South Carolina (USC), 173–174
University of South Carolina String Project (USCSP), 173–174
University of Washington, 227
Update: Applications of Research in Music Education, 228
Upper Arlington, Ohio orchestra, 82
USC (University of South Carolina), 173–174
USCSP (University of South Carolina String Project), 173–174

Validity, catalytic, 43
Variation theory, 243
Vernacular community music, 176–178
Video data or footage, 168
Vocal-general music, 26
Vocal music, 26

Walls, Billy G., 62
Wang, Shi-Hwa, 73
Watkins, Alfred, 62
Wenger, Etienne, 238
Williams Beuren syndrome, 195
Williams syndrome, 195, 196
Wilson, Bruce, 5
Winds, brass, percussion (instrumental music), 49–70
World music(s), 219–236
World music pedagogy, 224–225
World music studies
  in community context, 231–233
  in elementary school, 220–223
  in higher education, 226–229
  in high school, 225–226
  in middle school, 223–225
  in unclear or combined educational levels, 229–230
Writing
  researcher positioning, 39–41
  with video, 168
Writing assignments, 245–254
WS. *See* Williams syndrome

Zimmerman, J. R., 7
Zimmerman, M. P., 7
Zone of proximal development (ZPD), 254